THE KREMLIN STRIKES BACK

America and Europe responded to Russia's annexation of Crimea on March 18, 2014, by discarding their policy of East-West partnership and reverting intermittently to a policy of cold war. The West believes that this on-again/off-again second Cold War will end with Russia's capitulation because it is not a sufficiently great power, while the Kremlin's view is just the opposite; Vladimir Putin believes that if Moscow has strategic patience, Russia can recover some of the geostrategic losses it incurred when the Soviet Union collapsed. *The Kremlin Strikes Back* scrutinizes the economic prospects of both sides, driven by their industrial prowess, warfighting capabilities, and national resolve, addressing particularly hot-button issues such as increasing military spending, decreasing domestic spending, and other policies. Steven Rosefielde aims to objectively gauge future prospects and the wisdom of employing various strategies to address Russian developments.

Steven Rosefielde is Professor of Economics at the University of North Carolina, Chapel Hill. In 1997 he was inducted into the Russian Academy of Natural Sciences (RAEN). His recent publications include: *Russia in the 21st Century: The Prodigal Superpower* (2005), *Masters of Illusion: American Leadership in a New Age* (2007), *Russian Economy from Lenin to Putin* (2007), *Russia since 1980: Wrestling with Westernization* (2008), and *Transformation and Crisis in Central and Eastern Europe: Challenges and Prospects* (2016).

The Kremlin Strikes Back

Russia and the West after Crimea's Annexation

STEVEN ROSEFIELDE

University of North Carolina, Chapel Hill

CAMBRIDGE
UNIVERSITY PRESS

CAMBRIDGE
UNIVERSITY PRESS

One Liberty Plaza, 20th Floor, New York, NY 10006, USA

Cambridge University Press is part of the University of Cambridge.

It furthers the University's mission by disseminating knowledge in the pursuit of education, learning, and research at the highest international levels of excellence.

www.cambridge.org
Information on this title: www.cambridge.org/9781107572959
10.1017/9781316423301

First published 2017

Printed in the United States of America by Sheridan Books, Inc.

A catalogue record for this publication is available from the British Library.

ISBN 978-1-107-12965-8 Hardback
ISBN 978-1-107-57295-9 Paperback

In memory of my beloved son, David Rosefielde

Contents

Figures, Tables, and Maps

Figures

Tables

Maps

Preface

Russia and the West are once again at dagger points. America and Europe responded to Russia's annexation of Crimea on March 18, 2014, by discarding their policy of East-West partnership and reverting to the Cold War.[1] More than two years later, the dust has settled and the path forward for both sides is clear. The West has adopted the "who is afraid of the big bad wolf?" position that this time will be the same; that if America and the European Union stick more or less to business as usual, Cold War II will end with Russia's capitulation because it is not a sufficiently great power. The Russians aren't really coming. Strategic patience will assure victory. Crimea and the Donbas may be temporarily lost, and Putin may strike a few other nonlethal blows, but eventually there will be a happy ending. The West can safely divert its attention to more pressing matters such as the Islamic State (IS), because the countermeasures already adopted will suffice, or can be enhanced with little strain.

The Kremlin's view is just the reverse. Vladimir Putin is confident that this time will be different. He believes that if Moscow has strategic patience and plays a weak hand deftly, Russia can roll back some of the geostrategic losses it incurred when the Soviet Union collapsed, expand its sphere of influence to include Syria and the Middle East, blunt Western efforts at fomenting regime change on Putin's turf, and contest the West's unipolar ambitions.

Faith that this time will be the same is nearly universal among American and EU leaders. Putin's narrative and posture are dismissed as bluster and wishful thinking. Perhaps, history will validate the certitude. But faith isn't science, and many arguments advanced in support of the proposition that this time will be the same are spurious, especially claims that Russia's economy and military-industrial potential cannot sustain Putin's ambitions, and the West's economy is fundamentally sound.

The West's reluctance to discuss, let alone negotiate, a compromise Cold War II–ending new global order with the Kremlin, while simultaneously creating a cooperative façade in Syria, is a corollary of its faith in strategic patience and its "duty to prevail." It reflects a more general attitude taken by reigning administrations that foreign threats such as nuclear proliferation can be left to fester[2] if they require fundamental changes in domestic priorities. American and EU leaders speak as if they believe that they have a civilizing mission to spread democracy and Western cultural values through color revolutions and regime change across the globe (for example, their insistence that Assad must go). They do not consider this policy hostile or transgressive. Their faith in selective benign neglect, and their duty to prevail, real or disingenuous, however, is not determinative. Cold War II, regardless of how the West chooses to manage perceptions, will be costly and entails catastrophic risks that may justify sacrificing this or that noble principle for the greater good.

This volume attempts to evaluate whether the West's "this time will be the same" strategy in Crimea and the Donbas is prudent; whether it would be wiser to discuss and renegotiate the post-Soviet rules of East-West relations, adopt an interim Détente II policy, or upgrade defense and fundamentally modify the West's economic system. The task is accomplished by probing Putin's motives and stratagems and documenting his drive to restore Russia's great power in Crimea and the Donbas region of Novorossiya. A survey of the West's responses to Crimea's annexation and the Kremlin's countermoves follows establishing a benchmark for assessing the next phase. Correlation-of-forces analysis given this benchmark is applied to calibrate the prospect that this time will be the same, supplemented by a review of longer-term historical influences. The risks entailed by staying the course, renegotiating the world order, or adopting Détente II are then assessed. The analysis reveals that staying the course might be prudent if the West modifies its strategy, but that adopting Détente II as an interim policy is wisest because the West is reluctant to fund the military forces necessary to prevail; faces severe obstacles to extricating its economies from secular stagnation; and is not ready to comprehensively renegotiate the world order, expecting "this time to be the same." At the moment, it appears that the Syrian imbroglio is prodding the West toward informal Détente II, pending fresh surprises.

The narrative and analysis in this study employ the objective-subjective method (separating positive from normative issues) without attempting to comprehensively resolve conflicting claims about facts, causalities, and priorities. It is nonpartisan. The method acknowledges contending viewpoints, plumbs hidden agendas, and makes strong analytic judgments wherever reason and evidence permit.

The filter clarifies the basics. Russians aren't ten feet tall, nor are they midgets. They are tall enough to stand up to the West and push back, and Putin and the *siloviki* are intent on doing so, but the filter does not settle issues of motivation, merit, and justice, about which readers must ultimately decide.

The method also is inclusive, requiring expertise not only in international security affairs but also in economic theory. Foreign policy analysts understandably are uncomfortable with rigorous technical assessments of Western and Russian economic potential, but they deceive themselves if they suppose that they can safely disregard Western economic vulnerabilities and Russian strengths in assessing wise international security policy.

Notes

1 This is the case even though the Obama administration is disinclined to publicly characterize the contest as anything more than a squabble. Putin is embraced by the American White House as a comrade in arms against the Islamic State (IS) in Syria, despite the Kremlin's refusal to rescind Crimea's annexation. Cf. Stephen Cohen, *Should the West Engage Putin's Russia?: The Munk Debates*, New York: House of Anansi Press, 2016.

2 Non-signatories to the nonproliferation treaty who have active nuclear programs or are believed to be emerging nuclear powers are India, Pakistan, Iran, North Korea, and Israel. Elise Hu, "North Korea Says It Conducted Hydrogen Bomb Test," *NPR*, January 5, 2016. www.npr.org/sections/thetwo-way/2016/01/05/462098403/north-korea-says-it-conducted-hydrogen-bomb-test.

Acknowledgments

The Kremlin Strikes Back synthesizes a lifetime of research on Russia and the challenges it poses to the West. It owes a debt of gratitude to many who have worked in the vineyard of the discipline, my teachers, scholars, practitioners, and friends. Abram Bergson, Stephen Blank, William van Cleave, Bruno Dallago, Emil Ershov, Gottfried von Haberler, Stefan Hedlund, George Kleiner, Andrew Marshall, Quinn Mills, Alec Nove, Patrick Parker, Ralph W. Pfouts, Jan Rylander, Leonard Schapiro, and Vitaly Shlykov all contributed to my understanding of what was said, and what went unspoken.

The University of North Carolina provided a Senior Faculty Research and Scholarly Leave (Kenan, Pogue, William R. Kenan Jr., William N. Reynolds, and R. J. Reynolds Industries funds) to facilitate the project, and the Bank of Finland (BOFIT), the Stockholm Institute of Transition Economies (SITE), the Swedish Defence Research Agency (Totalförsvarets forskningsinstitut FOI), and the University of Trento hosted me as a visiting scholar. I especially wish to thank Executive Vice Chancellor James W. Dean Jr. and Vice Provost Ronald Strauss, Iikka Korhonen, Pekka Sutela, Laura Solanko, Jouko Rautava, Liisa Mannila, Tia Kurtti, Torbjorn Becker, Gun Malmquist, Lennart Samuelson, Sven Hirdman, Carolina Vendil Palin, Gudrun Persson, Johan Nordberg, Bruno Dallago, Gert Guri, and Lara Fiamozzini for their kind assistance.

My wife, Susan Rosefielde, and daughter, Justine Rosefielde, provided unstinting moral support.

Introduction

The post-Soviet world order that replaced the Yalta and Potsdam Agreements (February 11, 1945 and August 1, 1945) and the Cold War after 1991 blossomed during the 1990s in an era of compatible intentions.[1] Leaders in the Kremlin and the West wanted Russia to distance itself in varying degrees from Soviet-style authoritarianism, communism, and central planning in favor of democracy, the rule of law, and free enterprise.[2] These shared goals, driven in part by the changing "correlation of forces,"[3] formed the basis of their "partnership,"[4] and provided a framework for resolving differences.[5] Pride of place was given to ties that bound instead of latent disputes that divided. The age of geopolitics and polarization had yielded to "globalization."

It is doubtful that Boris Yeltsin and Vladimir Putin ever fully subscribed to Samuel Huntington's idea of the West (including true democracy,[6] free enterprise, and the "rule of law") underpinning the West's concept of globalization, even if the West faithfully practiced what it preached.[7] Both appear to have preferred Russian Muscovite culture,[8] and governance to Enlightenment principles, as Huntington surmised.[9] They accepted Western economic assistance in turbulent times as an adverse "correlation of forces" dictated,[10] but how would they behave when the shock of Soviet disunion faded, the realities of post-Soviet engagement set in,[11] and the tide turned? Yeltsin left office too soon to judge, but Putin's reaction is public record – he decided that America and the European Union were Russia's cynical adversaries, Western protestations to the contrary notwithstanding,[12] and that realpolitik had to replace the façade of post-Soviet "partnership."[13] The Kremlin's annexation of Crimea and the subsequent Moscow-led surrogate insurgency against Ukraine prove that Russia's and the West's premises and perhaps intentions today are incompatible, although Western leaders increasingly consider the spat a temporary aberration (teething pains). Putin contends that he has rediscovered the virtues of Russian imperial exceptionalism.[14] He has publicly declared his "disenchantment" and disgruntlement, asserting that he is no longer willing to abide by the West's rules and agenda. Putin intermittently insists that Russia and its post-imperial Western neighbors should cease cohabiting in a "common European home,"[15] and demands that the West respect Russia's imperial spheres of influence.[16] He condemns America for seeking global domination through soft power,[17] a stance endorsed by Mikhail Gorbachev, who asserts that he was betrayed by the West's perfidy,[18] and is "absolutely convinced that Putin protects Russia's interests better than anyone else."[19] The Kremlin isn't improvising.[20] It is methodically striking back![21]

The West consequently finds itself in the unhappy position of having to decide whether to stay the Cold War II course, renegotiate the post-Soviet world order framed by parameters hammered out at Yalta and Potsdam, make fundamental domestic policy adjustments, or opt for Détente II.[22] Although America and the European Union deride Putin's narrative[23] and portray themselves as the sword and shield of reason, social justice, diversity, minority rights, ethnic self-determination, global harmony, universal values, democracy, competition, Weberian efficiency, anticolonialism, and the rule of international law, they must still decide how to manage the Kremlin's challenge. Is it wiser to cajole and coerce Russia into becoming a compliant junior "partner" (acquiescing to the West-dominated post-Soviet world order of 1992–2008);[24] to de jure or de facto rewrite the terms of engagement (first phase of the post-Soviet order), taking account of recent changes in the "correlation of forces" (2002–2016); embrace an interim Détente II strategy; or bolster its military deterrent and restructure its economy?[25] Experts and think tanks have discussed these possibilities,[26] but their analyses often are incomplete because few fully grasp and take to heart contemporary Russia's resurgent economic and military industrial power,[27] its sophisticated approach to geopolitical domination,[28] and information warfighting capabilities.[29] They fail to adequately appreciate Putin's tenaciousness, his ability to repress dissent and[30] make opponents vanish,[31] and his willingness to play "Russian roulette."[32] And they tend to disregard the dangers of Western secular economic stagnation,[33] political paralysis, domestic disaffection, military decay,[34] and rollback of nuclear arms control.[35] As a consequence, American and EU statesmen have mostly played the role of mock avenging angels,[36] chiding the Kremlin for violating the written and implicit post-Soviet rules of the game (including the INF Treaty),[37] imposing slapdash economic sanctions,[38] and threatening military reprisals, including arming Ukrainian proxies,[39] while relying on "strategic patience,"[40] instead of prudently managing adverse changes in the correlation of forces, or changing them.[41] The West is inclined to disparage and disregard Putin's demands for spheres of influence, giving priority to rights of self-determination claimed by Eastern and Central Europe, Estonia, Latvia, Lithuania, Ukraine, Moldova, Transdnistria, Armenia,[42] Georgia, South Ossetia,[43] and Russia's own Westernizers.[44] Washington and Berlin also appear unwilling to leash their push for "color revolutions" on Putin's turf (Armenia, Azerbaijan, Belarus, Georgia, Moldova, Ukraine),[45] EU enlargement, and forward NATO military deployments in Russia's neighborhood. This places the Kremlin and the West on a Cold War II collision course where episodic confrontation, including proxy wars,[46] rather than partnership (globalization), is the de facto "new normal" across a broad spectrum of issues, including economic sanctions,[47] unless one side or the other blinks.[48]

The alternatives to staying the course under the guise of a "reset" are Western military strengthening and economic revitalization, Détente II, or a renegotiated world order formally establishing Western and Kremlin spheres of influence.[49] Détente II is an interim strategy that temporarily accepts Crimea's annexation,[50] and the "frozen conflict" in Novorossiya while both sides try to figure out whether to push for victory or to negotiate a compromise either behind the scenes,[51] or at a formal conference some Russian security experts call Yalta II ("new normalization").[52] The devil, as always, is in the process, details, and implementation,[53] but the costs of persevering with the globalization policies that provoked Crimea's annexation seem to vastly outweigh the benefits for the American and European people.[54] It is unrealistic to suppose that a new consensus world order can be swiftly achieved,[55] but America and the European Union should be able to orchestrate Détente II to achieve Cold Peace (mutual toleration) without abandoning legitimate ideals or fully discarding hidden agendas, if they cannot strengthen their militaries and economies.[56] Once the West makes some substantial concessions to terminate today's often veiled cold war (mutual intolerance),[57] and Putin's accepts the Cold Peace, he will be reluctant to press the envelope too far to avoid reverting to square one. The Kremlin will have struck back, but if properly managed, most of the former Soviet Union's vassals can retain their newly acquired territorial integrity, EU status, and NATO membership.[58]

Although partnership is best, Détente almost as good, and Cold Peace better than Cold War II, the latter is apt to prevail in the decade ahead because the world is entering a new epoch where the gains from cooperation no longer self-evidently exceed the expected benefits of bullying. During the 1990s and until the global financial crisis of 2008, authentic cooperation seemed the wisest course for most nations, despite lingering concerns about Western hegemonic intentions for a variety of compelling reasons. Global economic growth, spurred by the demise of command communism, EU monetary union, and American financial "liberalization," provided political support for cooperation, as did heady hopes for democratization, peace, solidarity, affirmative action, social justice, and universal harmony. This optimism is no longer convincing, especially in the Kremlin. Not only is economic growth decelerating in both the developed and developing worlds, auguring "secular stagnation,"[59] but "savvy" players appear to have concluded that domination is more important than small cooperative benefits. Berlin's ongoing effort to wrest control of Athens's public finances by threatening to destroy the Greek banking system, despite the European Union's praise for compassionate solidarity, is symptomatic of this "new normal."[60]

The triumph of willfulness over cooperation and the public good has become endemic in Russia and the West, making it difficult to restore general prosperity. Russia no longer is enticed by democratic free enterprise; the West is addicted to deficit spending and monetary stimulus as antidotes for efficiency-destroying over-taxation, overregulation, over-control, mandating, and executive orders.[61] China's growth is waning as it exhausts the advantages of economic development, and deflation (despite quantitative easing) threatens all countries dependent on secularly increasing natural resources prices. The West is going to be riven by fierce struggles for the division of its national pies that precludes parrying a Russian arms buildup.[62]

The Kremlin, for its part, will continue favoring "rent-granting" and the *siloviki* (power services) over civilian priorities, defending and expanding Russia's sphere of influence to bolster its legitimacy, despite high hopes in some quarters for "regime change."

The conjuncture of these forces and their persistence doesn't allow analysts to accurately predict short-term micro consequences, but it does shape contours. Russia's annexation of Crimea symbolizes the onset of "postglobalization," a war of attrition between intransigent foes speaking inspirationally about mutual accommodation, but struggling to expand their spheres of influence by all means fair and foul. Konstantin Sivkov has even argued for preventative tactical nuclear strikes.[63]

This prognostication is positive, not normative. Judgments about virtue and merit, right and wrong aren't required to know which way the wind is blowing or to gauge the new epoch's rhythms and perils. Nor is it essential to build a causal daisy chain explaining how partnership devolved into Cold War II. The crucial point for policy makers and analysts is that Cold War II has emerged with no politically viable easy fixes. It could verge toward a major armed conflagration or toward Cold Peace, depending on how conflicts are managed. Discord can be overcome, but may necessitate fundamental changes in the modus operandi of both sides that neither is yet sincerely willing to make.

Notes

1 Stalin shredded the Yalta and Potsdam Agreements in the late 1940s by reducing Eastern and Central Europe to the status of satellites, but they became default agreements when Gorbachev launched his "new thinking" (*novoe myshlenie*) in 1987, opening the possibility for dismantling the communist bloc and restoring Baltic independence. German reunification was settled by the Treaty on the Final Settlement on September 12, 1990.

2 Steven Rosefielde, Will Russia Embrace the Rule of Law? Paper presented at the University of Dallas, History and Theology Departments, September 12, 2014.

3 Correlation of forces is a Soviet concept closely related to the Western notion of balance of power.

4 "Partnership" is an outwardly amicable, mutually advantageous relationship overlaying latent conflicts. It shapes Russian geopolitical strategy. For a disingenuous interpretation of the phenomenon, see Ivan Kratsev and Mark Leonard, "Europe's Shattered Dream of Order," *Foreign Affairs*, May/June, Vol. 94, No. 3, 2015: 48–58. Europeans, they claim, believed that "So long as citizens could choose freely, the thinking went, governments would eventually embrace the European way. Russia shattered that assumption last year when it invaded Crimea." This formula pretends that the West avoided provoking the Kremlin.

5 Dmitri Trenin, "Russia and the United States: A Temporary Break or a New Cold War?" Carnegie Moscow, January 22, 2015. http://carnegie.ru/2014/12/08/russia-and-united-states-temporary-break-or-new-cold-war/hxw4?mkt_tok=3RkMMJWWfF9wsRoluaXPZKXonjHpfsX56OsvXqGg38431UFwdcjKPmjr1YACTsV0aPyQAgobGp5I5FEIQ7XYTLB2t60MWA%3D%3D. Trenin, in his testimony to the Duma, characterizes Russia's strategic vision and the correlation of forces as follows: "9. Strategic vision means understanding that: a. Russian-American relations now are different than during the Cold War; they do not determine world development by themselves, though they fully conform to its logic. b. The new competition is not 'a life and death struggle,' but a struggle to set the terms of future interaction, in other words, tough competition. c. The outcome of Russian-American confrontation will be determined not in Ukraine or Syria, but mainly in the areas of economics, science, and technology, social development, and, more broadly, the internal state of Russia."

6 True democracy (*demos kratos*) is a system of rule where the people's preferences govern public policies and private markets. True democracy requires elected officials to passively carry out the people's will without imposing their own preferences. Steven

Rosefielde and Quinn Mills, *Democracy and Its Elected Enemies: American Political Capture and Economic Decline*, Cambridge: Cambridge University Press, 2013.

7   Samuel Huntington, "The West: Unique, Not Universal," *Foreign Affairs*, Vol. 75, No. 6, 1996: 28–46; Samuel Huntington, *The Clash of Civilizations and the Remaking of World Order*, New York: Simon & Schuster, 1996; Steven Rosefielde and Stefan Hedlund, *Russia since 1980: Wrestling with Westernization*, Cambridge: Cambridge University Press, 2008. The same can be said about Mikhail Gorbachev.

8   Catherine Belton and Neil Buckley, "Businessmen Are 'Serfs' in Putin's Russia, Warns Sergei Pugachev," *Financial Times*, October 8, 2014. http://www.ft.com/cms/s/0/ab541ee8-4e4c-11e4-bfda-00144feab7de.html#axzz3Fexe6dBq.

Muscovite culture is traceable to Ivan III Vasilevich, known as Ivan the Great, Grand Prince of Muscovy (1440–1505). The Muscovite idea is that the ruler, whether he is called grand duke, tsar, vozhd (leader), general secretary, or president, is an autocrat who, de facto or de jure, owns all of the country's productive assets and governs for himself in the name of the nation. He is the law and rules by edict absolutely or behind a façade of parliamentary constitutionalism. Everyone else is a *rab* (slave of the ruler). Individuals of other stations may have private lives and may seek to maximize their happiness, but they are always subject to commands, edicts, and rules imposed from above by their supreme lord, without protection of the rule of law. They have no inviolable human, property, economic, political, or social rights. Whatever has been given can be rescinded, regardless of custom or precedent. Social welfare in this cultural framework is synonymous with the autocrat's welfare, given whatever allotment he chooses to share with his people.

On its face, universal autocratic ownership and governance seem intrinsically totalitarian. It is easy to imagine Ivan the Terrible (Ivan IV Vasilevich, 1530–1584, first tsar of Russia) assigning his servitors detailed economic, administrative, police, martial, and diplomatic tasks and meticulously monitoring their performance. However, comprehensive control was never feasible, even during Joseph Stalin's reign. Autocrats had only sketchy knowledge of their realm, its potentials, and the requirements for efficient utilization and were never successful at devising an honest and effective bureaucracy to do the job for them. Consequently, they were compelled by circumstances to grant servitors substantial independence in operating the autocrat's properties for their own benefit (*pomestie*) in return for tax and service obligations, while tolerating bureaucratic corruption and inefficiency. Autocrats were rent-grantors, and servitors were rent-seekers. As long as rulers received what they needed, they didn't concern themselves with overpaying or with their deputies' exploitation of the peasantry. This attitude, optimizing where possible and satisficing where circumstances dictated, was coercive, not totalitarian, even though in principle the scope of the tsar's authority was unbounded. It was a callous mechanism for squeezing taxes from a servile population, but not an instrument of comprehensive micro control. Russia's autocrats didn't systematically oppress the people or bother themselves about their plight. They simply permitted their servitors to get the job done, whatever that entailed. The arrangement was paradoxical. On paper, the tsar and the state were all-powerful, but they often were weak in practice. In times of crisis, pressure could be exerted to mobilize resources for defense or industrialization, but even then, outcomes depended more on the vagaries of rent-granting in a natural economy with underdeveloped markets, making Russia a colossus with clay feet. The Kremlin could struggle to keep up with the West, but remained forever backward. History, of course, isn't static. Servitors conspired to transform rent-granting into private property. Like paramours scheming for marriage, some of these stationary bandits (in Mancur Olson's terminology) were successful. However, a critical mass needed to achieve free enterprise under the rule of contract law or democracy was never reached, even though Catherine the Great relieved the nobility of lifetime service and Tsar Nicholas II's premier, Piotr Stolypin (1862–1911), tried to create peasant landownership in the *ukaz* of November 9, 1906. Patrimonialist Muscovy was always able to keep rent-granting in command through political intrigue, the secret police, and the army. It refused to serve Douglass North's role of credible enforcer for an autonomous, self-regulating society because sovereigns preferred autocracy to economic and political liberty.

Although the attributes of Muscovy varied from epoch to epoch, its footprint has remained unmistakable, the key traits being patrimonial rent-granting, based on the rule of men rather than the rule of law, where the ruler's optimization is narrowly circumscribed by a short span of control. These characteristics have made Russia a nation extraordinarily dependent on the machinations of the privileged and the tight supervision of the secret police. Effort is primarily mobilized through coercion rather than entrepreneurial initiative and market discipline, hindering catch-up with the Western high-productivity frontier. Conquest has often proven more gratifying to rulers than competitive national economic rivalry. They frequently have been content to live lavishly from natural resources–financed foreign imports rather than nurturing high value-added mass production. It is always possible that these cultural proclivities are teething problems and that the Kremlin will soon mature; however, until it does, the model will remain pre-enlightened.

9 Robert Kaplan, "Countering Putin's Grand Strategy: With Europe Weak and Distracted, only the U.S. can Thwart the Kremlin's Growing Ambitions," *Wall Street Journal*, February 11, 2015. Kaplan is a geographic determinist. See Robert Kaplan, *The Revenge of Geography: What the Map Tells Us about Coming Conflicts and the Battle Against Fate*, New York: Random House, 2010.

10 Mary Elise Sarotte, "A Broken Promise? What the West Really Told Moscow about NATO Expansion," *Foreign Affairs*, Vol. 90, September/October 2014. Cf. Joshua R. Itzkowitz Shifrinson, "Deal or No Deal? The End of the Cold War and the U.S. Offer to Limit NATO Expansion," *International Security*, Vol. 40, No. 4 (Spring 2016), 7–44. http://belfercenter.ksg.harvard.edu/files/003-ISEC_a_00236-Shifrinson.pdf

11 The term *engagement* in diplomatic parlance means one or many parties trying to strong-arm another through "friendly persuasion."

12 John Kornblum, "Time to Stop Letting Putin Win the War of Words," *Wall Street Journal*, February 8, 2015. http://www.wsj.com/articles/john-kornblum-time-to-stop-letting-putin-win-the-war-of-words-1423438339. "Western nations must start the turnaround by emphatically refuting one of Mr. Putin's favorite claims: that the West abrogated the promise of democratic partnership with Russia in the 1990 Paris Charter, a document produced by a summit that included European governments, the U.S. and the Soviet Union, convened as Communism crumbled across Eastern Europe. The U.S. and its allies didn't rush in after 1990 to exploit a proud but collapsing Soviet Union – a tale that Mr. Putin now spins. I took part in nearly every major negotiation of that era. Never was the idea of humbling Russia considered even

for a moment. The Russian leaders we encountered were not angry Prussian-style Junkers who railed against a strategic stab in the back. Many if not all viewed the fall of the Soviet Union as liberation rather than defeat. They saw Western democracy as the best path to security and freedom for their country." Mr. Kornblum, a former U.S. ambassador to Germany and former assistant secretary of state for European affairs, is senior counselor for Noerr LLP law firm in Berlin.

13 Andrei Kortunov, "The Splendours and Miseries of Geopolitics," *Valdai*, January 16, 2015. http://valdaiclub.com/russia_and_the_world/74960.html. Leon Aron, "Why Putin Says Russia Is Exceptional," *Wall Street Journal*, May 30, 2014. http://online .wsj.com/articles/why-putin-says-russia-is-exceptional-1401473667. "To Mr. Putin, in short, Russia was exceptional because it was emphatically not like the modern West – or not, in any event, like his caricature of a corrupt, morally benighted Europe and U.S. This was a bad omen, presaging the foreign policy gambits against Ukraine that now have the whole world guessing about Mr. Putin's intentions." "One of the most troubling aspects of this concept of Russian uniqueness is that it has been defined largely in opposition to an allegedly hostile and predatory West. According to Mr. Putin's favorite philosopher, the émigré Ivan Ilyin (1883–1954), 'Western nations don't understand and don't tolerate Russian identity. ... They are going to divide the united Russian "broom" into twigs to break those twigs one by one and rekindle with them the fading light of their own civilization.' Mr. Putin often quotes Ilyin and recently assigned his works to regional governors." "One can hear distinct echoes of Ilyin's views in the fiery speech that Mr. Putin delivered this past March after Russia's annexation of Crimea. The West, Mr. Putin said, 'preferred to be guided not by international law in its practical policies but by the rule of the gun' and wished to 'drive Russia into the corner.' He traced this hostility as far back as the 18th century and said that, in the post-Soviet era, Russia 'has always been deceived, has always been [confronted with] decisions made behind its back.'" Cf. Kathryn Stoner-Weiss, *Resisting the State: Reform and Retrenchment in Post-Soviet Russia*, Cambridge: Cambridge University Press, 2006; Peter Baker and Susan Glasser, *Kremlin Rising: Vladimir Putin's Russia and the End of Revolution*, New York: Scribner, 2005; Catherine Boyle, "Putin: West Guilty of 'Pure Cynicism' over Ukraine," *CNBC*, December 4, 2014. http://www.cnbc.com/id/102238208#.

14 Aron, "Why Putin Says Russia Is Exceptional." "In the winter of 2012, something surprising happened to Vladimir Putin: He discovered, as he wrote in a government newspaper, that Russia isn't just an ordinary country but a unique 'state civilization,' bound together by the ethnic Russians who form its 'cultural nucleus.' This was something new." "The pedigree of Russian exceptionalism stretches back to a 16th-century monk, Philotheus of Pskov, a city about 400 miles northwest of Moscow. Constantinople had fallen to the Turks a century earlier and Rome was possessed by the 'heresy' of Catholicism, so it fell to the Grand Duchy of Muscovy, Philotheus averred, to preserve, strengthen and expand the only real and pure Christianity: the Russian Orthodox faith."

15 Putin claims that the West reneged on promises to keep former Soviet republics and satellites out of NATO and the European Union. Sarotte reports with regard to East Germany that unwritten promises were made, but quickly shelved. See Sarotte, "A Broken Promise?" Despite this claim, Putin occasionally presses his plan for a Greater Europe co-led by Russia and others spanning the Atlantic to the Pacific.

Marek Menkiszak, *Greater Europe: Putin's Vision of European (dis)integration*, OSW Number 46, Warsaw, October, 2013. John Mearsheimer asserts that Putin's grievances are well founded. "The United States and its European allies share most of the responsibility for the crisis. The taproot of the trouble is NATO enlargement, the central element of a larger strategy to move Ukraine out of Russia's orbit and integrate it into the West. At the same time, the EU's expansion eastward and the West's backing of the pro-democracy movement in Ukraine – beginning with the Orange Revolution in 2004 – were critical elements, too. Since the mid-1990s, Russian leaders have adamantly opposed NATO enlargement, and in recent years, they have made it clear that they would not stand by while their strategically important neighbor turned into a Western bastion." See John Mearsheimer, "Why the Ukraine Crisis Is the West's Fault: The Liberal Delusions that Provoked Putin," *Foreign Affairs*, Vol. 90, September/October 2014.

16 The concept of a sphere of influence is a dubious basis for asserting power over others, but nonetheless is widely invoked by both sides across the East-West divide. Russia and the West have long claimed spheres of influence and asserted rights of hegemony. They both claim duties to intervene in the internal and foreign affairs of neighboring sovereign states, including obligations to foster regime change. Washington, Brussels, and Moscow contend that they reserve the right to employ armed forces against each other, independent nations, and non-state actors to further their national interests, while hypocritically contending that the world order is inviolable. The Kremlin never apologized for abetting the creation of people's republics, and Washington boasts about fomenting regime change (color revolutions) that suit its purposes.

The battle for Novorossiya and other parts of the former Soviet sovereign space is best understood from this perspective. Russia and the West are both trying to seize the moral high ground by justifying their actions on this or that universal principle, but they are merely perpetuating the traditional hegemonic game. The arguments advanced by both sides justifying their actions may persuade objective observers to support either antagonist, but the fundamental problem is a test of wills that the correlation of forces will ultimately determine. Claims of universal right are part of the correlation of forces and are unlikely to be determinative in the unfolding new cold war. The search for the conflict's peaceful resolution therefore must necessarily focus on encouraging both parties to soberly assess costs and benefits, including catastrophic risk given the correlation of forces, de-escalate, and sagely renegotiate the post-Soviet world order. Jean Tirole, "Country Solidarity in Sovereign Crises," *American Economic Review* 2015, 105(8): 2333–2363.

The new order will likely involve a spectrum of imperial authority running the gamut from annexation (Crimea by Russia and East Germany by West Germany) to Finlandization and lesser types of domestic intrusions and tribute. Neither Russia nor the West has to reconquer Novorossiya to settle their rival hegemonic claims. They have the option of negotiating less bellicose terms of mutual re-endearment behind a façade of uncompromising rhetoric.

This is best accomplished by both parties taking to heart the wisdom of compromising their contending claims, working out the particulars, and crafting face-saving rationales that placate constituents. The Germans appear willing to proceed in this manner, but Washington doesn't seem ready yet to concede anything beyond toning down its rhetoric. The White House insists on the inviolability of the implicit post-Soviet world order (the West's concept of globalization), categorically rejected by Putin with an important unintended consequence. The implicit rules of the new cold war are more elusive than those of the post-Stalinist world order, making risks correspondingly higher. Compromise in a post-ideological age should be easier, but ironically to date finding mutual grounds for agreements seems more difficult.

17 Olga Khvostunova, "Vladimir Putin's Valdai Show," *Institute of Modern Russia*, October 28, 2014. http://imrussia.org/en/opinions/2064-vladimir-putin%E2%80%99s-valdai-show. "Putin's answer to the question 'who is to blame?' is quite straightforward: 'It looks like the so-called "winners" of the Cold War are determined to have it all and reshape the world into a place that could better serve their interests alone. ... This is the behavior of the nouveau riche, who stumbled upon a great wealth – global leadership. Instead of managing it expertly and accurately, for their own benefit as well, they made a lot of blunders.'" Cf. Stephen Cohen, *Failed Crusade: America and the Tragedy of Post-Communist Russia*, New York: W.W. Norton, 2015; Stephen Cohen, *Should the West Engage Putin's Russia?: The Munk Debates*, New York: House of Anansi Press, 2016; Garry Kasparov, *Winter Is Coming: Why Vladimir Putin and the Enemies of the Free World Must Be Stopped*, New York: Public Affairs, 2015.

18 Nathan Gardels, "Why Gorbachev Feels Betrayed by the Post–Cold War West," *The World Post*, November 7, 2014. http://www.huffingtonpost.com/2014/11/07/gorbachev-post-cold-war-west_n_6116654.html. Note that Gorbachev may have a hidden agenda. He could be indicted for treason because of his role in fomenting *katastroika*. See "Russian Parliament Moves to Charge Gorbachev with Treason for Breaking Up U.S.S.R.," April 11, 2014.

19 Gardels, "Why Gorbachev Feels Betrayed by the Post–Cold War West." "On the 25th anniversary of the fall of the Berlin Wall, Mikhail Gorbachev, the last Soviet leader, remains a hero in the West. But the West is no longer in favor with Gorbachev. Already in 2005 when I sat down with him in Moscow to discuss the 20th anniversary of his reforms that ultimately led to the dissolution of the USSR, Gorbachev expressed anger and betrayal over what he regarded as America's 'victory complex' over Russia. Vladimir Putin and Mikhail Gorbachev could not be more different as leaders. But they are both proud Russians who don't think their nation is getting its due. They are like 'bent twigs springing back after being stepped on,' in the phrase Isaiah Berlin used to describe how resentment and aggressive nationalism are rooted in the backlash against humiliation. Gorbachev told Gardels, 'The Soviet Union used to be not just an adversary but also a partner of the West. There was some balance in that system. Even though the U.S. and Europe signed a charter for a new Europe, the Charter of Paris, to demonstrate that a new world was possible, that charter was ignored and political gains were pursued to take advantage of the vacuum. The struggle for spheres of influence – contrary to the new thinking we propounded – was resumed by the U.S. The first result was the crisis in Yugoslavia in which NATO was brought in to gain advantage over Russia. We were ready to build a new security architecture for Europe. But after the breakup of the Soviet Union and the end of the Warsaw Pact, NATO forgot all its promises. It became more of a political than a military organization. NATO decided it would be an organization

that intervenes anywhere on "humanitarian grounds." We have by now seen intervention not only in Yugoslavia, but in Iraq – intervention without any mandate or permission from the United Nations.'"

20 Matthew Schofield, "Russian News Report: Putin Approved Ukraine Invasion before Kiev Government Collapsed," McClatchy, February 21, 2015. http://www.mcclatchydc.com/2015/02/21/257386/russian-news-report-ukraine-invasion.html. The editor of *Novaya Gazeta*, Dmitri Muratov, claims to have an official government strategy document outlining the invasion of Ukraine that was prepared weeks before the Ukrainian government collapsed last year. Russia's commitment to rebuild its armed forces was already clear in its secret military modernization program of 2002, signed by Kasyanov. See Steven Rosefielde, *Russia in the 21st Century: The Prodigal Superpower*, Cambridge: Cambridge University Press, 2005. Cf. Andrew Weiss, "Putin the Improviser: The Ukraine Crisis Is even Scarier than You Think: Russia's Strongman Is Making it up as He Goes Along," *Carnegie Endowment*, February 20, 2015. http://carnegieendowment.org/2015/02/20/putin-improviser/i2q3.

21 Putin's position in all these regards is broadly supported by Stephen Cohen and Katrina van den Heuvel. See Cathy Young, "Putin's Pal," *Slate*, July 24, 2014. http://www.slate.com/articles/news_and_politics/foreigners/2014/07/stephen_cohen_vladimir_putin_s_apologist_the_nation_just_published_the_most.html. Richard Sakwa is also sympathetic. Richard Sakwa, *Frontline Ukraine: Crisis in the Borderlands*, London: I.B. Tauris, 2014. Cf. Jonathan Steele, Review of Frontline Ukraine: Crisis in the Borderlands, *Guardian*, February 19, 2015. http://www.theguardian.com/books/2015/feb/19/frontline-ukraine-crisis-in-borderlands-richard-sakwa-review-account. "Sakwa writes with barely suppressed anger of Europe's failure, arguing that instead of a vision embracing the whole continent, the EU has become little more than the civilian wing of the Atlantic alliance.

"A few months ago, at the height of the Russian-Ukrainian conflict over Crimea, Stephen F. Cohen, professor emeritus of Russian studies and politics at New York University and Princeton, acquired a certain notoriety as the Kremlin's No. 1 American apologist. As Cohen made Russia's case and lamented the American media's meanness to Vladimir Putin in print and on the airwaves, he was mocked as a 'patsy' and a 'dupe' everywhere from the conservative *Free Beacon* to the liberal *New York* and *New Republic*. Now, as the hostilities in eastern Ukraine have turned to the tragedy of Malaysia Airlines Flight 17, Cohen is at it again – this time, with a long article in the current issue of *The Nation* indicting 'Kiev's atrocities' in eastern Ukraine and America's collusion therein. The timing is rather unfortunate for Cohen and *The Nation*, since the piece is also unabashedly sympathetic to the Russian-backed militants who appear responsible for the murder of 298 innocent civilians. In the late 1980s, Cohen was an ardent enthusiast of Mikhail Gorbachev's perestroika reforms; he and his wife, Katrina van den Heuvel, now editor in chief of *The Nation*, co-authored *Voices of Glasnost: Interviews with Gorbachev's Reformers*, whose subjects – officials, journalists, and intellectuals – were all proponents of top-down change to bring about a kinder, gentler Soviet socialism. Those dreams ended in a rude awakening in 1991 with the demise of the Soviet Union. The Soviet collapse is generally seen as the result of the system's internal rot; Cohen, however, has blamed it on Boris Yeltsin's power-grabbing, aided by the pro-Western 'radical

intelligentsia' that 'hijacked Gorbachev's gradualist reformation.' His antipathy
to Yeltsin led him to sympathize with the views of those Russians who saw their
country during the 1990s as 'semi-occupied by foreigners – from shock-therapy
economists to human-rights advocates,' and who credited Putin with taking it
back. In *Newsweek's* February 2008 roundup of expert opinions on Putin and his
legacy, Cohen's contribution – entitled 'The Savior' – asserted Putin was the man
who 'ended Russia's collapse at home and re-asserted its independence abroad.' As
U.S.-Russian relations worsened, Cohen grew increasingly strident in his denuncia-
tions of the 'demonization' of Putin by the American media. Cohen's new article
in *The Nation* hits a new low. The charge Cohen makes is a serious one: that the
pro-Western Ukrainian government, aided and abetted by the Obama administration, the 'new Cold War hawks' in Congress, and the craven American media, is
committing 'deeds that are rising to the level of war crimes, if they have not done so
already.' He is referring to the Ukrainian military assaults on cities and towns held
by pro-Russian insurgents, including artillery shelling and air attacks."

22 The Yalta Agreement hammered out at Yalta in Crimea February 4–11, 1945 provided for the establishment of the United Nations as a cornerstone of the postwar
world order, settled various East-West territorial disputes, and established spheres
of influence of Germany, Austria, Poland, Czechoslovakia, Hungary, Romania, and
Bulgaria. The Soviet Union soon violated the accord by openly imposing communist regimes in Eastern and Central Europe, precipitating the Cold War world order
that lasted until December 25, 1991, when the Soviet Union was formally dissolved.
See Alexei Fenenko, "Options in Ukraine: Traditional Compromise, a Second Yalta
or Conflict in Intermarium," *Valdai*, September 4, 2014. http://valdaiclub.com/
near_abroad/71680.html.

23 Josh Rogin, "Europeans Laugh as Lavrov Talks Ukraine," *Bloomberg*, February
7, 2015. http://www.bloombergview.com/articles/2015-02-08/lavrov-s-comedy-
routine-on-ukraine-isn-t-funny-to-europe?cmpid=yhoo. "In the span of 45 min-
utes today, Russian Foreign Minister Sergei Lavrov rewrote the history of the Cold
War, accused the West of fomenting a coup in Ukraine and declared himself a
champion of the United Nations Charter. The crowd here in Germany laughed at
and then booed him, but he didn't seem to care." "Wolfgang Ischinger, chairman
of the Munich Security Conference, was moderating the question-and-answer
session on stage with Lavrov. He tried to find common ground, saying, 'The issues
we are discussing here are no laughing matter from any side.'
   "Actually, it was funny, but not because the fate of Ukraine should be trivialized.
The entire episode made it obvious that any notion that the West and Russia can
have a discussion on Ukraine, based on a shared vision of reality, is absurd."

24 "Russia Is 'Strategic Problem' for EU: Juncker," AFP Videos, December 4, 2014.
http://news.yahoo.com/video/russia-39-strategic-problem-39-190112992.html.
"Russia is now a 'strategic problem' for the EU amid the crisis in Ukraine, but
Brussels will work to make Moscow a partner again, European Commission president Jean-Claude Juncker said Thursday."

25 The term *correlation of forces*, borrowed from physics, is a multifactor version of
the balance of power concept widely employed by Soviet and Russian security analysts. Julian Lider, "The Correlation of World Forces: The Soviet Concept," *Journal*

of Peace Research, Vol. 17 No. 2, June 1980: 151–171. http://jpr.sagepub.com/content/17/2/151.abstract. Allen Lynch, *The Soviet Study of International Relations*, Cambridge: Cambridge University Press, 1989.

26 *PONARS Eurasia: Policy Perspectives*, Policy Conference, September 2014. Rajan Menon and Eugene B. Rumer, *Conflict in Ukraine: The Unwinding of the Post–Cold War Order*, Cambridge, MA: MIT Press, 2015.

27 Christopher Harress, "Russian Air Force and Navy to Receive 200 New Aircraft in 2015, more than Most World Air Forces Have," *Ibtimes*, February 4, 2015. http://www.ibtimes.com/russian-air-force-navy-receive-200-new-aircraft-2015-more-most-world-air-forces-have-1805100. "Shoygu also announced that the Russian air force will begin using the Su-35s Flanker multirole fighter jet in 2015. The twin-engine, single-seat fighter jet is undergoing tests, and 'this year the new aircraft should enter service,' Shoygu said during the conference call The aircraft, which will cost $85 million to buy at export price – far cheaper than Western counterparts – is considered to be a 4++ generation fighter, just short of the fifth-generation fighters, of which the United States' F-22 Raptor is the only operational example. However, Lockheed Martin's F-35 is in the final stages of becoming operational; the U.S. Marine Corps version should launch in December 2015. Russia's Sukhoi T-50 and China's Chengdu J-20 and Shenyang J-31, also fifth-generation fighters – defined by their use of stealth, or radar-evading features – are all still in testing."

28 Johan Norberg and Fredrik Westerlund, "Tailoring War: Russia's Use of Armed Force in Ukraine," draft paper prepared for the 46th Association for Slavic, East European, and Eurasian Studies Conference, San Antonio Texas, Friday, November 21, 2014. Cf. Eugene Rumer, "From Inside Putin's Parallel Universe, the Crisis Looks Bright," *Financial Times*, Op-Ed, December 22, 2014. http://carnegieendowment.org/2014/12/22/from-inside-putin-s-parallel-universe-crisis-looks-bright/hxsr?mkt_tok=3RkMMJWWfF9wsRolu67NZKXonjHpfsX56OsvXqGg38431UFwdcjKPmjr1YABSct0aPyQAgobGp5I5FEIQ7XYTLB2t60MWA%3D%3D.

"Russia's economic progress probably does not look too bad either when Mr Putin compares it with other leading powers. Who has done better in the past 15 years? Gross domestic product has increased sixfold. Income per head has risen sevenfold. Never before have Russians seen such prosperity. More currency reserves would be good, but $200bn is available immediately; and, by conservative measures, the same has been put in rainy day funds. The military has been rebuilt enough to instill fear in Europe, make the US pay attention once more and to make Russians proud."

29 Andrei Bystritsky, "War Is Peace," *Valdai*, February 26, 2015. http://valdaiclub.com/publication/75660.html.

30 Marc Bennetts, "The Latest Kremlin Crackdown on Opposition Is 'Unprecedented in Post-Soviet Russian History,'" *Business Insider*, February 8, 2015. http://www.businessinsider.com/the-latest-kremlin-crackdown-on-opposition-is-unprecedented-in-post-soviet-russian-history-2015-2. "If the West hoped economy-busting sanctions over the Kremlin's apparent military support for rebels in Ukraine would spark mass protests against Russian President Vladimir Putin's long rule, then – so far, at least – it was sadly mistaken. The Russian economy may be tanking and inflation may be rocketing, but discontent over the spiraling cost of living has been limited to online anger and small opposition rallies.

A controversial new law that came into force in July but is only now being implemented stipulates prison terms of up to five years for anyone detained more than
once in a period of 180 days at unsanctioned protests. Since the start of the year,
three opposition activists have been charged under the new law. The three men
facing years behind bars are Mark Galperin, a Moscow lawyer; Ildar Dadin, a
veteran political activist who took part in last year's Maidan uprising in Kiev; and
Vladimir Ionov, a 75-year-old activist. In late December, Russia jailed opposition
leader Alexei Navalny's younger brother, Oleg, in a ruling that seems designed
to keep up the pressure on Putin's biggest foe without turning him into a martyr.
On top of the Oleg jailing, a mother of seven was charged last week with treason
after calling the Ukrainian embassy to report a conversation she had overheard
about the possible deployment of Russian troops to the former Soviet republic –
even though Russia denies its forces are in Ukraine. Other laws have cracked
down on already shaky media freedoms. In case all that isn't enough to persuade
Russians to stay off the streets, a new pro-Kremlin movement, Anti-Maidan, has
been formed to counter any attempt to establish a Ukraine-style protest camp
in Moscow. A coalition of the Moscow-based Night Wolves biker gang, veterans
of Russia's wars in Chechnya and Afghanistan, as well as Cossacks and mixed
martial arts champions, the movement has already clashed with opposition supporters in Moscow. Anti-Maidan was formed by Dmitry Sablin, an ex-lawmaker
from Putin's United Russia party."

31 Alexander Winning, "Russian Opposition Leader Nemtsov Shot Dead in Moscow,"
Reuters, February 28, 2015. http://news.yahoo.com/russian-opposition-leader-
boris-nemtsov-shot-dead-moscow-220603814.html. "Boris Nemtsov, a Russian
opposition politician and former deputy prime minister who was an outspoken
critic of President Vladimir Putin, was shot dead meters from the Kremlin in central Moscow late on Friday. Putin condemned the killing and took the investigation
under presidential command, saying it could have been a contract killing and a
'provocation' on the eve of a big opposition protest that Nemtsov had been due
to lead in Moscow on Sunday. Nemtsov had been quoted as saying he was concerned that the president might want him dead over his opposition to the conflict in
Ukraine. Sunday's opposition march is intended as a protest against the war in east
Ukraine, where pro-Russian rebels have seized a swathe of territory."

32 Mikhail Lermontov, *A Hero of Our Time: The Fatalist*, 1841. http://www.eldritchpress
.org/myl/hero.htm. Cf. Ray Locker. "Pentagon 2008 Study Claims Putin has
Asperger Syndrome," *USA Today*, February 5, 2015. http://www.freep.com/story/
news/politics/2015/02/04/putin-aspergers-syndrome-study-pentagon/22855927/.
Asperger is an autism spectrum disorder characterized by significant social interaction and nonverbal communication difficulties. American Secretary of Defense
Ashton Carter portrayed Putin recently as a sensible patriot with whom the West
can find common ground. His statement no doubt is testing the ground for a
Washington led reset initiative "I'm frequently asked whether I know what Putin is
thinking. In fact, we all do, because he says what he thinks; he couldn't be clearer. He
regrets the demise of the Soviet Union. He wants respect for Russia's greatness. He
wants a voice in the world. And he wants a nonthreatening neighborhood." Carter
then adds, "Some aspects of that, or the manner in which he approaches it, could be
compatible with Western interests." "The Scholar as Secretary: A Conversation with

Ashton Carter," *Foreign Affairs*, Vol. 94, No. 5 (September–October 2015): pp. 72 ff., at page 75.

33 Steven Rosefielde and Quinn Mills, *Global Economic Turmoil and the Public Good*, Singapore: World Scientific Publishers, 2015. Alternatively, it has been suggested that Putin's misbehavior is explained by his Asperger's disease. Locker, "Pentagon 2008 Study Claims Putin has Asperger's Syndrome."

34 Francis Fukuyama, "America in Decay: The Sources of Political Dysfunction," *Foreign Affairs*, September/October 2014; Mackenzie Eaglen, "Politics Is Killing the Pentagon," November 12, 2014. http://www.aei.org/publication/politics-killing-pentagon/?utm_source=today&utm_medium=paramount&utm_campaign=111314. "Washington is in denial about two major realities: The U.S. military's technological edge is eroding, and politics is killing the Pentagon. All too soon, America won't be able to take on this range of challenges. Indeed, it's not even clear that we still can today." "At a recent Democratic Party event, President Obama boasted that, 'American military superiority has never been greater compared to other countries.' But the opposite is true. Earlier this year, the Pentagon acquisition chief contradicted his boss: 'Technological superiority is not assured, and we cannot be complacent about our posture. This is not a future problem; this is a "here now" problem.'"

35 Kalyan Kumar, "US, Russia Decide to Snap Nuclear Cooperation," *Australian Times*, January 26, 2015.
    http://au.ibtimes.com/us-russia-decide-snap-nuclear-cooperation-1414972. "Russia and the United States have reportedly called off their nuclear cooperation after Russia conveyed to the U.S. that it no longer needs the latter's assistance in safeguarding its nuclear sites. Russia-U.S. cooperation in the nuclear sector had been active in protecting weapons-grade uranium and plutonium from being stolen or sold unlawfully. The U.S. reportedly invested some $2 billion in the joint program and planned many joint initiatives through 2018."

36 *Saint Michael Vanquishing Satan*, Raphael, 1515, Louvre Museum, Paris.

37 Many in the arms control and disarmament community oppose America retaliation for Russia's admitted violation of the Intermediate Nuclear Forces (INF) treaty because they fear that this will give a green light to opponents urging the modernization of America's intermediate range missile capabilities. See David W. Kearn, "The INF Treaty and the Crisis in US-Russia Relations," *Huffington Post*, December 30, 2014. http://www.huffingtonpost.com/david-w-kearn/the-inf-treaty-and-the cr_b_6391032.html?ncid=txtlnkusaolp00000592.
    NATO has quietly matched Putin's saber rattling by Washington sending its nuclear-capable B-2 and B-52 to Europe for training missions with its NATO partners. It also continues to test intercontinental ballistic missiles, and the Western military alliance is currently modernizing the air-launched nuclear gravity bombs that fall under NATO's nuclear-sharing initiative. See Ian Kline, "NATO's Nuclear Relapse: Under the Public Radar," NATO Is Modernizing Its Tactical Nuclear Arsenal," *Aljazeera*, December 31, 2014. http://www.aljazeera.com/indepth/opinion/2014/12/nato-nuclear-relapse-2014123161917509924.html.

38 Alastair Cooke, "The Geo-financial War Places New Geo-political Facts on the Ground," *Valdai*, January 13, 2015. http://valdaiclub.com/russia_and_the_world/74880.html.

39 Peter Baker, "Debate on Arming Ukraine Fractures Washington Think Tank,"
    New York Times, February 6, 2015. http://www.nytimes.com/politics/first-draft/
    2015/02/06/debate-on-arming-ukraine-fractures-washington-think-tank/. "The
    Brookings Institution's president, Strobe Talbott, and one of his scholars, Steven
    Pifer, joined six other national security figures in a report on Monday calling on the
    Obama administration to provide arms to Ukraine's government to help it battle
    pro-Russian separatists. But ever since, other Brookings scholars have excoriated
    the idea. Jeremy Shapiro, a former State Department official now at Brookings,
    wrote on the institution's website that arming Ukrainians 'will lead only to further
    violence and instability, and possibly a dangerous confrontation.' Fiona Hill and
    Clifford Gaddy, two other Brookings scholars, added in *The Washington Post* that
    following their boss's advice would mean that 'the Ukrainians won't be the only
    ones caught in an escalating military conflict.' Mr. Talbott, a deputy secretary of
    state under President Bill Clinton, and Mr. Pifer, a former ambassador to Ukraine,
    responded to the friendly fire in their own follow-up posting on the Brookings
    site. 'If there's a better plan for settling the conflict, one that does not amount to
    wholesale Ukrainian capitulation, we would like to hear it,' they wrote."
40 Mark Salter, "Merkel Has a Strange View of How the Cold War Was Won," *Business
    Insider*, February 24, 2015. http://www.businessinsider.com/merkel-has-a-strange-
    view-of-how-the-cold-war-was-won-and-its-affecting-her-strategy-on-russian-
    aggression-2015-2. "Merkel reminded the audience that she was a little girl living
    in East Germany when the Soviets built the Berlin Wall in 1961 and the West had
    responded appropriately by patiently waiting 28 years for it to come down."
41 Henry Kissinger, *World Order*, London: Penguin Press HC, 2014; Henry Kissinger,
    "Henry Kissinger on the Assembly of a New World Order: The Concept that
    has Underpinned the Modern Geopolitical Era Is in Crisis," August 29, 2014.
    http://online.wsj.com/news/article_email/the-assembly-of-a-new-world-order-
    1409328075-lMyQjAxMTA0MDIwOTEyNDkyWj. "The contemporary quest for
    world order will require a coherent strategy to establish a concept of order within
    the various regions and to relate these regional orders to one another. These goals
    are not necessarily self-reconciling: The triumph of a radical movement might bring
    order to one region while setting the stage for turmoil in and with all others. The
    domination of a region by one country militarily, even if it brings the appearance of
    order, could produce a crisis for the rest of the world." "To play a responsible role in
    the evolution of a 21st-century world order, the U.S. must be prepared to answer a
    number of questions for itself: What do we seek to prevent, no matter how it hap-
    pens, and if necessary alone? What do we seek to achieve, even if not supported by
    any multilateral effort? What do we seek to achieve, or prevent, only if supported by
    an alliance? What should we not engage in, even if urged on by a multilateral group
    or an alliance? What is the nature of the values that we seek to advance? And how
    much does the application of these values depend on circumstance?"
42 Selcan Hacaoglu Sara Khojoyan, "Putin Seizes on Armenia Dispute to Buttress Iron
    Curtain Remains," *Bloomberg*, March 31, 2015. http://www.bloomberg.com/news/
    articles/2015-03-31/putin-seizes-on-armenia-dispute-to-buttress-iron-curtain-
    remains. "Armenia's decision in January was a victory for Putin after losing sway
    in Georgia, which signed an association agreement with the EU in 2013, and war-
    torn Ukraine. Yet the deal runs the risk of further isolation for Armenia under

Russia's protectorship, according to Alev Kilic, head of the Ankara-based Center for Eurasian Studies. 'While Ukraine turned its face toward the West at the risk of civil war, Armenia without any power was forced to bow to Putin,' Kilic said. The closed borders with Turkey and nearby Azerbaijan mean that without Russian support, 'life in Armenia would come to a standstill.' "

43 Max Delany, "Russia Stirs Anger with South Ossetia 'Annexation' Deal," *AFT*, March 18, 2015. http://news.yahoo.com/russia-stirs-anger-south-ossetia-annexation-deal-193229479.html. "President Vladimir Putin inked a deal in Moscow with South Ossetian leader Leonid Tibilov that officially makes Russia responsible for defending the self-declared republic, where the Kremlin has stationed thousands of troops since a war with Georgia there in 2008. The signing of the controversial pact came as Russia marked one year to the day since Putin signed off on the annexation of Ukraine's Black Sea republic of Crimea in a seismic shift slammed by Kiev and the West as an illegal land grab."

44 The West liberally construes the concept of self-determination to include covert assistance to preferred factions in Ukraine, Moldova, and Georgia. Azerbaijan and Armenia may also be added to this list. The concept of national self-determination isn't a Western monopoly, nor is the Kremlin's invocation of legitimating spheres of influence. The priority given these concepts by both sides depends on circumstances. For example, Putin's annexation of Crimea was justified by the popular will of the Crimean people. The West often asserts that this or that country falls into its sphere of influence.

45 The European Commission controls the Eastern Partnership (EaP). It is an initiative of the European Union governing its relationship with the post-Soviet states of Armenia, Azerbaijan, Belarus, Georgia, Moldova, and Ukraine, intended to provide a venue for discussions of trade, economic strategy, travel agreements, and other issues between the European Union and its Eastern neighbors. The project was initiated by Poland, and a subsequent proposal was prepared in cooperation with Sweden. It was presented by the foreign minister of Poland and Sweden at the EU General Affairs and External Relations Council in Brussels on May 26, 2008. The Eastern Partnership was inaugurated by the European Union in Prague on May 7, 2009. The Eastern Partnership consists of the post-Soviet states: Armenia, Azerbaijan, Belarus, Georgia, Moldova, Ukraine, and the European Union. Russia has voiced concerns over the Eastern Partnership, seeing it as an attempt to expand the European Union's "sphere of influence" in the quest for oil. Russia has also expressed concerns that the European Union is putting undue pressure on Belarus by suggesting it might be marginalized if it follows Russia in recognizing the independence of the Georgian breakaway regions of Abkhazia and South Ossetia. "Is this promoting democracy or is it blackmail? It's about pulling countries from the positions they want to take as sovereign states," Russian foreign minister Sergei Lavrov has stated. The European Commission portrays its actions as benign globalization; Russia sees the process as malevolent. Cf. Thomas de Waal and Richard Youngs, "Reform as Resilience: An Agenda for the Eastern Partnership," *Carnegie Endowment for Peace*, May 14, 2015. http://carnegieendowment.org/2015/05/14/reform-as-resilience-agenda-for-eastern-partnership/i8k4?mkt_tok=3RkMMJWW fF9wsRojuaTIZKXonjHpfsX56OsvXqGg38431UFwdcjKPmjr1YcIRct0aPyQAgob Gp5I5FEIQ7XYTLB2t60MWA%3D%3D. "After a year of diplomacy dominated by

the Ukraine-Russia conflict, the EU's Eastern Partnership (EaP) summit in Riga on May 21–22 will focus on the wider challenges of the surrounding region. Yet most EU member states appear reluctant to bring forward new agreements or promises to EaP states. … Since the current crisis erupted in 2013 with antigovernment protests in Ukraine, EU leaders have repeatedly asserted that the EaP needs to move into a higher gear. In practice, however, a number of factors are holding EU member states back from upgrading the partnership. While some member states talk of the Riga summit representing a last chance for the EaP, others hold positions that risk making it a nonevent. The EaP strategy has in some ways evolved and become more sophisticated. The 'more for more' concept – which the union has prioritized since 2011 and which promises bigger EU carrots in return for partners' stronger commitment to EU principles and values – is a sensible advance. This incentive has drawn a useful distinction between those states that have genuine affinities to the EU (Georgia, Moldova, and Ukraine) and those that do not (Azerbaijan and Belarus), with Armenia being something of a swing voter between those two positions." Raf Casert and Karl Ritter, "EU Careful not to Tread on Moscow's Toes at Eastern Summit," *Yahoo*, May 21, 2015. http://news.yahoo.com/eu-careful-not-tread-moscows-toes-eastern-summit-072445170.html. "On the eve of this year's summit, Russia again drew the line how far neighbors could go.

"'We don't see our neighbors' aspirations to strengthen ties with the European Union as a tragedy, but to make those processes develop positively they mustn't hurt the interests of the Russian Federation,' Foreign Minister Sergei Lavrov told the upper house of the Russian parliament." Dalibor Rohac, "Riga's Missed Opportunity," *AEI*, May 22, 2015. http://www.aei.org/publication/rigas-missed-opportunity/?utm_source=paramount&utm_medium=email&utm_content=AEITODAY&utm_campaign=052615. "Europe's lukewarm engagement with its eastern neighbors reflects a deeper crisis, illustrated also by the protracted fiscal and economic troubles in Greece and the rise of populist euroskepticism across the continent, typically with ugly nationalist undertones."

46 Michael Kofman, "How to Start a Proxy War with Russia," *National Interest*, February 5, 2015. http://nationalinterest.org/feature/how-start-proxy-war-russia-12187. "On Wednesday, Ashton Carter, the president's nominee for Secretary of Defense, made headlines when he told Congress that he was 'very much inclined' to arm the Ukrainian troops in order to combat pro-Russian rebels.

"Carter isn't alone in this regard. The release of a report this week calling for a vast expansion of U.S. military aid to Ukraine, titled 'Preserving Ukraine's Independence, Resisting Russian Aggression,' helped reignite the debate in Washington, DC, on the provision of lethal weapons and a reassessment of the U.S. role in the conflict. The authors are prominent former diplomats and highly respected members of the national-security establishment, including Michele Flournoy, Strobe Talbott and Steven Pifer, amongst others. As a result, the president's administration has come under heavy political pressure to reevaluate the existing policy of support for Ukraine. The prominence and experience of the political figures behind this report makes it impossible to ignore. It is a concise piece of argument, demanding the United States supply $1 billion per year in defense articles to Ukraine, ranging from anti-tank missiles to advanced air defense, and a variety of technical enablers for the Ukrainian military."

47 Kenneth Kopf, "Russia Sanctions: 'Ill-Planned, Ill-Timed and Foolhardy,'" *CNS News*, January 8, 2015. http://www.cnsnews.com/commentary/kenneth-kopf/ russia-sanctions-ill-planned-ill-timed-and-foolhardy. "Even if these 'capital sanctions' do have limited effect, it will not affect the nationalistic mentality (and thus annexation mentality), and will have a serious, long-term boomerang ripple effect on the rest of the world's economy, effectually prolonging the U.S. and EU recovery. The Administration's policy toward Russia is as short-sighted as its economic policies toward U.S. recovery." Alexander J. Motl, "Russia: It's Time for Regime Change," *Newsweek*, January 30, 2015. http://www.newsweek.com/ russia-its-time-regime-change-303399.

"Although 'regime change' has become a dirty phrase, the best thing that could happen to Russia, its neighbors and the world would be a change from Vladimir Putin's brand of strongman authoritarianism to some form of democracy." "Western hopes of resolving the Russo-Ukrainian war in eastern Ukraine by means of negotiations are therefore misplaced. Whatever Putin agrees to – even Ukraine's agreement never to seek NATO membership – will be at best a temporary retreat from his expansionist foreign policy. And Putin's choice of countries to pressure is large, extending from the Baltic states to Belarus, Moldova and Ukraine to Armenia, Azerbaijan and Georgia to the five Central Asian states. Russians or Russian speakers inhabit all these states and can, in principle, be used to justify Moscow's strong-arm tactics." "Ironically, the West is likely to face the prospect of regime change in Russia even though it desperately prefers not to think about such an eventuality. There is nothing that Western states can do to manage the inevitable decay of Putin's regime in Russia. But they can do a great deal to limit the damage that regime change will bring about by actively supporting Ukraine and other non-Russian states and thereby containing the instability to Russia."

48 Sergei Karaganov, "Russia and the U.S.: A Long Confrontation?" September 2014. www.globalaffairs.ru (republished at http://valdaiclub.com/usa/72040.html). "Russian-U.S. relations seem to have entered a long period of not just keen rivalry, but also confrontation." The acrimony is reflected in the claim that Russia is using racial slurs against Obama, prompting a call to arms to protect the West from Kremlin racism. See Mikhail Klikushi, "Russians Rage Against America Enduring Sanctions, Anger Turns to Hate: Racist Names for Obama and Putin Disses Coca-Cola," December 29, 2014. "Today, this country has a black President, and the Russians have a nickname for him too. He is called Maximka – after a character from a popular Soviet movie, made in 1952, which told the story of a black boy saved by the Russian sailors from the cruelty of the vicious American slave-traders who were terribly abusing him and calling him just that – 'Boy.' In the film, the saved boy was fed well by the Russian crew, given the name Maximka, and became one of their own in the end. But by the modern-day Russian legend, Maximka, unfortunately, has grown up into an ungrateful Russophobe." "US Department of State spokeswoman Jen Psaki has an anti-fan club of haters who consider her not to be very bright – they even invented their own anti-IQ unit called 1 Psaki. One who has 3 Psakis has a brain of a clam. The term 'psaking' in Russian political newspeak means to know nothing about the subject while saying something banal and politically correct." "Today, according to the respected Moscow 'Levada Center,' which measures political sentiment in Russian society, 74% of Russians have negative

feelings towards the USA. It hasn't always been like this; in the 1990s, 80% had positive attitude toward America. Currently, 76% of Russians hate Obama personally
and only a meager 2% like him. In 2009 only 12% of Russians had extremely negative feelings towards Obama." http://observer.com/2014/12/russians-rage-against-
america/.

49 Gary Schmitt, "NATO's Russian 'Reset': Less Is not More," *AEI*, February 10, 2015.
http://www.aei.org/publication/natos-russian-reset-less/?utm_source=today&utm_
medium=paramount&utm_campaign=021115. "Both US political parties have reinforced the reduced global strategic posture in order to address pressing domestic
issues. Obama administration officials, in particular, believed that rebalancing would
require not only winding down the wars in Iraq and Afghanistan but also building
new relationships with potential state competitors such as China and Russia. Hence,
the priority the administration gave in its early days to the 'reset' with Moscow and
enhanced engagement with Beijing." On the prospects for a second round of reset,
see "The Scholar as Secretary: A Conversation with Ashton Carter."

50 Leon Aron, "Spain 1936–1939; Ukraine, 2014– ?", *AEI*, February 20, 2015. http://
www.aei.org/publication/spain-1936-1939-ukraine-2014/. "Last week's Minsk
agreement, by which France and Germany in effect codified the cession to Russia
of Kiev's sovereignty over southeastern Ukraine, has temporarily taken the issue of
Russia's aggression in Ukraine off the table and thus off the conscience of the West."
"From 1936 to the defeat of the Republic three years later, Nazi Germany spent an
estimated $215 million – $3.6 billion in today's money – to provide the Nationalists
with 600 planes and 200 tanks and to pay the salaries of an estimated 16,000 German
'volunteers' of the Condor Legion. Encouraged by Germany, Mussolini sent the
Nationalists 660 planes, 150 tanks, 800 artillery pieces, 10,000 machine guns, and
240,000 rifles. In addition to providing arms, Germany trained 56,000 Nationalist
infantry, gunners, and pilots. The Luftwaffe pilots secured Nationalist dominance in
the air, strafing Republican troops and bombing Madrid with impunity, while the
Italian Navy controlled the Mediterranean and bombarded Malaga, Valencia, and
Barcelona.
    "Although no historical parallel is ever precise, the strangling of the Spanish
Republic suggests some lessons for today. First, one-sided embargoes stop neither
rebellion nor aggression, not to mention brutality. Will Mariupol, Debaltseve, or
perhaps soon Kharkiv, devastated by missiles from Russian Grad rocket launchers,
soon stain the reputation of the West as indelibly as Guernica, the Spanish town
where in April 1937 the Luftwaffe's Condor Legion killed 200–300 civilians?"

51 This may be impossible for the European Union and NATO, riven as they are by diverse
and incompatible national interests. Jeffrey Mankoff, "U.S.-Russian Relations: The
Path Ahead after the Crisis." Potomac Paper 22, December 2014. http://www.ifri
.org/sites/default/files/atoms/files/ifri_pp22jeffreymankoffusrussie.pdf. "In the longer term, containment needs to be supplemented by a real effort to reshape relations
between the West and Russia along less zero-sum lines." Jeffrey Mankoff, *Russian
Foreign Policy: The Return of Great Power Politics*, New York: Rowman & Littlefield,
2009. Eugene Rumer and Thomas Graham, "Arm Ukraine and You Risk Another
Black Hawk Down," *Financial Times*, February 3, 2015. http://carnegieendowment.
org/2015/02/03/arm-ukraine-and-you-risk-another-black-hawk-down/i139?mkt_
tok=3RkMMJWWfF9wsRolva7MZKXonjHpfsX56OsvXqGg38431UFwdcjKPmjr1
YAHT8J0aPyQAgobGp5I5FEIQ7XYTLB2t60MWA%3D%3D. "Sending weapons

to Ukraine could prolong the country's agony and distract it from the vital task of reconstruction. Ukraine cannot win this conflict now. It must be frozen. Ukraine's leaders should be told as much. It will deepen the tragedy if soldiers are sent to fight a hopeless battle. A free and independent Ukraine, a solid defence of the European order and a firm rebuff of Russian aggression are worthy goals. But they do not absolve us of our responsibility to consider the consequences of our actions. The current proposal to arm Ukraine does not meet that standard."

52 Fenenko, "Options in Ukraine."

53 Menon and Rumer, *Conflict in Ukraine*. "The current conflict in Ukraine has spawned the most serious crisis between Russia and the West since the end of the Cold War. It has undermined European security, raised questions about NATO's future, and put an end to one of the most ambitious projects of U.S. foreign policy – building a partnership with Russia. It also threatens to undermine U.S. diplomatic efforts on issues ranging from terrorism to nuclear proliferation. And in the absence of direct negotiations, each side is betting that political and economic pressure will force the other to blink first. Caught in this dangerous game of chicken, the West cannot afford to lose sight of the importance of stable relations with Russia."

54 Samuel Charap and Jeremy Shapiro, "How to Avoid a New Cold War," *Current History*, October 2014. http://scharap.fastmail.net/files/CurrentHistory.pdf. Rosefielde and Mills, *Democracy and Its Elected Enemies*; Samuel Charap and Jeremy Shapiro, "The Looming New Cold War and Its Consequences," *IISS*, February 5, 2015. http://www.iiss.org/en/politics%20and%20strategy/blogsections/2015-932e/february-2fea/the-looming-new-cold-war-and-its-consequences-9cca. "The administration's policy can be called the 'middle way' between these two extremes. It is defined by maintaining cooperation on key global issues while keeping up the pressure on Russia for its actions in Ukraine and supporting the new government in Kiev. It also is dependent on avoiding significant escalation on the ground in the Donbas and on the Kiev government managing to stay solvent.

"The middle way seems prudent today. But it cannot last. Obama's middle way will likely devolve into the very New Cold War that he is seeking to avoid. Politics in both Washington and Moscow and the interaction between them will make it be impossible to sustain over time in two key ways.

"First, it will become politically untenable to avoid escalation in Ukraine while maintaining cooperation on global issues. For the US, this dual-track approach – condemning Russia as an aggressor one day, and seeking to work with Moscow the next – creates regular opportunities for Obama's critics to decry him as weak and feckless. Indeed, cries of appeasement can be heard from Capitol Hill each time senior US and Russian officials meet to discuss global issues, or when the Obama administration takes steps to avoid escalation in Ukraine. In Moscow, officials are regularly criticised for having betrayed the Donbas, or for being too soft on the US by cooperating on other issues, such as arms control. And since these political dynamics play out in public and are picked up by the other side in real time, the hawks in each country tend to feed off each other, progressively raising tensions ever higher as time passes.

"Second, both countries' bureaucracies will prove incapable of resisting the urge to link their dispute in Ukraine to other aspects of bilateral interaction. The US began linking unrelated aspects of the relationship almost immediately after the annexation of Crimea in March 2014. All joint work considered non-essential – from the Bilateral Presidential Commission to most space cooperation – was suspended. But what remains of the relationship is therefore what matters the most to the US, from the Iran nuclear talks to the purchase of Russian rockets to launch US military satellites. Moscow has for the most part continued to cooperate on these issues, compartmentalizing them from the Ukraine dispute. But this mutual compartmentalization has already started to fray. In December, for example, Russia announced that it would not be attending the US-led Nuclear Security Summit. It is only a matter of time until the tsunami of tensions overwhelms the remaining islands of cooperation in the relationship."

55 Dmitri Trenin, "The End of Consensus: What does Europe Want from Russia?" *Carnegie Moscow Center*, December 17, 2014. http://carnegie.ru/eurasiaoutlook/ ?fa=57511&mkt_tok=3RkMMJWWfF9wsRoksq3IZKXonjHpfsX56OsvXqGg3843 1UFwdcjKPmjr1YEISsN0aPyQAgobGp5I5FEIQ7XYTLB2t60MWA%3D%3D.

"Berlin has increasingly become a public and unrelenting critic of Russia's domestic and foreign policy, shedding the image of Moscow's advocate and conduit into Western institutions that it enjoyed at the time of Gerhard Schröder and Helmut Kohl." "The pragmatic Ostpolitik that the Social Democrats formulated half a century ago has been replaced with the politics of moral principles and geopolitical interests." "At the same time, Germany itself is being closely watched by these countries and their friends in the United States to make sure that 'Molotov-Ribbentrop syndrome' does not repeat itself in any way. Washington, which entrusted the EU and Germany with the practical realization of the West's collective policy in Ukraine, expects Berlin to earn this trust." "The leadership on behalf of Europe also calls for competing against the Russian influence in the zone of conflicting interests. This zone does not only include Ukraine but also Moldova, Georgia, and other states in the Caucasus and Central Asia." "Germany also seeks to limit Russia's influence in the Balkan sphere of the EU interests – primarily in Serbia, as well as Bosnia." "Besides, Berlin is struggling against Moscow's influence among the EU members – the Czech Republic, Bulgaria, and Hungary. The seemingly long-forgotten traditional geopolitics is being resurrected right in front of our eyes, albeit in a new ideological incarnation and in different spheres – primarily in economy and information. The German-Russian consensus that worried the Eastern European countries is being replaced by new rivalries."

Karaganov, "Russia and the U.S.: A Long Confrontation?" Karaganov offers a Russian version of a negotiable solution: "

1. the eternal neutrality of Ukraine, codified in its constitution and guaranteed by external powers;
2. greater cultural autonomy for eastern and southeastern Ukraine;
3. economic openness of Ukraine to the East and the West (ideally, a compromise allowing Ukraine to be both in association with the EU and in the Customs Union);
4. Russian and German joint support for the economic development of Ukraine;
5. termination by all involved, including Russia, of support for the sides in the civil war, and an appeal to them to renounce the use of force;
6. evacuation of refugees and resistance fighters;
7. mutual renunciation of sanctions and counter-sanctions."

Sergei Karaganov is honorary chairman of the Presidium of the Council on Foreign and Defense Policy and dean of the School of World Economics and World Politics at the National Research University–Higher School of Economics.

56 Steven Rosefielde, "Cold Peace: 'Reset' and Coexistence," *The Northeast Asian Review*, Vol. 1, No. 3, March 2014: 39–50.

"Sam Charap: Is a Stable Agreement Possible Between Russia and Ukraine?" *IISS*, November 1, 2014. http://www.iiss.org/en/regions/ukraine/is-a-stable-agreement-possible-between-russia-and-ukraine-415c. "For Western policymakers, it is this factor – Russia's strong bargaining position, relative both to Ukraine and the West – that ultimately makes this crisis so different from others in the post-Cold War period. Never before have they faced a major nuclear power as an adversary in a regional dispute occurring in that power's backyard. In Kosovo, Russia was an opponent, but Kosovo barely registered in the hierarchy of Russian national-security imperatives. Ukraine, by contrast, ranks just short of national survival. And eastern Ukraine is one of a few places beyond Russia's borders in which Moscow can deliver the assets required to sustain an insurgency. Even if it were to receive the much-ballyhooed lethal military assistance from the West (and that does not seem likely), Ukraine cannot defeat such an insurgency if Russia remains determined to prevent it from doing so.

"Talking to Moscow is a policy of necessity; it is not one that any Ukrainian or Western leader would want to embrace publicly. For Ukraine to survive this crisis, however, they might not have a choice."

57 Robert Garver, "Putin Pulls Out of Post–Cold War Arms Treaty", *Yahoo*, March 10, 2015.

http://finance.yahoo.com/news/putin-pulls-post-cold-war-203200839.html. "At a time when European officials concerned about Russian aggression in Eastern Europe are openly calling for the creation of a Pan-European army, Moscow has announced it will cease all involvement in a major arms control treaty that was signed at the end of the Cold War. The Treaty on Conventional Armed Forces in Europe was an agreement signed in 1990 between the 16 North Atlantic Treaty Organization countries and six Warsaw Pact countries. It set caps on the number of soldiers, tanks, artillery pieces and other non-nuclear military assets that could be stationed in Europe." "'For years, the Russian side has been doing its best to maintain viability of the regime of control over conventional arms, it initiated talks on adapting the Treaty on Conventional Armed Forces in Europe, it ratified the agreement on Adapted CFE Treaty,' Mazur said, according to the Kremlin-owned news service ITAR-TASS. 'Regrettably, NATO countries have preferred to dodge CFE provisions by means of the alliance's expansion and use any pretexts to prevent the Agreement on Adapted CFE Treaty from coming into effect. This course pursued despite our repeated warning about its harmful impacts on the regime of control over conventional weapons led to the unavoidable result – Russia's suspending the CFE Treaty in 2007.'

"Russia had continued to participate in 'consultative' meetings with the signatories. However, Mazur said the Kremlin now sees further participation as 'pointless' from both political and practical points of view and as excessively costly from the financial and economic point of view."

58 Samuel Charap, "Why Ukraine Must Bargain for Peace with Russia," *Foreign Policy*, November 26, 2014. Samuel Charap advocates Ukrainians help America move toward a new world order by making concessions to Russia. "Vice President Joe Biden traveled to Kiev last week for his third visit to Ukraine's capital in the past seven months. He arrived bearing gifts: additional nonlethal military aid for the embattled Ukrainian government, including body armor, helmets, night-vision goggles, and counter mortar radar. The first three of 20 promised counter mortar radar systems were flown to Ukraine aboard a cargo plane accompanying Air Force Two the day the U.S. vice president arrived. Following the Nov. 3 separatist 'elections' reports of Russian tanks rolling across the border, and with the Minsk cease-fire agreements in tatters and almost 1,000 dead in the past two and a half months, this quite literal 'deliverable' for Biden's visit – combined with some tough words in public for Russian President Vladimir Putin ('Do what you agreed to do, Mr. Putin') – is certainly appropriate. But let's hope that the new kit and bravado gave Biden the public cover needed to make a far more important point to President Petro Poroshenko: Ukraine needs to make a deal with Russia if it wants to survive this crisis."

59 Rosefielde and Mills, *Global Economic Turmoil and the Public Good*.

60 Assaf Razin and Steven Rosefielde, "The European Project after Greece's Near Default," *Israel Economic Journal*, 2015; Steven Rosefielde and Yiyi Liu, "Limits of Country Solidarity in Sovereign Crisis," unpublished paper, September 2016.

61 Janet Yellen's recent quarter point increase in the Federal Reserve rate does alter the West's commitment to monetary accommodation.

62 Rosefielde and Mills, *Global Economic Turmoil and the Public Good*.

63 Gudrun Perrson, "Russian Strategic Deterrence – Beyond the Brinkmanship?" FOI, *RUFS Briefing* No. 29, September 17, 2015.

PART I

CRIMEA'S ANNEXATION

1

Vendetta

Introduction

The Euromaidan "revolution" in Ukraine that swept President Viktor Yanukovych out of power and into exile in February 2014 triggered Crimea's annexation. Vladimir Putin construed the event as an unacceptable plot the West had orchestrated to absorb Ukraine into the West's sphere of influence and immediately retaliated.

He had prepared for this contingency and did not vacillate because Russia had been sparring with the West over Ukraine since the late 1980s when Gorbachev began contemplating limited independence for Soviet republics. Euromaidan was only the proximate cause of Crimea's annexation. Putin's motivation was more complex, rooted in tsarist imperial precedent, the Soviet Union's collapse, post-Soviet "partnership," the reemergence of authoritarian identity, and Russian military modernization. During the quarter century separating Euromaidan from Gorbachev's scheme for republican independence, Putin discovered that he did not want Russia and its vassals to clone the West or to subordinate themselves to Western globalization. He became convinced that Russia could restore some of its lost great power, partly recover former spheres of influence, and defend itself against further Western encroachment, and concluded that these goals could not be achieved through friendly persuasion. The West would have to be deterred and pushed back not just in Crimea, but in Ukraine and a host of other contested territories.

Crimean annexation consequently should not be seen as Putin's end game. He perceives it as the starting point for a politically sustainable long-term struggle for internal and external control inside Russia and across its periphery. Even if the West accepts Crimea's annexation, Putin is likely to soldier on until the West comes to terms with the Kremlin's grievances (power) and negotiates an acceptable new world order.

This won't happen any time soon, with future outcomes depending on Russia's economy, rearmament, Western vulnerabilities, the West's willingness to substantively accommodate Kremlin power, and wild cards like the natural resources supercycle.[1] Putin's great power restoration project has strong legs, standing as it does on tsarist and Soviet tradition, energized by the power services' resentment against the West's role in Soviet disunion, *katastroika* (Gorbachev's catastrophic radical economic reform), and Russia's post-Soviet humiliation. Russia's power services distrust the West with some justification and won't be beguiled by American and EU professions of reason and goodwill.

Stab in the Back

The destruction of the Soviet Union was brought about by a series of ill-conceived (or perhaps intentional) radical economic and political reforms Mikhail Gorbachev and his counselors executed with the formal consent of the Communist Party. It was achieved with a two-pronged surgical strike against the established communist order that (1) devolved Communist Party power from the Kremlin to federal republics[2] and (2) abolished command planning.[3] The first action legalized partisan politics and agitation for republican secession,[4] leading directly to Soviet dismemberment.[5] The second compelled enterprises to fend for themselves (including embezzling state revenues and plundering assets) without competitive market assistance, causing economic chaos and collapse.[6] The dismantling of communism in Central Europe (Hungary, Poland, the Czech Republic, and Slovakia) followed a similar but less economically disastrous Austro-Hungarian pattern.[7]

Both actions were undertaken on Gorbachev's initiative. They were debated and approved by party and state authorities. Foreign powers did not inflict these lethal wounds. The responsibility was solely Gorbachev and his advisors'.

If their intentions were compatible with revitalizing Soviet power as Gorbachev claimed,[8] they botched the job. If command communism was deliberately discarded in favor of democratic free enterprise (as the West and Stanislav Shatalin urged),[9] their efforts failed. If they scuttled the Soviet Union to enrich and empower themselves, they succeeded at exorbitant cost to the Soviet people and the Muscovite cause.[10] Whichever interpretation(s) one prefers, it is easy to suspect that the Soviet Union, communism, the

Kremlin, and the people (*narod*) were "stabbed in the back" by Gorbachev's actions.

Grounds for suspicion are increased by the president's failure to reverse course when confronted with the adverse effects of devolving communist power from the Kremlin to the republics and abolishing command planning. The loss of East Germany on November 9, 1989, and of the Baltic states in September 1991 did not trigger recentralization of Communist Party power, and no effort was made to restore command planning after the economy swooned in 1990. Gorbachev and his supporters of course could and did argue that retreat was unwarranted and advance imperative, but it is difficult to understand how radical reformers maintained their faith amid the evidence to the contrary unless they subconsciously or consciously intended to destroy communism at any price.[11]

Gorbachev's power service adversaries weren't perplexed. They deduced that he was betraying the revolution and for the first time in Soviet history launched a palace coup d'état on August 19, 1991, aimed at persuading the General Secretary of the Soviet Communist Party to reject what they considered a destructive draft treaty on union. When he refused, Vice President of Russia's Defense Council Gennadi Yanayev signed a decree naming himself as acting USSR president on the pretext that Gorbachev was ill.[12] The abortive putsch failed with disastrous consequences from the power services' perspective.[13] It brought Yeltsin to power, accelerated Soviet disunion, and destroyed the USSR, but it also provided fodder for conspiracy theorists convinced that Gorbachev and his court had stabbed Russia in the back. Members of the State Emergency Committee (Gosudarstvenniy Komitet po Chrezvichaynomu Polozheniyu) never regretted their effort to save Soviet power; they only lamented that they botched the palace coup d'état by neglecting to arrest Boris Yeltsin in Kazakhstan on August 17, 1991.

Many of their successors in the power services continue to carry the torch, believing like their Weimar counterparts that the Soviet Union wasn't defeated by foreign armies or the people's will,[14] but was stabbed in the back by domestic traitors (Gorbachev)[15] and anti-Party opportunists (Yeltsin).[16] The *siloviki* liken Gorbachev and Yeltsin to Germany's republicans who traitorously overthrew the Kaiser (Soviet power).

The loyalty of the power services in 1991 was to communism and the Soviet state, in the same sense that German patriotic allegiance was to the crown and the House of Hohenzollern. However, as memories blurred in both Germany and Russia, many came to equate the defeat of the Kaiser and the Soviet Union with national ideals and homelands rather than the states they had served, a subtle psychological transference allowing new generations to share the old guard's sense of betrayal. Russia's power services and nationalists today seek the restoration of their country's former greatness partly because they feel that Russia, the Kremlin, Muscovy, and the *narod* (rather than the Soviet Union and communism) were treacherously brought to their knees.

This attitude, which puts Russia's conflict with the West in an instructive long-term historical context, sheds a shaft of light on why Vladimir Putin appears impelled to redress Gorbachev's and Yeltsin's "crimes against the Kremlin,"[17] even though he doesn't display nostalgia for communism or the Soviet state. Putin is the embodiment of Russia's power services mentality.[18] He joined the KGB in 1975 and was stationed in Dresden, East Germany from 1985 to 1990, where he coordinated efforts with the Stasi to track down and recruit foreigners. Following the collapse of the communist East German government, he returned to Leningrad, where, while still a KGB lieutenant colonel, he assumed a position with the international affairs section of Leningrad State University and was appointed an international affairs advisor to Mayor Anatoly Sobchak in June 1991. Soon thereafter he rose to a position as head of the Committee for External Relations of the Saint Petersburg Mayor's Office, with responsibility for promoting international relations and foreign investments. Putin resigned from the KGB with the rank of lieutenant colonel on August 20, 1991, on the second day of the KGB-led abortive putsch against President Gorbachev.[19]

In 1996, when Mayor Anatoly Sobchak lost his bid for reelection in Saint Petersburg, Putin transferred to Moscow and became deputy chief of the Presidential Property Management Department, working to recover foreign assets of the former Soviet Union (billions of dollars were traced to banks in New York City, but were never recovered).[20] On March 26, 1997, President Boris Yeltsin appointed Putin deputy chief of presidential staff, and chief of the Main Control Directorate of Presidential Property Management.

On May 25, 1998, Putin was appointed first deputy chief of presidential staff for regions. Soon thereafter he became head of the commission for the preparation of agreements on the delimitation of the power of regions and Moscow. On July 25, 1998, Yeltsin appointed Putin to head the Federal Security Service (FSB) (successor to the KGB),[21] a position Putin occupied until August 1999. He became a permanent member of the Security Council of the Russian Federation on October 1, 1998, and its secretary on March 29, 1999. On August 9, 1999, Putin was appointed first deputy prime minister, and later that day President Boris Yeltsin appointed him acting prime minister of the government of the Russian Federation. Yeltsin also announced that he wanted Putin to succeed him. Putin immediately agreed to run for the presidency. On August 16, the State Duma approved his appointment as prime minister.

Putin's intoxicating ascent testified to his nimbleness in the corridors of power. He parlayed an unspectacular KGB service record into a host of high government positions that gave him high-level experience in the domestic *apparat*, and a role in forging Russian military doctrine and military operations in Chechnya. He gained control over the secret police and the prime ministership and was designated presidential heir apparent. Most important, he mastered the dark art of *kompromat* (compromising rivals) as FSB head and allegedly used it against Tatyana Yeltsin (Tatyana Borisovna Yumasheva) to blackmail her father into designating Putin acting president on the last day of the old millennium.[22] In a whirlwind decade, Putin had achieved a palace coup d'état against the idealists and opportunists who he believed destroyed Soviet communism and betrayed the motherland. He became the power services' favorite son committed to settling old scores.[23]

Foreign Complicity

These old scores were in the first instance domestic. Gorbachev and Yeltsin's policies served their internal purposes; however, no flight of fancy is required to suspect that they had been influenced and/or abetted by the West. The Cold War was widely portrayed as a clash of civilizations (communism versus capitalism,[24] plan versus market),[25] where both sides claimed that its system was superlative and the other's doomed. Karl Marx foresaw the "death knell of capitalism,"[26] and Francis Fukuyama "the end of history."[27] The West preached the gospel of democratic free enterprise, freedom, rule of law, and national self-determination (for the Kremlin's East European satellites and each Soviet republic), contending that communism precluded *la dolce vita* and condemned the USSR to be an impoverished superpower.[28] The greyness of Soviet reality made the West's pitch credible to a large segment of the Communist Party, shaped contemporary perceptions of the "correlation of forces," and contributed to Gorbachev's and Yeltsin's advocacy of radical economic and political reform (*perestroika, demokratizatsiya,* and *novoe myslenie*).[29]

This makes the West guilty by association in the power services' eyes of stabbing Russia in the back, a conviction aggravated by suspicions of Western internal meddling. The Soviet Politburo and other members of the power establishment were fully aware that institutions they considered American front organizations were linked with Gorbachev and other key insiders. The Trilateral Commission funded the Gorbachev Foundation (founded December 1991),[30] and the Soros Foundation assisted Leonid Kravchuk.[31] The power services likewise knew that the Reagan administration strove to persuade Gorbachev to focus his attention on devising policies to improve living standards, foster democracy, and reduce the Soviet defense burden, and inferred that these initiatives contributed to the Kremlin's ruin.[32] The jump from the West's guilt by association to a belief that the West conspired with domestic liberals in stabbing Russia in the back was effortless for many members of Russia's power services. Putin's animus against America and the European Union therefore may well partly reflect his suspicion that the West was behind the Kremlin's humiliation. There are elements of double-thinking and irony in the power services' vendetta. They fully intended to subvert the West, but became sore losers when the tables were turned against them.

Stab in the Chest

The power services' grievances aren't limited to the domestic betrayal of Soviet power. This was a stab in the back. They also resent Yeltsin's war against them and the ascendance of his liberal advisors, construed as a stab in the chest against the Russian people, the Kremlin as the symbol of Muscovite power, the Federal Security Service of the Russian Federation (FSB),[33] the Ministry of the Interior of the Russian Federation (MVD),[34] the military-industrial complex (VPK),[35] and the Ministry of Defense.[36]

The same issues of guilt by association and Western complicity apply, but the allegations differ. Yeltsin, egged on by the West, is vilified for slashing weapons production by 90 percent,[37] cutting military manpower 80 percent,[38] crippling military readiness, and defanging the secret police.[39] These actions may reflect his chagrin at having been targeted for arrest by the State Emergency Committee (Gosudarstvenniy Komitet po Chrezvichaynomu Polozheniyu) in Kazakhstan on August 17, 1991, but the destruction of Russia's conventional warfighting capabilities and the leashing of its internal security forces also were Western dreams come true. Slashing weapons production, cutting military personnel, crippling readiness, and straitjacketing the FSB allowed the West to consolidate its hold over former spheres of Kremlin influence in Central and Eastern Europe and the Baltic states, prevented Moscow from protecting Serbs in Pristina, and compelled Russia to rely almost exclusively on decaying nuclear forces to deter Western and Chinese aggression.[40] America and the European Union didn't compel Yeltsin to do most of these things, but they applauded his efforts to create a rudderless Russian state stripped of its power-vertical.

Yeltsin, egged on by the West, is also accused of engineering Russia's catastrophic transition (*katakhod*) from 1992 to 2000,[41] and is blamed for 3.4 million hyper-depression-inflicted excess deaths.[42] Specifically, his economic guru Yegor Gaidar (first deputy prime minister and prime minister)[43] is charged with having stabbed Russia in the chest by promoting asset-grabbing, foreign economic penetration, and what Marshall Goldman has termed "oligarchic piratization,"[44] under the pretext of transitioning to Washington consensus-style, democratic free enterprise.[45] Yeltsin's prime minister insisted that the best method for constructing Russia's democratic market transition (*perekhod*) was "shock therapy,"[46] that is, instantaneous denationalization (privatization) of the means of production without an orderly transfer of assets into competent hands;[47] abolition of Gosplan,[48] ministerial controls, and managerial bonuses (Gorbachev previously had terminated command planning); the elimination of the turnover tax collection system (via the state bank credit/debiting mechanism); price decontrol; removal of capital controls to prevent capital flight;[49] withdrawal of state financial support; deferred wage payments to state employees; and foraging.[50] The people, in effect, were driven to barter,[51] and forced to fend for themselves in a lawless environment without preparation or assistance. Yeltsin's notion of transition was making billionaires out of his drinking buddies by allowing them to privatize media and natural resources processing companies,[52] supplemented with lucrative state contracts. Destroying the old economic order and reviving market Muscovite rent-granting were the sum and substance of his prosperity strategy, despite claims of "competitive market building" and democratization.[53] Everything was up for grabs, including the sale of nuclear power plants to China and Iran.[54]

Gaidar confidently proclaimed that the forces of supply and demand would automatically create a rule of commercial law and other missing institutional prerequisites needed to promptly transform Russia into a well-functioning, consumer-sovereign, competitively efficient, full-employment, macro-economically stable, financially sound engine of rapid growth and development.[55] The miracle never occurred. Russia's economy plunged into freefall. Industrial production plummeted 70 percent, unemployment swelled into the high double digits,[56] and suicides skyrocketed.[57] Distinguished Soviet academician and advisor to Gorbachev Yuri Yaremenko likened conditions in the early 1990s to Hitler's siege of Leningrad in 1941–1944.[58]

Gaidar and Yeltsin were unfazed. Like Nero, they chose to fiddle while the Russian Federation burned, and seemed content to allow the nation to languish. They kept repeating the "shock therapy" mantra during the years of freefall and the financial crisis of 1997,[59] until Yeltsin's bitter end, earning Gaidar the enmity of the power services. Vitaly Shlykov, co-chairman of Russia's Defense Council, despised him for needlessly impoverishing the Russian people.[60] The power services didn't have a coherent view about the hidden agenda motivating the Yeltsin administration's economic nihilism, including the shredding of the social safety network,[61] but they felt in their bones that Russia's White House had betrayed the motherland.

Their suspicions were whetted by the West's double standard, advocating "shock therapy" for Russia,[62] but not China,[63] as well as the meagerness of the financial assistance provided by the "Grand Bargain,"[64] the World Bank Group's inconsistent stance on macroeconomic stimulus, and failure to modify its advice in the face of *katakhod*. The West routinely employs Keynesian expansionary policies to combat recessions at home. *Austerity* is now a dirty word in America and the European Union,[65] but the World Bank Group dissuaded Yeltsin from public spending programs to bolster aggregate effective demand.[66] Shock therapy as the IMF and the World Bank construed the concept excluded pump priming in favor of promoting privatization, market building, and competition.

Gaidar's and the West's shock therapy and Grand Bargain for Russia can be defended on flimsy theoretical and international political economic grounds. Many eminent economists participated in the G-7's effort, providing generic "transition" (*perekhod*) assistance to all newly independent nations of the former Soviet Union,[67] and never ceased claiming success.[68] The IMF and the World Bank may well have jumped on the transition bandwagon to provide their institutions with a lucrative mission, and Western governments may have used them as goodwill symbols rather than engines of mass economic destruction. Putin and the power services he heads, however, have equally plausible grounds for suspecting that the West's unwavering toxic economic counsel and stingy assistance were intended to crush Russia.[69] The West assiduously consolidated its geopolitical gains from the Soviet Union's dismemberment and Russia's economic collapse and military disintegration until Putin reversed the Kremlin's fortunes by restoring the power vertical.[70] Putin was in a position in 1996–1999 under Yeltsin's command to directly experience the consequences of shock therapy and the Yeltsin administration's dereliction of duty to Muscovy. He saw firsthand how the policies the West advocated harmed the nation, and it would be surprising if he didn't draw the natural conclusion that Yeltsin and the West had stabbed Russia in the chest.[71] The world is full of odd bedfellows. Robert Gates, former CIA director and secretary of defense, sympathizes with Putin's suspicions.[72]

Notes

1 Richard Dobbs, Jeremy Oppenheim, Fraser Thompson, Sigurd Mareels, Scott Nyquist, and Sunil Sanghvi, "Resource Revolution: Tracking Global Commodity Markets," McKinsey Global Institute, September 2013. www.mckinsey.com/insights/energy_resources_materials/resource_revolution_tracking_global_commodity_markets. "It may be tempting to view recent declines in commodity prices as the end of the resource 'supercycle' – the period of sharp price rises and heightened volatility since the turn of the 21st century. Yet rumors of the supercycle's death are greatly exaggerated."

2 February 7, 1990. "Soviet Communist Party Gives up Monopoly on Political Power – History.com. This Day in History – 2/7/1990." History.com.

3 Law on State Enterprise, July 1987.

4 This action was tantamount to Lincoln accepting the South's secession on grounds that it reflected the will of Confederate legislatures.

5 See Chapter 2, this volume.

6 Steven Rosefielde and Stefan Hedlund, *Russia since 1980: Wrestling with Westernization*, Cambridge: Cambridge University Press, 2008.

7 Bruno Dallago and Steven Rosefielde, *Transformation and Crisis in Central Europe: Challenges and Prospects*, London: Routledge, 2016.

8 Mikhail Gorbachev, *Perestroika: New Thinking for Our Country and the World*, New York: Harpercollins, 1987.

9 Stanislav Shatalin, *Transition to the Market: 500 Days*, Moscow: Arkhangelskoe, 1990.

10 China's market transition proves that there was at least one better way.

11 Valery Boldin, *Ten Years that Shook the World*, New York: Basic Books, 1994. Cf. Robert Legvold, "Review of *Ten Years that Shook the World*," *Foreign Affairs* (July/August): 1994.

12 The State Emergency Committee (Государственный Комитет по Чрезвычайному Положению, ГКЧП, or Gosudarstvenniy Komitet po Chrezvichaynomu Polozheniyu, GKChP) had been created "to manage the country and to effectively maintain the regime of the state of emergency." The GKChP included the following members:

Gennady Yanayev (Vice President of the Soviet Defense Council)
Valentin Pavlov (Premier)
Vladimir Kryuchkov (Chief of the KGB)
Dmitriy Yazov (Defense Minister)
Boris Pugo (Internal Affairs Minister)
Oleg Baklanov (Deputy Chief of the Soviet Defense Council)
Vasily Starodubtsev (Chairman of the USSR Peasant Union)
Alexander Tizyakov (President of the Association of the State Enterprises and Conglomerates of Industry, Transport, and Communications)

On December 11, 1990, KGB Chairman Vladimir Kryuchkov made a "call for order" over central television. That day, he asked two KGB officers to prepare a plan of measures that could be taken in case a state of emergency was declared in the USSR. Later, Chief Kryuchkov brought Soviet Defense Minister Dmitriy Yazov, Internal

Affairs Minister Boris Pugo, Premier Valentin Pavlov, Vice President Gennady Yanayev, Soviet Defense Council Deputy Chief Oleg Baklanov, Gorbachev's Chief of Staff Valeriy Boldin, and CPSU Central Committee Secretary Oleg Shenin into the conspiracy.

On August 4, Gorbachev went on holiday to his dacha in Foros in the Crimea. He planned to return to Moscow in time for the Union Treaty signing on August 20.

On August 17, the conspirators met at a KGB guesthouse in Moscow and studied the treaty document. They believed the pact would pave the way for the Soviet Union's breakup, and decided it was time to act. The next day, Soviet Defense Council Deputy Chief Oleg Baklanov, Gorbachev's Chief of Staff Valeriy Boldin, CPSU Central Committee Secretary Oleg Shenin, and USSR Deputy Defense Minister General Valentin Varennikov flew to Crimea for a meeting with Gorbachev. The four demanded that Gorbachev either declare a state of emergency or resign and name Vice President of the Soviet Defense Council Yanayev as acting president so as to allow the conspirators "to restore order" in the country.

Yanayev signed the decree naming himself acting USSR president on the pretext of Gorbachev's inability to perform presidential duties due to "illness." These eight collectively became known as the "Gang of Eight."

Gorbachev has always claimed that he refused point blank to accept the ultimatum. Varennikov has insisted that Gorbachev said: "Do what you think is needed, damn you!" However, those present at the dacha at the time testified that Baklanov, Boldin, Shenin, and Varennikov had been clearly disappointed and nervous after the meeting with Gorbachev. With Gorbachev's refusal, the conspirators ordered that he remain confined to the Foros dacha; at the same time, the dacha's communication lines (which the KGB controlled) were shut down. Additional KGB security guards with orders not to allow anybody to leave the dacha were placed at its gates.

Yevgenia Albats and Catherine A. Fitzpatrick, *The State Within a State: The KGB and Its Hold on Russia – Past, Present, and Future*, New York: Farrar Straus & Giroux, pp. 276–293. Cf. Kathryn Stoner-Weiss and Michael McFaul, "Domestic and International Influences on the Collapse of the Soviet Union (1991) and Russia's Initial Transition to Democracy (1993)," CDDRL Working Papers, Number 108, March 2009. http://iis-db.stanford.edu/pubs/22468/No_108_Stoner-Weiss_domestic_and_international_influences_on_collapse_of_USSR.pdf.

13 Many claim that disunion and collapse were inevitable. China provides a compelling counterexample.

14 A referendum on the future of the Soviet Union was held on March 17, 1991. The question placed on the ballot was: "Do you consider necessary the preservation of the Union of Soviet Socialist Republics as a renewed federation of equal sovereign republics in which the rights and freedom of an individual of any nationality will be fully guaranteed?" The results showed 77.9 percent of the population voted to preserve the Soviet Union.

15 Boris Kagarlitsky, "Gorbachev the Traitor," *Moscow Times*, March 17, 2011. www.themoscowtimes.com/opinion/article/gorbachev-the-traitor/432703.html. Kagarlitsky exonerates Gorbachev on the ground that the Soviet collapse was putatively inevitable (like North Korea?). Gorbachev took office with a pledge to serve and defend the state. He cannot be blamed for the fact that a catastrophe

that had been brewing for two decades erupted during his reign. But, as the captain, he was obligated to "go down with the ship" and share the political fate of the country he governed. The problem is not that Gorbachev could have prevented the collapse and did not – he couldn't have under any circumstances – but that when the troubles came, he snuck away from the battlefield and went home to have dinner.

16 Yeltsin came to loathe the Soviet Communist Party. See Rosefielde and Hedlund, *Russia since 1980.* The stab-in-the-back thesis, widely believed in right-wing circles in Germany after 1918, contends that the German army did not lose World War I, but was instead betrayed by civilians on the home front, especially the republicans who overthrew the monarchy. Advocates denounced the German government leaders who signed the Armistice on November 11, 1918, as the "November Criminals." Rodger Chickering, *Imperial Germany and the Great War, 1914–1918,* Cambridge: Cambridge University Press, 2004.

17 Leon Aron, "What Makes Putin Tick? A Primer for Presidential Candidates," *AEI,* December 5, 2014. www.aei.org/publication/makes-putin-tick-primer-presidential-candidates/?utm_source=today&utm_medium=paramount&utm_campaign=120514. "What, then, does Putin want? What is his overarching agenda? What does he aspire to for his country and himself – the two undoubtedly merged inexorably in his mind? What makes Putin tick?

"The ultimate goal, which has motivated and guided him since he took over the presidency 14 years ago and which he has pursued with remarkable consistency and persistence, is to recover most, if not all, key assets – political, economic and geostrategic – lost in the collapse of the Soviet state. I call this overarching agenda the Putin Doctrine."

18 Peter Baker and Susan Glasser, *Kremlin Rising: Vladimir Putin's Russia and the End of Revolution,* New York: Scribner, 2005; Vladimir Putin, Nataliya Gevorkyan, and Natalya Timakova, *Vladimir Putin First Person: An Astonishingly Frank Self-Portrait by Russia's President,* New York: Public Affairs, 2000; Anna Politkovskaya, *Putin's Russia: Life in a Failing Democracy,* New York: Holt, 2007; Yuri Felshtinsky, *The Corporation: Russia and the KGB in the Age of President Putin,* New York: Encounter Books, 2009; Alexander Litvinenko and Yuri Felshtinsky, *Blowing Up Russia: The Secret Plot to Bring Back KGB Terror,* New York: Encounter Books, 2007.

19 Masha Gessen, *The Man without a Face: The Unlikely Rise of Vladimir Putin,* New York: Riverhead, 2012; Richard Sakwa, *Putin: Russia's Choice,* Abingdon, Oxon: Routledge, 2007.

20 Celestine Bohlen, "U.S. Company to Help Russia Track Billions," *New York Times,* March 3, 1992.

21 Федеральная служба безопасности Российской Федерации (ФСБ); Federal'naya sluzhba bezopasnosti Rossiyskoy Federatsii (FSB) succeeded the USSR's Committee of State Security (KGB).

22 The first presidential decree Putin signed, on December 31, 1999, was titled "On guarantees for the former president of the Russian Federation and members of his family." This ensured that "corruption charges against the outgoing President and his relatives" would not be pursued.

23 Daniel Treisman, "Putin's Silovarchs," *Orbis,* Winter (2007): 141–153.

24 John Lewis Gaddis, *The Cold War: A New History,* New York: Penguin, 2005.

25 Joseph Schumpeter, *Capitalism, Socialism and Democracy*, New York: Harper and
    Brothers, 1942; Abram Bergson, John Hazard, and Alexander Balinky et al., eds.,
    Market and Plan in the U.S.S.R. in the 1960s, New Brunswick, NJ: Rutgers University
    Press, 1967.
26 Karl Marx, *Das Kapital*, Vol. 1, Chapter 32. www.marxists.org/archive/marx/works/
    download/pdf/Capital-Volume-I.pdf.
27 Francis Fukuyama, *The End of History and the Last Man Standing*, New York: Free
    Press, 2006.
28 Henry Rowen and Charles Wolf Jr., *The Impoverished Superpower: Perestroika and
    the Soviet Military Burden*, San Francisco, CA: Institute for Contemporary Studies,
    1990. Moscow promised similar benefits in the fullness of time plus egalitarianism,
    proletarian solidarity, personal liberation, and socialist humanism.
29 Theodore Karasik and Thomas Nichols, *Novoe myshlenie and the Soviet Military: The
    Impact of Reasonable Sufficiency on the Ministry of Defense*, Santa Monica,
    CA: Rand, 1989.
30 The Trilateral Commission is a nongovernmental, nonpartisan discussion group
    David Rockefeller founded in July 1973 to foster closer cooperation among North
    America, Western Europe, and Japan. It is closely connected with Western policy
    makers. The current chairmen are former U.S. Assistant Secretary of Defense
    for International Security Affairs Joseph S. Nye Jr., former head of the European
    Central Bank Jean-Claude Trichet, and Yasuchika Hasegawa. The organization is
    controversial, but is referenced here only because the Soviet power services saw
    it as a front for Reagan's and Bush's engagement policies. See Anatoly Chernyaev,
    Notes from the Politburo Meeting, January 21, 1989, trans. Svetlana Savranskaya,
    The Archive of the Gorbachev Foundation, Cold War International History Project,
    Virtual Archive, CWIHP.
       "During the significant changes that were brewing in the Soviet Union and
    Eastern Europe in the 1980s, Mikhail Gorbachev (leader of the Soviet Union) met
    with members of the Trilateral Commission, a nongovernmental organization
    founded in 1973 by private citizens of Japan, North America, and Europe to foster
    mutual understanding and cooperation. In these notes from a Politburo meeting in
    January 1989, Gorbachev points to some of the questions and concerns that arose
    in his meeting with the former U.S. Secretary of State Henry Kissinger, the former
    president of France Valery Giscard d'Estaing, and the former Japanese prime min-
    ister, Yasuhiro Nakasone, all of who continued their involvement in foreign affairs
    and policies through this international commission. These notes show recogni-
    tion on the part of these leaders that the Soviet Union and Eastern Europe were
    on the verge of a new relationship with each other and with the rest of the world.
    Gorbachev acknowledges that Eastern European countries might break away from
    the Soviet Union, and points to the importance of working with these countries on
    economic and political reforms to avoid this break."
31 Kurt Nimmo, "Soros Admits Responsibility for Coup and Mass Murder in Ukraine,"
    May 27, 2014. www.infowars.com/soros-admits-responsibility-for-coup-and-mass-
    murder-in-ukraine/. "George Soros told CNN's Fareed Zakaria over the weekend he
    is responsible for establishing a foundation in Ukraine that ultimately contributed
    to the overthrow of the country's elected leader and the installation of a junta hand-
    picked by the State Department.

" 'First on Ukraine, one of the things that many people recognized about you was that you during the revolutions of 1989 funded a lot of dissident activities, civil society groups in eastern Europe and Poland, the Czech Republic. Are you doing similar things in Ukraine?' Zakaria asked Soros.

" 'Well, I set up a foundation in Ukraine before Ukraine became independent of Russia. And the foundation has been functioning ever since and play[s] an important part in events now,' Soros responded."

It is well known, although forbidden for the establishment media to mention, that Soros worked closely with USAID, the National Endowment for Democracy (now doing work formerly assigned to the CIA), the International Republican Institute, the National Democratic Institute for International Affairs, Freedom House, and the Albert Einstein Institute to initiate a series of color revolutions in Eastern Europe and Central Asia following the engineered collapse of the Soviet Union.

32 Aron, "What Makes Putin Tick?" "Most of all, the next American president should be guided by Reagan's unshakable conviction that the only way to fundamentally change Russia's policies is to create an inducement for domestic reforms." "The choice grows starker by the day: Go for deep institutional, decentralizing and liberalizing reforms that drastically improve the investment climate? Or, opt for the re-Stalinization of Russia in a reign of mass impoverishment and repression, inevitably leading to a collapse."

33 Федеральная служба безопасности Российской Федерации (ФСБ); Federal'naya sluzhba bezopasnosti Rossiyskoy Federatsii succeeded the USSR's Committee of State Security (KGB). In 2003, the FSB's responsibilities were widened by incorporating the previously independent Border Guard Service and a major part of the abolished Federal Agency of Government Communication and Information (FAPSI). The two major structural components of the former KGB that remain administratively independent of the FSB are the Foreign Intelligence Service (SVR) and the State Guards (FSO).

34 Министерство внутренних дел, МВД, Ministerstvo Vnutrennikh Del, (MVD) is the interior ministry of Russia. Its predecessor was founded in 1802 by Alexander I in Imperial Russia.

35 Now called the Defense Industrial Complex.

36 Министерство обороны Российской Федерации, Минобороны России, (informally abbreviated as Минобооронпром) exercises administrative and operational leadership over the Armed Forces of the Russian Federation.

37 Steven Rosefielde, *Russia in the 21st Century: The Prodigal Superpower*, Cambridge: Cambridge University Press, 2005.

38 Ibid. The CIA estimated that it had approximately 6 million military personnel in 1991; a number that may have fallen by 5 million in 2015, equivalently defined.

39 The FSB was downsized, dismembered, and kept on a short leash.

40 The Russian general staff was terrified of a Chinese attack during the 1990s. This changed to complacency as Putin consolidated power (personal conversations and closed conferences).

41 The term *katastroika* is often used to describe the reality of Gorbachev's *perestroika*. Aleksandr Zinov'ev, *Katastroika*, London: Claridge Press, 1991. Yeltsin called his economic strategy *perekhod* (transition) and distinguished it sharply from radical

economic reform. The reality of his *perekhod* therefore should be labeled *katakhod* (catastrophic transition) for precision.

42 Steven Rosefielde, "Premature Deaths: Russia's Radical Transition," *Europe-Asia Studies*, Vol. 53, No. 8 (December 2001): 1159–1176. For a Russian view of the phenomenon, see Sergei Glazyev and Rachel B. Douglas, *Genocide: Russia and the New World Order*, Executive Intelligence Review, 1999. Sergei Yurevich Glazyev was first deputy minister, and then minister of foreign economic relations of the Russian Federation. He also was a deputy in the State Duma and chief of the Russian Federation Security Council's Directorate of Economic Security. Rosefielde and Hedlund, *Russia since 1980*.

43 Gaidar was editor of *Kommunist* during the Gorbachev years, before joining forces with Yeltsin. While in government, he advocated shock therapy and free market economic reforms. He abolished price controls and cut military procurement and industrial subsidies, and reduced the budget deficit. Gaidar was the first vice-premier of the Russian government and minister of economics from 1991 until 1992, and minister of finance from February 1992 until April 1992.

44 Marshall Goldman, *The Piratization of Russia: Russian Reform Goes Awry*, London: Routledge, 2003.

45 John Williamson, "What Washington Means by Policy Reform," Washington, DC: Peterson Institute for International Economics, November 2002. Williamson's article provides a concise statement of the neoliberal approach to free market economic development. It eschews "shock therapy" in favor of prudent pro-competitive market institution building. Jeffrey Sachs disparagingly describes the "Washington Consensus" as Milton Friedman-style free enterprise. Jeffrey Sachs, "What I Did in Russia, March 14, 2012. http://jeffsachs.org/2012/03/what-i-did-in-russia/ He insists that "shock therapy" was intended to create a more social democratic outcome than the "Washington Consensus."

46 Yegor Gaidar, *Collapse of an Empire: Lessons for Modern Russia*, Washington, DC: Brookings Institution Press, 2007; Yegor Gaidar and Karl Otto Pöhl, *Russian Reform / International Money (Lionel Robbins Lectures)*, Cambridge, MA: MIT Press, 1995; Yegor Gaidar, Michael McFaul, and Jane Ann Miller, *Days of Defeat and Victory*, Seattle: University of Washington Press, 1999; Yegor Gaidar, *State and Evolution: Russia's Search for a Free Market*, Seattle: University of Washington Press, 2003.

Yegor Gaidar, ed., *The Economics of Russian Transition*, Cambridge MA: MIT Press, 2002.

Sergei Vasiliev and Yegor Gaidar, *Ten Years of Russian Economic Reform*, London: Centre for Research into Post Communist Economies, 1999.

47 James Buchanan explained to the author at a conference in 1993 that capital must be privatized to the most competent hands for economies to prosper. Privatizing to oligarchs is counterproductive.

48 The military-industrial component of Gosplan still exists within the VPK. My colleague Ivan Materov was a high-ranking official during the Yeltsin years.

49 Vladimir Tikhomirov, "Capital Flight from Post-Soviet Russia," *Europe Asia Studies* Vol. 49, No. 4 (1997): 591–615. Vladimir Tikhomirov, "Capital Flight: Causes, Consequences and Counter-Measures," in Klaus Segbers, *Explaining Post-Soviet Patchworks 2*. Aldershot, UK: Ashgate, 2001, 251–280.

50 Traffic police in Moscow, for example, stopped cars at random and demanded that drivers pay their "salary." Military forces in the Caucasus operated on the same principle.

51 Valerii Makarov and Georgii Kleiner, "Barter v ekonomike perekhodnovo perioda: Osobennosti i tendentsii." *Ekonomika i Matematicheskie Metody* Vol. 33, No. 2 (1997): 25–41.

52 The most influential oligarchs from the Yeltsin era were Boris Berezovsky, Alexander Smolensky, Mikhail Khodorkovsky, Alex Konanykhin, Mikhail Fridman, Anatoly Chubais, Vladimir Gusinsky, Vitaly Malkin, and Vladimir Potanin. Putin purged all of them except Potanin, Malkin, and Fridman.

53 The World Bank, IMF, and G-7 provided and promoted Yeltsin's cover agenda of constructing democratic free enterprise. Some may have been motivated by devotion to the "Washington Consensus," but breaking the back of communism was the hidden goal. John Williamson, "Development and the 'Washington Consensus,'" in *World Development* Vol. 21 (1993): 1239–1336.

54 Brando Fite, *U.S. and Iranian Strategic Competition: The Impact of China and Russia*, Washington, DC: Center for Strategic and International Studies, March 2012.

55 Alexander Gerschenkron famously taught that Gaidar's theory was fatuous. See Alexander Gerschenkron, *Economic Backwardness in Historical Perspective*, Cambridge, MA: Harvard University Press, 1962.

56 Steven Rosefielde, "The Civilian Labor Force and Unemployment in the Russian Federation," *Europe-Asia Studies*, Vol. 52, No. 8 (December 2000): 1433–1447.

57 Maria Fedorishina, "Suicide Rate Falls in Russia," *Russia and India Report*, October 17, 2014. http://in.rbth.com/society/2014/10/17/suicide_rate_falls_in_russia_39087.html. "Over the past 20 years, the number of suicides in Russia has almost halved. Where in 1993, 56,136 people committed suicide, the figure came down to 28,779 suicides in 2013, according to the Federal State Statistics Service (Rosstat).

"'Suicide rates are an objective indicator of social disadvantage,' said Boris Polozhiy, the head of environmental and social issues at the Serbsky State Scientific Centre for Social and Forensic Psychiatry. 'In the first half of the 90s, we saw a period of radical social and political reforms in Russia, and during this period the suicide rate rose. It reached its peak in 1994–95, aided by the prolonged complex social situation in the country,' he said."

58 Personal conversation with Yaremenko and Vitaly Shlykov, Moscow, winter 1994.

59 Steven Rosefielde, "Review of Andrey Vavilov, *The Russian Public Debt and Financial Meltdowns*, New York: Palgrave Macmillan, 2010, xi, 269 pp.," *Slavic Review*, 2011. The economy had modestly rebounded from its 1996 low in response to the massive devaluation of 1998 caused by the flimflam sale of dollar-denominated foreign debt, but any sustainable recovery to the Soviet era standard of living seemed hopelessly out of reach, due in part to the obsolescence and depreciation of Russia's capital stock driven in part by massive capital flight. Oligarchs went on a capital asset buying spree abroad because of the ever-present threat that the rents granted to them would be rescinded, and their assets confiscated.

60 Numerous private discussions.

61 Judith L. Twigg and Kate Schechter, editors, *Social Capital and Social Cohesion in Post-Soviet Russia*, New York: M.E. Sharpe, 2003; Murray Feshbach, "Russia's

Demographic and Health Meltdown," in *Russia's Uncertain Economic Future*, Washington, DC: Joint Economic Committee of Congress, 2002, 283–306; Mark Field, "The Health and Demographic Crisis in Post-Soviet Russia: A Two Phase Development," in Field and Twigg, eds., *Russia's Torn Safety Nets*, New York: St. Martin's Press, 2000, 11–43.

62   The primary advocate of shock therapy for Russia in the West was Jeffrey Sachs. See Jeffrey Sachs, "Goodwill Is not Enough," *The Economist*, December 1991. He was the one who advised Gaidar to abruptly abolish price controls. He excuses his failure in Russia by stressing the difficulties of Russia's plight, but displays no practical understanding of the Soviet Union's command economic system. He opposes public programs to stimulate aggregate economic activity and simultaneously criticizes the Washington Consensus. It is unclear what he really thought he was doing. See Sachs, "What I Did in Russia."

63   The Chinese Communist Party rejected shock therapy out of hand, and the West knew Deng Xiaoping could not be persuaded to abandon his gradualist approach to authoritarian market building. Instead of scuttling the command economy in one fell swoop, China chose to turbo-charge aggregate economic demand to ease the dislocations cause by orderly marketization. Now that the Chinese approach has been vindicated and shock therapy largely forgotten, Deng Xiaoping's strategy is lauded as the Beijing Consensus. See Stefan Halper, *The Beijing Consensus: How China's Authoritarian Model Will Dominate the Twenty-First Century*, New York: Basic Books, 2010.

64   Graham Allison, *Window of Opportunity: The Grand Bargain for Democracy in the Soviet Union*, New York: Pantheon, 1991; Graham Allison and Robert Blackwill, "America's Stake in the Soviet Future," *Foreign Affairs* Vol. 70, No. 3 (1991): 77–97. Robert Blackwill and Graham Allison, "On With the Grand Bargain," *Washington Post*, August 27, 1991. http://belfercenter.ksg.harvard.edu/publication/1301/on_with_the_grand_bargain.html. "The terms of the Grand Bargain remain unchanged: substantial Western support and financial assistance to motivate and facilitate Soviet reforms strictly conditioned upon the political and economic transformation of that vast conglomerate. Real Western resources committed not for Soviet promises, vague plans or repeated proclamations of the kind that Mr. Gorbachev took to the London Economic Summit. Real Western resources committed only after real Soviet economic reform, which, despite the momentous and thrilling events in Moscow, has not yet occurred." The author interviewed the Japanese official responsible for writing the Grand Bargain assistance checks to Russia. Although Japan had pledged $2 billion of assistance, it had not paid a single yen! Cf. Steven Rosefielde, "The Grand Bargain: Underwriting Katastroika," *Global Affairs* Vol. 7, No. 1 (1992): 15–35.

65   Steven Rosefielde and Quinn Mills, *Global Economic Turmoil and the Public Good*, Singapore: World Scientific Publishers, 2015.

66   The author discussed this option at the time with a senior American official, who asserted that if public spending programs succeeded, this might weaken Yeltsin's resolve to destroy communist-style big government, and might lead to a communist *revanche*.

67   Ronald McKinnon, *The Order of Economic Liberalization: Financial Control in the Transition to a Market Economy*, Baltimore, MD: John Hopkins University Press, 1991; Pekka Sutela, *The Road to the Russian Market Economy*, Helsinki: Kikkimora,

1998; Anders Aslund, *How Russia Became a Market Economy*, Washington, DC: Brookings Institution, 1995; Anders Aslund and Richard Layard, *Changing the Economic System in Russia*, New York: Palgrave Macmillan, 1993. Joseph Stiglitz was appointed World Bank senior vice president for development policy and its chief economist in 1997.

68 Anders Aslund, *Russia's Capitalist Revolution: Why Market Reform Succeeded and Democracy Failed*, Washington, DC: Peterson Institute of International Economics, 2007; Andrei Shleifer and Daniel Treisman, "A Normal Country," *Foreign Affairs* Vol. 83, No. 2 (2004): 20–39. Cf. Steven Rosefielde, "An Abnormal Country," *The European Journal of Comparative Economics* Vol. 2, No. 1 (2005): 3–16; Steven Rosefielde, "The Illusion of Westernization in Russia and China," *Comparative Economic Studies*, Vol. 49 (2007): 495–513; H. Alice, Jacek Kochanowicz, and Lance Taylor, *The Market Meets Its Match: Restructuring the Economies of Eastern Europe*, Cambridge, MA and London: Harvard University Press, 1994.

69 Many distinguished economists in Russia and abroad opposed shock therapy, and the World Bank Group's bogus claims of successful Russian market transition. Clifford Gaddy and Barry Ickes, *Russia's Virtual Economy*, Washington, DC: Brookings Institution Press, 2002.

70 This, however, doesn't mean that Yeltsin was a democrat. He rose to power championing fair electoral democracy, but called in the military to suppress the parliament when legislators rejected his autocratic constitution. His electoral victory in 1996 was assured by vote rigging, and in 2000, he appointed Vladimir Putin as his successor. Although Yeltsin is still lauded in the West as the father of Russian democracy, his promises remain unfulfilled. See Rosefielde and Hedlund, *Russia since 1980*. Cf. Leon Aron, *Yeltsin: A Revolutionary Life*, New York: St Martin's Press, 2000.

71 John Schindler, "Russia Is on A 'Holy Mission' and the West Doesn't Get It," *Business Insider*, January 27, 2015. http://www.businessinsider.com/russia-is-on-a-holy-mission-and-the-west-doesnt-get-it-2015-1. "As Russian troops are advancing deeper into Ukraine, fresh from victory at Donetsk, NYT asked what on earth is going on here; why would Russians want more war now that the cost of it all to their economy is becoming obvious? The explanation was proffered by a Moscow economist: 'The influence of economists as a whole has completely vanished,' he opined about the Kremlin: 'The country is on a holy mission. It's at war with the United States, so why would you bother about the small battleground, the economy?' It's increasingly clear that the security sector, what Russians term the special services, are running the show. They are Putin's natural powerbase, his 'comfort zone' in Western parlance, plus they are the guarantor of his maintaining power as the economic crisis worsens. Current reports indicate that Putin's inner circle now is made up entirely of *siloviki*, to use the Russian term, men from the special services: National Security Council head Nikolai Patrushev, Federal Security Service (FSB) head Aleksandr Bortnikov, Foreign Intelligence Service (SVR) head Mikhail Fradkov, and Defense Minister Sergei Shoygu. Patrushev headed the FSB from 1999, the beginning of Putin's presidency, to 2008, and was a previously a career KGB officer, serving in Leningrad counterintelligence just like Putin: and just like Putin, he is a Chekist to his core. Current FSB director Bortnikov, who took over from Patrushev in 2008, is another career Chekist who joined the KGB after college and, yet again, comes out of the Leningrad office. Fradkov is not officially a Chekist

by background, having spent the early years of his Kremlin career in foreign trade matters, but he was 'close' to the KGB during that time, and he has headed the SVR, the successor to the KGB's elite First Chief Directorate, since 2007; it says something about Putin's confidence in him that Fradkov survived the 2010 debacle of the exposure of the SVR's Illegals network in the United States, which was nearly as demoralizing to the SVR as the Snowden Operation has been for U.S. intelligence. The last, Shoygu, who has headed the powerful defense ministry since 2012, is not a military man by background, yet has longstanding ties to military intelligence (GRU).

"As Russia's economic crisis has mounted, Putin has unsurprisingly turned to fellow Chekists, some of them very like himself by background. They share a worldview which is conspiratorial and deeply anti-Western; they view America as their Main Enemy and now believe Obama is on a mission to destroy Russia.

"That they will not allow, and they will stop at nothing to halt what prominent Orthodox clerics recently have termed the 'American project' that wants to destroy Holy Russia. This volatile combination of Chekist conspiracy-thinking and Orthodox Third Rome mysticism, plus Russian xenophobia and a genuine economic crisis, means that 2015 promises to be a dangerous year for the world. The Kremlin now believes they are at war with the United States, an Orthodox Holy War in the eyes of many Russians, and that struggle is defensive and legitimate. It would be good if Obama and his staff paid attention. This is about much more than Ukraine."

72 Robert Gates, *Duty: Memoirs of a Secretary at War*, New York: Alfred A. Knopf, 2014.

2

Annexation

Recovering Lost Ground

Russia's annexation of Crimea on March 18, 2014, appears to herald the end of the post-Soviet world order founded on partnership and the West's Wilsonian idealist concepts of the rule of law, democracy, and the sanctity of national independence. It likely represents the opening phase of Putin's campaign to roll back post-communist geostrategic losses,[1] blunt NATO's eastward advance, repel fresh Western-backed color revolutions throughout the former Soviet space, and expand the Kremlin's sphere of influence.[2]

The tactics Russia employed in Crimea appear to presage things to come, and offer insight into how Putin expects to reestablish Russia's Soviet-era great power,[3] while holding the line against color revolutions,[4] cultural "infection," and NATO expansion.[5] He probably intends to gather low-hanging fruit, annex vulnerable territories, or transform them into vassal states by fomenting ethnic liberation, concocting historical pretexts,[6] employing highly trained Russian military "surrogates," and saber-rattling.[7] He has abandoned the Soviet-era concept of blitzkrieg invasions with massive tank armies,[8] choosing instead to achieve the same goal with subtler methods that lighten occupation costs and reduce the risks of conventional and nuclear war.[9] Putin understands Western political vulnerabilities and doubtlessly plans to exploit them by coaxing America and the European Union to temporize and appease the Kremlin de facto or de jure one concession at a time until he achieves a multipolar world order more to his liking.[10]

Why Crimea?

Putin began planning Crimea's annexation long before Euromaidan for sound geostrategic reasons.[11] He coveted Crimea because its acquisition extends the Kremlin's control over the Sea of Azov, part of the Black Sea, secures the Sevastopol naval base, and encloses Ukraine in a pincer with little risk and the hope of low occupation costs.[12] Crimea lies just across a narrow strait from Russia's Kuban region, and was part of both the Russian empire and the Soviet Union. Catherine the Great conquered the Crimean Khanate in the eighteenth century and incorporated Crimea as the Taurida Oblast in 1783. After the Russian Revolution of 1917, Crimea became a republic within the Russian Soviet Federative Socialist Republic in the USSR. In 1954, the Crimean Oblast was transferred to the Ukrainian Soviet Socialist Republic for the Kremlin's administrative convenience.[13] As a consequence, the Crimean Oblast inadvertently became the Autonomous Republic of Crimea under the control of independent Ukraine when the Soviet Union collapsed in 1991, while Sevastopol with its status as a closed military federal city retained its Russian administration. Crimea, from the Kremlin's perspective, rightfully belongs to Russia. According to Mikhail Gorbachev, it was only ceded to Ukraine in the Soviet divorce because the West gave him false assurance that Kyiv wouldn't join the European Union and NATO.[14] The Kremlin views Crimea's inclusion in post-Soviet Ukraine as a blunder and claims that Putin's re-annexation is a dream come true for Crimea's people.

Decision to Attack

Political events in Ukraine provided Putin with the golden opportunity to initiate his great power restoration campaign early in 2014. The civil unrest in Kyiv, President Viktor Yanukovych's flight to Russia on February 21, 2014 (known as the Ukrainian "revolution" or Euromaidan events), and ethnic strife gave him a compelling pretext to attack. The Kremlin immediately condemned the Euromaidan events as a coup d'état against Yanukovych. It demanded his reinstatement[15] and refused to acknowledge Oleksandr Turchynov's legitimacy.[16] These declarations sparked pro-Russia protests in Sevastopol two days later. Beginning on February 26, pro-Russia groups occupied strategic positions and infrastructure across the Crimean peninsula, assisted by special Russian security troops transferred from Sochi at the conclusion of the Winter Olympics.[17] A rump session of the Crimean parliament then dismissed the Ukrainian Crimean government and promptly called for a referendum on Crimea's autonomy. The vote held on March 16, 2014, was a ringing endorsement for annexation. Ninety seven percent of the Crimean electorate and 96 percent of Sevastopol's population officially chose secession.

This provided Moscow with the semblance of legitimacy it had been seeking, despite the West's and Kyiv's cries of foul play. The Crimean parliament declared its independence, and asked Putin to annex Crimea the next day. The deal was sealed March 18, 2014. Both the Republic of Crimea and Sevastopol acceded to the Russian Federation. The action was declared invalid by the West,[18] Ukraine, and a non-binding UN resolution.[19] Kyiv and its allies insist that Russia's occupation of Crimea is temporary, and demand that the Kremlin rescind its illegal annexation. Moscow's annexation of Crimea, however, is almost certainly a fait accompli on a par with Yanukovych's exile.[20] Putin freely admits that Russia conspired with Crimea's secessionists,[21] but this alters nothing. He is in a position to plausibly claim that Crimea should be Russian, that the Crimean people desire annexation, and that neither Kyiv nor NATO has the armed forces to restore the status quo ante. This makes the opening round of what appears to be Putin's great power restoration campaign a stunning triumph from the Kremlin's perspective. America, the European Union, and Ukraine's current president, Petro Poroshenko, were caught off guard because they failed to accurately comprehend Putin's intentions and[22] dismissed the possibility of the Kremlin's strike the day before it happened, although, like Pearl Harbor, they should have known better.[23] They had no operational contingency plan to repel Moscow's bold thrust,[24] have no viable military plans to deter further aggression,[25] are still preoccupied with Monday night quarterbacking,[26] and are pretending that the Kremlin will be pushed back and partnership rebooted on the West's terms.[27] Putin's realpolitik has trumped the West's rule of international law.[28]

Phase Two: Slow Motion Advance and Consolidation

American, the European Union, and Ukraine have only band-aid strategies for deterring a second phase of Russia's counteroffensive.[29] They are improvising with the Minsk II agreement, slapping Putin's wrist with economic sanctions, reprimanding him, demanding Crimea's return, and dismissing Putin's boast that time is on the Kremlin's side. NATO's failure to bolster its deterrent capabilities gives Moscow ample time to consolidate its control and establish the "new normal" in Novorossiya. Power today can override the rule of law. This is an important aspect of Putin's great power restoration initiative, and a new twist on Hitler's tactics in the late 1930s, when the West also assumed that time was on its side.[30]

Novorossiya was an Imperial Russian province (*guberniya*) from the eighteenth to the twentieth century, encompassing a large slice of contemporary

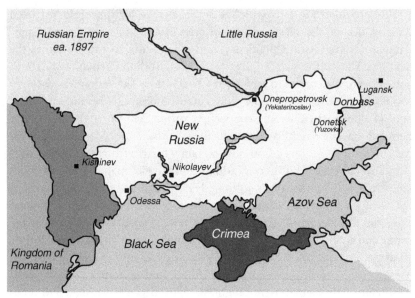

Map 2.1 Novorossiya, 1897.

Ukraine, administratively centered in Dnepropetrovsk (see Map 2.1). Its importance lies in Putin's claim that the region, whatever its ethnicity (Russia's tsarist empire was multiethnic) and boundaries, was Russia's before the Bolshevik coup d'état,[31] and therefore on historical grounds belongs to Russia today.[32] This claim, which presumes the legitimacy of empire in a mostly post-imperial age, provides him with a legal basis for applying his Crimean tactics along Russia's eastern border with Ukraine (Luhansk, Donetsk, Mariupol, and Kharkov). Following the Crimean precedent, local groups assisted by Russian special forces created people's republics in Luhansk and Donetsk, which subsequently merged into the federal state of Novorossiya.[33] Other "republics" may be added as the battlefield evolves.

Ukraine's impotent military gives Putin the ability to harry and intimidate Poroshenko's government in eastern Ukraine and extend operations to Odessa and Kharkov at Moscow's discretion (see Map 2.2).[34] Kharkov can be conquered by Russia's tank armies in the north, and naval operations can be launched against Odessa from Sevastopol, enabling Russia to control the hatched area from Mariupol to Odessa, denying Kyiv river access from the Dneiper to the Black Sea and the Sea of Azov.[35] Moreover, by linking a future Russian-annexed Odessa to Transdnistria, Novorossiya can be restored to the Kremlin in its fuzzy entirety.[36]

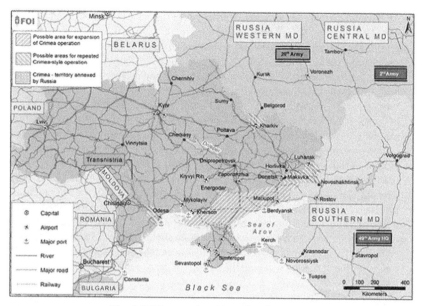

Map 2.2 Novorossiya, 2015: Conflict zones.

Military operations of these sorts entail risks. Although Russia's million-strong army outclasses any defense Kyiv can muster, and NATO is unlikely to fight in Ukraine, Moscow must be mindful of exposing its flank with China.[37] Putin's solution appears to be stealthy hybrid war, *maskirovka*,[38] nonlinear war and combined arms combat as situations dictate,[39] and the extensive use of soft power (nonmilitary means of influence) that mitigates out-of-theater dangers.[40] He will try to skirt red lines and avoid debilitating occupation costs, and can settle for half a loaf at his discretion because territory isn't the primary objective. It may be quite sufficient to partially roll back post-Soviet geostrategic losses, blunting NATO's eastward advance and repelling fresh Western-backed color revolutions throughout the former Soviet space. Perhaps, Putin's repeated references to Novorossiya are empty bluster, but after Crimea's annexation, it seems prudent to take his self-declared ambitions to heart.

Notes

1 Putin's plan includes influencing Western domestic politics. Athena Yenko, "Revealed: Vladimir Putin Plotting to Invade Europe – Report," *Australia International Business Times*, November 28, 2014. http://au.ibtimes.com/articles/574304/20141128/vladimir-putin-europe-germany-vienna.htm#.VHrmZ8lN9c4.

Cf. Raymond Aron, "What Makes Putin Tick? A Primer for Presidential Candidates," AEI, December 5, 2014. http://www.aei.org/publication/makes-putin-tick-primer-presidential-candidates/?utm_source=today&utm_medium=paramount&utm_campaign=120514. "Outside the country, the Putin Doctrine aims at Moscow's de facto veto power over domestic regimes and foreign and defense orientations of most post-Soviet states, with swift and unyielding pressure applied to those that attempt to resist. Globally, the doctrine has guided Putin's efforts to restore Russia to the status of a great power – defined in the quasi-Soviet way seen in much of Putin's thinking – mostly in opposition to the United States. Finally, his Russia must continue as the world's other nuclear superpower, which, in Putin's mind, is incompatible with any kind of European strategic missile defense." Aron advances the old saw that Putin will falter because he won't be able to provide Russia with both butter and guns. "The Kremlin is no longer capable of securing both guns and butter. The billion-dollar price tags for Crimea, Putin's pet new state of 'Novorossiya,' and a mammoth military modernization are coming due, not to mention the costs from Western sanctions. Russian cannot deal with these expenses without slashing budgets for healthcare and education, freezing pensions and salaries; that is, he can't deal with them without hitting his political base by reducing the incomes of tens of millions of pensioners and state employees."

2 Stephen Blank, "Telling the Truth about Ukraine," Unpublished manuscript, 2014. "Furthermore, Buchanan's argument that Russia has genuine grievances against Ukraine which justifies its aggression – such as the election of a pro-western government in Kiev this spring – is also completely off base. The evidence that this war is preplanned is also overwhelming. US analyst Reuben Johnson wrote that planning for this and a potential Moldovan operation started in 2006: 'Moscow has the political and covert action means to create in the Crimea the very type of situations against which Putin is offering to "protect" Ukraine if the Russian Fleet's presence is extended. Thus far such means have been shown to include inflammatory visits and speeches by Russian Duma deputies in the Crimea, challenges to Ukraine's control of Tuzla Island in the Kerch Strait, the fanning of "anti-NATO" – in fact anti-American – protests by Russian groups in connection with planned military exercises and artificial Russian-Tatar tensions on the peninsula.' Furthermore, Russian intelligence, military, economic, informational, ideological, and other forms of penetration of the Crimea to nullify Ukraine's de facto if not de jure sovereignty there along with warnings concerning Crimea's future have been long apparent. Russia also augmented its capabilities for covert and overt subversion by instituting a substantial program giving soldiers and officers in the Transnistrian 'Army' that occupies part of Moldova, Russian military service passports and rotating them through elite Russian officer training courses at Solnechegorsk. As one intelligence officer in a post-Soviet republic said: 'You do not try to cover up a training program of this size unless you are someday planning on using these people to overthrow or otherwise take control of a sovereign government. – The facility at Solnechegorsk is used by Russia to train numerous non-Russian military personnel openly and legally for peacekeeping and other joint operations. If then, in parallel, you are training officers from these disputed regions – officers that are pretending to be Russian personnel and carrying bogus paperwork – then it does not take an enormous leap of faith to assume that Moscow is up to no good on this one.'"

3 Jakob Kipp, "Russia, the European Union, and the Ukrainian Crisis: A European or a Eurasian Crisis?" Paper presented at the UNC Conference on a Global Perspective on the European Crisis, Chapel Hill, September 19, 2014. Roger McDermott and Jacob Kipp, "The Bear Went under the Mountain: Is Russia's Style of Warfare Really New?" European Leadership Network, December 15, 2014. http://www.europeanleadershipnetwork .org/the-bear-went-under-the-mountain-is-russias-style-of-warfare-really-new_ 2263.html. The authors explore the nuances of the master plan concept.

4 The term *color revolutions* describes popular demonstrations seeking regime change, with the further implication that color revolutionaries oppose authoritarianism and support democratic free enterprise. The Obama administration's ambassador to Russia, Michael McFaul, expressed his view that Putin's authoritarianism soon would give way to democracy. See Michael McFaul and Kathryn Stoner-Weiss, "Mission to Moscow: Why Authoritarian Stability Is a Myth," *Foreign Affairs*, January/February 2008. McFaul worked for the U.S. National Security Council as special assistant to the president and senior director of Russian and Eurasian affairs. McFaul is one of the architects of the "reset." See Leon Aron, "A Tormenting in Moscow," *AEI*, April 12, 2012. The West's approach to color revolution violates the Wilsonian concept of the rights of national self-determination and non-aggression against sovereign states, while holding Russia accountable to the same standards, but Western leaders disregard the contradiction.

5 Johan Norberg and Fredrik Westerlund, "Russia and Ukraine: Military-Strategic Options, and Possible Risks, for Moscow," FOI, Stockholm, April 7, 2014. http:// www.iiss.org/en/militarybalanceblog/blogsections/2014-3bea/april-7347/ russia-and-ukraine-3b92.

6 Elena Holodny and Michael B Kelley, "Putin-Backed Rebels just Made a Huge Move Right under Europe's Nose," *Business Insider*, February 6, 2015. http://finance.yahoo .com/news/putin-backed-rebels-just-made-213511522.html. "The self-proclaimed, largely unrecognized Donetsk People's Republic (DPR) moved closer to unifying with the other region that has forcefully broken away by declaring itself the legal successor of a 1918 self-proclaimed Soviet republic. 'We, the deputies of the Donetsk People's Republic, aware of our responsibility before the past and paving the road for the future, proclaim the continuation of the tradition of the Donetsk-Krivoy-Rog Republic and announce that the state of Donetsk People's Republic is her successor,' the memorandum stated, according to Gazeta.ru. The Donetsk-Krivoy-Rog Republic declared independence from Ukraine on Feb. 12, 1918. And then, 36 days later, it was incorporated into the Ukraine Soviet Republic – that is, one of the constituent republics of the Soviet Union.

"On Friday, the DPR's memorandum was sent over to another self-proclaimed state, [the] Luhansk People's Republic (LPR), according to a report from Interfax. One of the leaders of the DPR, Andrei Purgin, noted that the leadership of the LPR is in talks with Luhansk to synchronize the legislative activity.

"'Memorandum on state-building and continuity of the Donetsk-Krivoy Rog republic will be adopted also in LPR,' he said."

7 Stephen Cohen and his colleagues broadly support Putin's master plan. See Cathy Young, "Putin's Pal," *Slate*, July 24, 2014. http://www.slate.com/articles/news_and_ politics/foreigners/2014/07/stephen_cohen_vladimir_putin_s_apologist_the_ nation_just_published_the_most.html. "Is Cohen the one person in the world who

puts stock in the results of the Donetsk and Luhansk 'referendums', which even Russia did not formally recognize? Pre-referendum polls in both regions found that most residents opposed secession; they were also, as a U.N. report confirms, kept from voting in the presidential election by violence and intimidation from the insurgents. Nor does Cohen ever acknowledge the known fact that a substantial percentage of the 'resisters' are not locals but citizens of the Russian Federation – particularly their leaders, many of whom have ties to Russian 'special security services.' Their ranks also include quite a few Russian ultranationalists and even neo-Nazis – a highly relevant fact, given that much of Cohen's article is devoted to claims that Ukrainian 'neo-fascists' play a key role both in the Kiev government and in the counterinsurgency operation. On this subject, Cohen's narrative is so error-riddled that one has to wonder if *The Nation* employs fact-checkers. (According to *The Nation*'s publicity director, Caitlin Graf, 'All of *The Nation*'s print pieces are rigorously fact-checked by our research department.') Cohen asserts that after the fall of pro-Moscow President Viktor Yanukovych, the far-right Svoboda party, and the paramilitary nationalist group Right Sector got a large share of Cabinet posts, including ones for national security and the military, because Ukraine's new leaders were 'obliged to both movements for their violence-driven ascent to power, and perhaps for their personal safety.' In fact, Svoboda (which has tried to reinvent itself as a moderate nationalist party, despite a genuinely troubling history of bigotry and extremism) got its Cabinet posts as part of a European Union–brokered agreement between Yanukovych and opposition leaders, made shortly before Yanukovych skipped town. Right Sector has no such posts – early reports that its leader, Dmytro Yarosh, got appointed deputy minister for national security were wrong – and the government actually moved to crack down on the group in April. Cohen also neglects to mention that the Svoboda-affiliated acting defense minister, Ihor Tenyukh, was sacked in late March and replaced with a nonpartisan career military man.

"Cohen's claims about the 'mainstreaming of fascism's dehumanizing ethos' in Ukraine are equally spurious – and rely heavily on Russian propaganda canards. Thus, he asserts that Ukrainian Prime Minister Arseniy Yatsenyuk called the rebels 'subhumans'; in fact, even the pro-government Russian newspaper *Vzglyad* admits this was an English mistranslation of *nelyudi*, literally 'inhumans' or 'monsters.' (The word also exists in Russian, and Russian officials have freely used it toward their own 'resisters' in the Caucasus.) He reports that a regional governor (Yuri Odarchenko of the Kherson region) 'praised Hitler for his "slogan of liberating the people" in occupied Ukraine' in his speech at a Victory Day event on May 9. In fact, as a transcript and a video show, Odarchenko said that Hitler used 'slogans about alleged liberation of nations' to justify invading sovereign countries and 'the aggressor' today was using similar slogans about 'alleged oppressions' to justify aggression against Ukraine. And, in Cohen's extremely tendentious retelling, the May 2 tragedy in Odessa, where clashes between separatists and Kiev supporters led to a deadly fire that killed some 40 separatists, becomes a deliberate holocaust reminiscent of 'Nazi German extermination squads.' In a downright surreal passage, Cohen argues that Putin has shown 'remarkable restraint' so far but faces mounting public pressure due to 'vivid accounts' in the Russian state-run media of Kiev's barbarities against ethnic Russians. Can he really be unaware that the hysteria is being whipped up by lurid fictions, such as the recent TV1 story about a 3-year-old boy crucified in Slovyansk's main square in front of a large crowd and his own mother? Does Cohen not know that Russian disinformation and fakery, including old footage from Dagestan or Syria passed off as evidence of horrors in Ukraine, has been extensively documented? Is he unaware that top Russian officials, including Foreign Minister Sergei Lavrov and Putin himself, have publicly repeated allegations of war crimes that were quickly exposed as false, such as white phosphorus use by Ukrainian troops or a slaughter of the wounded in a hospital? But Cohen manages to take the surrealism a notch higher, earnestly citing the unnamed 'dean of Moscow State University's School of Television' (that's Vitaly Tretyakov, inter alia a 9/11 'truther') who thinks the Kremlin may be colluding with the West to hush up the extent of carnage in Ukraine."

8 Putin's tactics resemble Hitler's, but he rejects military conquest in Europe, with the possible exception of the Baltic states. See Christian Reiermann, "Fighting Words: Schäuble Says Putin's Crimea Plans Reminiscent of Hitler," *Spiegel*, March 30, 2014.

   http://www.spiegel.de/international/germany/schaeuble-compares-putin-moves-in-crimea-to-policies-of-hitler-a-961696.html.

9 The strategy is consistent with Lenin's concept of armed struggle and Clausewitz's views on small wars. In his famous "Bekenntnisdenkschrift" of 1812, he called for a "Spanish war in Germany" and laid out a comprehensive guerrilla strategy to be waged against Napoleon. It is also compatible with Clausewitz's famous aphorism that "War is merely the continuation of policy by other means." Carl von Clausewitz, *On War*, Princeton, NJ: Princeton University Press, 1976, chapter 1, Section 24.

10 Putin is focused on the West, but understands China's strategic importance.

11 Euromaidan refers to Euro Square (Maidan Nezalezhnosti) in Kyiv, which served as the geographical focus of a wave of Ukrainian demonstrations and civil unrest that began on November 21, 2013, with public protests demanding closer European integration.

12 This geostrategic motive is consistent with a top-secret document leaked and published in *Novaya Gazeta*. The authenticity of the document cannot be independently confirmed. The leak may have been pre-approved by Putin. See Damien Sharkov, "Top Secret Briefing Advising Putin on Break-Up of Ukraine Leaked," *Newsweek*, February 26, 2015. http://www.newsweek.com/top-secret-briefing-advising-putin-break-ukraine-leaked-309477. "A top secret Kremlin briefing purportedly intended for the eyes of Russian President Vladimir Putin on the eve of Ukraine's revolution which discusses how to co-opt regions of the country's east into the Russian Federation has been leaked, according to Russian media." "Point three of the document laments that the Ukrainian constitution doesn't contain mechanisms by which the country's eastern territories and Crimea might decide to secede and join the Russian Federation. The author therefore suggests that it is then right for Russia to 'play on the aspirations' of eastern Ukrainian regions with pro-Russian sentiments, to allow them 'ascension' to Russia" in one form or another.

"Thus, the author of the document highlights the need for Russia to first 'sign contracts' for cross-border cooperation [with these regions], after which [they can] establish direct government-agreed relations with these Ukrainian territories where there are durable pro-Russian electoral sympathies.

"The author highlights Crimea and Kharkiv as regions pro-Russian groups are already strong enough to push for 'maximum integration' with Russia, also listing Luhansk and three other eastern Ukrainian regions. Crimea was annexed by Russia in March last year, while pro-Russian separatists are currently battling pro-K forces for control of Luhansk.

"Interestingly the region of Donetsk, which has seen some of the most invigorated pro-Russian militias and fiercest fighting, is omitted from that list as the author believed local Ukrainian oligarch Rinat Akhmetov's control there was too strong.

"In *Novaya Gazeta*'s notes on the document, the paper highlights how pragmatic the document is, in juxtaposition with the image of the Ukrainian conflict which the Kremlin have presented to the world. 'There is no "spiritual-historical" justification for Russian interference in Ukraine [in the document]; Andrey Lipsky, *Novaya Gazeta*'s political editor writes. 'There are no arguments about "Novorossiya" [New Russia] or the protection of Russian-speakers, or the "Russian world" or the resurgent "Russian Spring." Only geopolitics and cold expediency.'

"Instead, the reason for Russian interference in regions of Ukraine given by the author is retaining control over Ukraine's gas pipelines and strengthening Russia's role in Eastern and Central Europe.

"Elsewhere Yanukovych is notably described rather negatively as an individual 'of inconsiderable moral will.' The author of the document does not believe he would stay in power for long, saying that there is no longer a need for 'the Russian federation to provide any political, diplomatic, financial or informational support.'

"According to Lilia Shevtsova, Kremlinologist and Russia expert at Moscow's Carnegie Endowment for Peace, the leaked document's publication is very significant.

"'This "plan" suggests that the attempts of the forces close to the Kremlin, apparently working on Kremlin orders, to find ways to subjugate Ukraine had been undertaken before Yanukovych's collapse, thus we are dealing with a certain strategy that fits Putin's new survival doctrine adopted in 2012–2013,' she says."

13 During World War II, the Crimean Soviet Republic was downgraded to an Oblast.

14 Nathan Gardels, "Why Gorbachev Feels Betrayed by the Post-Cold War West," *The World Post*, November 7, 2014. http://www.huffingtonpost.com/2014/11/07/gorbachev-post-cold-war-west_n_6116654.html.

15 Vladimir Soldatkin, "Putin Says Plan to Take Crimea Hatched before Referendum," *Reuters*, March 10, 2015. http://news.yahoo.com/putin-says-plan-crimea-hatched-referendum-140644857.html. "This was on the night of Feb. 22 through to Feb. 23. We finished around 7 in the morning. And, while saying goodbye, I told all the colleagues: 'We have to start the work on Crimea's return into Russia.'

"This account, broadcast on Sunday, appeared to be at odds with previous assertions from Russian officials that the annexation decision was taken only after the referendum on March 16, when Crimeans voted to become part of the Russian Federation."

16 Turchynov is the current chairman of the Ukrainian parliament. He was appointed interim president by the Rada on February 21, 2014, serving until Petro Poroshenko was elected president on June 7, 2014.

17 Stephen Blank, Lecture delivered at the 46th Association for Slavic, East European, and Eurasian Studies Conference, San Antonio, Texas, Friday, November 21, 2014.

18 "Germany: No Recognition for Russia's Crimea Annexation," Anadolu Agency, November 19, 2014. "Foreign Minister Steinmeier says Russia's taking over the Ukrainian region is a clear violation of international law." http://www.aa.com.tr/en/world/423300–germany-no-recognition-for-russias-crimea-annexation.

19 "United Nations A/RES/68/262 General Assembly," *United Nations*, April 1, 2014.

20 "German Politician Censured for Crimea Recognition Remarks," Ukraina.ru, "Читать далее: http://en.ukraina.ru/news/20141121/1011240840.html Former chairman of the Social Democratic Party Matthias Platzeck was criticized for suggesting that Crimea should be legally recognized as part of Russia and was accused of being a Putin sympathizer." Читать далее: http://en.ukraina.ru/news/20141121/1011240840.html.

21 "Direct Line with Vladimir Putin," kremlin.ru. April 17, 2014. "Of course, Russian servicemen backed the Crimean self-defense forces."

22 Josh Rogin and Eli Lake, "U.S. Told Ukraine to Stand Down as Putin Invaded," *Bloomberg*, August 21, 2015. http://www.bloombergview.com/articles/2015-08-21/u-s-told-ukraine-to-stand-down-as-putin-invaded?cmpid=yhoo. "As Russian President Vladimir Putin's forces took over Ukraine's Crimean peninsula in early 2014, the interim Ukrainian government was debating whether or not to fight back against the 'little green men' Russia had deployed. But the message from the Barack Obama administration was clear: avoid military confrontation with Moscow.

"The White House's message to Kiev was advice, not an order, U.S. and Ukrainian officials have recently told us, and was based on a variety of factors. There was a lack of clarity about what Russia was really doing on the ground. The Ukrainian military was in no shape to confront the Russian Spetsnaz (special operations) forces that were swarming on the Crimean peninsula. Moreover, the Ukrainian government in Kiev was only an interim administration until the country would vote in elections a few months later. Ukrainian officials told us that other European governments sent Kiev a similar message.

"But the main concern was Russian President Vladimir Putin."

"As U.S. officials told us recently, the White House feared that if the Ukrainian military fought in Crimea, it would give Putin justification to launch greater military intervention in Ukraine, using similar logic to what Moscow employed in 2008 when Putin invaded large parts of Georgia in response to a pre-emptive attack by the Tbilisi government. Russian forces occupy two Georgian provinces to this day."

23 Josh Rogin and Eli Lake, "U.S. Told Ukraine to Stand Down as Putin Invaded," *Bloomberg*, August 21, 2015. http://www.bloombergview.com/articles/2015-08-21/u-s-told-ukraine-to-stand-down-as-putin-invaded?cmpid=yhoo. "When Russian special operations forces, military units and intelligence officers seized Crimea, it surprised the U.S. government. Intelligence analysts had briefed Congress 24 hours before the stealth invasion, saying the Russian troop buildup on Ukraine's border was a bluff."

24 Ibid. "Looking back today, many experts and officials point to the decision not to stand and fight in Crimea as the beginning of a Ukraine policy based on the assumption that avoiding conflict with Moscow would temper Putin's aggression. But that was a miscalculation. Almost two years later, Crimea is all but forgotten,

Russian-backed separatist forces are in control of two large Ukrainian provinces, and the shaky cease-fire between the two sides is in danger of collapsing." "As U.S. officials told us recently, the White House feared that if the Ukrainian military fought in Crimea, it would give Putin justification to launch greater military intervention in Ukraine, using similar logic to what Moscow employed in 2008 when Putin invaded large parts of Georgia in response to a pre-emptive attack by the Tbilisi government. Russian forces occupy two Georgian provinces to this day."

25 Noah Barkin and Andreas Rinke, "Merkel Hits Diplomatic Dead-End with Putin," November 25, 2014. http://news.yahoo.com/insight-merkel-hits-diplomatic-dead-end-putin-135131306.html. Instead of acknowledging that Putin successfully annexed Crimea, this story spins things, pretending that Putin lost because he dug himself into a hole, and cannot extricate himself from it. http://valdaiclub.com/near_abroad/71680.html. "NATO Secretary-General Anders Fogh Rasmussen announced NATO's intention to draft a strategy to counter 'Russian aggression,' which provides, in part, for the deployment of NATO military assets in Eastern European member countries."

26 Rogin and Lake, "U.S. Told Ukraine to Stand Down." " 'Part of the pattern we see in Russian behavior is to test and probe when not faced with pushback or opposition,' said Damon Wilson, the vice president for programming at the Atlantic Council. 'Russia's ambitions grow when they are not initially challenged. The way Crimea played out, Putin had a policy of deniability, there could have been a chance for Russia to walk away.' " " 'I don't think the Ukrainian military was well prepared to manage the significant challenge of the major Russian military and stealth incursion on its territory,' Andrew Weiss, a Russia expert and vice president for studies at the Carnegie Endowment, told us. This was also the view of many in the U.S. military and intelligence community at the time."

27 Ibid. "McFaul said the ease with which Putin was able to take Crimea likely influenced his decision to expand Russia's campaign in eastern Ukraine: 'I think Putin was surprised at how easy Crimea went and therefore when somebody said let's see what else we can do, he decided to gamble.'

"The Obama administration, led on this issue by Kerry, is still pursuing a reboot of U.S.-Russia relations. After a long period of coolness, Kerry's visit to Putin in Sochi in May was the start of a broad effort to seek U.S.-Russian cooperation on a range of issues including the Syrian civil war. For the White House, the Ukraine crisis is one problem in a broader strategic relationship between two world powers."

28 Laura Mills and John-Thor Dahlburg," Change of Leadership in Crimea Means Property grab," *AP*, December 2, 2014. http://news.yahoo.com/change-leadership-crimea-means-property-grab-095405755.html. "Crimea's Russia-installed prime minister, Sergei Aksyonov, says the nationalization law enacted Aug. 8 seeks to right wrongs committed by officials in Ukraine, where a lot of state property was sold off at bargain prices because the government was broke, or to benefit cronies." "The biggest loser so far has been Ihor Kolomoisky, a Ukrainian oligarch and nationalist firebrand. Aksyonov's government has taken 65 of his properties, including all branches of Privatbank, one of the largest in Crimea."

29 Bill Gertz, "Russia, China, and Iran Are Mastering Unconventional Warfare – and the US Doesn't Have a Plan to Counter Them," *The Washington Free Beacon*, November 25, 2014. "Russia, China, Iran, and Islamists are waging unconventional

warfare around the world, and the United States currently lacks a clear strategy to counter the threat, according to a recent report by the Army Special Operations Command." " 'Russian unconventional warfare is thus the central, most game-changing component of a hybrid warfare effort involving conventional forces, economic intimidation of regional countries, influence operations, force-posturing all along NATO borders, and diplomatic intervention,' the report said." http://freebeacon.com/national-security/russia-china-iran-waging-unconventional-warfare-report-says/#ixzz3K7RQ5jYi   http://freebeacon.com/national-security/russia-china-iran-waging-unconventional-warfare-report-says/#ixzz3K7Qu-wrjU. Cf. Norberg and Westerlund, "Russia and Ukraine."

30 Ibid. "Russia has so far used its armed forces against Ukraine in three ways. First, they were used for direct – but semi-covert – intervention to capture Crimea. This prevented Ukraine, and other actors, from intervening by force. Second, a major readiness exercise was held in the Western and Central MDs from 26 February to 7 March. This served as a diversion that hindered Ukraine from focusing political and military attention on Crimea. An early Ukrainian military response in Crimea was likely to have been a Russian military concern. Finally, the stated size of the exercise signalled the potential to intervene on a larger scale, thus putting pressure on Ukraine."

31 Paul Sonne, "With 'Novorossiya,' Putin Plays the Name Game with Ukraine: Russia Brings Back Czarist-Era Name of 'New Russia' for Southeastern Ukraine," *Wall Street Journal*, September 1, 2014. http://online.wsj.com/articles/with-novorossiya-putin-plays-the-name-game-with-ukraine-1409588947.
The Kremlin has not issued an official map of Novorossiya to define its claims, preferring to wait future developments.

32 Ukrainian sources counter-argue that ethnicity and post-tsarist developments supersede Russia imperial arrangements, rendering Putin's claims irrelevant. See "5 facts about 'Novorossiya' you won't learn in a Russian history class," http://euromaidanpress.com/2014/10/17/5-facts-about-novorossiya-you-wont-learn-in-a-russian-history-class/.

33 The Federal State of Novorossiya is a self-proclaimed confederation of the Donetsk People's Republic and the Luhansk People's Republic, claiming the territory of Donetsk Oblast and Luhansk Oblast in eastern Ukraine. This echoes Bolshevik tactics during Russia's civil war (1917–1921). See Richard Pipes, *The Formation of the Soviet Union Communism and Nationalism, 1917–1923*, Revised Edition, Cambridge MA: Harvard University Press, 1997.

34 Johan Norberg, Ulrik Franke, and Fredrik Westerlund, "The Crimea Operation: Implications for Future Russian Military Interventions," in Niklas Granholm, Johannes Malminen, and Gudrun Persson (eds.), *A Rude Awakening: Ramifications of Russian Aggression Towards Ukraine*, FOI-R–3892–SE, June 2014, Swedish Defence Research Agency, pp. 41–49. Norberg and Westerlund, "Tailoring War."

35 Norberg and Westerlund, "Russia and Ukraine." Will Cathcart, "Putin's Power Projection: It's All about Energy and the Black Sea," *Daily Beast*, March 1, 2015. http://www.thedailybeast.com/articles/2015/03/01/putin-s-power-projection-it-s-all-about-energy-and-the-blacksea.html?utm_source=feedburner&utm_medium=feed&utm_campaign=Feed%3A+thedailybeast%2Farticles+%28The+Daily+Beast+-+Latest+Articles%29. This deal brings the fighting in eastern Ukraine full circle and explains how an eventual land bridge to Crimea is Putin's long-term

goal. He will slowly and methodically make his way there in between the ceasefires. Putin has the entire Black Sea to gain. This is why the Kremlin is seeking not just economic dominance of the Black Sea corridor and energy transit routes, but military dominance as well.

36 There are short-term constraints that require attention, but slow-motion conquest should be an effective antidote. See Norberg and Westerlund, "Russia and Ukraine." "The annexation of Crimea has, to a degree, diluted Russia's overall military capability. Securing Crimea militarily over time requires the reinforcement of the whole peninsula's air and coastal defences, and ensuring the capability for combined-arms ground operations, primarily for defending the peninsula. A ground force of two motor-rifle brigades reinforced by artillery, air-defence units and attack helicopters would be needed, as well as the command function of an all-arms army. Russia's Black Sea Fleet lacks the capability to command combined-arms ground operations. These assets would have to be taken from somewhere else in Russia."

37 Ibid. "Russian strategic and doctrinal documents reveal a world view that sees military threats and dangers from all directions. Apart from NATO expansion to Russia's west, instability looms in the Caucasus and Central Asia to the south. Furthermore, Russia's force posture in the Eastern Military District (MD) clearly shows that China is a military concern, requiring preparations to augment Russian forces there. Although the armed forces are geographically dispersed, Russia can concentrate forces for offensive operations to seize and hold territory but only in one strategic direction at a time."

38 Lucy Ash, "How Russia Outfoxes Its Enemies," *BBC*, January 28, 2015. http://www.bbc.com/news/magazine-31020283. The key principles of *maskirovka* are "Surprise, Kamufliazh (camouflage) – such as the white uniforms worn by Russian troops in snow during their invasion of Finland in World War II, Demonstrativnye manevry – manoeuvres intended to deceive, Skrytie – concealment, Imitatsia – the use of decoys and military dummies, Dezinformatsia – disinformation, a knowing attempt to deceive."

39 Jacob Kipp, "Russia, the European Union, and the Ukrainian Crisis: A European or a Eurasian Affair?" in John McGowan, Gert Guri, and Bruno Dallago (eds.), *A Global Perspective on the European Economic Crisis*, London: Routledge, 2016, 259–274.

40 Mike Winnerstig (ed.), *Tools of Destabilization: Russian Soft Power and Non-military Influence in the Baltic States*, Swedish Defense Organization, FOI-R–3990 – SE, December 2014. "The Russian aggression against Ukraine has generated considerable concerns in the Baltic states of Estonia, Latvia and Lithuania. They are NATO members and thus protected by the collective defence capabilities of the alliance, but also in many ways the most vulnerable members of the alliance. This has led to an increased interest in other issues than traditional military threats against the Baltic states, in particular Russian 'soft power' and other means of non-military influence. To wield soft power might be a more effective tactic in a conflict than a traditional military attack – especially if the target is protected militarily through an alliance with bigger and more important actors. The results of the report indicate that a substantial number of actors, backed by the Russian federal government, are engaged in the implementation of a soft power strategy in the Baltic states. Central pieces of this strategy are a) the

Russian Compatriots policy, that actively supports all Russian-speaking people outside of Russia proper, b) a campaign aimed at undermining the self-confidence of the Baltic states as political entities, and c) interference in the domestic political affairs of the Baltic states. All this is reinforced by systematic Russian attempts to portray the Baltic states as 'fascist.' The results of the Russian actions are so far rather limited. For example, the majority of the Russian-speakers in Estonia are nowadays Estonian citizens, and a relatively small number are 'stateless.' In all three Baltic countries there are new younger generations today, with Russian as their mother tongue but increasingly identifying themselves as loyal citizens of their country of residence. In that sense, the Russian wielding of soft power against the Baltic states has been a failure. In other areas, such as the energy sector, Russian non-military power has been more successful, but there are signs indicating that the Baltic states are coming to grips with that situation as well."

PART II

RESURGENT COLD WAR

3

Punitive Measures

The Kremlin's annexation of Crimea took the West by surprise. It didn't anticipate Putin's boldness, whether the strike was premediated or an ad hoc response to Maiden, and consequently American and European leaders needed time to discuss and coordinate full-spectrum countermeasures. In the interim they fell back on protocol, chastising Moscow and imposing slap-on-the-wrist economic sanctions,[1] some of which replicated Jackson-Vanik controls the Obama administration had rescinded less than two years earlier on December 20, 2012.[2]

Neither scolding nor perfunctory sanctions induced the Kremlin to repent.[3] Sanctions included: export restrictions on technologies and services regulated under the U.S. Munitions List, blocking property of fourteen defense companies and individuals in Putin's inner circle;[4] the limiting of certain financing to six of Russia's largest banks and four energy companies, prohibiting the provision, exportation, or re-exportation of goods, services, or technology in support of exploration or production for deep-water, Arctic offshore, or shale projects. Other adverse economic developments likewise had no visible chastening effect. Plummeting petroleum prices, the voluntary withdrawal of Western business from Russia's market,[5] and a 31 percent export drop in the first quarter of 2015 fell like water off a duck's back.[6] Nothing persuaded Moscow to abandon its imperial claims[7] or to rescind Crimea's annexation.[8] The West also found it difficult to forge a consensus in favor of military intervention, diplomatic retaliation, or summit-level Yalta II negotiations. Instead, leaders gradually escalated their rhetoric and added fresh economic sanctions, to no avail.[9] It is therefore worth pondering whether Russia's economy is resilient enough to withstand any sanctions regime the West can politically muster.[10]

The evidence suggests that the Kremlin's economy is more resilient to sanctions within limits imposed by WTO rules[11] than many hope[12] due to circumvention,[13] new sources of funding like Saudi Arabia,[14] and fundamental systemic changes inside the military-industrial complex (VPK).[15] Perhaps sanctions will keep the Kremlin from misbehaving in Novorossiya and the Baltic.[16]

American and European Union (EU) authorities are schizophrenic (double-thinking) on this subject. They confidently insist that economic pressure will compel the Kremlin to abide by the West's rules,[17] but at the same time contend that stronger punitive action, including military force, may be required to prevent additional Ukrainian territorial losses.[18]

This ambivalence is understandable. The historical record is perplexing. During the Cold War (1947–1987), the USSR managed to persevere despite stringent Western economic sanctions (Jackson-Vanik amendment,[19] CoCom[20]).[21] By contrast, Moscow was brought to its economic knees during the Gorbachev and Yeltsin years when East-West relations were cordial.[22]

Precedent thus doesn't inspire confidence that economic sanctions (as distinct from economic war)[23] will stay Putin's hand, or restore his respect for the world order.[24] Nonetheless, many international relations experts seem to take for granted that Russia's market economic system is crucially dependent on its exports to Europe (mostly petroleum),[25] and Western direct investment and finance.[26] They correctly perceive that the Kremlin cannot import goods and finance the state budget at past levels given today's low natural resources prices – something, they insist will have to give. Russia doubtlessly is being compelled to make unpleasant cuts in its domestic spending. But will this condemn the nation to depression, recession, stagnation, or intolerably slow economic growth, or consign Russia to the Soviet Union's fate? Will the pain compel Putin to throw in the towel?[27]

There are two fundamental grounds for skepticism. First, long-term economic growth depends on scientific and technological progress, achieved domestically and through technology transfers.[28] Neither economic sanctions nor economic war within the limitations imposed by the prevailing WTO rules can permanently prevent Russia's future economic progress. The Kremlin's Muscovite system impedes the full realization of Russia's economic potential, but the additional burden of Western sanctions cannot prevent Russia from achieving sustained economic growth. Second, the Kremlin has recently made its economic model more sanctions-resilient than it was in 2008, a transformation few analysts grasp.[29]

Russia's economy both now and before the global financial crisis is ruled by Putin and a small circle of oligarchic insiders, often referred to as *kleptocrats*.[30] The state support provided to the companies that they control in both the private and public sectors encourages inefficiency that until recently made the Kremlin susceptible to Western persuasion. But Putin discovered in the wake of the 2008 global financial crisis that Russia could rouse its lethargic oligarchs by tying state support to the fulfillment of procurement targets (contracts), enabling the Federation to reduce Moscow's dependency on the West. The new plan-constrained incentive system with stringent financial controls is a market-friendly version of Soviet command planning that promotes resource mobilization and modernization instead of indulgent kleptocracy, especially in the military-industrial complex (see Chapter 10). The initiative's success is attributable primarily to improved incentive design (performance-based contracting), but its effectiveness also reflects the rise of a new post-Yeltsin breed of oligarchs drawn from the power services.[31]

The revised weapons-first approach doesn't transform kleptocrats into virtuous, market-disciplined, Western corporate managers. Russia's oligarchs always have been free to efficiently compete, but were dissuaded from doing so by lavish state support that made it more attractive to satisfice (wallow in luxury). These privileges remain, but they have been made contingent on achieving concrete results (delivery of for-profit contracted weapons), particularly in the military-industrial complex (VPK). Managers in the defense sector during the first decade of the twenty-first century focused on R&D at the expense of high-volume weapons production. They enjoyed the free ride, but circa 2010 Putin put their heels to the fire more or less in line with Kasyanov's 2002 military modernization plan.[32] They were free to choose. Weapons manufacturers could satisfy Putin's demands for rapid military rearmament retaining ample perks, or be cashiered.

The tactic wasn't failsafe, but its potential can be illuminated by drawing an analogy between Russian oligarchic enterprise and Western "workably competitive" big business in an expanded Baumol-Simon comparative static framework.[33] Baumol has shown that workably competitive enterprise managers ignorant of their rivals' reaction functions (bounded rationality) achieve satisfactory results by wagering on profit maximizing, sales maximizing, or hedging subject to market demand. Even though they cannot optimize, they can earn adequate profits by employing various rules of thumb and Kremlin managers, and can do even better by rent-seeking.[34] Details are provided in Appendix 3.1.

The upshot of this mathematic demonstration is that oligarchs who may be neither profit nor revenue maximizers under bounded rational constraint can operate sub-optimally with government support. They don't have to function as workably competitive Western oligopolists (Baumol managers). They do not have to profit-seek, sales maximize, or hedge within the oligopolist framework, or even minimize losses because oligarchs can enrich themselves at their firms and the public's expense via subsidies, mandates, executive orders, and lucrative government contracts. This makes Russia's oligarchs and Kremlin public policy inherently less efficient and productive than their Western counterparts.

The deficiency was particularly glaring during Boris Yeltsin's *katakhod* (catastrophic economic transition, 1992–2000) and the first few years of the new millennium, but it lessened as Putin methodically restored state discipline and renationalized a substantial segment of the "commanding heights," especially the military-industrial complex (VPK). A substantial portion of the monies poured into the R&D for the development of fifth-generation weapons from 2002 to 2009 went down the drain, but starting in 2010 the Kremlin began demanding a rapid arms build-up as the price for its rent-grants.[35] The ploy succeeded in transforming a passive military-industrial complex-affiliated oligarchy into a market-assisted resource mobilization model of the type KGB chief Yuri Andropov originally sought in the late 1970s.[36]

The obligation imposed on oligarchs for mass arms production and the high-volume supply of other products doesn't assure full employment and rapid economic growth. The system remains severely inefficient, but it also has become more robust and economic sanctions resilient by making resource mobilization a condition of oligarchic tenure. The same objective was accomplished during the Soviet era with plan commands that got the job done at great expense in terms of foregone household consumption (guns over butter).[37] Contemporary oligarchy in the service of resource mobilization suffers from the same defect. However, the losses are less severe because the non-oligarchic component of Russia's market is workably competitive, making Putin's system a better mousetrap.[38] Russia is no longer a structurally militarized[39] "economy of shortage."[40] It has the capacity for military-driven moderate economic growth and gradually rising living standards (like America during the Second World War).

The transformation from passive to resource-mobilizing kleptocracy is the key to understanding the resilience of Putin's market economy to Western sanctions. Both the Soviet command model and oligarchic market regime sacrifice microeconomic efficiency for the fulfilment of a narrow set of missions and macroeconomic robustness.[41] The Kremlin's economy is underproductive, under-efficient, and growth retarding just as critics contend, but its resource-mobilizing characteristic and power service agenda make it strongly resilient to foreign-imposed financial restrictions, retaliatory tariffs, and embargoes. Putin, the *genstab* (Russian General Staff),

VPK, and *siloviki* are willing to accept austerity as the price for great power. They know that Western economic sanctions necessarily diminish Russia's growth prospects and tighten state budget constraints, but this doesn't countervail the positive effects of Putin's enhanced oligarchic model from the power services' perspective.

This claim, as documented in Chapters 7 and 10, is supported by World Bank Group's (WGB). Despite sanctions (asset freezes and visa bans) for dozens of high-ranking government officials, prohibitions on doing business with a number of Russian (and Crimea-based) companies and banks, including a ban against Visa and MasterCard dealings with these banks, prohibitions against long-term borrowing in U.S. capital markets on certain state-controlled oil companies, banks, and defense sector companies, bans on sales of certain defense-related products and services, bans on certain oil and gas sector exploration and production technologies;[42] a more than 67 percent plunge in petroleum prices that broke the Kremlin's budget[43] and severely diminished domestic wealth, a 50 percent ruble devaluation,[44] capital flight,[45] soaring interest rates,[46] double-digit inflation,[47] and dyspeptic global economic demand, GDP has fallen only modestly, supported by continued growth in industrial production (mostly weapons).[48] The aggregate effect of these diverse shocks was a zero to 1.5 percent drop in Russia's national income in 2014 with the WBG forecasting a return to positive growth by the end of 2015 (see Figure 7.3). Growth in 2015 was more negative than anticipated, but the WBG now contends that positive growth will be achieved in 2016, or, at the latest, 2017.

This resilient picture is confirmed by Vladimir Popov's index of Russian industrial production,[49] although some, like Anders Aslund, are still predicting a catastrophic Russian depression (10 percent decline in GDP).[50] Economic sanctions in some small part no doubt contributed to a "great recession" recession,[51] but the impact must be assessed in the appropriate perspective. The 3.7 percent GDP decline in 2015 is miniscule compared with the 8 percent fall in GDP occasioned by the 2008 global financial crisis. Russia's economy apparently is far more robust than it was eight years ago, and the impacts of the West's economic sanctions obviously have been insufficient to deter Putin's ambitions.

Although some Russian economists contend that 2016 could be worse due to a further decline in petroleum prices begun in mid-December 2015,[52] the data still support the hypothesis that the Russian economy switched from passive kleptocracy to a resource-mobilizing oligarchy (based on for-profit defense contracting) circa 2010. The Kremlin may well be better positioned to expand its influence in Novorossiya and the Baltic states and to endure a renewed cold war than it was during the first two terms of Putin's presidency because the old oligarchic model has been significantly improved. Linking profit-driven resource mobilization to insider privilege has enhanced macroeconomic robustness, significantly diminishing Russia's vulnerability to Western economic sanctions both with respect to aggregate economic activity and the power services perception of acceptable cost. This doesn't mean that economic pressure should be abandoned to punish Putin for violating international norms, or deter further Kremlin expansion, even taking account of the pain caused by Kremlin retaliatory sanctions.[53] Nonetheless, Western policy makers are ill advised to count on economic sanctions to halt Putin's great power restoration campaign, constrain his territorial ambitions in Novorossiya, or ultimately rescind Crimea's annexation.[54] Putin recognizes that sanctions necessarily cost Russia something, that falling petroleum prices are a far greater obstacle, and that the economy nonetheless is weathering the storm better than his opponents are predicting.[55]

Notes

1   The term *economic sanctions* refers to peacetime punitive measures, short of "economic war." Policy makers impose economic sanctions to chasten adversaries by denying them access to factors of production, products, technology, and finance. Export subsidy stratagems (beggar-thy-neighbor policies) can be utilized to similar effect, but are usually excluded from the concept because rivals can easily deflect them with quotas. High-intensity economic sanctions combatants employ during peace and wartime are commonly called *economic warfare* (blockades, blacklisting, preclusive purchases), even though the prohibitions have the same character as lower-intensity punitive measures. There is a large literature on economic warfare that stresses its reciprocal character and inconclusiveness. See, for examples, Frances Cappola, "U.S. Sanctions on Russia Are Financial Warfare," *Forbes*, July 18, 2014. http://www.forbes.com/sites/francescoppola/2014/07/18/u-s-sanctions-on-russia-are-financial-warfare/. Percy W. Bidwell, "Our Economic Warfare," *Foreign Affairs*, April 1942. https://www.foreignaffairs.com/articles/united-states/1942-04-01/our-economic-warfare. The use of counter-value conventional and nuclear strikes against C^3 (command, communications, and control), transport, and industrial targets is more effective than economic sanctions in compelling adversaries to yield, but hardly guarantees success.
2   "New Era in Russia-US Trade Relations: Obama Scraps Jackson-Vanik Amendment," *RT*, December 20, 2012. http://on.rt.com/6pxru6.
3   Jen Psaki, "United States Expands Export Restrictions on Russia," US State Department, April 28, 2014. www.state.gov/r/pa/prs/ps/2014/04/225241.htm. "Today, in response to Russia's continued actions in southern and eastern Ukraine, the United States is implementing additional restrictive measures on defense

exports to Russia. Accordingly, the Department of State is expanding its export restrictions on technologies and services regulated under the U.S. Munitions List (USML). Effective immediately, the Department's Directorate of Defense Trade Controls (DDTC) will deny pending applications for export or re-export of any high technology defense articles or services regulated under the U.S. Munitions List to Russia or occupied Crimea that contribute to Russia's military capabilities. In addition, the Department is taking actions to revoke any existing export licenses which meet these conditions. All other pending applications and existing licenses will receive a case-by-case evaluation to determine their contribution to Russia's military capabilities. The United States will continue to adjust its export licensing policies toward Russia, as warranted by Russia's actions in Ukraine. We urge Russia to honor the commitments it made in Geneva on April 17 to deescalate the situation in Ukraine." Susanne Oxenstierna and Per Olsson, *The Economic Sanctions against Russia: Impact and Prospects of success*, FOI-R–4097 – SE, September, 2015. The main conclusion of the report is that the targeted economic sanctions of the EU and the US have contributed to imposing a cost on the Russian economy in combination with other factors, but have so far not persuaded Russia to change its behaviour towards Ukraine. Oxenstierna and Olsson provide a complete listing of EU sanctions in their Appendix 2.

4   "U.S. Sanctions Russia's State-Owned Arms Exporter Rosoboronexport," *Reuters*, September 3, 2015. http://news.yahoo.com/u-sanctions-russias-state-owned-arms-exporter-rosoboronexport-165633514–business.html. "The United States has imposed sanctions on Russian and Chinese companies, including Russian state-owned arms exporter Rosoboronexport, for violating a U.S. law restricting weapons trade with Iran, North Korea and Syria." These sanctions apparently were imposed for violating U.S. law, unconnected with Crimea's annexation.

5   Maria Kiselyova and Gleb Stolyarov, "Russia's GAZ in Talks with Foreign Car Makers to replace GM," *Reuters*, June 20, 2015. http://news.yahoo.com/russias-gaz-talks-foreign-car-makers-replace-gm-175823896--finance.html. "Russian businessman Oleg Deripaska's GAZ Group is in talks with at least six foreign car producers to let them use its idle capacity after General Motors Co pulled out of the market, GAZ Chairman Siegfried Wolf said."

6   Mark Adomanis, "Russia's Foreign Trade Is Collapsing," *Forbes*, March 25, 2015. http://www.forbes.com/sites/markadomanis/2015/03/25/russias-foreign-trade-is-collapsing/. The decline is mostly attributable to the collapse of petroleum prices.

7   David Herszenhorn, "A Diplomatic Victory, and Affirmation, for Putin," *New York Times*, May 15, 2015. http://www.nytimes.com/2015/05/16/world/europe/a-diplomatic-victory-and-affirmation-for-putin.html?_r=0. "Mr. Obama led the charge by the West to punish Mr. Putin for his intervention in Ukraine, booting Russia from the Group of 8 economic powers, imposing harsh sanctions on some of Mr. Putin's closest confidants and delivering financial and military assistance to the new Ukrainian government. ... In recent months, however, Russia has not only weathered those attacks and levied painful countersanctions on America's European allies, but has also proved stubbornly important on the world stage. That has been true especially in regard to Syria, where its proposal to confiscate chemical weapons has kept President Bashar al-Assad, a Kremlin ally, in power, and in the negotiations that secured a tentative deal on Iran's nuclear program."

"Mr. Putin, who over 15 years as Russia's paramount leader has consistently con-founded his adversaries, be they foreign or domestic, once again seems to be emerg-ing on top – if not as an outright winner in his most recent confrontation with the West, then certainly as a national hero, unbowed, firmly in control, and having sur-rendered nothing, especially not Crimea, his most coveted prize."

8 Adrian Croft, "EU Extends Trade and Investment Ban on Crimea," Reuters, June 19, 2015. http://www.reuters.com/article/2015/06/19/us-ukraine-crisis-eu-sanctions -idUSKBN0OZ1B920150619. "EU governments extended for a year a ban on trade and investment with Crimea on Friday, meaning European help for Russian Black Sea oil and gas exploration and visits by European cruise ships will remain outlawed." This judgment holds even if, as some suspect, the West conspired to drive petro-leum prices down to cripple Russia's economy. The West may even encourage this sort of speculation to persuade Putin that it is the arbiter of Russia's economic well-being. Cf. Anjli Raval, "Saudi Claims Oil Price Strategy Success," *Financial Times*, May 13, 2015. http://www.ft.com/intl/cms/s/2/69350a3e-f970-11e4-be7b-00144feab7de.html#axzz3a7307zHU. "Saudi Arabia says its strategy of squeezing high-cost rivals such as US shale producers is succeeding, as the world's largest crude exporter seeks to reassert itself as the dominant force in the global oil market."

9 "Ukraine and Russia Sanctions," http://www.state.gov/e/eb/tfs/spi/ukrainerussia/. Russia and Ukraine Sanctions, Department of the Treasury

On March 6, 2014, President Obama signed Executive Order 13660 that autho-rizes sanctions on individuals and entities responsible for violating the sovereignty and territorial integrity of Ukraine, or for stealing the assets of the Ukrainian people. These sanctions put in place restrictions on the travel of certain individuals and offi-cials and showed our continued efforts to impose a cost on Russia and those respon-sible for the situation in Crimea.

On March 17, 2014, President Obama issued Executive Order 13661 under the national emergency with respect to Ukraine that finds that the actions and poli-cies of the Russian government with respect to Ukraine – including through the deployment of Russian military forces in the Crimea region of Ukraine – undermine democratic processes and institutions in Ukraine; threaten its peace, security, stabil-ity, sovereignty, and territorial integrity; and contribute to the misappropriation of its assets.

On March 20, 2014, the President issued a new Executive Order, "Blocking Property of Additional Persons Contributing to the Situation in Ukraine," expanding the scope of the national emergency declared in Executive Order 13660 of March 6, 2014, and expanded by Executive Order 13661 of March 16, 2014, finding that the actions and policies of the Government of the Russian Federation, including its pur-ported annexation of Crimea and its use of force in Ukraine, continue to undermine democratic processes and institutions in Ukraine; threaten its peace, security, stabil-ity, sovereignty, and territorial integrity; and contribute to the misappropriation of its assets, and thereby constitute an unusual and extraordinary threat to the national security and foreign policy of the United States.

Utilizing these Executive Orders, the United States has steadily increased the dip-lomatic and financial costs of Russia's aggressive actions towards Ukraine. We have designated a number of Russian and Ukrainian entities, including 14 defense com-panies and individuals in Putin's inner circle, as well as imposed targeted sanctions limiting certain financing to six of Russia's largest banks and four energy companies. We have also suspended credit finance that encourages exports to Russia and financing for economic development projects in Russia, and are now prohibiting the provision, exportation, or re-exportation of goods, services (not including financial services), or technology in support of exploration or production for deep-water, Arctic offshore, or shale projects that have the potential to produce oil in the Russian Federation, or in maritime area claimed by the Russian Federation and extending from its territory, and that involve five major Russian energy companies.

These actions, in close coordination with our EU and international partners, send a strong message to the Russian government that there are consequences for [its] actions that threaten the sovereignty and territorial integrity of Ukraine. The United States, together with international partners, will continue to stand by the Ukrainian government until Russia abides by its international obligations. The United States is prepared to take additional steps to impose further political and economic costs. A secure Ukraine, integrated with Europe and enjoying good relations with all its neighbors, is in the interests of the

United States, Europe, and Russia.

Executive Orders

12/19/14 EO 13685; Blocking Property of Certain Persons and Prohibiting Certain Transactions With Respect to the Crimea Region of Ukraine

03/20/14 EO; Blocking Property of Additional Persons Contributing to the Situation in Ukraine

03/17/14 EO 13661; Blocking Property of Additional Persons Contributing to the Situation in Ukraine

03/06/14 EO 13660; Blocking Property of Certain Persons Contributing to the Situation in Ukraine.

Sanctions Overview (from March 2014) United States, EU, and other OECD member sanctions on Russia:

- Asset freezes and visa bans for dozens of high-ranking government officials.
- Prohibition on doing business with a number of Russian (and Crimea-based) companies and banks, including a ban against Visa and MasterCard dealings with these banks.
- Prohibitions against long-term borrowing in U.S. capital markets on certain state-controlled oil companies, banks, and defense sector companies.
- Ban on sales of certain defense-related products and services.
- Ban on certain oil and gas sector exploration and production technologies.

Russian countersanctions against the West:

- Visa bans for dozens of Western officials.
- Bans on certain food imports (meat, dairy, fish, nuts, and produce) from the United States, the European Union, Norway, Canada, and Australia valued at about $9 billion.

10 "Italy and Russia: How Sanctions Affect Bilateral Commercial Relations," *Valdai*, July 1, 2015. http://valdaiclub.com/economy/78880.html. "Among other things, Russia also suffers a substantial outflow of capital (estimated at $151 billion in

2014), which contributed to the gradual depreciation of the ruble. Recently, the American rating agency Standard & Poor's has rated the creditworthiness of Russia BB +, Moody's assigned Ba1, while Fitch has considered the Russian outlook still negative, BBB-. Nevertheless, the current account balance remains positive, supported by exports of energy resources and metallurgical production, accounting for 75% of total Russian exports." "Italy is the third largest trading partner of the Russian Federation. According to the latest available data, the Italian FDI in Russia amounts to 51 billion euros. The main Italian investment destination remains the energy sector. The Italian presence also is growing in other areas – defense, household appliances, food processing." "Unfortunately, the first months of 2015 confirm this negative trend with Italian exports declining by 25% in the first quarter of 2015 compared to the same period of the last year, mainly due to the effects of sanctions against Russia. Particularly affected were the micro and small businesses. According to figures provided by Confartigiana, in the period between March 2014 and March 2015, the value of products exported by micro and small businesses totaled 102.4 billion euros, equal to 6.2% of Italian GDP. There was a real collapse (−34.6%) in exports by Italian small businesses to Russia. According to analysts, without sanctions the total exports of micro and small Italian companies to Russia would record a potential growth rate by 5.4%.

"Approximately 570 Italian companies are present now in Russia, particularly dealing with energy, automotive industry, food processing and telecommunications. As to the energy sector, Italy has a fruitful partnership with the Russian government, sharing real interdependence and common interests. ENI, ENEL, Saipem and Finmeccanica are very active in the country. In particular, it is necessary to mention the SuperJet International project, which is the joint venture created in 2007 between the Italian company Alenia Aermacchi (Finmeccanica group), which holds 51% of stakes, and the Russian Sukhoi Holding, which owns 49% of the capital. This is the civil aviation partnership program, the most important project ever concluded between Europe and Russia.

"Russia is among the main energy suppliers to Italy. Between January and February 2015 Italy purchased from Russia natural gas for about 39% of our imports and crude oil for about 30% of imports. Russia traditionally has been a reliable supplier, whom Italy could rely upon in case of difficulties with other energy producers.

"In industrial and high-tech sectors such Italian companies as Finmeccanica collaborate successfully with Russian firms. Significant are investments from Pirelli, Danieli, Marcegaglia Group, Ferrero, Indesit, Cremonini, Coeclerici, Marazzi, and Barbaro. In spite of difficulties Russian Rosneft continues to keep strong ties with Pirelli. The two companies recently signed another cooperation agreement.

"This agreement provides the establishment of new Pirelli stores in Rosneft service stations, the construction of a flagship store entirely dedicated to Pirelli tires. The agreement will allow Rosneft to expand the portfolio of products offered in its own service stations and Pirelli would strengthen its strategic commercial presence in Russia, where the company has already two plants in Voronezh and Kirov. By the end of 2015, the two companies plan to open up to 15 stores in the Moscow area, while by 2019 there should be at least 200 Pirelli stores.

"The present sanctions did not bring particular benefits to European economies, but analysts envisage limited consequences. It is claimed that the majority of exports are not affected by sanctions and the impact on the European economy is relatively small and manageable. European companies, even those of the agricultural sector, have now redirected exports to other countries. However, according to the WIFO calculations, the European Union is preparing an extreme scenario with possible loss of more than 2 million jobs and 100 billion euros in added value. The forecasts are based on data of the first quarter of 2015, when many countries felt the collapse of exports to Russia. Germany alone in the short term could lose half a million jobs and 27.6 billion euros in added value; Italy may lose 80 thousand jobs and over 4 billion euros of added value. According to the WIFO analysis, the agriculture and food industry of the European countries will record the most damage. For example, the Italian consortium Parmigiano Reggiano may not export its production not only in Russia but also in other countries such as Germany, Netherlands and France. This is because of the dairy market overproduction in Europe.

"On the other hand, European sanctions against Russia could encourage competitors from China and other countries to exploit the situation. This is the scenario for the near future."

11 Russia became a member of the World Trade Organization on December 15, 2011.

12 Jacques Sapir, "Russian Successes," *Valdai*, May 19, 2015. https://russeurope.hypotheses .org/3826. "This diplomatic victory, Vladimir Putin owes it to the resistance of the Russian economy to the 'sanctions' and to sundry destabilizing manoeuvres. The decision, announced on May 14th, to officially resume foreign currency purchases on the currencies exchange market, confirms that Russia has retaken the upper hand on financial and monetary questions. Forthwith, the question is no longer on putting a brake to the depreciation of the ruble, but on the contrary to slow down its appreciation and to stabilize the exchange rate around 50 rubles to the US dollar."

13 Bruno Dallago believes that the most active conspirators in the circumvention for the Italians are Latvia, Bosnia, and Belorossiya. July 2, 2015.

14 Sneha Shankar, "Russia Signs Agreement to Get $10B Investment from Saudi Arabia amid Western Sanctions," *International Business Times*, July 7, 2015. http:// www.ibtimes.com/russia-signs-agreement-get-10b-investment-saudi-arabia-amid- western-sanctions-1997306. "Saudi Arabia signed a commitment to invest up to $10 billion in Russia within four to five years, Kirill Dmitriev, head of Russian Direct Investment Fund (RDIF), told Sputnik News, a state-run news agency, on Monday. Dmitriev added that the money from Saudi Arabia's Public Investment Fund (PIF) is the largest foreign investment for Russia." "In May, Russia and China signed a $2 billion investment fund to develop agricultural projects in the two countries and form a free-trade zone between their major farming belts." President Obama has been snubbing Saudi Arabia for more than a year, thereby creating this new source of foreign direct investment for the Kremlin.

15 Michael Ellman, "Russia's Current Economic System: From Delusion to Glasnost'," *Comparative Economic Studies* (2015): 1–18. "However, whereas many commentators and financial officials consider military spending a burden on the economy, the current Russian leadership considers stimulating defense industry as an effective way of stimulating the economy as a whole. As Putin put it in August 2012, the Defense Sector (*oboronka*) has always served as the locomotive which pulls the other branches of the economy behind it." p. 12.

16 Richard Connolly, "Troubled Times Stagnation, Sanctions and the Prospects for Economic Reform in Russia," *Chathamhouse*, February 2015. http://www.chathamhouse.org/sites/files/chathamhouse/field/field_document/20150224TroubledTimesRussiaConnolly.pdf. Western economic sanctions thus far, despite a great deal of hyperbole, have been levied against individuals or have focused on the financial sector. The exceptions involve prohibitions against high-tech energy and defense exports that provide anticompetitive protection to the West's energy industry, or bolster national security. Annie Fixler, Mark Dubowitz, and Juan Zarate, "'SWIFT' Warfare," *FDD* Press, July 7, 2015. http://www.defenddemocracy.org/media-hit/cyber-enabled-swift-warfare/. See more at: http://www.defenddemocracy.org/media-hit/cyber-enabled-swift-warfare/#sthash.Ft5KetRw.dpuf.

17 Clifford Gaddy, "One Year of Western Sanctions against Russia: We Still Live in Different Worlds," *Brookings*, March 9, 2015. http://www.brookings.edu/blogs/order-from-chaos/posts/2015/03/09-one-year-western-sanctions-against-russia-gaddy. "The sanctions policy was destined to fail because it was based on false assumptions about how most Russians think – in particular, how they think about security." "The current official Western view is that sanctions are a way to punish Russia for violating the rules of the international order and to thereby correct its behavior in the future. The Russians believe the sanctions are designed to weaken Russia and reduce its ability to defend itself." "Our Western view is that security in an interconnected world has to be based on cooperation, dialogue, and trust. It can only be guaranteed by everyone adhering to a rules-based system. Russia rejects that idea of security. It believes that the only real guarantee of its own security and sovereignty is its independent ability to defend itself. No multinational or supranational organization can guarantee that." "We are therefore caught in a trap, one of our own making. We adopted a policy that could never work as it was intended, namely, as a way to force Russia to change its behavior and obey the rules of our order." Western analysts brush aside the potential effectiveness of Putin's countermeasures, but may be too dismissive. Krystof Chamonikolas and Agnes Lovasz, "Putin Scores Victory over Ukraine Allies in Bond Market Collapse," *Bloomberg*, February 25, 2015. http://www.bloomberg.com/news/articles/2015-02-26/putin-scores-victory-over-ukraine-allies-in-bond-market-collapse?cmpid=yhoo. "Russia is damaging Ukraine's economy faster than the U.S. and its European allies can provide support. That's the conclusion of investors, who have sent the price of Ukrainian bonds to record lows even as the country awaits $17.5 billion of emergency loans from the International Monetary Fund. Its currency, the hryvnia, has lost about a half of its value this month, forcing the central bank to tighten capital controls to keep money from fleeing the country."

18 "Should the United States Provide Military Assistance to Ukraine? PONARS Eurasia Experts Weigh In," *Ponars Eurasia*, February 6, 2015. http://www.ponarseurasia.org/article/should-united-states-provide-military-assistance-ukraine.

19 The Jackson-Vanik Amendment is a 1974 provision in U.S. federal law, intended to affect U.S. trade relations with countries with non-market economies (originally, countries of the Communist bloc) that restrict freedom of emigration and other human rights. It is believed that it was a response to the Soviet Union's "diploma taxes" levied on Jews attempting to emigrate. The law, which made the Soviet

Union and later Russia ineligible for normal trade relations, programs of credits, credit guarantees, investment guarantees, or commercial agreements, was repealed together with the adoption of the Magnitsky Act by President Obama on December 14, 2012. The Magnitsky Act prohibits Russian officials thought to be responsible for the death of Sergei Magnitsky from entering the United States and using its banking system.

20 CoCom (Coordinating Committee for Multilateral Export Controls) was established by Western bloc powers in the first five years after the end of World War II, during the Cold War, to put an arms embargo on COMECON countries. It was rescinded March 31, 1994.

21 For a good summary of the literature on the effectiveness of sanctions, see Mark Kramer, "Exclusive: Sanctions and Regime Survival," *Ponars Eurasia*, March 11, 2015. http://www.ponarseurasia.org/article/sanctions-and-regime-survival. "In a study of 136 countries from 1947 to 1999, Nikolay Marinov sought to determine whether 'economic sanctions hurt the survival of government leaders in office.'[2] After comparing the longevity of leaders in countries that were targeted by sanctions with the longevity of leaders in countries that were not targeted, he concluded that sanctions do in fact 'destabilize the leaders they target.'" "Escribà-Folch and Wright find that although economic sanctions do, on average, contribute to the destabilization and removal of personalistic dictators, sanctions do not have any appreciable effect on the longevity of single-party regimes and military juntas." "A different take on this question comes in a study coauthored by William Kaempfer, Anton Lowenberg, and William Mertenis that relies on a model derived from public-choice theory. [4] The three authors claim that 'damaging economic sanctions can have the counterproductive effect of encouraging the ruling regime and its supporters while at the same time undermining the political influence of the opposition.'" "One of the implications of this approach is that sanctions cannot be effective in precipitating the downfall of the regime unless 'there exists within the target country a reasonably well-organized opposition group whose political effectiveness potentially could be enhanced as a consequence of sanctions.'" "Even in this case, however, the sanctions might still have debilitating effects on the opposition."

"In the case of the Soviet regime and the sanctions imposed by the Carter administration in 1980 after the Soviet invasion of Afghanistan, we know for sure from declassified CPSU Politburo transcripts that Soviet leaders hated the sanctions and resented their effects. The sanctions did not, however, produce any near-term change in Soviet policy in Afghanistan." "Hence, assessing the longer-term effects of the 1980 sanctions is inherently difficult. The sanctions may have had a small deterrent effect on subsequent Soviet foreign policy decisions (e.g., during the crisis in Poland), but they did not change fundamental Soviet goals. Gorbachev's adoption of a vastly different approach to foreign policy is not directly traceable to the impact of past sanctions (though indirectly they may have played a small role).

"In the case of the Russian Federation today, the U.S. and EU sanctions have not produced any discernible change in Russian policy vis-à-vis Crimea and eastern Ukraine, and Putin's regime has given no indication that it will back down even if the sanctions are tightened. Will the sanctions help to bring about a change of regime? With Putin's popularity ratings at 85 percent and few if any signs of a debilitating split in the ruling elite, this goal, too seems elusive, at least for now.

Although one cannot fully rule out a longer-term impact on the stability of the regime, that seems a distant prospect at best." Susan Hannah Allen, "The Domestic Political Costs of Economic Sanctions," *Journal of Conflict Resolution*, Vol. 52, No. 6 (December 2008): 916–944, esp. 916–917; Nikolay Marinov, "Do Economic Sanctions Destabilize Country Leaders?" *American Journal of Political Science*, Vol. 49, No. 3 (July 2005): 564–576; Abel Escribà-Folch and Joseph Wright, "Dealing with Tyranny: International Sanctions and the Survival of Authoritarian Rulers," *International Studies Quarterly*, Vol. 54, No. 2 (June 2010): 334–359, which builds on David Lektzian and Mark Souva, "An Institutional Theory of Sanctions Onset and Success," *Journal of Conflict Resolution*, Vol. 51, No. 6 (November 2007): 848–871; William Kaempfer, Anton Lowenberg, and William Mertens, "International Economic Sanctions against a Dictator," *Economics and Politics*, Vol. 16, No. 1 (March 2004): 29–51. See also William Kaempfer and Anton Lowenberg, "The Theory of International Economic Sanctions: A Public Choice Approach," *American Economic Review*, Vol. 78, No. 4 (December 1988): 786–793.

22 There was a Soviet economic slowdown after 1968 that could be ascribed to Jackson-Vanik sanctions after 1974, but most analysts contend Soviet growth retardation is fully explained by domestic factors. See Abram Bergson, *Planning and Productivity under Soviet Socialism*, Columbia University Press, New York, 1968. Cf. Steven Rosefielde, "Tea Leaves and Productivity: Bergsonian Norms for Gauging the Soviet Future," *Comparative Economic Studies*, Vol. 47, No. 2, June (2005): 259–273. The West's assistance to Russia after 1987 didn't cause the Soviet Union's collapse, but it didn't obviously ameliorate hyper-depression either.

23 Economic sanctions reduce gains from international trade and technology transfer. Economic warfare (blockades and bombing industrial targets) is value-subtracting and destroys assets.

24 Samuel Charap and Bernard Sucher, "Why Sanctions on Russia Will Backfire," *New York Times*, March 5, 2015. http://www.nytimes.com/2015/03/06/opinion/why-sanctions-on-russia-will-backfire.html?_r=0. "The American objective of integrating Russia into the global economy has been fundamentally undermined. Second, the use of sanctions broadcasts to others the strategic hazard of integrating into the American-led global financial system. Third, while there is no question that sanctions have inflicted real costs on the leading state-owned and state-affiliated companies and harmed Mr. Putin's cronies, the collateral damage to independent, private enterprise in Russia is incomparably worse. Fourth, by imposing sanctions on Russia when it was already falling into a downward economic spiral, Washington has given Mr. Putin a powerful political instrument to deflect blame for the consequences of his own baleful decisions in Ukraine."

25 This shoe pinches Europe more than Russia. Rashid Husain Syed," Can the West Afford an 'Oil War' with Russia?" *Epoch Times*, May 22, 2014. http://www.theepochtimes.com/n3/689056-can-the-west-afford-an-oil-war-with-russia/.

26 The supposed dependency didn't deter Germany's inking a new Baltic Sea gas pipeline deal with Moscow. "Gazprom Inks Plan for New Gas Pipeline to Germany," AFP, June 18, 2015. http://news.yahoo.com/gazprom-inks-plan-gas-pipeline-germany-131244934.html. "Russian gas giant Gazprom on Thursday agreed on a plan with Shell, E.ON and OMV aimed at building a new gas pipeline to Germany, the companies said in a statement. In the memorandum of understanding, Germany's E.ON,

Austria's OMV and Anglo-Dutch Shell would join up to construct the new route under the Baltic Sea from Russia with a capacity of 55 billion cubic metres per year, the statement said. The project – for which no timeframe was given – would double the capacity of the existing Nord Stream pipeline currently linking the two countries. The announcement comes as Russia seeks more routes to deliver its gas to the European Union avoiding crisis-hit Ukraine, despite the 28-nation bloc insisting it wants to cut its dependence on Russia."

27 Torbjörn Becker, *Russian Economy and Trade*, Stockholm Institute of Transition Economics (SITE), September 3, 2015.

28 Robert Solow, "A Contribution to the Theory of Economic Growth," *Quarterly Journal of Economics* (Oxford), Vol. 70, No. 1, February (1956): 65–94; Robert Solow, "Technical Change and the Aggregate Production Function," *Review of Economics and Statistics*, Vol. 39, No. 3 (1957): 312–320; Trevor Swan, "Economic Growth and Capital Accumulation," *Economic Record*, Vol. 32, No. 2, November (1956): 334–361; David Romer, "The Solow Growth Model," in *Advanced Macroeconomics*, New York: McGraw-Hill, 2011, 6–48; Daron Acemoglu, "The Solow Growth Model," in *Introduction to Modern Economic Growth*, Princeton, NJ: Princeton University Press, 2009, 26–76.

29 See Chapter 4 for a complete discussion of Russia's economic model. Ellman, "Russia's Current Economic System: From Delusion to Glasnost.'" Steven Rosefielde, *Russia's Military Industrial Resurgence: Evidence and Potential*, U.S. Army War College, Carlisle Barracks, 2016.

30 Karen Dawisha, *Putin's Kleptocracy*, New York: Simon and Schuster, 2014.

31 Rosefielde, *Russia's Military Industrial Resurgence*.

32 Kasyanov's 2002 military modernization plan postponed rebuilding Russia's arsenal until after fifth-generation weapons were developed. Vitaly Shlykov confirmed this to the author. Enterprise managers weren't pressured to increase arms output. Vast sums were spent on RDT&E, but few weapons were produced. This was a matter of policy, not systems failure. Russia's ability to re-achieve Soviet levels of weapons production hinged on whether leaders chose to revert to the command principle or could successfully substitute for-profit based contracts. Putin chose the second route. The command economy hasn't been restored, but weapons production has substantially increased.

33 John Maurice Clark, *Competition as a Dynamic Process*, Washington, DC: The Brookings Institution, 1961. William Baumol, *Business Behavior, Value and Growth* (rev. ed.), New York: Macmillan, 1959; Herbert Simon, "A Behavioral Model of Rational Choice," in Simon, *Models of Man: Social and Rational-Mathematical Essays on Rational Human Behavior in a Social Setting*, New York: Wiley, 1957; Herbert Simon, "A Mechanism for Social Selection and Successful Altruism," *Science*, Vol. 250, No. 4988) (1990): 1665–1668; Herbert Simon, "Bounded Rationality and Organizational Learning," *Organization Science*, Vol. 2, No. 1 (1991): 125–134; Gerd Gigerenzer and Reinhard Selten, *Bounded Rationality*, Cambridge, MA: MIT Press, 2002; Ariel Rubinstein, *Modeling Bounded Rationality*, Cambridge, MA: MIT Press, 1998; Clem Tisdell, *Bounded Rationality and Economic Evolution: A Contribution to Decision Making, Economics, and Management*, Cheltenham, UK: Brookfield, 1996; Daniel Kahneman, "Maps of Bounded Rationality: Psychology for Behavioral Economics," *The American Economic Review, Vol. 93*, No. 5 (2003): 1449–1475.

34 For a semi-dynamic extension, see Steven Rosefielde and Ralph W. Pfouts, *Inclusive Economic Theory*, Singapore: World Scientific Publishers, 2014, appendix 4, "Realist Profit and Revenue Seeking: Multi-firm Interaction Effects." Dynamic analysis adds valuable insights, but doesn't alter the conclusion that when the axioms of virtuous rationality underlying Simon's neoclassical "satisficing" construct are violated, outcomes cannot be "second best" in a narrow technical sense, and in the real world are likely to be very bad.

35 http://books.sipri.org/files/FS/SIPRIFS1304.pdf

36 Yuri Vladimirovich Andropov headed the KGB from 1967 to 1982, when he became General Secretary of the Communist Party of the Soviet Union.

37 Steven Rosefielde, *Russian Economy from Lenin to Putin*, New York: Wiley, 2007; Charles Wolf Jr. and Henry Rowen, *The Impoverished Superpower: Perestroika and the Soviet Military Burden*, San Francisco, CA: Institute for Contemporary Studies, 1990.

38 John M. Clarke, "Toward a Concept of Workable Competition," *American Economic Review*, June (1940): 231–256.

39 Vitaly Shlykov, "Nazad v budushchee, ili Ekonomicheskie uroki kholodnoi voiny," Rossiia v Global'noi Politike, Tom 4, No. 2, Mart–April' 2006, pp. 26–40. Shlykov, "Nevidimaia Mobilizatsii," *Forbes*, No. 3, March (2006): 1–5; Shlykov, "Globalizatsiia voennoi promyshlennosti – imperativ XXI veka," *Otechestvennye zapiski*, No. 5 (2005): 98–115.

40 Igor Birman, Экономика недостач, Нью-Йорк: Chalidze Publications, 1983.

41 The West uses Keynesian deficit spending and QE (quantitative easing) for the same purpose; that is, buttressing aggregate effective demand.

42 Kenneth Kopf, "Russia Sanctions: 'Ill-Planned, Ill-Timed and Foolhardy,'" CNS News, January 8, 2015. http://www.cnsnews.com/commentary/kenneth-kopf/russia-sanctions-ill-planned-ill-timed-and-foolhardy. "The current economic sanctions imposed by the United States were aimed at specific Russian individuals (and their companies). These sanctions were, ostensibly, intended to deter Putin from continuing [his] illegal and immoral incursion into Ukraine. But a question could be raised as to what the true Obama administration intent was given the evident, resultant effects of these sanctions. A question could be raised whether those sanctions were adequate, properly designed or effectively implemented. If the true intent was to bring Russia to its knees – economically – then it was a good start. If it was, as we are told, to stop the Ukraine incursion, and bring them to 'the table,' then it was, in my opinion, misguided and totally ineffective."

43 Oil and gas revenues account for more than 50 percent of the federal budget revenues. U.S. Energy Information Administration, March 2014. http://www.eia.gov/countries/cab.cfm?fips=RS. Unless petroleum prices reverse swiftly, Moscow may be compelled to slash government spending by as much as 25 percent, deplete its foreign reserves, or secure compensatory financing at home and abroad. Darya Korsunskaya and Elena Fabrichnaya, "As Oil Falls, Russia Choked by Military, Social Spending," Reuters, December 30, 2014. http://www.reuters.com/article/2014/12/30/russia-crisis-budget-idUSL6N0UD1AE20141230. Russia sells its natural resources for dollars. Plummeting dollar prices reduce the proceeds from natural resources sales. The budgetary impact, however, can be mitigated or exacerbated by fluctuations in the foreign exchange rate. Small devaluations will assure that

falling dollar natural resources prices have a substantial budgetary impact. If natural resources prices and the value of the ruble drop *pari passu*, then the budget will be unaffected.

44 http://www.bloomberg.com/quote/USDRUB:CUR

45 Bryan Rich, "No Repeat of 1998: Russia Capital Flight Good for Dollar and Stocks," *Forbes*, December 17, 2014. http://www.forbes.com/sites/greatspeculations/2014/12/17/capital-flight-from-russia-good-for-dollar-and-stocks/.

46 Alanna Petroff, "Russia Fights Ruble Crash with 5th Rate Rise," CNN, December 11, 2014. http://money.cnn.com/2014/12/11/news/economy/russia-interest-rates-ruble/index.html. "The central bank hiked interest rates for a fifth time this year on Thursday, taking them up to 10.5%. That compares with 5.5% at the start of 2014."

47 Mihail Mokrushin, "Russian Inflation Rate for 2015 to Remain Same as 2014 at 12%: Kudrin," *Sputnik*, December 22, 2014. http://sputniknews.com/russia/20141222/1016104685.html.

48 Vesa Korhonen, Zuzana Fungacova, Laura Solanko, Iikka Korhonen, and Heli Simola, *BOFIT Policy Brief*, July 2015. *BOFIT Weekly*, July 31, 2015. *BOFIT Forecast for Russia 2015–2017*, September 24, 2015.

49 Vladimir Popov, "Will the Russian Economy Accelerate in 2015?" *Ponars Policy Memo 361*, March 2015. http://www.ponarseurasia.org/memo/will-russian-economy-accelerate-2015.

"Paradoxically, some healthy economic developments occurred in Russia in 2014 owing to its conflict with the West and the decline in oil prices. The 'forced' reversal of some mistaken economic policies of the past – an overvaluation of the ruble and virtually tariff-free imports of food – has created an upward push for the national economy that may be stronger than the downward push caused by the outflow of capital, decline in oil prices, and Western economic sanctions.

"The longer-term impact of sanctions on the Russian economy is still indeterminate. Western sanctions against Russia since its incorporation of Crimea in March 2014 have been rather modest, even symbolic (See Appendix – Sanctions Overview). By comparison, Russia's response in August 2014 banning food imports totaling $9 billion annually from the EU, United States, Canada, Australia, and Norway was harsh. If a scalpel was the Western instrument, Russia used an axe. Hit hardest were the export markets of Poland (fruits and vegetables), Norway (salmon), the Netherlands (cheese), and Spain (fruits and vegetables).

"But the devaluation that resulted from the fall in oil prices (which was not linked to the conflict) and outflow of capital, combined with measures to protect domestic food production, have had a large stimulation effect on the Russian economy. After extremely sluggish GDP growth in relatively favorable 2012–13 (3.4 percent in 2012 and 1.3 percent in 2013) and almost no growth at all in 2014 (0.6 percent), Russia may finally see an acceleration of growth in 2015 and beyond."

50 Anders Aslund, "Russia's Output Will Slump Sharply in 2015," *American Interest*, January 15, 2015. http://www.the-american-interest.com/2015/01/15/russias-output-will-slump-sharply-in-2015/. Cf. Paul Roderick Gregory, "A Russian Crisis with No End in Sight, Thanks to Low Oil Prices and Sanctions," *Forbes*, May 14, 2015.

http://www.forbes.com/sites/paulroderickgregory/2015/05/14/a-russian-crisis-with-no-end-in-sight-thanks-to-low-oil-prices-and-sanctions/3/. "Unlike the

2008/9 financial crisis, Russia faces a long and deep recession because the underlying causes are unlikely to go away in the near term."

51 The Great Recession is a term devised in the West to describe a period of general economic decline observed in world markets during the late 2000s and early 2010s. The scale and timing of the recession varied from country to country. The International Monetary Fund judged it to be the worst global recession since World War II.

52 Former Russian finance minister Alexei Kudrin's prediction of a 3.6 percent drop offers an alternative "worst case" scenario. Korsunskaya and Fabrichnaya, "As Oil Falls, Russia Choked by Military, Social Spending." The Brent oil benchmark price on December 19, 2015 was $37 per barrel.

53 Kenneth Rapoza, "Here's What Putin's Counter-sanctions Did To E.U. Exporters," *Forbes*, April 17, 2015.http://www.forbes.com/sites/kenrapoza/2015/04/17/heres-what-putins-counter-sanctions-did-to-e-u-exporters/2/. EU food exporters are expected to lose a billion dollars in food export sales to Russia due to Putin's retaliatory sanctions.

54 International sanctions are seldom decisive. America has been trying unsuccessfully for decades to halt nuclear proliferation with international sanctions. See John Bolton, "To Stop Iran's Bomb, Bomb Iran," *AEI*, March 26, 2015. http://www.aei.org/publication/to-stop-irans-bomb-bomb-iran/?utm_source=paramount&utm_medium=email&utm_content=AEITODAY&utm_campaign=032715. "In theory, comprehensive international sanctions, rigorously enforced and universally adhered to, might have broken the back of Iran's nuclear program. But the sanctions imposed have not met those criteria." Oxenstierna and Olsson, *The Economic Sanctions against Russia*. "The authoritarian nature of the regime and its anti-Western propaganda, which manipulates public perceptions of the conflict issue, make the regime less exposed to the full effects of the economic decline. The West's political measures that complement the sanction regimes need to address this threat and manage the risks it poses to the Western objectives. The conflict over Ukraine is important for both Russia and the West."

55 "Western Sanctions 'Severely' Harming Russia: Putin," *AFP*, January 11, 2016. http://news.yahoo.com/western-sanctions-severely-harming-russia-putin-112746316.html. "President Vladimir Putin acknowledged Monday in an interview with German daily *Bild* that Western economic sanctions over the Ukraine crisis are affecting Russia." "Putin said, however, that 'the biggest harm is currently caused by the decline of the prices for energy.'" "Putin said Russia was now 'gradually stabilising our economy.'"

    "Last year, the gross domestic product had dropped by 3.8 percent. Inflation is approximately 12.7 percent. The trade balance, however, is still positive." "'For the first time in many years, we are exporting significantly more goods with a high added value, and we have more than $300 billion in gold reserves.'"

    "No Need for Anti-crisis Plan for 2017, Russia Moving 'Toward Economic Growth,'" http://sputniknews.com/business/20160903/1044921703/russia-economy-2017-plan.html.

    "Russian Economic Development Minister Alexei Ulyukayev said Saturday August inflation in the country was close to 0 percent while by the end of the year it was expected to reach 6.8 percent on a year-on-year basis against 7.2 percent in 2015."

Appendix 3.1: Attractors and Bounded Rationality

William Baumol, on the basis of his consultant experience, concluded that "optimizing" businessmen (firm managers) in monopolistic enterprises were more interested in maximizing sales than profits once an acceptable level of profit had been attained, prompting him to infer that they wanted to maximize revenue subject to a profit constraint. Since this also requires knowledge of product and factor-demand equations, it cannot be done ideally, but it is possible for a firm by lowering price to increase revenue and thus perhaps increase market share.[1]

Consider a limited plane space denoted by Γ and a subspace within Γ denoted by Ω. We also consider a type of motion that takes place within Γ. If motion of this type starts within Γ but not within Ω and always ends within Ω, then Ω is an attractor. We will return to this definition after developing an example devised by Edward Beltrami.[2]

Figure 3.A1 depicts the non-ideal (and imperfectly competitive) consumer product demand and producer factor cost curves of a monopolistic firm. It can be estimated, but for practical and econometric reasons, the monopolistic firm knows that it is unreliable. Ideal Samuelson type demand curves don't exist.[3]

p_1 and p_2 are the implied (but non-determinable) ideal (or short run imperfectly competitive ideal) profit-maximizing and revenue-maximizing prices, respectively. Suppose the firm, unable to locate p_1 and p_2 set the price p^* above the profit-maximizing price. The management may find that this price is too high evaluated from the standpoint of bounded rational product demand and factor supply curves because the quantity sold is small and profits are not as large as expected. They may decide to lower the price a small amount. This will set a price nearer the bounded rational profit-maximizing and the revenue-maximizing price. Clearly this is a desirable result, since both profit and revenue are larger.

The success invites repetition that will continue until a price lower than p_1 but larger then p_2 is fixed. A further reduction will reduce profit and increase revenue. A price decrease no longer increases both. The firm is in its attractor.

If the firm had started with a price of p^{**}, price increases would raise both profit and revenue until the price had been raised above p_2. If the price is greater than or equal to p_2 and less than or equal to p_1 the firm is in the attractor.

It will set a price at or below the profit-maximizing price and at or above the revenue-maximizing price. In other words, it will operate at one of the maximizing prices or at a price between them. If it sets prices outside this price interval, it can increase both profit and revenue by moving toward the interval. This closed interval from p_1 to p_2 inclusive is the firm's attractor. The firm will always seek to be operative within its attractor.

This example meets the definition of an attractor given earlier. The space Γ is the demand curve between intersections with the axis or other extreme points. The type of motion is changing the production level and the attractor, corresponding to Ω, is the demand curve from and including p_1 to p_2.

Why should a monopoly care about revenue and satisfying? Shouldn't it care only about profit? Not necessarily because satisficing discourages potential competition.

Although the firm does not know the precise location of either the ideal or the bounded rational demand curve, it can find out when it is in the attractor by varying its price. If profit and revenue change in the same direction, it is not in the attractor. If they change in opposite directions, or if one objective does not change, they are in the attractor. These points may easily be verified by reference to Figure 3.A1.

If the firm is in its attractor and lowers its price, with the lower price also within the attractor, it will increase revenue and lose profit. Revenue will increase because bounded rational demand is elastic (marginal revenue is positive) in the attractors. Profit will decline to the right of the profit-maximizing price's marginal cost because marginal cost in this region is greater than marginal revenue.

On the other hand, if the firm when it is in the attractor raises its price, the new price also being in the attractor, revenue will decline and profit will increase. Revenue will decline with the higher price because demand is elastic. Profit will increase because selling fewer units lowers cost, and since marginal cost is greater than marginal revenue, profit will increase. These points may be verified by reference to Figure 3.A1.

The behavioral rules of thumb here are straightforward. If a price change causes both profit and revenue to increase, firms should change price again in the same direction. If a price change causes both profit and revenue to decrease, firms should change price in the opposite direction. If a price change results in either profit or revenue increasing while the other decreases, the firm in the attractor must decide which goal is best. If either profit or revenue remains the same and the other one increases, the firm is at or near the maximum point for the unchanged objective. Again a decision is required.

Suppose that the monopolist's worst fear is realized and a competing firm enters the market. This alters the original firm's estimated demand

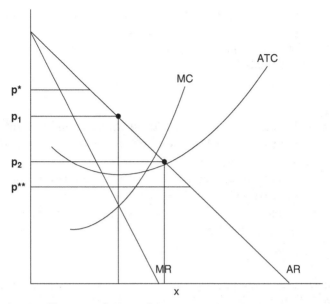

Figure 3.A1 Feasible monopolistic production.

equation, and the estimated demand curve will shift each time the competitor changes its price. Thus the attractor changes with the competitors' price changes. But the attractor remains attractive. Following its self-interest will still lead the firm toward and into the new attractor. In short, satisficing supply side theory shows that monopolistic firms (and competitive ones too) can behave diversely in what seems to be ideally rational ways without nudging the state of the system toward ideal competitive or imperfectly competitive equilibrium. It could be true that each firm may believe that it is optimizing, but as Baumol fails to adequately appreciate, this cannot be so for the ideal system in its entirety. Suppliers under this sort of regime are responsive to bounded rational consumer demand, and don't have any ideally reliable way of choosing between profit and market share maximizing.[4]

Firm Revenue and Profit in a Competing Group

Let us now consider the general case of rival, not necessarily identical firms. Assume that the number of firms is small enough so that each firm can affect the market by changing its price, but there is more than one firm. A bounded rational product demand equation exists for each firm, but no firm knows it with precision. The same principle holds for primary and intermediate factor supply curves behind the scenes.

A product demand equation for each of the n firms in the competing group can be formulated as:

$$x_i = f_i(p_1, \ldots, p_n, m), \forall_{i=1}^n$$

Where x_i is the quantity sold by the ith firm, the p's indicate the prices charged by the firms and m indicates the income of the buyers. We also specify that $\partial x_i / \partial p_i < 0, \partial x_i / \partial p_i > 0$, $j \neq i$, and $\partial x_i / \partial m > 0$ Because buyer's income is exogenous to the market and we are interested in interactions within the market, we will ignore income terms.

Each firm is interested in revenue because it contributes to profits and market share. Revenue for firm is

$$R_i = p_i x_i$$

Firms interested in gaining market share will try to increase revenue by lowering their prices. The change can be shown as:[5]

$$dR_i = x_i dp_i + p_i \frac{\partial x_i}{\partial p_i} dp_i + \sum_{k \neq i} \frac{\partial x_i}{\partial p_k} dp_k \qquad (1)$$

Income terms are ignored because we assume that demand is elastic for small competitive firms. Note that if price is reduced by firm i, the first term on the right will be negative, but the second term will be positive. The second will be larger in absolute amount if and only if the firm is operating at a point at which its demand is elastic in its attractor.

The summation in (1), the third term on the right, shows the effect on firm [i]'s revenue of price changes by competing firms. Clearly, this summation must be considered when the firm is trying to anticipate the effects of its own price change. If the firm lowers its price to increase revenue or increases its price to increase profit, the summation of the effects of other firms' price changes may offset its effort in whole or in part. Of course, since the firm does not know its demand equation, it does not know the mathematical statement of the summation, but it will know that the forces represented by the summation are operating even though it cannot measure their effects.

During the presentation and discussion of the attractor, it was assumed that if the firms are in their attractors and if $dp_i < 0$, then $dR_i > 0$; i.e. that other firms' price changes effect the firm's revenue but do not offset completely the effect of the firm's own price change on its own revenue when firm [i] is in its attractor. This permits the firm to set prices with the direction of the result being the same in the absence of competitors. Of course the magnitude of change will vary with competitors' actions, but the direction will not. The effects of price changes on competitors' revenues are discussed elsewhere.[6] It also can be argued that $dp_j < 0$ implies $dR_i > 0$ will often be empirically accurate.

To deal with profit we introduce cost. The total cost for firm is shown by

$$k_i = k_i(x_i, w_1, \ldots, w_q),$$

While incremental cost is

$$dK_i = \frac{\partial K_i}{\partial x_i} \cdot \frac{\partial x_i}{\partial p_i} dp_i + \frac{\partial K_i}{\partial x_i} \sum_{k \neq i} \frac{\partial x_i}{\partial p_k} dp_k \qquad (2)$$

The w's being the prices of factors of production, which we assume to be constant throughout our discussion. Also $\partial K_i / \partial x_i > 0$. Profit can now be written as

$$\pi_i = p_i f_i(p_1, \ldots, p_n, m) - K_i(x_i, w_1, \ldots, w_q)$$

Ignoring income effects as before, we write the profit differential as

$$d\pi_i = x_i dp_i + p_i \frac{\partial x_i}{\partial p_i} dp_i + p_i \sum_{k \neq i} \frac{\partial x_i}{\partial p_k} dp_k$$

$$-\frac{\partial K_i}{\partial x_i} \frac{\partial x_i}{\partial p_i} dp_i - \frac{\partial K_i}{\partial x_i} \sum_{k \neq i} \frac{\partial x_i}{\partial p_k} dp_k \qquad (3)$$

$$dR_i - dK_i,$$

Or as

$$d\pi_i = x_i dp_i + \left(p_i - \frac{\partial k_i}{\partial x_i} \right) \frac{\partial x_i}{\partial p_i} dp_i + \left(p_i - \frac{\partial k_i}{\partial x_i} \right) \sum_{k \neq i} \frac{\partial x_i}{\partial p_k} dp_k, \qquad (4)$$

The effects of competitors' price changes on profits also must be considered. Just as it was assumed in the revenue case that $dp_i < 0$ implies $dR_i > 0$, it can be assumed likewise that $dp_i < 0$ implies $d\pi_i > 0$.[7] It can be argued that the assumption often will be valid.

The Attractor

As in the case of a simple monopoly, the attractor is the range of product prices and values bounded by the profit-maximizing price and the revenue-maximizing price for each firm.[8]

Let $\bar{p}_1$ be the profit-maximizing price; then, according to (3), this is the price at which $dR_i = dK_i$. Since this is the profit-maximizing point, at a price higher than $\bar{p}_1$, $dR_i > dK_i$. Thus if the firm lowers its price but still has a price higher than $\bar{p}_1$, it increases revenue and profit. At a price lower than $\bar{p}_1$ but still in the attractor, we have $dR_i > dK_i$. Thus revenue has increased because the price is lower, but the cost has increased even more. Consequently profit is reduced.

As price is lowered from $\bar{p}_1$ revenue will increase by smaller and smaller amounts until $dR_i = 0$, which locates the price, call it $\hat{p}_i$ at which revenue is maximized.

Thus we have $\bar{p}_1$, the highest point of firm ^{i}'s attractor, and $\hat{p}_i$, the lowest. For points outside the attractor, prices higher than $\bar{p}_1$ or lower then $\hat{p}_i$, a price move toward the attractor increases both revenue and profit. Such a move generates $d\pi_i\, dR_i > 0$.

Within the attractor, i.e. at prices between $\bar{p}_1$ and $\hat{p}_i$ inclusive, a price decline increases revenue and increases cost more than revenue, thus lowering profit. For a price increase within the attractor, revenue decreases but cost decreases even more, thus increasing profit. Hence for either a price increase or decrease in the attractor, $d\pi_i\, dR_i \leq 0$.

The heuristics are the same as in a monopoly case. The question of whether all firms can be in their attractors at the same time is critical because satisficing theory depends on all firms seeking their attractors and remaining in them. It is analogous to the general equilibrium question: Can all firms optimize simultaneously? The issue for bounded rationality is whether all firms can reach satisfactory levels simultaneously.

To answer the question, recall that in a firm's attractor, incremental cost and incremental revenue are equal only at the profit-maximizing point, the attractor's highest point. At all other points in the attractor, incremental cost is positive and larger than incremental revenue.

In turn incremental revenue is positive at all except the lowest point of the attractor, at which it is zero. This last is the revenue-maximizing point.

Consequently the attractor can be described by the following statements:

$$dK_i > 0$$

$$dR_i > 0$$

$$dK_i - dR_i \geq 0,\ \forall_{i=1}^{n} \tag{5}$$

The first two inequalities assure that the equality in (5) will hold only when, $dK_i = dR_i$, i.e., only at the profit-maximizing point the highest point in the attractor. At other points, $dK_i > dR_i$.

The second inequality requires that $dR_i = 0$ only at the revenue maximum. This is the lowest point in the attractor. Beyond this point, at lower prices, $dR_i < 0$.

Thus we have a description of the attractor in the inequalities written earlier. The only remaining question is whether (5) can hold for all firms at the same time. To answer this question, we need to examine the inequalities,

$$dK_i - dR_i = \frac{\partial K_i}{\partial x_i} \frac{\partial x_i}{\partial p_i} dp_i + \frac{\partial K_i}{\partial x_i} \sum_{k \neq i} \frac{\partial x_i}{\partial p_k} dp_k$$

$$-x_i dp_i - p_i \frac{\partial x_i}{\partial p_i} dp_i - p_i \sum_{k \neq i} \frac{\partial x_i}{\partial p_k} dp_k \geq 0. \forall_{i=1}^n$$

We simplify the notation:

$$a_{ii} = \frac{\partial K_i}{\partial x_i} \frac{\partial x_i}{\partial p_i} - x_i - p_i \frac{\partial x_i}{\partial p_i},$$

$$a_{ij} = \frac{\partial K_i}{\partial x_i} \frac{\partial x_i}{\partial p_j} - p_i \frac{\partial x_i}{\partial p_j},$$

and form the matrix

$$A = \begin{bmatrix} a_{11} & \cdots & a_{1n} \\ \vdots & \ddots & \vdots \\ a_{n1} & \cdots & a_{nn} \end{bmatrix},$$

Which we will argue is non-singular.

Now the inequality in (5) can be shown as

$$\begin{bmatrix} a_{11} & \cdots & a_{1n} \\ \vdots & \ddots & \vdots \\ a_{n1} & \cdots & a_{nn} \end{bmatrix} \begin{bmatrix} dp_1 \\ \vdots \\ dp_n \end{bmatrix} \geq O$$

or as

$$A dp \geq O, \tag{6}$$

O being the zero column vector.

To parse the subject further we rewrite (5) as

$$\text{Adp} = \alpha \qquad\qquad (7)$$

Here α is a vector whose elements are either zeros or positive numbers. This is true because they are the differences between incremental cost and incremental revenue; in other words, they satisfy (5) and consequently they cannot be negative. Each row in A represents the dK_j, dR_i for each company; that is, each competitor is represented by a row in A. Since the competitors do not know their demand equations, they cannot maximize profit exactly. Therefore, a zero will appear in α only when the firm has stumbled on the precise maximization of profit. Otherwise, the elements of α are the positive differences between incremental cost and incremental revenue, and (5) shows they will be positive. Even though they may not think of it this way, every firm wants to be in its attractor. This is true simply because they can increase both profit and revenue by moving into their attractor. But what do they do once they are there?

A firm could increase price in an attempt to increase or even maximize profit. If profit is already judged satisfactory, this is likely to be unattractive because it involves shooting in the dark. That is, the firm does not know its demand equation, and it may not know how competitors will respond. Thus it faces two kinds of uncertainty about the outcome, which makes price increases unattractive if profit is at an acceptable level.

If profit is judged as meager, a price increase might be considered, especially if the firm's price appears low in comparison to competitors'. But this also involves shooting in the dark and carries with it a loss of revenue and perhaps market share. Price increases are likely to be undertaken with caution.

It is not unusual for the senior executives of a company to speak publicly about their uncertainty about whether they should raise price and thus increase profit, or lower price to increase market share. In each case they are contemplating, the anticipated outcome is in their attractors.

The firm could consider a price decrease to bolster market share. This, however, is shooting in the dark and risks a price war. Price competition and price changes generally therefore are likely to be undertaken with caution, except in special types of markets.

Advertising may offer an alternative to price competition. Unfortunately, it is often futile because competitors respond in kind, even though firms may feel compelled to advertise for defensive reasons. Curtailing or shunning advertising may appreciably reduce sales.

Price changes and advertising are short-run moves and consequently are limited in their ability to change the attractors of the firms, even though each firm may want to change its own and its competitors' attractor to win its rivals' expense. Price changes will not do this, and advertising is unlikely to be predictably more effective.

Oligarchs and Public Rent-Grantors

The attractor illustrated in Figure 3.A1 is confined to the range of product prices and values bounded by the profit-maximizing and revenue-maximizing prices because competition limits managers' degrees of freedom. Russian oligarchs (like the mafia) by contrast have more choice because they can control prices, marginal revenues, and marginal costs with coercive methods, and they can expand their options further by colluding with public rent-grantors to bar or deny market entry to rivals, mandate consumer purchase of insider products, and control prices and marginal revenues. These actions will shift demand and marginal revenue curves outward and favorably affect their slopes. Public rent-grantors can assist oligarchs further with subsidies that lower the marginal cost curve, and supplementary rents and lump sum transfers that augment kleptocratic wealth.

Oligarchs who may neither be profit nor revenue maximizers under bounded rational constraint can operate at suboptimal points inside or outside the attractor on a transitory basis or permanently with government support. Consequently, satisficing insider in the bounded rational universe don't have to operate as workably competitive restrained Baumol managers. They do not have to operate profitably, sales maximize, or hedge within the monopolist framework, or even minimize losses because insiders can enrich themselves at their firms' expense, and public policy makers can subsidize their activities out of general and specific tax revenues, impose mandates, and issue executive orders and government purchase contracts on any terms they desire. Consequently, in these cases, neither private enterprise nor public policies will be efficient in any meaningful neoclassical sense whenever objective functions and methods lie outside the virtuous axiomatics of Baumol's neoclassical bounded rational framework.[9]

The obligation imposed on oligarchs to produce high volumes of weapons and other products for the power services can be interpreted in Figure 3.A1 as a movement initially within the attractor along the horizontal access (sales/output) and then substantially beyond as the demand curve shifts outward and Putin dictates. This same objective was accomplished during the Soviet era with plan commands that got the job done, but only at great expense in terms of foregone household consumption (guns over butter).[10]

Notes

1   There are at least three definitions of market share: profit share, output share, and revenue share. Maximizing profits is consistent with maximizing profit share, so no conflict between firm behavior and the assumption of profit maximization arises. Output share is subject to an "apples and oranges" problem because the products of different firms may be heterogeneous with regards to design and, as perceived by buyers, quality. Therefore, in the formal model, it is assumed that market share is measured as the share of industry revenues. First, it sometimes happens that the volume of future sales depends on prior achieved levels. For example, the sale of razor blades often depends on the number of razors and therefore razor blades in use. Similarly, adopting Word instead of WordPerfect should be preferable because Word's large market share allows users greater scope for document sharing. Second, increasing market share may discourage would-be competitors. If it appears that entrants might face stiff competition from dominant firms, prospective new entrants may decide that discretion is the better part of valor. Third, managers may succumb to moral hazard, placing their private interest above firm owners'. Managers are not "residual claimants," and therefore may be more interested in market share than profits because this usually increases their compensation. See Adolf Berle and Gardner Means, *The Modern Corporation and Private Property*, New York: Macmillan, 1932. Fourth, large market share sometimes makes it easier to raise capital on private equity markets because investors equate size with success, or anticipate that lending to this type of firm will make it an attractive takeover candidate.

2   Edward Beltrami, *Mathematics for Dynamic Modeling*, Boston, MA: Academic Press, 1987, 208.

3   Paul Samuelson, *Foundations of Economic Analysis*, Cambridge, MA: Harvard University Press, 1947.

4   The same problem held in a more extreme form in Soviet enterprises. See Steven Rosefielde, *Russian Economy from Lenin to Putin*, New York: Wiley, 2007.

5   Many of the relationships that will be developed could be stated in elasticity terms. E.g. if $dp_i < 0$ and $dR_i > 0$ then using (1) we can easily obtain

$$(1 + \epsilon_{ii}) \frac{dp_i}{p_i} > \sum_{k \neq i} \epsilon_{ik} \frac{dp_k}{p_k}$$

Here ϵ_{ii} is good i's own price elasticity coefficient and ϵ_{ik} is the cross elasticity of i with respect to the price of good k. It seems more straightforward to use price and quantities rather than elasticity coefficients.

6 Steven Rosefielde and Ralph W. Pfouts, *Inclusive Economic Theory*, Singapore: World Scientific Publishers, 2014, appendix 4, "Realist Profit and Revenue Seeking: Multi-firm Interaction Effects."
7 Ibid.
8 The attractors that we derive are not "strange attractors." The latter require the presence of a fractal and sensitivity to initial conditions. Our attractors do not meet either of these requirements.
9 The same principle applies for other Simon-type bounded rational cases.
10 Rosefielde, *Russian Economy from Lenin to Putin*; Charles Wolf Jr. and Henry Rowen, *The Impoverished Superpower: Perestroika and the Soviet Military Burden*, San Francisco, CA: Institute for Contemporary Studies, 1990.

4

Minsk II Protocol

It is widely acknowledged that Ukraine teeters on the brink of becoming a "failed state" with a comatose economy. This facilitates further Russian advances in Novorossiya. The West, recognizing Kyiv's parlous state, has responded to Putin's territorial ambitions in Novorossiya by initiating a conflict resolution process called the Minsk I and Minsk II Protocols to restore peace and partnership in the region, and by encouraging Ukraine's rapid transition to democratic free enterprise. The successful achievement of both goals would strengthen Ukraine's independence and dim prospects for Putin's campaign to restore Russia's spheres of influence. Failure would have the opposite effect, assisting the Kremlin to annex parts of Novorossiya. It would check new Western inroads, and expand Russia's hegemonic sway. Putin is betting that President Petro Poroshenko will fail, that the Kremlin will successfully subjugate large portions of Novorossiya while paying lip service to Ukraine's sovereign autonomy. The West hopes that Minsk I and II will upset Putin's applecart. The outcome for both sides therefore depends significantly on the West's management of the Minsk process and Kyiv's political and economic reforms.

The results to date aren't encouraging and don't inspire confidence in the West's and Kyiv's resolve. The Minsk Protocol was drawn up by the Trilateral Contact Group comprised of Ukraine, Russia, and the Organization for Security and Co-operation in Europe (OSCE)[1] with the informal participation of the Donetsk and Luhansk People's Republics on September 5, 2014, as a framework for resolving the Russo-Ukrainian conflict.[2] It resembled President Petro Poroshenko's "fourteen-point peace plan" of June 20, 2014,[3] and contained twelve points:[4]

1. To ensure an immediate bilateral ceasefire.
2. To ensure the monitoring and verification of the ceasefire by the OSCE.

3. Decentralization of power, including the adoption of the Ukrainian law "On Temporary Order of Local Self-Governance in Particular Districts of Donetsk and Luhansk Oblasts."
4. To ensure the permanent monitoring of the Ukrainian-Russian border and verification by the OSCE with the creation of security zones in the border regions of Ukraine and the Russian Federation.
5. Immediate release of all hostages and illegally detained persons.
6. A law preventing the prosecution and punishment of persons in connection with the events that have taken place in some areas of Donetsk and Luhansk Oblasts.
7. To continue the inclusive national dialogue.
8. To take measures to improve the humanitarian situation in Donbas.
9. To ensure early local elections in accordance with the Ukrainian law "On Temporary Order of Local Self-Governance in Particular Districts of Donetsk and Luhansk Oblasts."
10. To withdraw illegal armed groups and military equipment as well as fighters and mercenaries from Ukraine.
11. To adopt a program of economic recovery and reconstruction for the Donbas region.
12. To provide personal security for Minsk I participants.[5]

Few of these points were implemented in the ensuring months, underscored by the Luhansk and Donetsk People's Republics wresting significant new territories from Kyiv. The Minsk I Protocol completely collapsed in January 2015, but was swiftly revised in the form of a new agreement called Minsk II by the leaders of Ukraine, Russia, France, and Germany.[6] Minsk II resembles Minsk I, but adds an OSCE-observed unconditional ceasefire from February 15, 2015, withdrawal of heavy weapons from the front line, release of prisoners of war, and constitutional reform in Ukraine.[7]

It has been partially effective, with some hopeful signs.[8] The ceasefire in Donbas has not prevented thousands of people from losing their lives since February 2015, in addition to the 5,000 fatalities inflicted during Minsk I. The fighting escalated for a while, but tanks and light weapons were removed from Donetsk in October 2015.[9] Heavy weapons are still positioned close to the ceasefire line, and are active. The constitutional reform dialogue the Minsk II Protocol mandated hasn't produced significant results, and Kyiv has refused to pardon and amnesty those it deems "terrorists." Prisoners and hostages have been incompletely exchanged. Humanitarian assistance has trickled in, and social and economic transfers, including pensions and taxes, have only been partially restored.[10]

The restoration of Kyiv's control of the Ukrainian–Russian border has been blocked. No evidence has emerged of a pullout of foreign forces and weapons or the disarmament of illegal groups. Russia's support for the "people's republics" is unflagging. Constitutional reform in Ukraine aimed at drawing up a new basic law for the country by the end of 2015, but nothing was achieved, prompting Putin to declare in June 2016 that "It would be absurd to expect Russia to implement Minsk peace deal. … Key issues of the implementation of the Minsk agreements are now in the hands of our Kyiv partners, the Kyiv authorities. We can do nothing without them. We cannot amend the Ukrainian constitution, we cannot enforce the law on special forms of government in certain territories. We cannot sign the law on amnesty for the Ukrainian president."[11]

This record is unimpressive, but it more or less should have been expected, official rhetoric notwithstanding. Ukraine, Russia, and the European Union (via the OSCE, German chancellor Angela Merkel, and French president Francois Hollande) knew they could not achieve a satisfactory settlement with Russia in September 2014, and decided to stall for time while maintaining the illusion of progress. They devised a framework agreement that provided political cover for all, and obligated no one to anything. Poroshenko signed because his armed forces could not dislodge the Russians and he hoped to enrich himself along the way with Western assistance. Putin rightly calculated that Ukraine's state would deteriorate, expanding his options while awaiting the most opportune moment to attack.[12] Germany and France sought to avoid military escalation. They took the position that a framework agreement diminished political and military risk, and offered an opportunity to test the efficacy of punitive economic sanctions. The European Union renewed existing sanctions.[13] Washington announced it was contemplating fresh sanctions;[14] on October 21, 2015, America stated that it would send modified counter-battery radar to Ukraine;[15] and Belgium and France sequestered Russian assets to pay disputed claims by former shareholders of the Yukos corporation,[16] thus far as of September 2016 all to no avail.[17]

The West seems to have embraced Minsk I and II because leaders decided that it was better than chaos, even if it obstructed the attainment of a just outcome. The merit of the ploy depends on whether the breathing room gained has been used wisely and bears constructively on the next step. If as seems possible, Minsk I and Minsk II have postponed the day of reckoning without vouchsafing Novorossiya's security or successfully pressuring the Kremlin to revoke Crimea's annexation, then it will have appeased Russia to no avail and encouraged fresh aggression. The West may be deluding itself that a perpetual Minsk process will freeze the conflict in place,[18] or that its tepid actions are a prelude to a more ultimate victory,[19] but thus far Putin is hanging tough.

The game isn't over. The Kremlin might capitulate. However, if it doesn't, the correlation of forces will tilt strongly in Russia's favor, forcing the West to decide whether to risk armed confrontation or to acquiesce to Putin's version of the "new normal."[20] Minsk I and Minsk II's only consolation in this adverse case will lie in the hope "strategic patience" provides.

Notes

1 OSCE is the world's largest security-oriented intergovernmental organization. Its mandate includes issues such as arms control and the promotion of human rights, freedom of the press, and fair elections. It has its origins in the 1975 Conference on Security and Co-operation in Europe (CSCE) held in Helsinki, Finland.

2 The signatories were Swiss diplomat and OSCE representative Heidi Tagliavini, former president of Ukraine and Ukrainian representative Leonid Kuchma, Russian ambassador to Ukraine and Russian representative Mikhail Zurabov, and DPR and LPR leaders Alexander Zakharchenko and Igor Plotnitsky.

3 "Ukraine Crisis: Details of Poroshenko's Peace Plan Emerge," *BBC News*, June 20, 2014. http://www.bbc.com/news/world-europe-27937596.

4 "Minsk Protocol," Organization for Security and Co-operation in Europe, September 5, 2014.

5 The Protocol was supplemented with a memorandum on September 19, 2014; to wit all parties agreed to: pull heavy weaponry 15 kilometers (9.3 miles) back on each side of the line of contact, creating a 30-kilometer (19-mile) buffer zone; ban offensive operations; ban flights by combat aircraft over the security zone; withdraw all foreign mercenaries from the conflict zone; set up an OSCE mission to monitor implementation of the Minsk Protocol.

6 The signatories were Vladimir Putin, Ukrainian president Petro Poroshenko, German chancellor Angela Merkel, French president François Hollande, DPR leader Alexander Zakharchenko, and LPR leader Igor Plotnitsky.

7 "Ukraine Peace Talks Yield Cease-Fire Deal," *Wall Street Journal*, February 12, 2015. The full text of the agreement is as follows:[23][24]

> 1. Immediate and full ceasefire in particular districts of Donetsk and Luhansk oblasts of Ukraine and its strict fulfilment as of 00:00 midnight EET on 15 February 2015.
>
> 2. Pullout of all heavy weapons by both sides to equal distance with the aim of creation of a security zone on minimum 50 kilometres (31 mi) apart for artillery of 100 mm calibre or more, and a security zone of 70 kilometres (43 mi) for multiple rocket launchers (MRLS) and 140 kilometres (87 mi) for MLRS Tornado-S, Uragan, Smerch, and Tochka U tactical missile systems:
>
>> for Ukrainian troops, from actual line of contact;
>>
>> for armed formations of particular districts of Donetsk and Luhansk oblasts of Ukraine, from the contact line in accordance with the Minsk Memorandum as of 19 September 2014

The pullout of the above-mentioned heavy weapons must start no later than the second day after the start of the ceasefire and finish within 14 days.

This process will be assisted by OSCE with the support of the Trilateral Contact Group.

3. Effective monitoring and verification of ceasefire regime and pullout of heavy weapons by OSCE will be provided from the first day of pullout, using all necessary technical means such as satellites, drones, radio-location systems etc.

4. On the first day after the pullout a dialogue is to start on modalities of conducting local elections in accordance with the Ukrainian legislation and the Law of Ukraine "On Temporary Order of Local Self-Governance in Particular Districts of Donetsk and Luhansk Oblasts," and also about the future of these districts based on the above-mentioned law.

   Without delays, but no later than 30 days from the date of signing of this document, a resolution has to be approved by the Verkhovna Rada of Ukraine, indicating the territory which falls under the special regime in accordance with the law "On Temporary Order of Local Self-Governance in Particular Districts of Donetsk and Luhansk Oblasts," based in the line set up by the Minsk Memorandum as of 19 September 2014.

5. Provide pardon and amnesty by way of enacting a law that forbids persecution and punishment of persons in relation to events that took place in particular districts of Donetsk and Luhansk oblasts of Ukraine.

6. Provide release and exchange of all hostages and illegally held persons, based on the principle of "all for all." This process has to end – at the latest – on the fifth day after the pullout (of weapons).

7. Provide safe access, delivery, storage and distribution of humanitarian aid to the needy, based on an international mechanism.

8. Define the modalities of a full restoration of social and economic connections, including social transfers, such as payments of pensions and other payments (income and revenue, timely payment of communal bills, restoration of tax payments within the framework of the Ukrainian legal field).

   With this aim, Ukraine will restore management over the segment of its banking system in the districts affected by the conflict, and possibly, an international mechanism will be established to ease such transactions.

9. Restore control of the state border to the Ukrainian government in the whole conflict zone, which has to start on the first day after the local election and end after the full political regulation (local elections in particular districts of Donetsk and Luhansk oblasts based on the law of Ukraine and Constitutional reform) by the end of 2015, on the condition of fulfilment of Point 11 – in consultations and in agreement with representatives of particular districts of Donetsk and Luhansk oblasts within the framework of the Trilateral Contact Group.

10. Pullout of all foreign armed formations, military equipment, and also mercenaries from the territory of Ukraine under OSCE supervision. Disarmament of all illegal groups.

11. Constitutional reform in Ukraine, with a new constitution to come into effect by the end of 2015, the key element of which is decentralisation (taking into account peculiarities of particular districts of Donetsk and Luhansk oblasts, agreed with representatives of these districts), and also approval of permanent legislation on

the special status of particular districts of Donetsk and Luhansk oblasts in accordance with the measures spelt out in the attached footnote,[note 1] by the end of 2015.

12. Based on the Law of Ukraine "On Temporary Order of Local Self-Governance in Particular Districts of Donetsk and Luhansk Oblasts," questions related to local elections will be discussed and agreed upon with representatives of particular districts of Donetsk and Luhansk oblasts in the framework of the Trilateral Contact Group. Elections will be held in accordance with relevant OSCE standards and monitored by OSCE/ODIHR.

13. Intensify the work of the Trilateral Contact Group including through the establishment of working groups on the implementation of relevant aspects of the Minsk agreements. They will reflect the establishment of working groups on the implementation of relevant aspects of the Minsk agreements. They will reflect the composition of the Trilateral Contact Group.

"Package of Measures for the Implementation of the Minsk Agreements," Organization for Security and Co-operation in Europe, 12 February 2015.

8 *CSIS Ukrainian Timeline*, October 22, 2015. http://csis.org/ukraine/index.htm#248.

9 Andrew Kramer, "Attacks, and Accusations, Escalate in Eastern Ukraine," *New York Times*, August 18, 2015. http://www.nytimes.com/2015/08/19/world/europe/fighting-intensifies-along-eastern-ukraine-cease-fire-line.html. "Fighting between government forces and Russian-backed rebels in eastern Ukraine has escalated sharply in recent days, with each side blaming the other for the violence. At least nine people were killed in artillery strikes on Monday in villages and towns on both sides of a cease-fire line, and United States officials have said that one three-day period of fighting along the front last week was the most intense since a February cease-fire."

10 Dmitri Trenin, "Harsh Realities in Ukraine," *Carnegie Moscow Center*, June 16, 2015. http://carnegie.ru/2015/06/16/harsh-realities-in-ukraine/ianl?mkt_tok=3Rk MMJWWfF9wsRojvK7AZKXonjHpfsX56OsvXqGg38431UFwdcjKPmjr1YYCRcd 0aPyQAgobGp5I5FEIQ7XYTLB2t60MWA%3D%3D.

11 Putin: Absurd to Expect Russia to Implement Minsk Agreements," June 24, 2016. http://uatoday.tv/politics/putin-it-is-absurd-to-expect-russia-to-implement-minsk-agreements-678855.html.

12 CSIS, The Ukrainian Crisis Timeline, December 18, 2015. http://csis.org/ukraine/index.htm.

"Ukraine Places Moratorium on Russia Debt Repayment. Ukraine stated definitely today that it will place a moratorium on the repayment of its $3 billion debt to Russia that the IMF classified as an official loan earlier this week. Ukraine claims that it has engaged in good faith negotiations with Russia by offering the Kremlin the same terms agreed to with Ukraine's private creditors – terms that Russia has categorically rejected. Ukrainian Prime Minister Arseniy Yatsenyuk said today that the moratorium will remain in place 'until the acceptance of our restructuring proposals or the adoption of the relevant court decision.' Ukraine is thus set to default on the debt on December 20th when it is set to mature.

"IMF officials stated today that Ukraine's bailout program may be in threat, though not because of the decision to default on the $3 billion debt to Russia. Instead, IMF first deputy director David Lipton stated that the possible failure of the Rada to pass a proposed tax code and budget for 2016 that are consistent with the terms of the bailout program may 'interrupt the program and inevitably disrupt the associated international financing.'"

13　Raf Casert, "EU to Extend Russia Sanctions by 6 months," AP, June 17, 2015. http://news.yahoo.com/eu-extend-russia-sanctions-6-months-170708837.html.

14　Keith Johnson, "Europe Deals a Double Blow to Putin's Russia," *Foreign Policy*, June 17, 2015. Bradley Klapper, "US, EU Ready Tough Russia Sanctions, in Case They're Needed," *AP*, June 18, 2015. http://foreignpolicy.com/2015/06/17/europe-deals-a-double-blow-to-putins-russia-sanctions-yukos-rosneft/ http://news.yahoo.com/us-eu-ready-tough-russia-sanctions-case-theyre-195742831.html. "The penalties could start with banning more Russian government officials and businessmen from traveling and doing business in the West, U.S. and European officials said. But they can climb dramatically to include new measures to crimp the country's all-important fuel exports, cut Russian banks off from international financial transactions and severely limit the capacity of Russian businesses to engage in lucrative business deals overseas."

15　*CSIS Ukrainian Timeline*, October 22, 2015. http://csis.org/ukraine/index.htm#248.

16　"Moscow Says Russian Embassy Accounts Frozen in Belgium," *YahooNews*, June 18, 2015. http://news.yahoo.com/moscow-says-russian-embassy-accounts-frozen-belgium-154310476.html. "Moscow on Thursday reacted furiously to a move by Belgium to freeze the accounts of Russian diplomatic missions and other organisations, summoning the Belgian ambassador over the 'openly hostile act.'" "Russian state-run news agency RIA Novosti reported that Belgian authorities had frozen official accounts in relation to legal claims by shareholders of defunct oil firm Yukos." "Former Yukos shareholders were awarded $50 billion in damages against Russia by an international arbitration court in 2014 over the dismemberment of the firm. Russia stripped apart the oil firm after making in 2003 a high-profile arrest of Yukos chief executive Mikhail Khodorkovsky. The company – which had a market capitalisation of some $21 billion in 2003 – was sold off in a series of opaque auctions between 2004 and 2006, with state-owned Rosneft buying up most of its operations."

17　Donetsk People's Republic (DPR) and Lugansk People's Republic (LPR) elections were postponed to November 6, 2016.

18　Trenin, "Harsh Realities in Ukraine." "A frozen conflict in Donbass is not what the European Union wants. Europe insists on full implementation of the Minsk accords. However, it needs to face up to the harsh realities. Donbass rebels want a confederal status within Ukraine, complete with a veto on the country's potential NATO membership. Kiev wants to crush the rebellion, punish its leaders and activists, and end Russian interference in Ukraine. No compromise between the two seems possible. Minsk II is definitely headed for a train wreck. Its likely failure, however, must not be allowed to lead to a resumption of the large-scale hostilities that we saw last summer and winter."

19　Klapper, "US, EU Ready Tough Russia Sanctions." "Secretary of State John Kerry told reporters this week that imposing additional sanctions on Russia 'depends on what happens on the ground' and on President Vladimir Putin's support for fully implementing a February cease-fire in Ukraine. If violence stops and separatists can reach a political agreement with Ukraine's Western-backed government in Kiev,

sanctions can be rolled back, he said. But, 'if President Putin chooses to play a double game and continues to allow the separatists to press forward, then obviously we
have a very big challenge ahead of us.'"

20 Trenin, "Harsh Realities in Ukraine." "To avert looming disaster, the parties to the
Minsk agreement and the United States need to focus on those elements of it which
can be implemented: stabilizing the ceasefire; pulling back heavy weapons; and
exchanging prisoners. This means in practice much tighter control of the forces
physically confronting each other across the line of contact."

5

Partnership to Cold War

Russia's annexation of Crimea abruptly ended the West's post-Soviet partnership with the Kremlin. The West immediately changed the concept governing its relationship with Russia from partnership to confrontation. The new posture is a de facto cold war symbolized by the expulsion of Russia from the G-8,[1] with some renewed elements of cooperation and partnership. Cold War I had a similar mixed character with armed confrontation coexisting with Détente, arms control, and disarmament agreements, and bouts of confidence building. Policy makers haven't formally declared Cold War II, and equivocate about calling a spade a spade, but the underlying reality became transparent when the West demanded the revocation of Crimea's annexation and Moscow scoffed. Swords were crossed.

But what sort of cold war had erupted? Is it a resurrection of Cold War I framed by the class struggle between communism and capitalism in a new guise, or something less grandiose? The situation at first was obscure, but has gradually come into focus. There is renewed cold war between old adversaries, but its scope and ideology have changed. The West continues to champion global democratic free enterprise, but Russia no longer acts as the leader of the non-capitalist world. It speaks only for Muscovy and Putin doesn't express any desire to impose Russia's system on the West, China, India, or others.

Cold War II is a regional dispute between the West and the Kremlin over hegemony in Russia's neighborhood cast in the West as a battle between authoritarian expansionism and the rule of international law. It is being fought with the same tools employed in the Cold War I struggle between capitalism and communism, but is geographically confined and more tractable because Putin doesn't feel any ideological compulsion to bury the West.[2] He only wants to limit and partially push back its sphere of influence.

Washington and Brussels, for their part, are trying to tame Russia anew with tried and true engagement tactics, and as before are prepared to be strategically patient even if Russia fends off greater EU and NATO expansion and Western-sponsored color revolutions for decades.[3] The West's approach assumes that mutually assured nuclear destruction precludes World War III, and that Russian authoritarianism cannot be competitive in the long run. The game as seen in Washington and Brussels is a matter of strategic patience that provides the West with a high probability to win, without serious risk of losing.[4] The strategy worked well in the late 1980s because communist leaders in Moscow and throughout the Soviet bloc were persuaded that the West's quality of life was superior, and dashed for the exits.[5]

Vladimir Putin, by contrast, seems to believe that contemporary Russian authoritarianism and his mixed market economy are better than the Soviet Union's. He appears confident that this time will be different, that the Kremlin can partially recapture some of Russia's historical sphere of influence lost after 1988. His Cold War II strategy echoes Stalin's, but is less ambitious. He seeks to win at the West's expense by rolling back some of the West's post-Soviet geostrategic gains, forging a new global order more to his own liking, and won't be content with the status quo.

Both sides are operating at cross purposes and are playing to win because they believe that they can prevail. Their convictions have hardened and are unlikely to be affected by minor setbacks. Putin won't morph into Gorbachev and the West won't be disheartened by his resilience. The West might even stick to its guns if the Kremlin annexes Novorossiya and the Baltic states.

Smiles, however, can only paper over the differences.

The initial economic and political repercussions of Crimea's annexation in Russia and the West have been symmetric. Both sides are unwilling to alter their strategic trajectories and have returned to Cold War jousting. They are preparing for a long-term engagement, the West halfheartedly and Putin with zeal.

Russia for its part is focused on holding the line without abandoning its aspirations for great power restoration.[6] The Kremlin has chosen to consolidate its positions in Luhansk and Donetsk rather than immediately pressing forward to Mariupol. It has chosen to compete with the West in Syria as an ostensible ally, while otherwise parrying Western economic sanctions and diplomatic maneuvers. It is rapidly building up its Revolution in Military Affairs (RMA) combined with arms warfighting capabilities in vulnerable theaters of military operations (TVDs), accompanied by intimidating military gestures.[7] Putin's behavior is reminiscent of the Soviet Union's posture during the early expansionary phase the Cold War. The Kremlin is on the offense, regardless of how events play themselves out.

The West is on the defense, trying to preserve its post-Soviet sphere of influence, but also on the offense insofar as it refuses to abandon its color revolution policy, NATO expansion, its quest for Crimean de-annexation, and the Eastern Partnership in the newly independent states of the former USSR.[8]

This split vision plays to Putin's advantage. Stalin's ambitions in the late 1940s and early 1950s were checked because the West chose to contain him, but this time around the Kremlin has a freer hand because Washington and the Europeans are hoping that Putin will fade away without having to be militarily deterred.

The main difference between Russia's and the West's strategies in the early fencing is war preparation. Russia is building up its armed forces, while Western military expenditures are declining. Russia is planning to fight, win, and hold territory in Novorossiya, and, perhaps, the Baltic states, while the West is dilatorily going through the motions of deterrence. The West, for its part, continues to doggedly press for regime change, while the Kremlin is equally committed to fighting back, not just along Russia's periphery, but in Syria and other parts of the Middle East.

Putin appears to be succeeding on some scores. Western economic sanctions and plummeting natural resources prices haven't brought Russia's economy to its knees. Putin hasn't lost his grip on power and has retained his great power restoration project. The Russian people by and large have rallied around the flag. The Kremlin is expanding its sphere of influence and forging authoritarian alliances in China, the Balkans, Syria, Iran, and other parts of the Middle East. Russia has paid a diplomatic and material price for Crimea's annexation in terms of foregone transition possibilities, but the benefit outweighs the cost from Putin's perspective. He opposes Moscow and Eurasia's hegemonic absorption by the West. The Kremlin wants Russia to be a self-sufficient, great power and is succeeding without provoking significant regime threatening social discord.

The West too hasn't suffered any catastrophic setbacks after Crimea's annexation. Some ground has been lost in Luhansk and Donetsk, and Russia has garnered political support in Hungary, Serbia, Slovenia, and Greece. The Kremlin's strengthened presence in Syria and Iran should be counted as negatives, but Russia's economic counter sanctions have had no significant impact on EU employment, production, and growth,[9] despite howls from special constituencies because the consumer goods that Russia imports from the West are being discounted and sold to alternative buyers by European suppliers.[10] Things could have been worse. The Kremlin could have cut off natural gas and petroleum supplies to Europe,[11] if sanctions had escalated into economic war, but a burgeoning global petroleum glut stayed Putin's hand. Both sides nipped,[12] but neither drew much blood.

This standoff in the aftermath of Crimea's annexation and territory losses in Luhansk and Donetsk, nonetheless, on balance can be counted as a victory for Russia and a loss for the West. The Kremlin has won by making its great power claims credible, impeding the West's eastward expansion,[13] and using shock-and-awe tactics, including cyberwarfare to sow fear and dissension. America and the European Union have lost because their aura of global invincibility has been punctured,[14] and their concept of world order violated. Globalization on Western terms before March 2014 was taken for granted. Now not only does multi-polarization seem more plausible,[15] redrawing spheres of influence in Europe itself has appeared on the radar screen as a serious possibility. Serbia, Montenegro and Macedonia are no longer intimidated by EU "manifest destiny," and for multiple reasons including Grexit and Brexit, EU solidarity is crumbling.

Once upon a time, the European Union and greater EU projects seemed unstoppable, despite the 2008 financial crisis and its aftermath. Now Greece,[16] Britain, Hungary, and Spain are visibly displaying their doubts,[17] splintering the European Union's political cohesion and opening the door for Kremlin mischief making.

America and the European Union are vulnerable to these machinations because their economies have malfunctioned since 2008, Europe is plagued by a burgeoning refugee crisis, and global politics have turned confrontational. Putin cannot be blamed for the West's economic malaise. Excessive national indebtedness, monetary debasement, lax financial regulation, asset price speculation, intractable high unemployment and underemployment, economic stagnation, power and privilege-seeking, burgeoning inequality, welfare dependency, educational deterioration, illegal immigration,[18] the mass influx of Syrian, Iraqi, African, and South and Central Asian refugees,[19] and ethnic and religious conflict are homegrown problems. Nonetheless, Kremlin antics raise fears and aggravate domestic discontent, facilitating Moscow's meddling in the West's increasingly fractious internal politics. The center-left EU establishment is under assault from a host of populist parties that make it difficult to responsibly govern and effectively engage Russia's geopolitical assertiveness.[20] A Pew survey indicates that the majority of Europeans oppose honoring NATO commitments to defend members under attack (Latvia, Lithuania, Estonia) if Russia is the aggressor.[21]

It didn't have to happen this way. The West could have used the Russian peril as an excuse for getting its house in order. Nations often rally around the flag when externally threatened, setting aside self-seeking and parochial squabbles for the common good, but this hasn't occurred. There has been a great deal of talk about strengthening national security, but no meaningful public military, political, or societal response. Those who oppose increased military spending have by and large prevailed, and advocates of ever-greater deficit spending, monetary expansion, miss regulation, and abusive entitlements are still at the helm and are being pushed by new parties to do more. These macroeconomic and microeconomic expansionary policies were supposed to reinvigorate and unite America and the European Union. They were supposed to leverage the "peace dividend"[22] and its blessings through economic, political, social, and military strength, but the lessons of persistent stagnation and discord continue to be disregarded. The post-Soviet peace dividend has been exhausted, and the West cannot square the circle. It cannot count on "strategic patience," repel Kremlin pushback, or prevent Putin from exploiting the West's vulnerabilities for Russia's benefit. In the worst case, it may be on a slow track to becoming a failed civilization.[23]

Crimea's annexation has fundamentally changed the East-West paradigm, replacing partnerships with an undeclared cold war of attrition, where winning from Putin's perspective means sowing discord among Russia's enemies, and demanding accommodation (non-reciprocal access, assistance, influence, and territory). This is a complex game focused on dividing and weakening the European Union from within rather than destroying it, while simultaneously seeking accommodation. A prosperous, self-confident, unified, expansionary European Union threatens the Kremlin, as might the restoration of a nationalities-based prewar European order. Moscow prefers a third way. Its interests are best served by a bickering and enfeebled Europe that degrades NATO's military credibility, encourages unilateral concessions, and strengthens Russia's sphere of influence.

This divide-harry-and-weaken-from-within strategy works by pitting Greece, the United Kingdom, France, Italy, Hungary, and Serbia against Germany;[24] and Eastern and Central Europe and the Baltic states against the Mediterranean. Russia supports the Portugal, Italy, Ireland, Greece, and Spain (PIIGS) quest for debt postponement and forgiveness.[25] It praises Hungary's irredentist ambitions and anti-immigrant policies.[26] It sympathizes with Scottish separatism, and wherever it can encourages domestic political gridlock that weakens Europe, hampers resistance to Kremlin ambitions, tarnishes democracy, and discredits the "idea of the West." Muscovite authoritarianism is unappealing, but may seem like the lesser evil to some of the disaffected.

Putin's Greater Europe Plan

Putin enjoys fishing in troubled waters, even when he knows there is little chance the West will immediately rise to the bait. One little-known but instructive gambit for simultaneously engaging Europe and Eurasia was laid out by Vladimir Putin in 2011,[27] and can be extended to encompass America via the "Euro-Atlantic security community."[28] It starts from Gorbachev's premise that Russia and Europe share a common home ("new thinking," *novoe myslenie*), which can be revived on the basis of Enlightenment, humanist, and socialist cultural principles, including democracy, private property, free enterprise, the rule of law, civil liberties, minority rights, entitlements, multiculturalism, affirmative action, egalitarianism, national independence, anticolonialism, and anti-imperialism.[29] Putin, building on Yeltsin's prior embellishments of Gorbachev's "common European home doctrine,"[30] claims that nothing fundamental separates the two camps, that a peaceful and prosperous "Greater Europe" stretching from the Atlantic to the Pacific can be readily negotiated and implemented.[31] In his view, Russia's deeds qualify it for accession to Greater Europe. It has discarded one-party Communist rule for electoral democracy, privatized the means of production on a freehold basis, created competitive markets, relaxed constraints on international trade, finance, and labor migration, established freedom of speech, press, and religion, curbed the FSB, and emptied the Gulag of its political prisoners.

The Greater Europe framework is compatible with Yalta II, but broader and more subversive because it explicitly includes a supranational option;[32] that is, Russian Trojan Horse membership and a leading role in an enlarged European Union,[33] Eurozone,[34] and NATO.[35] Greater Europe as Putin envisions it won't be the United States of "Europe, Russia and Eurasia." It will be a transnational federation with a clear division of responsibilities among its supranational,[36] shared,[37] and independent member jurisdictions.

The European Union is a supranational entity, and Putin's Greater Europe gambit will adhere to the same principle. Supranationality is a hybrid form of multinational government that requires members to transfer some aspects of their national sovereignty like foreign trade, international capital flows, foreign exchange policy, monetary policy, or fiscal policy to superior transnational bodies, while retaining other equally important sovereign powers like national defense. It differs fundamentally from America's federative form of government where sovereignty over critical powers is held centrally,[38] with authority over subsidiary matters like public education reserved to subordinate states.[39] Supranationalists, including Putin, argue that sharing of vital powers among transnational, national, and local authorities is better than traditional unified national arrangements,[40] but they disagree about the fine print.

Transnational, national, and local governing bodies in supranational regimes can be authoritarian or democratic in varying degrees and mixes. The scope and competencies of transnational, national and local authorities, including policy making, can be configured in a kaleidoscope of ways. Conflict adjudication can take multiple forms. Membership can be unitary (with all nations and localities treated equally), stratified, or divided into blocs (spheres of influence). Laws, rules, rights, social and cultural policies, and jurisdictions can apply uniformly or may be differentiated. National member states can retain control over money, banking, exchange rates, minorities, religion, education, foreign policy, and defense, or these powers can be ceded to transnational authorities. Putin's advocacy of Greater European supranationality allows him to retain ample degrees of freedom to do more or less as he pleases at his partners' expense within a seemingly benign framework.

If Putin's gambit were to succeed, he would make himself *vozhd* over Greater Europe's transnational realm masked with Surkovian democracy. He would govern by edict (rule of men) behind a constitutional façade, and rent-grant wherever possible at the expense of market competition. He would foster the *siloviki*'s cultural values, curb civil liberties, and prioritize guns over butter. In short, if dreams came true under Putin's plan, Russia would subjugate Europe, Eurasia, and America (via the Euro-Atlantic security community) in a vast Russian empire euphemistically called Greater Europe. Kim Jong-un advocates Korean unification in the same spirit.

Of course, Putin knows that the European Union and America won't fall into his trap, and that the turmoil surrounding Brexit and Grexit has taken the subject off the table. The purpose of his Greater Europe Plan isn't to achieve the impossible. The goal is to eventually provide a second track for negotiating condominium that allows the Kremlin to retain, defend, and perhaps expand Russia's sphere of influence working from within a supranational framework,[41] rather than as an adversarial outsider seeking a Yalta II accord.

The approach has two advantages. It is ostensibly non-confrontational, and offers better prospects for defusing the post-Crimea annexation conflict by providing Moscow, Brussels, and Washington with greater scope for

bargaining. It may be possible to trade political for organizational concessions. The European Union has invited Russia to join it and to participate
in NATO in the past, and could do so again, but this should not be considered a panacea.[42] Any strategy the West chooses to reverse Russia's annexation of the Crimea and restore the status quo ante will encounter staunch
resistance. The *siloviki*-friendly Kremlin is going to energetically engage the
West under the twin banners of Greater Europe and Yalta II until it is convinced further struggle is futile.[43]

American and European leaders, like Neville Chamberlain before them,
don't want to appease authoritarianism; however, Putin is betting they will.

The West is already restoring Putin's diplomatic legitimacy by partnering with him in Syria.[44] He appears to understand the West better than its
insiders, but even if he is wrong, the Kremlin should be expected to wage
a vigorous campaign to encourage condominium by dividing and inter-
nally weakening its adversary (enlisting America against Turkey in Iraq).[45]
Crimean annexation's aftermath is becoming an undeclared war of attrition
against the West.

Notes

1 Jim Acosta, "U.S., Other Powers Kick Russia Out of G8," *CNN*, March 24, 2015.
    http://www.cnn.com/2014/03/24/politics/obama-europe-trip/index.html.
2 Nikita Khrushchev used the phrase "Мы вас похороним!" in a speech addressing
    Western ambassadors on November 18, 1956.
3 Julianne Smith, "A Transatlantic Strategy for Russia," *Carnegie Foundation Task
    Force on U.S. Policy Toward Russia, Ukraine, and Eurasia Project*, August 29, 2016.
    http://carnegieendowment.org/2016/08/29/transatlantic-strategy-for-russia-
    pub-64416?mkt_tok=eyJpIjoiTTJJMk1tTTNObUV5WmpObSIsInQiOiJrUnQ-
    xd0JuaHp3OUhLQ3R3aG5ienJDcUpmMW5MZzZ6YWt6YzNVYU9LeHlTTVJX-
    bWs1RnI5R2ZPeWFxbGY3Znp4amR6MzIybFlnU1JJMmozWjhuV0xQN09YRn
    V6YTlMcDJSKzRHMnY2eW42WT0ifQ%3D%3D. "Europe and the United States
    deserve kudos for the series of measures they have taken together in response to
    Russia's aggression. Although those policies have not (yet) succeeded in signifi-
    cantly improving Russia's relations with its neighbors or the West, no one should
    conclude that the policies themselves should be abandoned. The transatlantic
    partners just need to ensure that they are doing everything they can to position
    themselves for long-term success. That means they should assess both their policy
    victories and policy failures over the last two years, reaffirm and message the tenets
    of their shared strategy, and make some adjustments in both substance and style."
4 Gopal Ratnam, "White House Unveils Call for 'Strategic Patience,'" *Foreign Policy*,
    February 5, 2015. http://foreignpolicy.com/2015/02/05/white-house-to-unveil-call-
    for-strategic-patience-russia-ukraine-syria-iraq-china-asia/.
5 Bruno Dallago and Steven Rosefielde, *Transformation and Crisis in Central Europe:
    Challenges and Prospects*, London: Routledge, 2016.

6 Barbara Taasch, "Russia Is Reviewing the 'Legality' of Baltic States' Independence," *Business Insider*, June 30, 2015. http://finance.yahoo.com/news/russia-reviewing-legality-baltic-states-200136322.html. "The Russian Prosecutor General's office began checking the legality of the recognition of the independence of the Baltics.

"Estonia, Latvia, and Lithuania were Soviet republics until the dissolution of the USSR back in 1991.

"The report comes one week after the transfer of Crimea to Ukraine in 1954 – back when Nikita Khrushchev was in power – was declared unconstitutional." "Lithuania's foreign minister Linas Linkevicius called the investigation an 'absurd provocation,' according to the BBC."

7 "'If Russia Plans to Attack Ukraine, It Will Do So in the Next Several Weeks,' Says Paul Goble." http://windowoneurasia2.blogspot.com/2016/08/if-russia-plans-to-attack-ukraine-it.html.

"Staunton, August 28, 2016 – It remains unclear whether Moscow intends to launch a full-scale military attack on Ukraine, Pavel Felgengauer says; but if it plans to, there are compelling reasons – deteriorating weather in the fall and the new round of the Russian military draft in October – to think that it will begin in the next several weeks.

"The Russian military analyst says that 'Russian forces have been brought to full military readiness and moved up to the borders of Ukraine.' And while this at one level at least is only 'saber rattling,' it is clear that it is possible that this will lead to a full-scale military conflict (apostrophe.com.ua/article/politics/2016-08-27/nastuplenie-na-ukrainu-doljno-nachatsya-v-blijayshie-neskolko-nedel/7021).

"Indeed, if such an expanded invasion doesn't begin, then it is far from understandable 'why all this is being organized because the forces that have been moved forward are very serious.' To be sure, Moscow has not called up the reserves, but it doesn't have to because 'even without them,' Moscow can assemble 'more than 100,000 men' for an attack.

"Russian generals are in command of the forces of the Donbass, the so-called first and second corps of the DNR and LNR. And all of these are subordinate to the Southern Military District. But the forces in the Donbass will not move independently in any 'principally new' direction without support from their Russian rear.

"Everything that is taking place now, Felgengauer says, 'is very dangerous, but whether there will be a war is something we shall have to wait and see. It won't be long. Various scenarios are possible,' but 'the main thing for Russia will be to achieve strategic and tactical surprise.'

"'And if it does not do that now, then it will be [too] late,' the analyst says: In October, the weather will change for the worse, and the fall draft into the Russian army will introduce problems for commanders, including the rotation out of soldiers who have served their time, that would make any attack difficult if not impossible."

8 The European Union's erstwhile former Soviet partners are Ukraine, Georgia, Moldova, Armenia, Azerbaijan, and Belarus. See Alistair Macdonald, "As Russia Growls, EU Goes Cool on Eastern Promises," *Yahoo News*, May 24, 2015. http://news.yahoo.com/russia-growls-eu-goes-cool-eastern-promises-151727068.html.

9 Neil MacFarquhar and Alison Smaleaug, "Russia Responds to Western Sanctions with Import Bans of Its Own," *New York Times*, August 7, 2014. http://www.nytimes.com/2014/08/08/world/europe/russia-sanctions.html. "Russia retaliated

on Thursday for Western sanctions against Moscow, announcing that it was banning imports of a wide range of food and agricultural products from Europe and the United States, among others." "After the United States, Russia is the biggest market for European agricultural exports, worth about 11.8 billion euros last year, or roughly $15.7 billion, according to Eurostat, the European Union's statistics agency. That is about 10 percent of European agricultural trade; the vast majority of that commerce stays within the 28-nation bloc." "The most noticeable American food import to Russia is chicken. But even there, Russia currently *accounts for just 7 percent of United States poultry export volume, compared with 40 percent* of the total in the mid-1990s, according to the National Chicken Council. But the council said the sanctions would not have much of an impact."

10 "Italy's Veneto Calls for End to Russia Sanction," *The Ghana News*, March 15, 2015. http://todayghananews.com/2015/03/15/italys-veneto-calls-for-end-to-russia-sanctions/. "The governor of Italy's northern province of Veneto says the region is suffering losses of up to 500 million euros amid EU sanctions on Russia and its tit-for-tat food embargo, calling for an end to the anti-Moscow bans.

"The Kremlin also has retaliated against American travel restrictions on key Russian officials." Charles Onians, "Russia Releases 89-Name EU Travel Blacklist," *AFP*, May 30, 2015. http://news.yahoo.com/russia-issues-blacklist-bars-eu-politicians-dutch-pm-164848974.html.

11 Arthur Neslen, "Europe's Dependency on Russian Gas May Be Cut Amid Energy Efficiency Focus," *Guardian*, September 8, 2014. http://www.theguardian.com/world/2014/sep/09/europe-dependency-russian-gas-energy-efficiency-eu. Colin Chilcoat, "Russian Gas: There Is No Alternative for Europe," *Yahoo Finance*, May 16, 2015. http://finance.yahoo.com/news/russian-gas-no-alternative-europe-215815154.html. "Securing supply is an even greater headache. The shale gas revolution in Europe has turned out to be anything but. The majors have pulled out of Poland and Ukraine – two of the more promising countries – though marginal hopes still remain in Denmark and the UK. US liquefied natural gas is still years away, and even then is unlikely to satisfy Europe's thirst. Cheniere Energy's Corpus Christi LNG is the only prospective terminal to have signed contracts with Europe. By 2018 at the earliest, the terminal will deliver about 7.3 billion cubic meters (bcm) of LNG annually – or approximately 1.7 percent of Europe's demand. Turkmen gas – via the southern corridor – is not expected until 2019. Turkmen officials believe deliveries could account for between 2 and 7 percent of Europe's annual demand. Russia's Turkish Stream pipeline is expected to be operational in 2016, though it is unclear whether or not infrastructure on the Greek side will be ready then. In the meantime, the EU and Sefcovic will broker an interim Russia-Ukraine gas deal to last until a Stockholm arbitration court rules on Gazprom and Naftogaz's debt dispute. A positive result there would, for a time, reduce the risk of any supply stoppage. Nearly 20 bcm of gas has already transited through Ukraine this year. Russian gas is here to stay. Not because the EU's Energy Union is still far from the solidarity it seeks, but because the alternatives don't make sense."

12 "Putin Signs Russian Law to Shut 'Undesirable' Organizations," Yahoo News, May 24, 2015. http://news.yahoo.com/putin-signs-russian-law-shut-undesirable-organizations-040632637.html, "President Vladimir Putin Signed a Bill into Law

Saturday Giving Prosecutors the Power to Declare Foreign and International Organizations 'Undesirable' in Russia and Shut Them Down."

13 Alexander Baunov, "Not Against Russia: Why the Eastern Partnership Makes Increasingly Less Sense," *Carnegie Moscow Center*, June 1, 2015. http://carnegie.ru/ eurasiaoutlook/?fa=60256&mkt_tok=3RkMMJWWfF9wsRojvK3AZKXonjHpfsX5 6OsvXqGg38431UFwdcjKPmjr1YYCRMV0aPyQAgobGp5I5FEIQ7XYTLB2t60M WA%3D%3D.

14 Ibid.

15 Stephen Blank, "Does Russo-Chinese Partnership Threaten America's Interests and Policies in Asia?" *Orbis*, Vol. 60, No. 1, 2016, http://www.fpri.org/article/2016/01/ does-russo-chinese-partnership-threaten-americas-interests-in-asia/.

16 Sandy Macintyre and Nataliya Vasilyeva, "Putin: Russian Pipeline Project to Help Greece Pay Its Debt," *AP*, June 20, 2015. http://news.yahoo.com/greece-signs-deal-russia-build-gas-pipeline-100934561–finance.html.

17 Raphael Minder, "Vote Fails to Settle Dispute on Secession by Catalonia," *New York Times*, September 28, 2015. http://www.nytimes.com/2015/09/29/world/europe/ election-fails-to-resolve-fight-over-catalonias-direction.html?_r=0.

18 Sylvia Poggioli, "As Migrants Stream in, Italy and the EU Are at Odds," NPR, June 15, 2015. http://www.npr.org/2015/06/15/414561558/steady-stream-of-migrants-heightens-tensions-between-italy-and-eu-partners?utm_medium=RSS&utm_campaign=world. "Europe Migrant Crisis Was to Be 'Expected': Putin," *AFP*, September 4, 2014. http://news.yahoo.com/europe-migrant-crisis-expected-putin-095320325.html. "Russian President Vladimir Putin on Friday called Europe's migrant crisis a predictable result of its policies in the Middle East and said he had personally warned of the consequences."

19 Somini Segupta, "Refugee Crisis in Europe Prompts Western Engagement in Syria," *New York Times*, September 30, 2015. http://www.nytimes.com/2015/10/01/world/ middleeast/europe-refugee-crisis-syria-civil-war.html?_r=0.

20 Mike Peacock,
   "The European Center-Left's Quandary," *Yahoo News*, May 24, 2015. http://news .yahoo.com/european-center-lefts-quandary-071004412--business.html. "In an age when austerity still holds sway, the center-left faces a choice of embracing painful structural reforms or trying to protect traditional supporters from the economic winds blowing across the world." "The rise of new parties across Europe has also shattered the calculation that the moderate left could take its traditional supporters for granted as they had nowhere else to go. Now they do – to Syriza, the National Front, UKIP and Podemos to name but a few."
   "'The political game has changed from a fundamental left/right contest over the role of the state in the economy to a question of how much and in what ways to protect the losers of globalization through the welfare state and limits on migration,' said Heather Grabbe, Director of the Open Society European Policy Institute in Brussels." Monika Scislowska, "Polish President Concedes Defeat after Exit Poll Released," *Yahoo News*, May 24, 2015. http://news.yahoo.com/poles-vote-cliff-hanger-presidential-election-runoff-062402489.html. "Polish President Bronislaw Komorowski conceded defeat in the presidential election Sunday after an exit poll showed him trailing Andrzej Duda, a previously little-known right-wing politician."

21 Michael Gordon, "Survey Points to Challenges NATO Faces over Russia," *New York Times*, June 10, 2015. http://www.nytimes.com/2015/06/10/world/europe/survey-points-to-challenges-nato-faces-over-russia.html?_r=0. "'At least half of Germans, French and Italians say their country should not use military force to defend a NATO ally if attacked by Russia,' the Pew Research Center said it found in its survey, which is based on interviews in 10 nations."

22 Richard Nixon, "Save the Peace Dividend," *New York Times*, November 19, 1992. http://www.nytimes.com/1992/11/19/opinion/save-the-peace-dividend.html. "EBRD warns post-Cold War 'peace dividend' at risk", *Reuters*, May 17, 2015. http://finance.yahoo.com/news/ebrd-warns-post-cold-war-165624611.html;_ylt=A0LEVikZclhVchYADj4nnIlQ;_ylu=X3oDMTByNXQ0NThjBGNvbG8DYmY xBHBvcwM1BHZ0aWQDBHNlYwNzcg--.

"The European Bank for Reconstruction and Development warned on Thursday that the crisis over Ukraine could erode some of the economic 'peace dividend' eastern Europe gained when the Cold War ended." "'The region is in the heavy shadow of the Ukraine/Russia crisis,' said EBRD Chief Economist Erik Berglof. 'Permanently higher military spending ... in response to the renewed geopolitical risks, could erode the peace dividend from the dissolution of the Soviet Union,' the EBRD said. The West has accused Russia of sending in troops and weapons to bolster separatist rebels in eastern Ukraine in more than five months of fighting that has killed over 3,000 people. A shaky ceasefire is now in place. Russia denies sending in troops. After months of conflict Ukraine's economy is now expected to shrink by 9 percent this year versus 7 percent forecast in May."

23 Steven Rosefielde and Quinn Mills, *Global Economic Turmoil and the Public Good*, Singapore: World Scientific Publishers, 2015.

24 "Hungary's Orban: Migrant Crisis Is German, not European Problem," *AFP*, September 3, 2015. http://news.yahoo.com/hungarys-orban-insists-migrant-crisis-german-not-european-090532730.html. "Hungarian Prime Minister Viktor Orban insisted Thursday the migrant crisis was a German problem, not a European one as he defended his government's handling of thousands of refugees flooding into his country.

"'The problem is not a European problem, the problem is a German problem,' Orban told a press conference with European Parliament President Martin Schulz in Brussels. 'Nobody wants to stay in Hungary, neither in Slovakia, nor Poland, nor Estonia. All want to go to Germany. Our job is just to register them.'"

25 John Browne, "Geopolitics Will Trump Economics in Greece," *Town Hall Finance*, June 18, 2015. http://finance.townhall.com/columnists/johnbrowne/2015/06/18/geopolitics-will-trump-economics-in-greece-n2013825. "Despite Greece's almost complete lack of financial integrity, neither NATO nor the EU can afford the political cost of a Greek exit from the EU.

"The unacceptable specter lurking behind the EU negotiators is that, if Greece is shown the door by the EU, Russia or even China might step in to provide financing to Greece in return for a strategic foothold in Western Europe and gateway to the Eastern Mediterranean. This is a possibility that Europe cannot abide. In short, international political ramifications will trump any economic or financial issues."

26 Nina Lamparski, "Hungary Halts Key EU Asylum Rule, Saying 'the Boat Is Full,'" Yahoo News, June 24, 2015. http://news.yahoo.com/hungary-suspends-key-eu-asylum-claim-rule-official-163612981.html.

27 "It is my firm conviction that in today's rapidly changing world, in a world witnessing truly dramatic demographic changes and an exceptionally high economic growth in some regions, Europe also has an immediate interest in promoting relations with Russia. No one calls in question the great value of Europe's relations with the United States. I am just of the opinion that Europe will reinforce its reputation of a strong and truly independent center of world politics soundly and for a long time if it succeeds in bringing together its own potential and that of Russia, including its human, territorial and natural resources and its economic, cultural and defense potential." President Putin's address to the Bundestag, September 25, 2001. http://archive.kremlin.ru/eng/speeches/2001/09/25/0001_type82912type82914_138535.shtml.

Cf. "I am deeply convinced: united Greater Europe from the Atlantic to the Urals, and in fact all the way to the Pacific Ocean, the existence of which will be based on universally recognized democratic principles, offers a unique chance for all the nations of the continent, including the Russian nation. Europeans can fully rely on Russia in the pursuit of this chance for a peaceful, prosperous and dignified future, as they could in the struggle against Nazism. We also believe that Russia's efforts to develop integration bonds with both the EU member states and the members of the Commonwealth of Independent States are a single, organic process which should lead to a considerable expansion of harmonious common spaces of security, democracy and business co-operation in this gigantic region." Vladimir Putin, "Lessons from the Defeat of Nazism: Mastering the Past to the Construction of a Secure Human Future." http://www.mid.ru/nspobeda.nsf/304a70a9f8af-4383c3256eda00378036/c3256eda00375761c3256fb0030159b?OpenDocument.

Putin's Greater Europe Plan has five points:

1. "A harmonised community of economies, from Lisbon to Vladivostok," which in future could perhaps transform into a free trade area or even pursue more advanced forms of economic integration. This community would be built in gradual steps that would include Russia's membership in the WTO, harmonization of legislation, customs procedures, and technological standards and elimination of bottlenecks in pan-European transport networks.
2. "A common industrial policy based on a synergy between the technological and resource potentials of the EU and Russia." This policy would be implemented through joint projects to support small and medium enterprises and, even more important, "a fresh wave of industrialization based on the establishment of strategic sectoral alliances in the shipbuilding, automobile, aviation, space, medical and pharmaceutical industries, nuclear energy and logistics."
3. "A common energy complex in Europe." The complex would comprise extended energy infrastructure and the Nord Stream and South Stream gas pipelines, and would be governed by the new regulations, including a new energy treaty proposed by Russia, which would balance the interests of suppliers, buyers, and final consumers of energy. Russian and European companies would share energy

assets, and cooperation would be developed at all stages (from exploration and extraction to delivery to end consumers). Cooperation would also extend to education and personnel training, creation of engineering centers, and implementation of energy efficiency and renewable energy projects.

4. Cooperation in science and education. It would include, among other measures, the implementation of joint research projects, especially for applications in high-technology industries based on a shared financing effort, as well as exchanges of researchers and students, traineeships, etc.

5. Elimination of barriers impeding human and business contacts. This objective would be achieved by abolishing visas for travelers between the European Union and Russia based on a clear plan and definite time schedule.

28 Robert Legvold, "A Melting Arctic in a Frozen Russia-West Relationship," *Valdai*, May 6, 2015. http://valdaiclub.com/russia_and_the_world/77220.html. On the Euro-Atlantic Security Initiative (EASI), see http://www.nti.org/about/projects/euro-atlantic-security-initiative-easi/. The Transatlantic Economic Council advances EU-US economic integration by bringing together governments, the business community, and consumers to work on areas where regulatory convergence and understanding can reap rewards on both sides of the Atlantic. Chaired by the EU Trade Commissioner and the US Deputy National Security Adviser for International Economic Affairs, the TEC provides a high-level forum to address complex areas like investment, financial markets, accounting standards, and secure trade, along with more technical issues.

Vladimir Putin, "Russia and Europe: From Assimilating the Lessons of the Crisis to a Higher Stage of Partnership," November 25, 2010. http://archive.premier.gov.ru/eng/events/news/13088/ Cf. Richard Sakwa. "The New Atlanticism," *Valdai Papers*, No. 17, May 2015. "This meant that the Atlantic system was increasingly unable to reflect critically on the geopolitical and power implications of its own actions, a type of geopolitical nihilism that in the end provoked the Ukraine crisis. From a defensive alliance established to resist the Soviet Union, the new Atlanticism is both more militant in advancing its interests and more culturally aggressive, setting itself up as a model of civilisational achievement. It is unable to accept geopolitical pluralism in Europe, and thus has become an increasingly monistic body. Although it is an 'empire' by invitation (although the invitation was not extended to Russia) and retains considerable internal divergence, the exclusion of the greatest power in Europe meant that it is unable to escape the constraints of its Second World War and Cold War origins, and instead perpetuates the monist logic of earlier years."

29 Mikhail Gorbachev, *Perestroika: New Thinking for Our Country and the World*, New York: Harper and Row, 1987. Cf. Eugene Rumer, "The German Question in Moscow's 'Common European Home': A Background to the Revolutions of 1989," *Rand*, 2009. http://www.rand.org/content/dam/rand/pubs/notes/2009/N3220.pdf.

30 Boris Yeltsin outlined his vision of Greater Europe during a Council of Europe summit in Strasbourg on October 10, 1997. He said on that occasion: "We are now poised to begin building together a new greater Europe without dividing lines; a Europe in which no single state will be able to impose its will on any other; a Europe in which large and small countries will be equal partners united by common democratic principles. This Greater Europe can now become a powerful community of

nations with a potential unequalled by any other region in the world and the ability to ensure its own security. It can draw on the experience of the cultural, national and historical legacies of all of Europe's peoples. The road to greater Europe is a long and hard one but it is in the interest of all Europeans to take it. Russia will also help to realize this goal." http://www.coe.int/aboutCoe/index.asp?page=nosInvites&l=ca&s p=yeltsin.

31 Cf. Gary J. Schmitt and Jeffrey Gedmin, "Why Georgia's Quest for Euro-Atlantic integration Matters More than Ever," *AEI*, August 28, 2015. http://www.aei. org/publication/why-georgias-quest-for-euro-atlantic-integration-matters-more-than-ever/?utm_source=paramount&utm_medium=email&utm_content=AEITODAY&utm_campaign=083115. Schmitt and Gedmin argue that Georgia should be admitted to NATO to unilaterally preempt a Russo-West condominium.

32 Wolfram Kaiser and Peter Starie, eds., *Transnational European Union: Towards a Common Political Space*, London: Routledge, 2009; Richard Baldwin and Charles Wyplosz, *The Economics of European Integration*, 4th ed., New York: McGraw Hill, 2012.

33 Russia became a member of the Council of Europe in February 1996, and the EU-Russia Partnership and Cooperation Agreement came into force in 1997.

34 The Eurozone officially called the euro area is an economic and monetary union (EMU) of 17 EU member states that have adopted the euro (€) as their common currency and sole legal tender. The Eurozone currently consists of Austria, Belgium, Cyprus, Estonia, Finland, France, Germany, Greece, Ireland, Italy, Luxembourg, Malta, the Netherlands, Portugal, Slovakia, Slovenia, and Spain. Other EU states (except for the United Kingdom and Denmark) are obliged to join once they meet the criteria to do so.

35 Russia signed the Founding Act in cooperation with NATO, establishing a new format of relations between Russia and the NATO Alliance (May 1997). The Russia–NATO council was created in 2002 for handling security issues and joint projects. Cooperation between Russia and NATO now develops in several main sectors: fighting terrorism, military cooperation, cooperation in Afghanistan (including transportation by Russia of nonmilitary International Security Assistance Force freight [see NATO logistics in the Afghan War] and fighting local drug production), industrial cooperation, non-proliferation, and others. On April 1, 2014, NATO unilaterally decided to suspend practical cooperation with the Russian Federation, in response to the Ukraine crisis.

36 The governing bodies of the European Union's supranational governance tier are the European Parliament, the Council of the European Union, the European Commission, the European Council, the European Central Bank, the Court of Justice of the European Union, and the European Court of Auditors.

37 Supranational bodies have exclusive competence over: 1) the "customs union," 2) competition policy, 3) Eurozone (EZ) monetary power, 4) a common fisheries policy, 5) a common commercial policy, 6) conclusion of certain international agreements. They also have the right to shared competence in 7) the internal market, 8) social policy for aspects defined in the treaty, 9) agriculture and fisheries, excluding the conservation of marine biological resources, 10) environment, 11) consumer protection, 12) transport, 13) trans-European networks, 14) energy, 15) the area of

freedom, security, and justice, 16) common safety concerns in public health aspects defined in the treaty, 17) research, development, technology, and space, 18) development, cooperation, and humanitarian aid, 19) coordination of economic and social policies, 20) common security and defense policies. Additionally, supranational bodies enjoy supporting competence in 21) protection and improvement of human health, 22) industry, 23) culture, 24) tourism, 25) education, youth sport, and vocational training, 26) civil protection (disaster prevention), and 27) administration.

38 Assaf Razin and Steven Rosefielde, "Currency and Financial Crises of the 1990s and 2000s," *CESifo Economic Studies*, Vol. 57, No. 3 (2011): 499–530; Rosefielde and Assaf Razin, "A Tale of a Politically-Failing Single-Currency Area," *Israel Economic Review*, Vol. 10, No. 1 (2012): 125–138; Rosefielde and Assaf Razin, "What Really Ails the Eurozone?: Faulty Supranational Architecture," *Contemporary Economics*, Vol. 6, No. 4, December (2012): 10–18; Steven Rosefielde and Assaf Razin, "PIIGS," in Steven Rosefielde, Masaaki Kuboniwa, and Satoshi Mizobata, eds., *Prevention and Crisis Management: Lessons for Asia from the 2008 Crisis*, Singapore: World Scientific Publishers, 2012; Steven Rosefielde and Ralph W. Pfouts, *Inclusive Economic Theory*, Singapore: World Scientific Publishers, 2014.

39 States do not have the right to secede.

40 Europeans contend that concentrated federal sovereignty at the "commanding heights" in American-type systems is antidemocratic because representatives are too far removed from the electorate. Putin has not discussed the issue. Their leaders have been trying to prove they are right by gradually constructing a well-functioning supranational regime since the late 1940s (European Union [EU]), culminating with the Maastricht Treaty (1993) and a partial monetary union in 2002 (Eurozone [EZ]). Daniel Gros and Niels Thygesen, *European Monetary Integration*, London: Longman, 1999. After the demise of the Bretton Woods system in 1971, most EEC members agreed to maintain stable foreign exchange rate parities. Fluctuations were restricted to no more than 2.25 percent (the European "currency snake"). The system was replaced by the European Monetary System (EMS), and the European Currency Unit (ECU) was defined. It fixed parities, set an ERM, extended European credit facilities, and created a European Monetary Cooperation Fund that allocated ECU to member central banks in exchange for gold and U.S. dollar deposits. The German Deutsche Mark was the de facto anchor because of its relative strength and the country's low-inflation policies. In the early 1990s, the EMS was strained by conflicting macroeconomic policies in Germany and England. Britain and Italy withdrew in 1992. Speculative attacks on the French franc led to widening the band to 15 percent in August 1993. European Commission, "A Blueprint for a Deep and Genuine EMU," Brussels, November 28, 2012. Available at http://ec.europa.eu/commission_2012-2014/president/news/archives/2012/11/pdf/blueprint_en.pdf   (EC 2012).

41 "Europe needs its own vision of the future. We propose to shape it together, through a Russia-EU partnership. It would be our joint bid for success and competitiveness in the modern world. ... To alter the situation, we should exploit the advantages and opportunities available to both Russia and the EU. This could be a truly organic synergy of two economies – a classic and established EU model, and Russia's developing and new economy, with growth factors that complement each other well. We have modern technology, natural resources and capital for investment. Above all,

we have unique human potential. Finally, Russia and the EU have ample cooperation experience. And I am happy to say that Germany, the engine of European integration, is setting an example of leadership in the area." Putin, "Russia and Europe."

42   There is no ideal supranational system, even a democratic one, because it is impossible for member states' ordinal preference functions (which of course don't exist)
to be combined in a fashion compatible with exhaustive optimization. The most
they can validly contend is that "satisficing" solutions for both transnational
authorities (EU government) and independent national members are attainable if
transnational bodies and national family members are individually and mutually
accommodating. A vast EU literature addresses the possibility of optimizing and
satisficing collaboration designed to forge ideal free trade areas, economic communities, and economic unions. Most of it treats members as independent sovereigns,
like individuals in the marketplace, who agree to abide by common rules overseen
by impartial transnational national supervisors. Transnational administrators don't
make the law for their own purposes. They merely abide by the democratic will of
members, enforcing freely negotiated contracts. This characterization of the contracting process, including oversight and judicial enforcement, stresses the Pareto
advantages of intra-member and inter-member liberalization, while simultaneously
assuming that participants behave like a harmonious family. Rosefielde and Pfouts,
Inclusive Economic Theory; Baldwin and Wyplosz, *The Economics of European
Integration*; Robert A. Mundell, "A Theory of Optimum Currency Areas," *American
Economic Review*, Vol. 51, September (1961): 657–664; Ronald I. McKinnon,
"Optimum Currency Areas," *American Economic Review*, Vol. 53, No. 4 (September
1963): 717–725; Peter B. Kenen, "Toward a Supranational Monetary System," in G.
Pontecorvo, R. P. Shay, and A. G. Hart, eds., *Issues in Banking and Monetary Analysis*,
New York: Holt, Reinhart, 1967; Paul De Grauwe, "The Greek Crisis and the Future
of the Eurozone." "The structural problem in the Eurozone is created by the fact
that the monetary union is not embedded in a political union." Eurointelligence,
November 3, 2010. See also Paul De Grauwe, *Economics of Monetary Union*,
New York: Oxford University Press, 2000.

43   Richard Sakwa has pointed out that EU members like the United Kingdom can
forge parallel supranational arrangements that allow them to situationally pick
and choose the rules they prefer. "The new Atlantic community is reinforced
by attempts to give greater institutional form to economic links. The idea of a
Transatlantic Trade and Investment Partnership (TTIP) has recently been given a
new impetus, above all by the British, as part of the continuing stratagem to dilute
the integrative impulse of the EU and to undermine lingering continentalist
(Euro-Gaullist) aspirations. TTIP is the successor to the Multilateral Agreement
on Investment (MAI), which was defeated after massive public mobilisation in
1998. On the face of it, consumers will only gain from the establishment of a free
trade area and the removal of complex regulatory and other restrictions on the
movement of goods and services. It would allow European companies to enter
the notoriously complex and restrictive US market. However, TTIP plans to go
far further to entrench the power of markets against states. The US and 14 EU
members plan to establish a separate judicial system exclusively for the use of
corporations, thus granting them a privileged legal status. Corporations will be
able to sue governments in these special tribunal made up of corporate lawyers.

National laws can be challenged and compensation sought if the laws are considered to threaten their 'future anticipated profits.' The 'investor-state dispute settlement' (ISDS) system could undermine the ability of governments to protect health systems from the depredations of the market, the environment, labour rights, and social welfare programmes." Sakwa, "The New Atlanticism." Brexit has cast TTIP into limbo.

44 Michael Gordon and Gardiner Harris, "Obama and Putin Play Diplomatic Poker over Syria," *New York Times*, September 28, 2015. http://www.nytimes.com/2015/ 09/29/world/middleeast/obama-and-putin-clash-at-un-over-syria-crisis.html.

45 Roberta Rampton, "Obama Urges Turkey's Erdogan to Withdraw Troops from Iraq: White House," *Reuters*, December 18, 2015. http://www.reuters.com/article/ us-mideast-crisis-obama-erdogan-idUSKBN0U12JK20151218.

6

War of Attrition

The Kremlin's undeclared Cold War of attrition against the West triggered by Crimea's annexation is spilling over into Asia, the Middle East, and elsewhere across the globe.[1] Authoritarians of all descriptions – despots, communists, socialists, nationalists, and religious fundamentalists – find common cause in supporting Putin's push back against the West's brand of globalization in their own backyards. Putin's machinations in Syria, purportedly in support of Assad's secular state, are endorsed by Shite Islamic Iran. Kim Jong-un is warming his relationship with Moscow,[2] and the Chinese have sent an aircraft carrier to join the Russian fleet off Syria.[3] Most nations outside America's and the European Union's sphere of influence have no intention of deploying combatants to Russia's Western periphery to stare down NATO's democratic legions, but they are prepared to cooperate with the Kremlin by forging alternative institutions (Shanghai Cooperation Organization, Asian Infrastructure Investment Bank, Eurasian Economic Community, etc.), increasing their influence in the United Nations (World Bank, IMF, ASEAN, APEC), providing other forms of mutual cooperation and support, and challenging the West militarily in regional theaters (China Sea, Syria, Iran, Iraq, Afghanistan).[4]

Authoritarian cooperation lessens Moscow's dependence on the West, giving Russia more degrees of freedom to harry opponents and weather punitive sanctions. Authoritarian confrontation in Asia, the Middle East, and Africa aids Russia by stretching America's and the European Union's resources to the breaking point.[5] It tilts the correlation of forces against the West, testing America's and the European Union's flexibility and pressuring them to rein in their ambitions.[6]

Then and Now

Putin's undeclared war of attrition differs fundamentally from Stalin's and Hitler's authoritarian programs and their strategies of dictatorial coalition building during the interwar years. Stalin, in the Marxist-Leninist tradition, sought the triumph of world communism; that is, global proletarian victory under Moscow's hegemony. He used the Third Communist International (Comintern) Lenin founded in 1919 to enlist the aid of communists everywhere.[7] Although the USSR was compelled to settle for Russia's traditional sphere of influence by the Third Reich and Imperial Japan until June 20, 1941, Stalin harbored greater ambitions. He aspired to become the overlord of a global communist empire.

Hitler wanted to rule the world too, but in the name of a different cause – the principle of Aryan supremacy, domination, and extermination of inferior races. He allied with authoritarians, but wasn't prepared to accept Mussolini, Franco, and Hirohito as fascist equals. Europe's dictators were expected to obey Germany's Fuhrer.

The Second World War consequently wasn't really a death dance between democracy and authoritarianism, or a trilateral struggle among the forces of capitalism, socialism, and fascism. It was a contest among three narrower ideologies: democratic market enterprise, Muscovite communism, and Aryan despotism.

Only one survived. Aryan despotism was pulverized and Soviet communism later succumbed to auto-euthanasia, but new forms of authoritarianism have arisen outside of Germany and in Russia that eschew world conquest. The age of ideology has given way to an amorphous joust among Western globalizing ideocrats,[8] nationalists, theocrats, and sundry non-state actors, not to a war pitting democracy against Russian fascism, as some have recently suggested.[9]

Putin doesn't see his sparring with the West as Stalin did in terms of an apocalyptic, kill-or-be-killed (*kto kovo*) struggle for global supremacy. He doesn't covet Asia, Africa, the Middle East, and Latin America, or perceive himself as the sword and shield of authoritarianism. He is an authoritarian, but this isn't his raison d'etre. He is Russia's symbolic national champion using traditional Muscovite methods to defend and gradually expand the realm whenever targets of opportunity emerge.

His post-Crimean annexation strategy therefore should not be framed as a clash of civilizations or a struggle between irreconcilable systems, but less menacingly as the Kremlin's refusal to knuckle under to Western hegemony even if Washington and the European Union are right about the superiority of democratic free enterprise/democratic socialism. Putin doesn't care if the West wants to be the West as long as the West grudgingly accepts coexistence and a partial restoration of the status quo ante. He approaches his dealings with other authoritarians like China in the same manner.[10]

His war of attrition against the West both within Europe and beyond therefore is most likely to be pragmatic and fluid without decisive or apocalyptic pitched battles. The West won't be destroyed, and the reach of Russian authoritarianism will be circumscribed. Things, however, won't be the same. The West's globalist ambitions are going to be thwarted, and its leaders are going to have an identity crisis that complicates the task of keeping the European Union and the Atlantic Alliance from coming unglued.[11] Cold War II also means reduced global stability and an increased risk of unintended large-scale armed conflict.

Polarization and Fragmentation

The challenge is obscured by drawing false analogies between the Cold War Soviet past and today's realities. The world was polarized before 1991, but the divisions were different. During the communist era when the East was largely "red," the West struggled against the USSR, China, North Korea, Vietnam, Cambodia, Laos, Cuba, and socialist movements in vulnerable Third World nations. The globe was divided into two ideological camps.

The planet today is fragmented, not polarized. The West as before is opposing the Kremlin and authoritarianism,[12] but the antagonisms across the globe are primarily national, religious, cultural, migratory, and historical rather than ideological. Russia and China are imperial rivals striving to expand their spheres of influence and territory. Japan, India, and Brazil are great powers with regional aspirations seeking their independent places in global governance, business, and finance. The postcolonial Third World (including the Middle East, Southeast Asia, Africa, Latin America, and non-state actors like IS) is a crazy quilt of conflicting agendas.

The Kremlin's and arguably China's undeclared cold wars of attrition against the West therefore should be conceived as pieces of the game,[13] not the great game itself.[14] The globe is fragmented with a multitude of powerful players trying to cope with defending and advancing their interests. Japan, India, Brazil, the postcolonial Third World, and non-state actors are affected both by the West's decline and the East's resurgence, which in the final analysis boils down to the diminishment of America's and the European Union's global reach. This means that the West, in failing to respond adequately to Putin's (and Beijing's) challenge, is likely to sustain further losses to America's and the European Union's national interests.

Strategic Vision

The broad erosion of the West's hegemony has not gone unnoticed, but few analysts have sorted out the phenomenon's positive and normative aspects. Leaders intuit the main trend and gauge whether it is tolerable without carefully investigating objective possibilities (positivist causal analytics), weighing the merit of alternatives (normative analytics), and analyzing their interplay.[15]

Many pluralist options exist within both the democratic and authoritarian frameworks.

Positive/Normative

On the positive side, Western analysts can estimate the microeconomic, macroeconomic, and financial costs of the new trajectory and feasible alternatives. Political, geopolitical, social, civic, and cultural possibilities can also be calibrated, providing policy makers with a complete mapping of prospective outcome streams. The possibilities are strictly objective (positive). They can be generated regardless of individual, social, and transcendent merit.

The right choice among alternatives, allowing for interactive effects and transfers, is a normative matter subject to democratic public debate.[16] If properly informed, the people can determine for themselves whether they want tranquility through strength in the West's relations with Russia, and the fragmented world of emerging great powers, developing nations, and non-state actors, or prefer to bear the price of inattentiveness.

Today's crop of Western leaders laud their professional competency, thoroughness, due diligence, transparency, democratic process, and wisdom, but don't comprehensively do any of these things.[17] The bureaucracies, institutes, and NGOs they oversee work according to jurisdictional protocols without a coherent overview. They aren't guided by a lucid strategic vision and are fixated on muddling through and spinning reality to please their political masters.

Betting on the West's Adaptive Failure

Putin knows this and is betting on the West's adaptive failure. He has counted on it from the beginning and has not been disappointed. The Kremlin, like Iran's mullahs, understands the twin virtues of obstinacy and patience when dealing with adversaries who lack genuine strategic vision, have short attention spans,[18] are corrupt, and feel convinced that they can manage electorates with pan-gloss concepts like "new-normal."

Putin also knows that he can play the game episodically, seizing Crimea and halting, grabbing Luhansk, and promising never again until he pounces on Mariupol without taking excessive risk because Western leaders cannot discipline themselves to preserve tranquility through strength.[19]

Notes

1   Michel Gordon and Eric Schmitt, "U.S. Fears Russia Ramping Up Support for Assad." *New York Times*, September 5, 2015. http://www.nytimes.com/2015/09/05/world/middleeast/russian-moves-in-syria-pose-concerns-for-us.html?_r=0.   "Stepped-up Russian military support for the Syrian government could pose a problem for the United States in several ways. If Mr. Putin's intention is to support not just the Syrian government but also Mr. Assad, that could undercut Mr. Kerry's contention that the Syrian president needs to leave power as part of any political solution to the conflict. And if Russian pilots carried out airstrikes, administration officials say, the choice of targets might further aggravate the growing chaos. Russian strikes on Islamic State militants could interfere with, or at least complicate, the air operations that the United States-led coalition is already conducting in Syria against the group. But if Russia targets rebel groups that are opposed to Mr. Assad, they might be striking some of the moderate Syrian fighters who have been trained by the C.I.A. and the Pentagon."

2   Damien Sharkov, "North Korea's Kim Jong Un Wants to Develop Ties with Russia's Vladimir Putin," *Newsweek*, August 15, 2016. http://www.newsweek.com/putin-north-korea-visit-friend-ally-support-kim-jong-un-china-xi-jinping-thaad-490357.

3   Dmitri Trenin, "Putin's Syria Gambit Aims at Something Bigger than Syria," Carnegie Moscow Center, October 13, 2015. http://carnegie.ru/2015/10/13/putin-s-syria-gambit-aims-at-something-bigger-than-syria/ij2j.

"It is also not irrelevant here that, further away from the Syrian battlefield, Russia-China strategic coordination is growing closer, with both countries' leaders sharing a common worldview, a similar resentful attitude toward the United States, and a range of security and other interests. Islamist extremists, in particular, threaten both Russia and China. The failure of U.S. military engagements in the Middle East and Afghanistan leaves it to Moscow and Beijing to try to sort out the resulting mess in the areas of their vital national interest. In both cases, Russia takes the lead in the security domain, due to its regional experience, military capabilities, and willingness to take risks, but China observes the Russian actions closely. It may be remembered that early in 2015, when the decision on intervention in Syria must have already been taken in Moscow, Chinese and Russian navies engaged in joint exercises in the eastern Mediterranean. Now a Chinese aircraft carrier has joined the Russian fleet off the coast of Syria. With Moscow no longer looking at Washington and NATO as security partners, but rather as sources of trouble, new Eurasian security arrangements are being created on the basis of bilateral and multilateral relations involving Russia, China, Iran, India, and Central Asian countries."

4 Alexander Gabuev, "The Silence of the Bear: Deciphering Russia's Showing at Shangri-La Dialogue," *Carnegie Moscow Center*, June 1, 2015. http://carnegie.ru/eurasiaoutlook/?fa=60263&mkt_tok=3RkMMJWWfF9wsRojvK3AZKXonjHpfsX56OsvXqGg3 8431UFwdcjKPmjr1YYCRMV0aPyQAgobGp5I5FEIQ7XYTLB2t60MWA%3D%3D.
   "Triumphant summits between Vladimir Putin and Xi Jinping may end with propaganda fanfare and dozens of signed documents, but multilateral meetings are where one can really measure the progress of Russia's "pivot to Asia." Moscow's showing at the recent Shangri-La Dialogue hosted by IISS and the government of Singapore, the prime platform of formal and informal exchanges between the region's top security policymakers, is an indicative example. The quantity of Russian participants and the quality of the official presentations speak volumes about Moscow's ability to navigate a complex security environment in a region, which the Kremlin wants to see as a new driver of economic growth to replace the hostile West."

5 Stephen Blank, "Does Russo-Chinese Partnership Threaten America's Interests and Policies in Asia?," *Orbis*, forthcoming, 2016.

6 Michael Auslin, "China Is Gambling Obama Doesn't have Will to Respond to Its Massive Land Grab," AEI, June 2, 2015. http://www.aei.org/publication/china-is-gambling-obama-doesnt-have-will-to-respond-to-its-massive-land-grab/?utm_source=paramount&utm_medium=email&utm_content=AEITODAY&utm_campaign=060215.
   "China has engaged in a massive reclamation project, dredging up sand and creating islands on shallow reefs. The US government estimates that up to 2,000 acres of new land has been built. On these 'fantasy' islands, China is building airstrips and ports, erecting barracks and establishing radar systems. Guns and fighter jets are next. Beijing is militarizing its new land and then claiming it as sovereign territory, demanding that other countries stay out of what was once international waters. For years, Washington ignored treaty allies like the Philippines, which called it 'a creeping invasion.' Instead, the Obama administration, like others before it, has bent over backward to try and improve relations with China, even inviting it to our biggest naval exercises. Much like the supposed Russian 'reset,' that goodwill has been spurned. Secretary of Defense Ash Carter last week publicly rebuked Beijing, demanding that it stop its reclamation activities and warning China that it is isolating itself in the eyes of the world community. More concretely, Carter and other officials have stated that the US will ignore China's claims and will fly military planes over the islands' airspace and will sail within the 12-mile limit claimed by China. Though no US ships have yet ventured inside that ring, the line has been drawn. For its part, Beijing is not backing down. Indeed, not only have Chinese officials criticized Washington's response, a state run newspaper, The Global Times, warned that a 'US-China war is inevitable,' if Washington tries to force China to halt its activities. Official Chinese military doctrine is also ominously changing to reflect the new reality, stating that Beijing's forces will no longer focus solely on territorial defense, but will project power far beyond its borders." Joschka Fischer, "Europe's Last Chance," Project Syndicate, August 29, 2016. https://www.project-syndicate.org/commentary/europe-needs-bold-leaders-by-joschka-fischer-2016-08?utm_source=Project+Syndicate+Newsletter&utm_campaign=3ad03442fc-Leonard_Playing_Defense_Europe_4_9_2016&utm_medium=email&utm_term=0_73bad5b7d8-3ad03442fc-93559677. "One thing is clear: Political and economic power is shifting

from the Atlantic to the Pacific, and away from Europe. This leaves many open questions: Which power (or powers) will shape this future world order? Will the transition be peaceful, and will the West survive it intact? What kind of new global-governance institutions will emerge? And what will become of the old Europe – and of transatlanticism – in a 'Pacific era?'"

7 The Communist International, or Comintern, was founded after the 1915 Zimmerwald and after the 1916 dissolution of the Second International. The Comintern had seven World Congresses between 1919 and 1935. Joseph Stalin officially dissolved it in 1943.

8 Ideocracies are systems governed by ideas and ideals, rather than purportedly complete, determinist ideologies. They are almost invariably dangerous to individual and social welfare insofar as people are beguiled, rather than dispassionately convinced. Ideocracy provides a benevolent face masking hidden agendas of disturbed and unscrupulous insiders that illuminate why bad government is more the rule than the exception. Cf. Martin Malia, *The Soviet Tragedy: A History of Socialism in Russia, 1917–1991*, New York: Free Press, 1994.

9 Robert Garver, "Putin Isn't Reviving the USSR, He's Creating a Fascist State," *Fiscal Times*, May 26, 2015. http://finance.yahoo.com/news/putin-isn-t-reviving-ussr-101500375.html.

10 Stephen Blank, "Does Russo-Chinese Partnership Threaten America's Interests and Policies in Asia?" *Orbis*, Vol. 60, No.1, 2016. http://www.fpri.org/article/2016/01/does-russo-chinese-partnership-threaten-americas-interests-in-asia/.

11 Leonid Bershidsky, "Obama Tries to Out-Putin Putin," *Bloomberg*, January 21, 2015. http://www.bloombergview.com/articles/2015-01-21/obama-s-bravado-on-russia-has-a-hollow-ring.

    "According to his State of the Union address, U.S. President Barack Obama has solved the Russia problem. His brief passage on the subject shows he's either blind to the dangers of the deteriorating relationship between Moscow and the West or merely too quick to take credit for a victory that is not even on the horizon. Here's what Obama had to say about the biggest threat to European stability since the fall of the Berlin wall 25 years ago: 'We're upholding the principle that bigger nations can't bully the small – by opposing Russian aggression, supporting Ukraine's democracy and reassuring our NATO allies. Last year, as we were doing the hard work of imposing sanctions along with our allies, some suggested that Mr. Putin's aggression was a masterful display of strategy and strength. Well, today, it is America that stands strong and united with our allies, while Russia is isolated, with its economy in tatters. That's how America leads – not with bluster, but with persistent, steady resolve.' Every one of these sentences is, to put it mildly, a stretch."

12 "Full Text: Obama's Address to the UN General Assembly," *ViralPH.com*, September 28, 2015. http://viralph.com/2015/09/29/full-text-obamas-address-at-the-un-general-assembly/.

13 Hiroshi Yamazoe, "The Prospects and Limits of the Russia-China Partnership," *RUFS Briefing* No. 32, December 3, 2015. http://nyhetsbrev.foi.se/v4_idrweb .asp?q=1D54-8DB-5BD2-53. "Russia's 'pivot to Asia' did not start in 2014. Since the Gorbachev era Russia has wanted to develop its Far East territory and integrate it into the regional economy. In the years 2012–2013 Russia intensified its efforts to strengthen its Armed Forces in the Eastern Military District. It also

upgraded ties with both China and Japan. In 2012, Russia's fleet joined the Sino-Russian Maritime Coordination-2012 joint naval exercise, the first in a series, and also the RIMPAC (the Rim of the Pacific) exercise around Hawaii hosted by the US Pacific Fleet. Russia also sent Nikolai Patrushev, the secretary of the Russian Security Council and one of President Vladimir Putin's closest associates, to start bilateral security talks with Japan. And in April 2013 the new Prime Minister Shinzo Abe visited Putin in Moscow to upgrade bilateral ties, resulting in a unique '2+2' foreign and defence ministers' meeting in Tokyo in November. The year 2013 also witnessed the Sino-Russian Maritime Coordination-2013 exercise, and, just after that, a much larger Russian military exercise in the form of a snap inspection of the Eastern Military District. Russia's approach to Asia is clear: nurture the partnership with China while enhancing Russia's own military presence and its ties with other countries in the region to avoid dependence on China." "Cases in Russian arms exports also show the not-so-smooth nature of Russia-China cooperation. For example, Vietnam continues to receive Kilo-class submarines and training support from Russia. At the same time, Russia has been eager to sell weapons to China, but negotiations on concrete terms have always been tough. In April 2015 Russia announced that it had signed a contract for the sale of the S-400 air defence system. Meanwhile, negotiations for the sale of the Su-35 fighter aircraft trade have a long history of disagreement over the number, price, and technical details of the aircraft. Early in 2014 the top political leaders intensified collaboration in all areas, but it took a long time of further bargaining before the signing of the contract was announced in November 2015.

"On a more symbolic level, Russia has been using the Moscow military parade in May to underline its political interpretation of history and to support its contemporary legitimacy, whereas China did the same in the Beijing parade in September 2015. By reciprocal visits they wanted to show their solidarity on historical issues. However, Putin did not endorse the way China blames contemporary Japan. Clearly, Russia does not want to be bound to China's position. Nor does it take sides concerning disputes in the East China Sea or the South China Sea, which involve China, Japan, the Philippines, and Vietnam.

14 Michael Klare, "The Next Cold War Is Here: China, Russia and the Ghosts of Dwight Eisenhower: As America Lurches from Crisis to Crisis, our Foreign Policy Elites Can't even Agree on our Principal Adversary," *TomDispatch*, July 2, 2015. http://www.salon.com/2015/07/02/the_next_cold_war_is_here_china_russia_and_the_ghosts_of_dwight_eisenhower_partner/. "For many in the Obama administration, however, it is not Russia but China that poses the greatest threat to American interests. They feel that its containment should take priority over other considerations. If the U.S. fails to enact a new trade pact with its Pacific allies, Obama declared in April, 'China, the 800-pound gorilla in Asia, will create its own set of rules,' further enriching Chinese companies and reducing U.S. access 'in the fastest-growing, most dynamic economic part of the world.'"

15 For example, the normative judgment that pressing a policy of democratic free enterprise takes precedence over a cooperative international environment diminishes the scope of free trade and may divert resources from the production of butter to increased military expenditures.

16 Abram Bergson, *Essays in Normative Economics*, Cambridge, MA: Harvard University Press, 1966.

17 Abram Bergson, "Social Choice and Welfare Economics under Representative Government," *Journal of Public Economics* 6, 3 (October), 1976, 171–190.

18 Attention deficit/hyperactivity disorder (ADHD).

19 "NATO Defense Spending to Fall this Year Despite Russia Tensions," Reuters, June 23, 2015. http://news.yahoo.com/nato-defense-spending-fall-despite-russia -tensions-190453734--business.html. "Military spending by NATO countries is set to fall again this year in real terms despite increased tensions with Russia and a pledge by alliance leaders last year to halt falls in defense budgets, NATO figures released on Monday showed. The figures showed defense spending by the 28 members of the alliance is set to fall by 1.5 percent in real terms this year after a 3.9 percent fall in 2014.

"The fall comes at a time when tension between NATO and Russia is running high over the Ukraine conflict. Russia has sharply raised its defense spending over the past decade.

"It also comes in spite of a pledge by NATO leaders, jolted by Russia's annexation of Ukraine's Crimea region, last September to stop cutting military spending and move toward the alliance's target of spending 2 percent of their economic output on defense within a decade.

"Garry Kasparov has puts the asymmetry in a nutshell. Contrasting Obama's and Putin's speeches to the UN General Assembly September 28, 2015, he writes 'Mr. Obama's speech was routine because he knows he will not act. Mr. Putin's speech was routine because he knows he will act anyway.'" Garry Kasparov, "Putin Takes a Victory Lap While Obama Watches," *Wall Street Journal*, September 29, 2015. https://video.search.yahoo.com/yhs/search;_ylt=A0LEVrgc2AtWGu4AIEInnIlQ;_ ylu=X3oDMTByMjB0aG5zBGNvbG8DYmYxBHBvcwMxBHZ0aWQDBHNlYw NzYw--?p=%E2%80%9CPutin+Takes+a+Victory+Lap%2C%E2%80%9D+Wall+Str eet+Journal&fr=yhs-mozilla-003&hspart=mozilla&hsimp=yhs-003.

PART III

CORRELATION OF FORCES

7

Putin's Economy

Introduction

Putin isn't a hostage of the *siloviki*'s vendetta. The grudge they harbor against those who stabbed the Kremlin in the back and then in the chest partly explains Putin's desire for revenge, but other aspects of the strategic balance also codetermine his actions. One of the most important of these factors – "correlation of forces" – is the state and potential of Russia's contemporary economic system. Western authorities double-talk on the subject without embarrassment. On one hand, they claim that Russia is a "normal middle-income developing economy" thanks to Jeffrey Sachs's and Yegor Gaidar's "shock therapy."[1] Some describe it as an economic miracle.[2] On the other hand, many of the same authorities contend that Russia's kleptocratic economy dooms Putin's ambitions.[3] Either way, the Kremlin is beholden to the West. It can enjoy the benefits of democratic free enterprise, or it can be disciplined by economic sanctions and firm military deterrence.[4] All these assertions are partial truths. Yes, Russia (like its Soviet predecessor) can be considered a "middle-income developing country,"[5] but it is "abnormal."[6] Yes, Russia can enhance its living standards by deeper economic integration with the West, but regional hegemony may bring higher returns. Yes, Russia's economy is warped by kleptocracy,[7] but its market system is better than Soviet administrative command planning. Yes, Western sanctions will inflict pain on the Kremlin, but they also will reciprocally harm the West,[8] and they won't deter Putin from pursuing the *siloviki*'s vendetta. Yes, living standards are important, but they can be finessed by Russia's nationalist remilitarization.[9]

A balanced assessment of the Kremlin's staying power cannot be deduced directly from neoclassical economic principles. A coherent picture can be constructed, but requires Sherlock Holmes's interpretative assistance.

The View from H Street

The World Bank Group (WBG) and many "shock therapy" advocates claimed that Russia's market transition had succeeded and predicted fair weather ahead until the Kremlin annexed Crimea.[10] The WBG was also often optimistic about Russia's burgeoning democracy.[11] Then suddenly on March 18, 2014, the notion that Russia had become a "normal democratizing and developing country" with above-average growth prospects collided with policy makers' wishful thinking about how to manage Putin's Crimean annexation challenge.[12] When partnership was Washington's and Brussels's primary theme, Russia was portrayed as a success story. Now, with the onset of Cold War II, Western leaders insist that that Russia's mixed-market economy cannot support Putin's geostrategic ambitions.[13] They are beating the tom-toms to spread the news, and have developed an acute case of selective amnesia about their previous ebullient assessments of the Kremlin's economic prospects.[14] "Shock therapy," hopes for improved Russian market competitiveness, and burgeoning democracy all have vanished from the headlines, replaced by the conviction that Russia's markets and embryonic democracy are on life support, plagued by endemic structural problems, plunging oil prices, and plummeting ruble foreign exchange rates.[15] The emerging consensus, as during the late Cold War I period, is that Russia's defective economy precludes Kremlin victory,[16] and makes transition inevitable.[17] Is today's orthodoxy any sounder than the WGB's upbeat pre-Crimean annexation assessment? Should Putin take the West's post-annexation consensus to heart, or advance confident that his brand of authoritarianism and Russia's weakly competitive market economy are good enough to support the restoration of Kremlin great power?

The Illusion of Western Economic Superiority

The claim that Putin's economy cannot support his hegemonic aspirations, preventing global repolarization, is overdrawn. Russia's blend of imperfectly competitive markets, rent-granting, and military-industrial oligopolistic competition almost certainly means that its consumers will be worse off than their brethren in the West, but this doesn't settle matters. The Kremlin's contest with the West is no longer about whether central planning can provide politically potent groups with the good life they covet (one of the primary forces behind Gorbachev and Yeltsin's anti-Soviet palace coup d'état); it turns on prospects for military-industrial mobilization and the economic discontent of ordinary citizens. Putin (touted by the Kremlin as "Person of the Year")[18] can prevail if Russia's imperfectly competitive market and state command over resources allow the Kremlin to maintain superior conventional combat forces in pertinent theaters of military operation (TVD),[19] while providing enough candy to placate his loyal supporters and the common man.[20] This contest isn't just about comparative international living standards and economic growth.[21] In Putin's view, it is about national identity and military power.[22] The West could continue to provide better-quality lives for its people, but still fail to parry Russian patriotism and Moscow's warfighting capabilities.[23]

Most analysts today, as during Cold War I, gloss the distinction between quality of life on one hand, and nationalism and military might on the other, in drawing large conclusions about the inferiority of Russia's economic system.[24] They contend that kleptocracy and low oil prices doom Russia's hegemonic aspirations.[25] It is important therefore to grasp why this litmus test is erroneous at a high theoretical level.[26] Putin may fail, but disparities in Russia and the West's commercial competitiveness need not be decisive.[27]

High Economic Theory

The presumption that the superiority of Western economic systems necessarily precludes the success of Putin's master framework is misguided because it conflates ideal markets and "doing-the-job-right" government with reality.[28] It is true that perfect democratic free enterprise guided by popular sovereignty and Adam Smith's deft "invisible hand" is superior to imperfect authoritarian market systems in all respects, including military-industrial efficiency, judged from the consumer's (and the people's) point of view (democratic Pareto optimality),[29] but neither Western democracy nor free enterprise are perfect. Western markets and state governance, like their Russian counterparts, are imperfect. Russia's markets and state governance may be more imperfect than the West's, but this is an empirical matter where specific sector asymmetries may be decisive, not an issue that can be adjudicated solely on the basis of rational actor theory.[30] Apples must be compared with apples. Apples (ideal) and oranges (real) should not be mixed.[31]

Many analysts, who acknowledge the need for common standards, try to salvage the situation by contending that neoclassical economic theory provides guidance about both ideal and real Western systems. They claim the West's economies are almost perfect, classifying them as "second best"[32] and hence inherently superior to Russia's "second worst" markets.[33] Their judgment, founded on Herbert Simon's "realist" concepts of "bounded rationality" and "satisficing," is appealing,[34] but also deceptive because it exaggerates Western economic efficiency.

The "bounded rationality" nuance doesn't save the day because it still presumes that rational actors abide by Enlightenment principles of honesty, fairness, free market access, equal opportunity, and free choice. Monopoly, oligopoly, corporate miss-governance, state miss-regulation, miss-taxation, and miss-mandating, authoritarian executive orders, power-seeking, coercion, corruption, and incompetence warp the West's private sector and impair its government programs more than Herbert Simon's "satisficing" (limited information, analytic indeterminism, incomplete preference formation, and real-time computational feasibilities) allows.[35] Western economies aren't Simon's "second best." They are more accurately described as "second worst" in the same broad sense as "second best" because their inefficiencies go far beyond competitive "bounded rationality" and "satisficing." Western economies underperform both their "first best" (ideal) and "second best" potentials,[36] and are financially unstable[37] and unjust to boot (see Appendix 3.1).[38] Consumers and the people (*demos*) aren't in command because their sovereignty is co-opted by private and government insider power- and wealth-seeking.[39] The blithe presumption that Western economic systems are fundamentally sound and virtuous is wishful thinking cultivated by government and private business.

True Lies: Prism of Deceptive Statistics

The comparison of the West's and Russia's "second worst" economies is fraught with difficulties. It is more necromancy than science because data often miss-measure value added;[40] Russian defense statistics are untrustworthy; and civilian data are frequently distorted by "hidden inflation," "sweetheart deals," and value imputed to unobserved activities ("second economy").[41] The term *hidden inflation* means that statisticians erroneously impute price increases to value added (GDP). An old Soviet joke illustrates the point. A comrade inquires, "What is the difference between one-star and five-star cognac?" The "red director" replies, "The number of stars on the label!" The distiller in this anecdote stopped manufacturing one-star cognac. He is now selling the same beverage in a five-star bottle at a much higher price. The ruse makes it appear as if consumers are buying more valuable cognac (and hence adding more value to GDP), when they are really being overcharged. There are supposed to be safeguards against price gouging, but anyone acquainted with the pricing of medical and educational (dis)services in America can readily appreciate that rising prices often greatly overstate value added, and by extension provide a misleading impression of national prosperity.

"Sweetheart" deals refer to opaque transactions that unduly favor insiders; a concept that can be broadened to include all transactions distorted by economic and political power. For example, Putin often awards state contracts to oligarchs on favorable terms that allow recipients to overbill the government (Sochi Olympic fiasco).[42] Official contracts make it appear as if payments are for services rendered and therefore count as value added in GDP, when they are really "payoffs" (under-the-table gifts that should be excluded from the gross domestic product). The phenomenon, which is widespread, can be viewed as a disguised form of Muscovite rent-granting.[43] It is compounded by the market power oligarchs, monopolists, and oligopolists wield in Russia's private sector.[44] The economies of Russia and the West are "second worst," not "second best," precisely because both are warped by monopoly, oligopoly, corporate mis-governance, state mis-regulation, mis-taxation, and mis-mandating, abusive executive orders, power-seeking, corruption, and incompetence, which mostly overstate reported GDP.[45]

Russia's GDP has another defect largely ignored by those who imagine that the viability of Putin's great power restoration campaign is easily deduced from standard measures of economic performance and potential. Twenty-three percent of Russia's official GDP is based on no information whatsoever![46] Roskomstat (the Russian Statistical Agency) doesn't deny it.[47] Its statisticians merely explain that they suspect that nearly a quarter of Russia's value-adding activity conducted in the "second economy" goes unreported, and have decided that it is better to guess the figure than ignore it. Perhaps they are right. Some account should be taken of the second economy,[48] but this doesn't alter the fact that both the size and growth of Russia's published GDP could be extraordinarily misleading.[49]

Many strategies have been devised to cope with the biases infecting official indicators of comparative Russian and Western economic performance. During the Cold War, Abram Bergson and the CIA audited, adjusted, and recomputed Soviet gross national product (GNP) series.[50] Other analysts fell back on anecdotes like "figures don't lie; but liars figure." This is a variant of *caveat emptor*. Alec Nove invoked a rule of thumb called the "law of equal cheating" to suggest that although statistics were corrupt, one can still draw inferences about comparative size and trends.[51] Andrei Shleifer and Daniel Treisman used the term "normal" to justify their claim that Russia's economic performance is as "transparent" as most "middle-income developing countries."[52] And of course, if all else fails, experts can simply ignore the

Table 7.1 *Comparative national income growth, 1961–1986*
(average annual growth: percent)

	USSR	USA
1961–1986	5.5	3.1
1971–1975	4.3	3.4
1981–1985	3.6	2.5
1986	4.1	2.5

Source: *Narodnoe khoziaistvo SSSR za 70 Let*, Finansy i Statistika, Moscow, 1987, p. 654.

problem and carry on as if statistics are reliable and prove that "the USSR was one of the most successful developing economies of the 20th century."[53]

Soviet precedent, however, is sobering. Anyone who accepted official *Goskomstat* statistics at face value (like the World Bank Group does Russian numbers today) might have wagered on communism's economic and military worldwide triumph.[54] Official Soviet national income growth outpaced the West throughout the postwar period, including the fatal 1980s, as did its weapons production (U.S. Defense Intelligence Agency weapons counts).[55] Table 7.1 provides *Goskomstat*'s perception of comparative Soviet and American national income growth.

CIA comparisons based on its adjustment of Soviet data reduced the Soviet growth advantage, but still showed the USSR expanding faster than the West (Table 7.2).[56]

Soviet industrial growth was impressive, especially in chemicals and machine building (Table 7.3).

Public services flourished (Table 7.4).[57]

Gertrude Schroeder's (CIA) consumption estimates indicated rapidly rising Soviet living standards (Table 7.5).[58]

And Soviet per capita consumption surged ahead at a pace equal to or greater than many Western market economies (Table 7.6).[59]

The USSR ostensibly was catching up with, and perhaps was destined to overtake the West on both official and CIA versions of the facts,[60] just as Nikita Khrushchev boasted in his infamous "We shall bury you!" speech.[61] Moreover, the CIA finessed the Soviet military threat by juxtaposing time series indicating high defense burdens (cost) with flat weapons production.[62] There was a military danger, but the Agency's Soviet weapons procurement series suggested that the peril was neither imminent nor unmanageable.[63]

Bergson, Nove, Schroeder, and the CIA had firsthand experience in the Soviet Union at the highest levels, and had other good reasons for being

Table 7.2 *Comparative Soviet and Western GNP growth*

	1951–1955[a]	1956–1960	1961–1965	1966–1970	1971–1975	1976–1979	1951–1979[a]
Total OECD	NA	NA	5.2	4.8	3.1	4.0	NA
Of which							
Canada	5.2	4.0	5.7	4.8	5_0	3.7	4.8
United States	4.2	2.3	4.6	3.1	2.3	4.4	3.4
Japan	7.2	8.6	10.0	12.2	5.0	5.9	8.3
Australia	3.8	4.0	4.8	6.0	3.5	2.4	4.2
New Zealand	3.8	4.0	4.9	2.7	4.0	0.3	3.3
Finland	5.0	4.1	4.8	4.8	3.9	2.5	4.2
France	3.7	5.0	5.8	5.4	4.0	3.7	4.6
West Germany	9.2	6.5	5.0	4.4	2.1	4.0	5.1
Italy	5.6	5.5	5.2	6.2	2.4	3.8	4.8
Netherlands	5.9	4.0	4.8	5.5	3.2	3.1	4.4
Norway	3.8	3.3	4.8	3.7	4.6	4.2	4.1
Spain	5.2	3.2	8.5	6.2	5.5	2.5	5.3
Sweden	3.4	3.4	5.2	3.9	2.7	1.1	3.4
Switzerland	4.9	4.3	5.2	4.2	0.8	0.9	3.5
Turkey	8.1	4.6	4.8	6.6	7.5	4.1	6.0
United Kingdom	3.9	2.6	3.1	2.5	2.0	2.4	2.7
USSR	5.5	5.9	5.0	5.2	3.7	3.0	4.8

[a] Data in column 1 for Japan and the United Kingdom are for 1953–1955; for Finland, France, West Germany, Italy, and the Netherlands – 1952–1955; and for New Zealand and Spain – 1955 only. The corresponding data in column 7 are for 1953–1979, 1952–1979, and 1955–1979, respectively. NA = not available.

Sources: OECD data are from *National Accounts of OECD Countries*, OECD, Paris, 1981, except for the value for total OECD for 1961–1965. The latter value is from the 1980 edition of the same publication. USSR data are from table A.5.

chary, but misread the undeniable reality in plain sight,[64] ultimately revealed by the USSR's self-destruction.

Through a Glass Darkly: Soviet Reality

What precisely was the reality that they misread? Can anything useful be deduced about the Soviet experience for gauging Russia's contemporary economic prospects through the fog of "true-lie" statistics? The situation is challenging, but not hopeless.[65] The Soviet communist experiment provides many useful, albeit imprecise lessons. The USSR's criminalization of private property, markets, and entrepreneurship, together with the Kremlin's military priorities, made the Soviet Union an impoverished superpower.[66]

Table 7.3 *Soviet industrial growth*

	1951–1960	1961–1970	1971–1980	1981–1987	1951–1987
Total industry					
CIA[a]	8.6	6.3	4.0	2.2	5.5
Soviet[b]	1 1:7	8.6	5.9	3.9	7.8
Ferrous metals					
CIA[a]	9.5	6.4	2.5	1.3	5.2
Soviet[b]	10.4	6.8	3.5	1.9[c]	6.3[c]
Fuels					
CIA[a]	9.3	6.0	4.2	1.4	5.5
Soviet[b]	9.3	6.2	4.4	1.6	5.6
Electric power					
CIA[a]	12.3	9.7	5.8	3.3	8.1
Soviet[b]	13.7	10.6	6.1	3.7	8.9
Machinery					
CIA[a]	7.4	6.6	5.1	2.4	5.6
Soviet[b]	15.4	12.1	9.9	6.3	11.2
Chemicals					
CIA[a]	10.7	10.0	5.6	3.8	7.8
Soviet[b]	14.7	13.3	8.1	5.0	10.6
Wood, pulp, and paper					
CIA[a]	6.4	2.7	1.0	2.7	3.2
Soviet[b]	8.0	5.3	3.3	3.6	5.2
Construction materials					
CIA[a]	15.7	5.9	3.1	2.3	7.0
Soviet[b]	18.4	8.6	4.5	3.4	9.0
Light industry					
CIA[a]	8.0	4.5	2.5	1.6	4.3
Soviet[b]	9.6	5.5	4.0	1.5	5.4
Food industry					
CIA[a]	9.1	6.4	2.7	1.1	5.1
Soviet[b]	8.9	6.6	3.4	3.8	5.8

[a] Growth of total industry is calculated from indexes of branch growth, weighted by value added at 1982 factor cost. Branch growth is calculated from indexes of gross output by sub-branch, weighted by value added in 1982 producers' prices (established prices, excluding turnover taxes and subsidies).

[b] Growth of total industry and its branches is calculated from values of gross output in comparable producers' prices (established prices, excluding turnover taxes and subsidies) of a series of linked base years (1952, 1955, 1967, 1975, and 1982).

[c] End year is 1984.

Table 7.4 *Soviet public sector growth*

	1951–1960	1961–1970	1971–1980	1981–1984
Housing				
CIA[a]	4.0	3.5	2.5	2.5
Prell[b]	7.7	5.6	5.2	4.9
Education				
CIA[a]	2.8	4.8	2.4	0.9
Prell[b]	4.1	5.5	3.8	2.5
Health				
CIA[a]	4.5	3.7	2.0	1.6
Prell[b]	5.9	4.7	4.0	3.6
Science				
CIA[a]	10.2	7.7	4.6	1.8
Prell[b]	7.7	6.9	4.6	2.2
Government administration				
CIA[a]	−4.2	3.5	3.5	1.5
Prell[b]	−2.1	4.3	3.9	1.7

[a] Estimates cited by Prell, based on earlier data than rest of estimates in this paper.

[b] See Mark Prell, *The Role of the Service Sector in Soviet GNP and Productivity Estimates* (PhD dissertation, Massachusetts Institute of Technology, 1987), pp. 218–224, 231–232.

Command communism was a Cold War I economy that provided its subjects with no-frills consumption and military might. It was able to produce things and grow (even cancer grows and metastasizes), some Western predictions to the contrary notwithstanding,[67] but the deliberate separation of consumer demand from supply assured that the system did not provide people with the goods they wanted (it was Pareto inefficient). Soviet designers neither knew nor cared about the product characteristics consumers preferred (quality). The micro assortments of the 27 million odd products Red directors manufactured were haphazardly determined by plans, bonus incentives, and party intervention, and then rationed at the wholesale and retail levels with little regard for consumer demand.

These deficiencies were compounded by what Igor Birman called the "economy of shortage";[68] a pernicious consequence of the Kremlin's prioritization of the military-industrial complex (Shlykov's "structural militarization").[69] The economy of shortage manifested itself most conspicuously in poorly stocked retail stores, shoddy merchandise (goods with inferior characteristics), and endless queues. Inventories were meager, shelves sometimes bare, and lines interminable for anything of value. Few starved

Table 7.5 *CIA (Schroeder) indexes of consumption in the USSR*

Indexes (1950 = 100)			Average Annual Rates of Growth (Percent)		
	Soviet Index of Real Incomes per Capita [a]	CIA Index of Real Per Capita Consumption [b]		Soviet Index	CIA Index
1950	100	100			
1955	142	125	1951–1955	7.3	4.5
1958	173	143	1956–1960	5.6	4.0
1960	187	151	1961–1965	3.6	2.4
1964	209	163	1966–1970	5.9	5.1
1965	223	171	1971–1975	4.4	2.9
1966	236	179	1976–1980	3.4	2.2
1967	252	189			
1968	268	200	1951–1960	6.5	4.2
1969	281	210	1961–1970	4.7	3.8
1970	297	219	1971–1980	3.9	2.5
1971	310	226			
1972	323	229	1951–1980	5.0	3.5
1973	339	236			
1974	352	244			
1975	368	252			
1976	384	257			
1977	397	263			
1978	408	269			
1979	419	276			
1980	435	282			

[a] The index was put together from indexes for various periods given in *Narkhoz* 1965, p. 593; *Narkhoz* 1967, p. 674; *Narkhoz* 1970, p. 537; *Narkhoz* 1975, p. 567; and *Narkhoz* 1980, p. 380.
[b] Table A-2. Growth rates were calculated from unrounded data.

because necessities were sold in factory canteens, and the privileged lived better, sometimes opulently on the state's tab, supplemented by back-channel (*kanaly*) access to superior goods and facilities purchased at bargain prices.[70] The consumer cornucopia implied by official Soviet and Schroeder's indices was a mirage. Westerners didn't flock to the East for *la dolce vita*.

Public goods like housing, health care, education, suburban transportation, domestic airports, telecommunications, and recreational facilities

Table 7.6 *Soviet and Western per capita consumption growth*

	1951–1955	1956–1960	1961–1965	1966–1970	1971–1975	1976–1979	1951–1979
Total OECD	NA	NA	3.7	3.7	2.8	3.1	NA
Of which							
Canada	2.5	2.1	2.6	2.7	5.2	2.4	2.9
United States	1.5	1.0	2.8	2.7	2.0	3.4	2.2
Japan	7.0	6.8	7.9	8.6	4.8	3.9	6.6
Australia	0.4	0.9	2.5	2.9	2.5	1.1	1.7
New Zealand	NA	NA	1.5	0	1.2	0.1	0.7
Finland	3.7	2.0	5.0	4.1	3.6	1.5	3.4
France	3.7	3.2	4.5	4.0	4.1	3.6	3.9
West Germany	8.1	5.5	4.1	4.0	2.6	3.7	4.6
Italy	3.9	4.1	5.3	6.1	1.8	2.6	4.0
Netherlands	3.4	2.3	4.9	4.9	2.3	3.3	3.5
Norway	1.8	2.2	2.6	2.9	3.2	1.9	2.5
Spain	4.6	1.5	7.3	4.8	4.8	1.6	4.1
Sweden	1.8	1.8	3.6	2.3	2.3	0.9	2.2
Switzerland	1.4	2.3	3.1	3.0	1.4	2.1	2.2
Turkey	5.4	1.9	1.8	3.0	4.5	1.7	3.1
United Kingdom	3.9	2.2	2.0	1.6	2.0	2.4	2.2
USSR	**3.1**	**3.8**	**2.1**	**4.3**	**2.6**	**1.7**	**3.0**

Data in column 1 for Japan and the United Kingdom are for 1953–1955; for Finland, France, West Germany, Italy, and the Netherlands – 1952–1955; and for Spain – 1955 only. The corresponding data in column 7 are for 1953–1979, 1952–1979, and 1955–1979, respectively. The value in column 7 for New Zealand is for 1961–1979.

NA= not available.

Sources: See sources to table 1 for the OECD consumption data. The USSR consumption data are from table A-9. The population data for all countries are from *World Population 1979*, U.S. Bureau of the Census, Government Printing Office, Washington, DC, 1980, and *Demographic Estimates for Countries With a Population of 10 Million or More: 1981*, U.S. Bureau of the Census, Government Printing Office, Washington, DC, 1981, and *World Population 1977*, U.S. Bureau of the Census, Government Printing Office, Washington, DC, 1978.

were primitive and poorly maintained, but adequate for many purposes (Table 7.4).[71]

Life for the vast majority was straitjacketed, Spartan, and gray, despite the existence of a parallel "second economy."[72] Few had hope for significantly brighter futures, and many became "inner emigres."[73] Most were resigned to their fate, solaced by job security, a barebones social safety net, and price stability. Official statistics and Schroeder's consumer goods growth indices told a rosier story, but as Mikhail Gorbachev, Abel Aganbegyan, and Girsh Khanin contended, the reality for households was stagnation (*zastoi*).[74]

A concise summary impression of this mixed performance can be visual-
ized with the aid of CIA Figure 7.1, which misleadingly purports to show
rapid persistent Soviet economic progress in industry, agriculture, and
GNP in the period 1950–1987. The steep positive slopes reflect the combined effects of physical output and hidden inflation. The true slopes as
Russians experienced them purged of hidden inflation were much lower.
The people received fewer and shoddier goods than Figure 7.1 indicates,[75]
and the dearth was compounded by the command economy's failure to provide people with the things they wanted. This was the reality of the USSR's
economy of shortage (a plan-constrained incentive and rationing-driven
system with stringent financial controls)[76] behind the façade of official
and CIA statistics. Soviet men and women understood in accordance with
Orwellian doublethink that rapid official economic growth was *zastoi* (stagnation), and that overtaking the West meant remaining forever backward.[77]

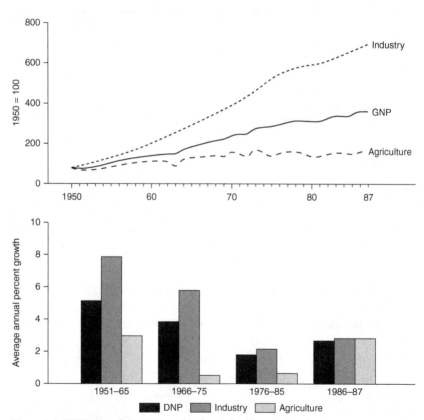

Figure 7.1 USSR: Trends in GNP and industrial and agricultural output, 1950–1987.

There was more to the Soviet experience, however, than the economy of shortage. Russians were acutely aware that the USSR was structurally militarized. Uniformed militia (MVD), secret police (KGB), and soldiers were omnipresent. Most people knew employees of the military-industrial complex (VPK), the media featured martial themes, and everyone was familiar with annual May Day arms parades in Red Square. The CIA and Vitaly Shlykov estimated that the USSR had 6 million men in arms (the Soviets acknowledged only 1 million), and Igor Birman estimated that there were more than 10 million military-industrial workers.[78] Satellite photo intelligence and other "national technical means" revealed that the Soviet arsenal was at least twice as large as America's. It included 52,000 nuclear weapons.[79] This made the USSR a military superpower, a fact widely acknowledged both in the East and the West, even though few people were fully acquainted with the facts. Most Russians were proud of the Soviet Union's military might and accepted the sacrifice entailed in their living standards, estimated by Vitaly Shlykov and the Office of the American Secretary of Defense to account for between a quarter and a third of Soviet value added.[80] They recognized, as Charles Wolf Jr. and Henry Rowen aptly put it, that the USSR was an "impoverished superpower,"[81] but were prepared to soldier forward. The Soviet economy worked in precisely this sense. It provided just enough material sustenance and nationalist esteem to plod along without fomenting a counterrevolution from below. The system was invulnerable to organized non-party opposition and external military threats, and would still be with us today if Gorbachev's liberals had not outmaneuvered his power services (counterrevolution from above).

Post-Soviet Reality

Russian reality changed in some important fundamentals glimpsed through a glass darkly after the Soviet Union dissolved. During the years of Boris Yeltsin's *katakhod* (catastrophic failed transition) (1992–2000) (see Figure 7.2), GDP, living standards, and military power plummeted, followed by a full economic recovery under Vladimir Putin (2000–2008), and modest growth after the 2008 financial crisis from 2010 to 2014. Russian living standards, military might, and national self-confidence crashed throughout the 1990s, but recovered after Putin's restoration of the power vertical. This description is consonant with Russian and Western perceptions, as well as with Angus Maddison's (OECD) statistics (Figure 7.2). It is also consistent with WGB series displaying more spectacular performance after 2005–2008 (18.9 percent per annum),[82] purged of an undisclosed and

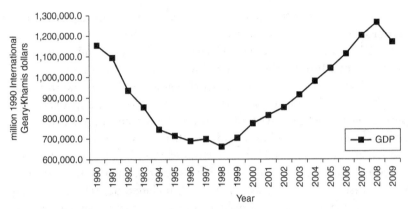

Figure 7.2 Russian GDP decline and recovery, 1990–2009.
Source: Angus Maddison, *The World Economy: Historical Statistics*, OECD, 2003, pp. 558–563, 566. http://www.ggdc.net/maddison/Historical_Statistics/horizontal-file_03-2009xls (last updated: March 2009).

misleading adjustment for the ruble appreciation caused by the post-9/11 petroleum price bubble.

The consensus reflecting WBG data is first that the Russian people today enjoy a higher living standard than they did a quarter century ago (similar GDP, lower population, fewer weapons), even though OECD statistics show scant improvement from 1990 to 2009, and CIA series indicate a sharp decline.[83] Second, the Kremlin is making progress in restoring its military superpower. It has the world's largest nuclear arsenal. Scuttling administrative command planning, restoring private ownership of the means of production, and decriminalizing markets seem to have helped post-recovery Russia to outperform the Soviet Union by providing the nation with substantially more butter without relinquishing military superpower.[84]

This perception is confirmed by congested urban highways, lavish home renovations, abundant luxuries, mushrooming consumer goods, unrestricted foreign travel, and the proliferation of services compared with the Soviet standard. The WBG classifies contemporary Russia as high income (upgraded from medium income: non-OECD country), sporting a $2 trillion economy, with a $14,200 per capita income.[85] Demand today governs consumer supply, not vice versa; the Soviet and Yeltsin era economies of shortage are faded memories in most urban centers, and citizens enjoy greater personal freedom.

These positives are marred by extreme income and wealth disparities among individuals and regions that accompanied Russia's anticompetitive marketization. Oligarchs and kleptocrats have captured the lion's share of the spoils at everyone else's expense, and city lights conceal the plight of those left behind outside of Moscow and a few other important metropolises. WBG Gini coefficients confirm the perception.[86]

Oligarchs and kleptocrats are also viewed negatively because they impair market competition. Until March 18, 2014, the WBG was broadly optimistic about Russia's long-term growth and catch-up potential,[87] but predicted moderate progress after 2010 because of the restraining effects of anti-competitiveness.

Nonetheless, the consensus net assessment despite these blemishes was that post-Soviet Russia had been transformed into a "normal" middle- to high-income developing country capable of groping its way toward OECD standards of prosperity, with or without high petroleum prices, but that it was susceptible to the "middle-income trap."[88] Convergence wouldn't happen immediately, but the Kremlin was on the right path. Russia's post-Communist economic system was believed to provide better results than its predecessor and appeared to offer superior prospects.

Thus despite the fog of true lies, it can be said with considerable confidence that

1) Russia is no longer an impoverished superpower.
2) Russia has ceased being an economy of shortage.
3) Russia is a military superpower.
4) Russia is a survivor (it endured extreme economic adversities).
5) Putin's authoritarianism didn't prevent recovery and growth.
6) Russia's oligarchs and klepocrats didn't prevent recovery and growth.
7) Russian rent-granting didn't prevent recovery and growth.
8) Russia's rearmament program didn't prevent recovery and growth.
9) Further rearmament need not impoverish the country.
10) Russia's mixed economy can support some of Putin's efforts to forge the new world order of his dreams.

Russia's Growth Potential

The economic feasibility of Putin's ambitions depends on Russia's mixed economy's ability to provide an adequate stream of guns and butter. Neoclassical economic theory teaches that market economies (and command systems) can increase the production of guns and butter if policy makers discover ways to increase the supply of primary factors of production (labor, capital, and land), improve skills and technologies, without these gains being offset by intensifying microeconomic market inefficiencies and diminishing aggregate effective demand (macroeconomic factors).

This means, in Russia's case, that if the anti-competitiveness of the Kremlin's imperfect market system doesn't intensify and plummeting petroleum prices don't cause mass involuntary unemployment, Putin can anticipate positive economic growth to the extent that the labor supply and investment increase; education, skills, and factor mobility improve; institutions become more efficient; domestic innovation flourishes; and technology is transferred from abroad. The precise impact of each of these influences depends on the form of the production function, which is difficult to discern through the fog of true lies; nonetheless, for the purposes at hand, it is easily appreciated that the Kremlin should be in a position to favorably influence economic growth. The mixed character of Russia's imperfectly competitive market economy should be sufficient to provide Putin with more guns and butter, unless the Kremlin policies stifle productivity. The imperfect competitiveness of Russia's market economy isn't enough to preclude sustained economic and military industrial growth.[89]

The WBG concurs. It forecasted a 3.5 percent GDP advance in 2011 based on the progress it foresaw in the Kremlin's ability to mobilize and increase factor supplies, diminish inefficiencies, spur innovation, and expedite technology transfers. Better results were also predicted in accordance with Russia's relative economic backwardness,[90] if the leadership initiated bold reforms, reduced the nation's budgetary dependency on petroleum revenues, improved the investment climate,[91] closed large infrastructure gaps, diversified exports, reformed the tax structure, broadened the economic base, improved governance, and strengthened institutions.[92] In the WBG's opinion, the Russian economy was not only in a position to grow, but to advance more rapidly than the West because the Federation's subpar investment climate, laggard infrastructure, natural resources–intensive exports, archaic tax structure, narrow economic base, and weak institutions left room for substantial improvement.[93] Russia's vices, from the WBG's perspective, weren't fatal. They were a gauge of its growth potential.[94]

Growth Retardation

The "true lies" evidence displayed in the WBG graphic (Figure 7.3) suggests that Russia's economic performance for 2011 was above target (4 percent per annum), but that the reforms the Kremlin claimed it made failed thereafter, driving achieved rates of growth down to the vicinity of 1 percent

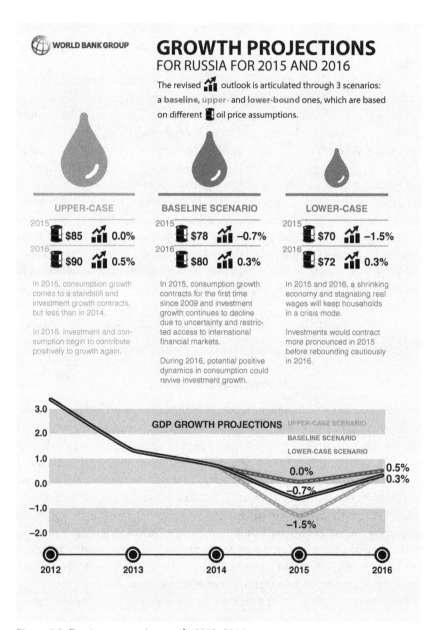

Figure 7.3 Russian economic growth, 2012–2016.
Source: http://www.worldbank.org/en/news/press-release/2014/12/08/world-bank-revises-its-growth-projections-for-russia-for-2015-and-2016

in 2012, 2013, and 2014 (more or less in line with the West's anemic GDP growth), long before plummeting petroleum prices became a significant factor.

The failure of the Kremlin's civilian economic reforms appears to have had two distinct aspects. First, Russia forewent anticipated productivity gains, and second, it incurred productivity losses from intensified anti-competitiveness. Both types of failure should have been expected. Fruitlessly going through the motions of reform is a hoary Kremlin tradition,[95] and returns to the regime's consolidation of the power vertical were bound to diminish and turn negative.[96] Putin's renationalization of the military-industrial complex and the re-imposition of stern production discipline in a for-profit, competitive contractual environment still seems to be working well, judged by what appears to be a swelling volume of arms procurement (see Chapter 10), but renationalization, intrusive regulation, mandates, executive orders, capricious rent-granting, and asset seizures outside the VPK are having a countervailing negative impact.[97] These cross tendencies echo the Soviet pattern in the late 1970s and 1980s, raising the specter of protracted growth retardation and secular stagnation (*zastoi*), unless Putin curbs Russia's systemic anti-competitiveness.

Macroeconomic Shocks

Russia's near-term economic outlook is clouded further by collapsed petroleum prices. The price of benchmark Brent crude plummeted 50 percent in the second half of 2014, jeopardizing Kremlin spending programs. It zigzagged thereafter through 2015, plummeting another 30 percent in the final quarter before falling 15 percent in early 2016. It is currently at the low end of the range beneath $46 per barrel.[98] Russia's economy is highly dependent on its hydrocarbons. Oil and gas revenues account for more than 50 percent of federal budget revenues.[99] Unless petroleum prices reversed, it seemed that Moscow might be compelled to slash government spending by more than 25 percent,[100] but this was avoided by tapping its foreign reserves, and securing compensatory financing at home and abroad.[101]

Russia still isn't out of the woods. First, like all petro nations, it has incurred windfall income and wealth losses. Per capita income and purchasing power have declined on this account and will continue until the wind shifts direction. If petroleum prices stay unchanged, Russia can resume its economic growth from the new achieved level by mobilizing and increasing factor supplies, diminishing inefficiencies, spurring innovation, and expediting technology transfers. Low petroleum prices don't destroy Putin's great power aspirations; they only pressure him to delay their implementation.

Second, the near-term impact of reduced government spending (austerity), trade-destroying economic sanctions, embargoed technology transfers, ruble devaluation, high interest rates, capital flight, financial turmoil, and cascading bankruptcies depends on a host of factors, including the robustness and nimbleness of Russia's imperfectly competitive mixed economic system. The command aspect of the Russia economic mechanism over the VPK, natural resources, utilities and financial sectors, together with ample foreign currency reserves, has helped Putin weather the storm.[102] Russia's military modernization program can also be viewed as a macroeconomic plus because it reduces the risk of mass involuntary unemployment by providing strong demand for military industrial employment.

Catastrophic outcomes (black swans) cannot be excluded.[103] The 2008 global financial crisis caused Russian GDP to plunge 8 percent in 2000,[104] but an encore hasn't occurred, even though petroleum prices fell to extremely low levels as some producing nations increased output to offset lost revenue.[105]

The World Bank's current baseline scenario anticipates a further contraction of 1.9 percent in 2016, before growth is expected to resume at a modest rate of 1.1 percent in 2017.[106]

The long-term effects of the burst petro bubble, permanent trade-destroying economic sanctions, embargoed technology transfer (like CoCom during the Cold War),[107] and ruble devaluation will be milder, and non-regime threatening (North Korea continues to persevere, despite Western sanctions).[108] Russia's potential stream of future national income will be reduced by the first three factors, but these losses will be partially offset by trade creation and diversion, and alternative sources of foreign technology transfer.[109] Russian finance minister Anton Siluanov even sees the crisis as an opportunity for the country to escape the "Dutch disease," that is, excessive social welfare expenditures and sluggish economic growth attributed to speculative energy prices and ruble overvaluation.[110] Although sanctions and lower natural resources prices has increased the domestic economic burden of Putin's great power restoration campaign, the Kremlin has not been daunted by the sticker shock. The Soviets successfully withstood America's refusal to recognize the USSR (1917–1933), and low natural resources prices during the Great Depression. They survived Cold War I sanctions, and Russia can persevere today because its economic system isn't critically dependent on its adversaries' solicitude.

Russia's Imperfectly Competitive Economic System

The parallels between Soviet and Russian economic performance and potential aren't accidental. Russia's growth retardation from 2012 to 2016 (see Figure 7.3) is mimicking the USSR's industrial production trajectory after 1970 (see Table 7.3), in part because the Kremlin's economic order today more closely resembles its Soviet twin than America or the European Union, despite repeated WGB claims that Russia has successfully transitioned from command communism to democratic free enterprise. Russian public and private sector economic governance remains predominantly authoritarian. The state is the freehold owner of the Federation's natural resources, the VPK, and most of the energy sector. This gives it the right to control production, finance, and sales in public sector enterprises. The president, not the people, determines all public programs, mandates, edicts, regulations, laws, and sensitive judicial decisions.[111] Putin exercises his authority with the support of the power services, guided by a paper constitution that he can breach with impunity. Private property is confiscated at his discretion,[112] and civil liberties are routinely abridged.[113] Russia is a soft authoritarian, martial police state. This means that the leader and his power services rather than the Duma and the courts are in command, but aren't despotic. The regime operates under the rule of men rather than the rule of law, just like its Soviet predecessor. Contemporary Russian authoritarianism is milder than Stalin's, Brezhnev's, and even Gorbachev's, however edict still trumps the domestic market and the people's will.

The most distinctive characteristic of Russian soft authoritarianism is rent-granting. Today's Kremlin is neither totalitarian nor tyrannical by Stalinist standards.[114] It doesn't harshly micro-direct the nation's economy. It relies instead on outsourcing; that is, the delegation of economic management to favored individuals (servitors, oligarchs, kleptocrats) who mostly run businesses as they please (except in the VPK) in return for transferring a share of their usufruct (rents, revenues, incomes, and capital gains) to the Kremlin, paying taxes and providing political support and state service. Rent-granting has been Russia's preferred governance strategy since Ivan the Great (1440–1505) became grand prince of Moscow in 1462, and constitutes the core of the Kremlin's Muscovite model.[115]

Profit seeking, consumer choice, markets, and even planning under this scheme are harnessed to Putin's great power restoration program. The Kremlin's preeminent concern is mobilizing labor, capital, and land to provide the regime with output, revenue, and essential political support. It cares little how these goals are accomplished outside the VPK.

Rent-grantees can be wasteful and extravagantly over-compensated as long as the Kremlin receives sufficient revenue, support, and military-industrial compliance. When the leader (*vozhd*) is displeased, he cavalierly revokes his agent's privileges and transfers the outsourcing lease to another servitor.[116] Neither private property nor rent grants are sacrosanct. Lip service is paid to productivity, efficiency, ethics, and the rule of law, but the benefits of rent-granting in the consumer sector trump them in the regime's eyes.

This means that the imperfectness of Russian competition goes deeper than the conventional notion of monopoly and oligopoly market power.[117] Western corporations overcharge consumers and underpay factors to augment profits by manipulating supplies whenever they can. This is a truism of neoclassical theory.[118] Oligarchs, kleptocrats, and rent-grantees, often in league with the mafia and the Federal Security Service (FSB), in Russia do the same, but they also employ supplementary anticompetitive methods. They receive privileged state contracts, exclusive rental and price-fixing rights, regulatory and judicial support, and de facto license to suppress competitors (poachers). This not only allows them to gain exorbitant unearned income (Marx's surplus value), but enables Roskomstat to treat price gouging, inferior goods, and worthless and phantom services as value added in official GDP statistics.

Russia's rent-granting economy, even in its contemporary resource-mobilizing form, is intrinsically corrupt, profoundly inefficient, and impervious to the curative powers of Adam Smith's invisible hand. It is indisputably

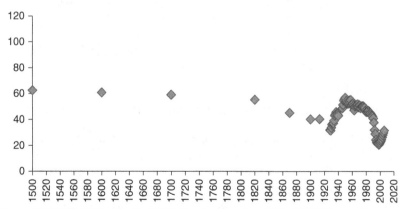

Figure 7.4 USSR-EU per capita GDP: Comparative size, 1500–2006 (Western European benchmark).
Source: Angus Maddison, *The World Economy: Historical Statistics*, OECD, 2003, pp. 558–563, 566.

inferior to Western imperfect competition (which to a lesser degree displays similar perverse traits) from the standpoint of Pareto efficient consumer sovereignty, but the Kremlin isn't perturbed because the Muscovite model serves the regime's great power purposes better than democratic free enterprise,[119] and provides a workable platform for Putin's great Russia project. The system offers Moscow affluence for its servitors, weapons, an adequate supply of necessities, and patriotism to fend off regime change.[120]

This explains why most Western analysts who insist that Russia's economic inferiority must ultimately compel the Kremlin to embrace democratic free enterprise and an America-led world order are barking up the wrong tree. Yes, democratic free enterprise does and should continue to provide higher per capita income growth in the long run in the West than in Russia, but Moscow is unimpressed. Superior Western living standards won't deter Putin from trying to recover territory and spheres of influence surrendered to America and the European Union after 1989.[121]

Nor is he daunted by the danger of a liberal-led palace coup d'état because ordinary people allegedly have lost hope for brighter tomorrows.[122] Market Muscovy provides Russians with more butter and higher expectations than command communism because it is modestly responsive to consumer demand, making it difficult for the regime's opponents to foment popular discontent and persuade the power services to tolerate another bout of liberal-orchestrated economic mayhem. Putin isn't invulnerable, but he is justified in believing that Russia's transformation from command communism to market Muscovy diminishes his and the Kremlin's exposure to systemic political risk. Market Muscovy is a better mousetrap, a fact recognized by most Russians who blame the West and Saudi Arabia for the regime's current economic woes,[123] but today's Western leaders are unimpressed. They don't consider improvements good enough to allow the Kremlin to win Cold War II.[124]

Potential Achilles Heel

Russia's Muscovite economy has constrained Kremlin ambitions for more than a half millennium. It is a negative component of the correlation of forces from Moscow's perspective. Figure 7.4 shows that the West's per capita income (territories of Austria, Belgium, Denmark, Finland, France, Switzerland, Germany, Italy, Netherlands, Norway, Sweden, and the United Kingdom) was 67 percent than higher Russia's (territory of the USSR) in 1500 during the reign of Ivan the Great, and steadily increased to 400 percent in the year 2000.

This didn't prevent Russia's living standard from significantly rising during the course of the past five centuries. In the WGB view, contemporary Russia has achieved the status of a high-income, non-OECD country, but it still lags far behind Portugal, and, other things equal, the gap is unlikely to be closed in the foreseeable future. This is an important disparity and could be the Kremlin's Achilles heel. However, subduing Russia is hardly inevitable. Russia's military-industrial productivity is closer to the West's high frontier, making it a potent adversary, as history attests. Peter the Great vanquished Charles XII at Poltava in 1709. Catherine the Great extended Russia's borders, absorbing Novorossiya, Crimea, Northern Caucasus, Right-Bank Ukraine, Belarus, Lithuania, and Courland. Alexander I contributed to Napoleon's defeat in 1812, and Stalin destroyed Hitler. The strength of the Kremlin's Muscovite economy is its ability to produce guns, and this may yet prove sufficient to support Putin's imperial agenda.

Notes

1 Yegor Gaidar, *State and Evolution: Russia's Search for a Free Market*, Seattle: University of Washington Press, 2003. Jeffrey Sachs, "What I Did in Russia, March 14, 2012." http://jeffsachs.org/2012/03/what-i-did-in-russia/.

2 Eugene Rumer, "From Inside Putin's Parallel Universe, the Crisis Looks Bright," *Financial Times*, Op-Ed, December 22, 2014. "http://carnegieendowment.org/2014/12/22/from-inside-putin-s-parallel-universe-crisis-looks-bright/hxsr?mkt_tok=3R kMMJWWfF9wsRolu67NZKXonjHpfsX56OsvXqGg38431UFwdcjKPmjr1YABSct 0aPyQAgobGp5I5FEIQ7XYTLB2t60MWA%3D%3D. "From inside Putin's parallel universe, the crisis looks bright. Russia's economic progress probably does not look too bad either when Mr Putin compares it with other leading powers. Who has done better in the past 15 years? Gross domestic product has increased sixfold. Income per head has risen sevenfold. Never before have Russians seen such prosperity."

3 Andrei Shleifer and Robert Vishny, *The Grabbing Hand: Government Pathologies and Their Cures*, MIT Press, 2000; Karen Dawisha, *Putin's Kleptocracy: Who Owns Russia*, New York: Simon and Schuster, 2014; Bertrand Guay Bill Browder, *Red Notice: A True Story of High Finance, Murder, and One Man's Fight for Justice*, New York: Simon and Schuster, 2015; Boris Rumer, "Russia – A Different Kind of Threat," *Carnegie Endowment for International Peace*, July 20, 2015. http://carnegieendowment.org/2015/07/20/russia-different-kind-of-threat/idml?mkt_tok =3RkMMJWWfF9wsRoguazKZKXonjHpfsX56OsvXqGg38431UFwdcjKPmjr1YY JSst0aPyQAgobGp5I5FEIQ7XYTLB2t60MWA%3D%3D.

4 Alastair Cooke, "The Geo-financial War Places New Geo-political Facts on the Ground," *Valdai*, January 13, 2015. http://valdaiclub.com/russia_and_the_world/74880.html. "In an interview with NPR on 29 December, President Obama said of Russia that 'their economy was already contracting and capital was fleeing even before oil collapsed. And part of our rationale in this process was that the only thing keeping that economy afloat was the price of oil.' ... He continued: 'And if, in fact, we

were steady in applying sanction pressure, which we have been, ... over time it would make the economy of Russia sufficiently vulnerable that if and when there were disruptions with respect to the price of oil ... they'd have enormous difficulty managing it. ... [On] an issue like Ukraine, we have to be firm with the Russians [as] ultimately, the big advantage we have with Russia is we've got a dynamic, vital economy, and they don't. They rely on oil; we rely on oil and iPads and movies and you name it.'" Andrew Kuchins, "Will Economy Be Putin's Downfall?" December 7, 2014. http://www.cnn .com/2014/12/07/opinion/kuchins-putin-economy-problems/. Priyanka Boghani, "What's Been the Effect of Western Sanctions on Russia?" January 14, 2015. Anders Aslund misleadingly attributes most of Russia's economic plight to the effectiveness of America's financial sanctions. http://www.pbs.org/wgbh/pages/frontline/foreign-affairs-defense/putins-way/whats-been-the-effect-of-western-sanctions-on-russia/.

5 Andrei Shleifer and Daniel Treisman, "A Normal Country," *Foreign Affairs*, March/April, Vol. 83, No. 2 (2004): 20–39.

6 Steven Rosefielde, "An Abnormal Country," *The European Journal of Comparative Economics, Vol.* 2, No. 1 (2005): 3–16.

7 Putin may be the biggest kleptocrat of them all. According to Bill Browder, the CEO of Hermitage Capital Management, formerly Russia's largest foreign investor, Putin's net worth is approximately $200 billion, more than double Bill Gates'. "Putin's networth is $200 billion, says Russia's once largest foreigner investor," *CNN*, February 15, 2015. http://cnnpressroom.blogs.cnn.com/2015/02/15/putins-net-worth-is-200-billion-says-russias-once-largest-foreigner-investor/.

8 Cooke, "The Geo-financial War." "France: Europe Hurting from Russia Sanctions, Needs to Act," *AP*, January 7, 2015. http://abcnews.go.com/International/wireStory/france-europe-hurting-russia-sanctions-act-28050002. "France's economy minister says Europeans should work together to pressure Russia for a solution over Ukraine so that all sides can ease sanctions that are hurting European economies."

9 Some outside the power services, like Finance Minister Anton Silianov, oppose stepping up defense spending, preferring butter to guns. "Силуанов: военные расходы России высоки, их нужно перераспределять," *РИА Новости*, December 25, 2014. http://ria.ru/economy/20141226/1040300620.html#ixzz3N5JvAxHS.

10 World Bank, *Country Partnership Strategy (CPS) for the Russian Federation*, Report No. 65115-RU, November 2011. Another version of the same document is titled: *Russian Federation – Country Partnership Strategy for the period 2012–2016* (English). "Russia is a middle income country (MIC) that strives to move to a high income status. In the period since 2005, the per capita GDP of Russia doubled to approximately US$10,500 in 2010, and the country moved to an upper MIC status. The current country context was formed in the course of a decade of turbulent adjustment following the transition from a centrally planned to a market economy and another decade of rapid economic growth driven largely by natural resources, interrupted by the 2008–2009 global financial and economic crisis. As a result of a strong fiscal and monetary counter-cyclical package, the country emerged from the global recession with lower than expected unemployment and poverty and has returned to moderate growth rates. To escape the 'middle income trap,' Russia's government pursues economic policy and institutional development that aim to modernize, diversify, and increase the competitiveness of the economy and improve the well-being of its citizens," p. 2.

11 "According to the 1993 Constitution, Russia is a democratic federal law-governed state with a republican form of government, comprising 83 federal subjects." "The next parliamentary elections will be held on December 4, 2011, to be followed by presidential elections on March 4, 2012. President Dmitry Medvedev came to power in March 2008 and appointed Prime Minister Vladimir Putin. This ruling tandem has operated well since then. According to recent polls, the approval ratings for both the president and prime minister remain high, albeit lower than in 2010. The ruling party, United Russia, dominates the State Duma by holding 315 seats. The 2011 parliamentary elections will be the sixth in the history of modern-day Russia. Vladimir Putin announced that he will run for president. According to latest public opinion polls, the political situation is not likely to change significantly after the elections, with the four leading parties retaining their dominance in the Duma." World Bank, *Country Partnership Strategy (CPS) for the Russian Federation*, p. 2. Anders Aslund, group e-mail, December 12, 2011. Nonetheless, Aslund remains hopeful that democracy will triumph soon. "Yet, I think Putin and his regime were effectively finished on December 10. I do not think it possible for Putin to serve as the next president, and I also think that Medvedev has no future role to play. Common slogans are directed against Putin: 'Russia without Putin,' 'Putin is a thief,' 'Putin to prison,' and 'Out with Putin!' Both the Russian people and authorities have shown that Russia is ready for a new democratic breakthrough."

12 Andrei Shleifer, *A Normal Country: Russia after Communism*, Cambridge, MA: Harvard University Press, 2005.

13 Susanne Oxenstierna, ed., *The Challenges for Russia's Politicized Economic System*, London: Routledge, 2015. "During the early 2000s the market liberalization reforms to the Russian economy, begun in the 1990s, were consolidated, but since the mid 2000s economic policy has moved into a new phase, characterized by more state intervention with less efficiency and more structural problems. Corruption, weak competitiveness, heavy dependency on energy exports, an unbalanced labour market, and unequal regional development are trends that have arisen and which, this book argues, will worsen unless the government changes direction." Susanne Oxenstierna, "Future Growth of the Russian Economy," *Baltic Rim Economies*, No. 6, December 2014, p. 44. "Russia experienced high growth in the 2000s up to the economic crisis in 2009 when GDP contracted by almost eight per cent. The economy recovered in 2010–2011, with yearly growth rates of over four per cent, but in 2012 growth declined to 3.4 per cent and in 2013 to 1.3 per cent. For 2014 the forecasted GDP growth was revised downwards from 3–4 per cent to 1–2 per cent during the year. Finally, in October 2014, IMF predicted growth of only 0.2 percent in 2014 and 0.5 per cent in 2015." "I would argue that the main reasons behind the decline of the growth rate are found in deeper systemic and structural elements that have characterized the economy under President Vladimir Putin."

14 Kuchins, "Will Economy Be Putin's Downfall?"

15 Sudeep Reddy, "Oil Collapse, Russia Woes Reshape White House's International Economic Policy," *Wall Street Journal*, December 19, 2014. http://blogs.wsj.com/washwire/2014/12/19/oil-collapse-russia-woes-reshape-white-houses-international-economic-policy/?mod=WSJ_Politics_Blog. Erin McClam, "Oil Prices, Sanctions and Currency Collapse

Put Putin in a Bind," NBC News, December 16, 2014. http://www.nbcnews.com/news/world/oil-prices-sanctions-currency-collapse-put-putin-bind-n269486.

16 During the 1960s and early 1970s, many worried that Soviet socialism was a superior economic growth engine that would render "capitalism" obsolete. See Abram Bergson, "The Great Economic Race," *Challenge Magazine*, Vol. 11, No. 6 (March 1963): 4–6. Attitudes began reversing in the late 1970s. Abram Bergson, "The Soviet Economic Slowdown," *Challenge Magazine*, Vol. 20, No. 6 (January–February) (1978): 22–33.

17 Alexander Gerschenkron took a more cautious position during the Soviet period, arguing that the deficiencies of administrative command planning were insufficient to compel the Kremlin to abandon its Muscovite culture. Alexander Gerschenkron, *Economic Backwardness in Historical Perspective*, Cambridge, MA: Harvard University Press, 1962.

18 "Putin Named Times' International Person of the Year," *RT*, December 30, 2013. ttps://www.rt.com/news/putin-times-person-year-979/.

19 театр военных действий, teatr voennykh deistvii. Cf. Carl von Clausewitz, *On War*, London: Oxford University Press, 2007.

20 Adam Chandler, "Putin's Popularity Is Much Stronger than the Ruble," *The Atlantic*, December 16, 2014. http://news.yahoo.com/putins-popularity-stronger-ruble-201100735 politics.html;_ylt=A0LEVrgscJVU5rkAjDUPxQt. "The Russian ruble is currently in the midst of an historic landslide; Russia's central bank jacked interest rates up nearly seven points on Tuesday to counter the currency's two-day, 20-percent fall. And yet today also brought news that the Russian president had emerged from a public-opinion poll as the country's 'Man of the Year' – for the fifteenth straight year."

21 Abram Bergson, "The USSR Before the Fall: How Poor and Why?" *Journal of Economic Perspectives*, No. 5, Fall (1991): 29–44. Abram Bergson, *Planning and Performance in Socialist Economies*, London: Unwin and Hyman, 1989.

22 Vladimir Isachenkov, "Putin: Russia Military Modernization to Go Ahead," *AP*, December 19, 2014. http://news.yahoo.com/putin-russia-military-modernization-plan-154457979.html. "Speaking at a meeting with Russia's top military brass, Putin said the nation's nuclear forces are a 'major factor in maintaining global balance,' adding that 'they effectively preclude the possibility of a large-scale aggression against Russia.'
"Putin said the military is set to receive 50 new intercontinental ballistic missiles – a significantly higher number than in previous years. The huge military buildup is continuing despite the country's economic woes, triggered by a combination of Western sanctions against Russia and the slumping prices of oil." "Минобороны потратит 1,74 трлн рублей на военную технику в 2015 году К Ведомство направит 52,7% бюджета на закупку и модернизацию техники," Izvestia, December 26, 2014. "– Доля расходов на военную технику в структуре нашего бюджета увеличивается из года в год – с 37% в 2013-м до прогнозируемых 58,8% в 2017-м, – пояснили в министерстве. Всего на оборонные расходы в следующем году планируется потратить 3,3 трлн рублей."

23 Johan Norberg and Fredrik Westerlund, "Tailoring War: Russia's Use of Armed Force in Ukraine," draft paper prepared for the 46th Association for Slavic, East European, and Eurasian Studies Conference, San Antonio Texas, Friday November

21, 2014. Christopher Harress, "Russia Will Have 55 Stealth Sukhoi T-50 Fighters by 2020, but Are They as Good as the US Stealth Jets?" *International Business Times*, December 19, 2014. http://www.ibtimes.com/russia-will-have-55-stealth-sukhoi-t-50-fighters-2020-are-they-good-us-stealth-jets-1763583. "According to retired U.S. Air Force Gen. David Deptula, who was deputy chief of staff of the USAF, the T-50 is a 'pretty sophisticated design' and has 'greater agility and a more aerodynamic design' than the F-35."

24 Abram Bergson, "Socialist Economics," in H. Ellis (ed.), *A Survey of Contemporary Economics*, Homewood, IL: Richard D. Irwin, 1948, 412–448; Abram Bergson, "Market Socialism Revisited," *Journal of Political Economy*, Vol, 75, No. 4 (October 1967): 655–673. Abram Bergson, "Soviet Economic Perspectives: Toward a New Growth Model," *Problems of Communism*, Vol. 32, No. 2 (March–April) (1973): 1–10.

25 Karen Dawisha, *Putin's Kleptocracy*, New York: Simon and Schuster, 2014. Masha Gessen, "The Myth of the Russian Oligarchs," *New York Times Op Ed*, December 11, 2014. http://www.nytimes.com/2014/12/11/opinion/masha-gessen-the-myth-of-the-russian-oligarchs.html?_r=1. "Conventional wisdom – or conventional hope – among many of the people who would like to see the end of the Putin regime has long been that a turn for the worse in the Russian economy will make the moneyed elite turn on the Russian president. Journalists, pundits and Mr. Putin's political opponents in Russia have predicted that Western sanctions and the economic disaster they hasten will result in a coup d'état staged by oligarchs. There is just one problem with that argument: There are no oligarchs anymore." "When Mr. Putin became acting president 15 years ago this month, Russia was an oligarchy – indeed the oligarchs, a small group of men who had grown very rich in the preceding decade, were instrumental in picking Putin out of obscurity and installing him at the helm. But within months, he made the oligarchs an offer they could not refuse: give up all of their political power and some of their wealth in exchange for safety, security and continued prosperity, or else be stripped of all power and assets." "Over these years of helping Mr. Putin solidify his regime, the Russian rich have not only become entrenched in this corrupt system, but they have lost the very ability to form and pursue a political agenda. Those who predict an imminent coup – a coup by oligarchs as independent actors who can form a coalition to pursue their economic interests – are far off the mark." "Russia's economic troubles probably mean that the moneyed elite will suffer, with more of its members going into exile or even to jail while their assets are redistributed. As for the rest of the Russian population, more than 140 million people, bad economic news is just bad economic news: It spells out-of-control inflation and real daily hardship. But neither the self-cannibalizing rich nor the newly poor are likely to pose a challenge to Mr. Putin's power."

26 Abram Bergson, "The Communist Efficiency Gap: Alternative Measures," *Comparative Economic Studies*, Vol. 36, No. 1, Spring (1994): 1–12.

27 Richard Pipes, *The Formation of the Soviet Union: Communism and Nationalism, 1917–1923*, Cambridge MA: Harvard University Press, 1964.

28 Steven Rosefielde and Quinn Mills, *Global Economic Turmoil and the Public Good*, Singapore: World Scientific Publishers, 2015.

29 Steven Rosefielde and Ralph W. Pfouts, *Inclusive Economic Theory*, Singapore: World Scientific Publishers, 2014. The Pareto presumption with regard to military-industrial

production is that the *demos* is fully informed and makes the wisest choices at the margin through a democratic process. Cf. Kenneth Arrow, *Social Choice and Individual Values*, 2nd ed. New York: Wiley, 1963.

30 Idealist neoclassical theory essentially is a beguiling tautology in Ludwig Wittgenstein's demanding sense (given its premises, true under all circumstances; it cannot be negated). Pareto optimality assumes that everyone is comprehensively rational and omni-competent, and then gives its claims a scientific patina by analytically deducing from the construct's premises that outcomes are ideal (everyone maximizes his or her utility within the constraints of voluntary exchange). Idealist neoclassical theory is empirically testable, but results are mixed. The disconfirmation is widely disregarded while maintaining the fiction that Pareto analysis is behaviorally true. Idealist neoclassical theory should be more accurately called neoclassical 'tauto-nomics.'" Perhaps Samuelson grasped the nuance in titling his magnum opus *Foundations of Economic Analysis*. Ludwig Wittgenstein, "Logisch-philosophiche Abhandlung," *Annalen der Naturphilosophie* (Leipzig), v. 14, 1921, pp. 185–262, reprinted in English translation as *Tractatus logico-philosophicus*, New York and London, 1922. Rhetorical tautologies state the same thing twice, while appearing to state two or more different things; logical tautologies state the same thing twice, and must do so by logical necessity. The inherent meanings and subsequent conclusions in rhetorical and logical tautologies or logical necessities are very different. By axiomatic necessity, logical tautologies are neither refutable nor verifiable under any condition. Herbert Simon's realist (behavior) neoclassical theory often is constructed from controlled behavioral experiments and therefore constitutes theory rather than tautology.

31 The same issue arose in the Soviet-era literature. Abram Bergson found that the comparative merit of Soviet and Western systems couldn't be deduced from the principles of perfect planning and perfect markets. The performance of Soviet and Western economies had to be directly compared. See Abram Bergson, "Socialist Economics," 234–236. On the welfare dimension, see Abram Bergson, "A Reformulation of Certain Aspects of Welfare Economics," *Quarterly Journal of Economics*, Vol. 52, No. 1 (1938): 310–334. Abram Bergson, "The Concept of Social Welfare," *Quarterly Journal of Economics*, Vol. 68, No. 2 (May 1954): 233–252.

32 Richard Lipsey and Kelvin Lancaster, "The General Theory of Second Best," *Review of Economic Studies*, Vol. 24, No. 1 (1956): 11–32. "Making the Second Best of It," *Economist*, August 21, 2007. http://www.economist.com/blogs/freeexchange/2007/08/making_the_second_best_of_it.

33 Steven Rosefielde, "Economic Theory of the Second Worst," *Higher School of Economics Journal (HSE)*, (Moscow), 2015, pp. 30–44.

34 Rosefielde and Pfouts, *Inclusive Economic Theory*; Rosefielde, "Economic Theory of the Second Worst"; Rosefielde, "Economic Theory of the Second Worst"; Paul Samuelson, *Foundations of Economic Analysis*, Cambridge, MA: Harvard University Press, 1947; Herbert Simon, *Models of Man: Social and Rational-Mathematical Essays on Rational Human Behavior in a Social Setting, Social and Rational-Mathematical Essays on Rational Human Behavior in a Social Setting*, New York: Wiley, 1957.

35 Herbert Simon, "A Behavioral Model of Rational Choice," in Simon, *Models of Man*; Herbert Simon, "A Mechanism for Social Selection and Successful Altruism," *Science*,

Vol. 250, No. 4988 (1990): 1665–1668; Herbert Simon, "Bounded Rationality and Organizational Learning," *Organization Science, Vol.* 2 , No. 1 (1991): 125–134; Gerd Gigerenzer and Reinhard Selten, *Bounded Rationality*, Cambridge, MA: MIT Press, 2002; Ariel Rubinstein, *Modeling Bounded Rationality*, Cambridge, MA: MIT Press, 1998; Clem Tisdell, *Bounded Rationality and Economic Evolution: A Contribution to Decision Making, Economics, and Management*, Cheltenham, UK: Brookfield, 1998; Daniel Kahneman, "Maps of Bounded Rationality: Psychology for Behavioral Economics," *The American Economic Review, Vol.* 93, No. 5 (2003): 1449–1475.

36 Robert Shiller, *Irrational Exuberance*, Princeton NJ: Princeton University Press, 2000. Also, Irving Fisher showed long ago that ideally efficient financial markets should not be crisis prone. His analysis holds in Simon's world too, but not where willfulness, power-seeking, unscrupulousness, and corruption rule. See Irving Fisher, *The Theory of Interest*, Clifton, NJ: Augustus M. Kelley, 1930.

37 Michael Snyder," Plummeting Oil Prices Could Destroy the Banks that Are Holding Trillions in Commodity Derivatives," December 3, 2014. http://theeconomiccol-lapseblog.com/archives/plummeting-oil-prices-destroy-banks-holding-trillions-commodity-derivatives. "It has been estimated that the six largest 'too big to fail' banks control $3.9 trillion in commodity derivatives contracts. And a very large chunk of that amount is made up of oil derivatives. By the middle of next year, we could be facing a situation where many of these oil producers have locked in a price of 90 or 100 dollars a barrel on their oil, but the price has fallen to about 50 dollars a barrel. In such a case, the losses for those on the wrong end of the derivatives con-tracts would be astronomical."

38 Amartya Sen, *The Idea of Justice*, London: Penguin, 2010; Amartya Sen, "Personal Utilities and Public Judgements: Or What's Wrong with Welfare Economics," *Economic Journal*, Vol. 89, No. 355 (1979): 537–588.

39 Rosefielde and Pfouts, *Inclusive Economic Theory*. Value is a utilitarian concept. The mismeasurement at stake refers to discrepancies between utilities' experience and what is recorded in national income statistics. In the case of sweetheart deals, national utility is diminished by anticompetitive income maldistribution.

40 Steven Rosefielde, "The Riddle of Postwar Russian Economic Growth: Statistics Lied and Were Misconstrued," *Europe-Asia Studies*, Vol. 55, No. 3 (2003): 469–481.

41 The European Union includes criminal activity as value added in its GDP accounts. Harry Alsop, "Italy to Boost GDP Figures with Drugs and Prostitution: Inclusion of Black Market in GDP Figures will Boost Italian Economy by around 1.3 per cent," *Telegraph*, May 24, 2014. http://www.telegraph.co.uk/news/worldnews/europe/italy/10853756/Italy-to-boost-GDP-figures-with-drugs-and-prostitution.html.

42 Joshua Yaffa, "The Waste and Corruption of Vladimir Putin's 2014 Winter Olympics," *Bloomberg Business Week*, January 2, 2014. http://www.businessweek.com/articles/2014-01-02/the-2014-winter-olympics-in-sochi-cost-51-billion. Cf. Henry Meyer, Ilya Arkhipov, and Alan Katz, "Putin's Friends Reap Billions in Deals as Economy Teeters," Bloomberg, December 11, 2014. http://finance.yahoo.com/news/putins -friends-reap-billions-deals-210100557.html. " 'Putin has been masterful at distrib-uting the rents to all the relevant people, but now he's monopolizing all the rents,' said Anders Aslund, a senior fellow at the Peterson Institute for International Economics in Washington." " 'Under Yeltsin, it was an oligarchy, but it was balanced among big groups,' Aslund said. 'Now, Putin just squeezes them out.' "

43   Steven Rosefielde, "Russia's Aborted Transition: 7000 Days and Counting," *Institutional'naya ekonomika razvitie*, 2010.

44   Steven Rosefielde and Quinn Mills, *Democracy and Its Elected Enemies: American Political Capture and Economic Decline*, Cambridge: Cambridge University Press, 2013. Rosefielde and Mills, *Global Economic Turmoil and the Public Good*.

45   Abram Bergson tried to obfuscate the issue by correctly insisting that excess profits in all sectors are partly offset from the standpoint of the relative prices used to form real GDP indexes. This nuance, however, doesn't alter the fact that market power causes the allocation of resources and distribution of goods to depart from the Paretian efficiency ideal.

46   Confirmed to the author by academician Valerii Makarov (director of TsEMI).

47   Personal interviews with Emil Ershov, former head of the audit division of Roskomstat, confirmed by Alexei Ponomarenko (Roskomstat).

48   The second economy refers to value-adding activities that take place beneath the state's statistical radar system.

49   Russian GDP rose slightly in 1996 for the first time in a decade. Valery Makarov explained that this was accomplished by increasing the estimated growth of the invisible second economy! This means that there was no uptick, just a political directive to show a positive result.

50   Abram Bergson, "Soviet National Income and Product in 1937," parts I and II, *Quarterly Journal of Economics*, Vol. 64, Nos. 2, 3, (May/August) (1950): 208–241, 408–441; Abram Bergson, "Reliability and Usability of Soviet Statistics: A Summary Appraisal," *American Statistician*, Vol. 7, No. 3 (June–July) (1953): 13–16; Abram Bergson, *Soviet National Income and Product in 1937*, New York: Columbia University Press, 1953; Abram Bergson (with Hans Heymann Jr.), *Soviet National Income and Product, 1940–1948*, New York: Columbia University Press, 1954. Abram Bergson, *The Real National Income of Soviet Russia since 1928*, Cambridge, MA: Harvard University Press, 1961. Abram Bergson, "National Income," in Bergson and Simon Kuznets (eds.), *Economic Trends in the Soviet Union*, Cambridge, MA: Harvard University Press, 1963. Abram Bergson, "Comparative National Income in the USSR and the United States," in J. D. Daly (ed.), *International Comparisons of Prices and Output, Studies in Income and Wealth*, Vol. 37, New York: National Bureau of Economic Research, 1972, 145–185; Abram Bergson, "Soviet National Income Statistics," in V. Treml and J. Hardt (eds.), *Soviet Economic Statistics*, Durham, NC: Duke University Press, 1972, 148–152.

51   Alec Nove, *The Soviet Economic System*, London: Allen and Unwin, 1977, 352.

52   Shleifer and Treisman, "A Normal Country."

53   Robert Allen, *Farm to Factory: A Reinterpretation of the Soviet Industrial Revolution*, New Brunswick, NJ: Princeton University Press, 2015. "In a startling reinterpretation, Robert Allen argues that the USSR was one of the most successful developing economies of the 20th century. He reaches this provocative conclusion by recalculating national consumption and using economic, demographic, and computer simulation models to address the central questions of Soviet history." Garbage in/garbage out!

54   Steven Rosefielde, *Russia in the 21st Century: The Prodigal Superpower*, Cambridge: Cambridge University Press, 2005.

55   *Narodnoe Khoziastvo SSSR*, various issues. Steven Rosefielde, *Russian Economy from Lenin to Putin*, New York: Wiley, 2007.

56 *Measures of Soviet Gross National Product in 1982 Prices*, Joint Economic Committee of Congress, Washington, DC, November 1990. Rosefielde, *Russian Economy from Lenin to Putin*.

57 *Measures of Soviet Gross National Product in 1982 Prices*; Rosefielde, *Russian Economy from Lenin to Putin*.

58 Gertrude Schroeder and Elizabeth Denton, "An Index of Consumption in the USSR," in *USSR: Measures of Economic Growth and Development*, Joint Economic Committee of Congress, Washington, DC, December 8, 1982, 217–401.

59 *Measures of Soviet Gross National Product in 1982 Prices*; Rosefielde, *Russian Economy from Lenin to Putin*.

60 Abram Bergson and most specialists during the 1980s argued that diminishing Soviet factor productivity most likely would prevent the Soviet Union from overtaking the West. See Steven Rosefielde, "Tea Leaves and Productivity: Bergsonian Norms for Gauging the Soviet Future," *Comparative Economic Studies*, Vol. 47, No. 2, June (2005): 259–273.

61 "Whether you like it or not, history is on our side. We will dig you in" ("Нравится вам или нет, но история на нашей стороне. Мы вас закопаем"). Soviet premier Nikita Khrushchev, address to Western ambassadors at a reception at the Polish embassy in Moscow on November 18, 1956. "Khrushchev Tirade Again Irks Envoys," *New York Times*, November 19, 1956, p. 1.

62 Rosefielde, *Russia in the 21st Century*.

63 The CIA's series failed to take adequate account of the improvements made to Soviet weapons. As in America, the main source of procurement growth is the qualitative enhancement of the subsystems carried by planes, missiles, ships, tanks, etc.

64 Bergson, "The USSR Before the Fall"; Donald Firth and James Noren, *Soviet Defense Spending: A History of the CIA Estimates 1950–1990*, College Station: Texas A&M University Press, 1998.

65 Economics isn't a reliable predictive science, even with full and accurate information, but this isn't critical for gauging comparative Russian and Western systems' potential. See Rosefielde and Pfouts, *Inclusive Economic Theory*. Alexander Rosenberg, *Mathematic Politics or Science of Diminishing Returns*, Chicago: University of Chicago Press, 1994. "None of our models of science really fit economics at all."

66 Charles Wolf Jr. and Henry Rowen, *The Impoverished Superpower: Perestroika and the Soviet Military Burden*, San Francisco, CA: Institute for Contemporary Studies, 1990.

67 Ludwig von Mises, *Socialism*, London: Jonathan Cape, 1936; Fredrich A. von Hayek, *Collectivist Economic Planning: Critical Studies on the Possibilities of Socialism*, London: George Routledge & Sons, 1935; Lionel Charles Robbins, *An Essay on the Nature and Significance of Economic Science*, London: Macmillan, 1932.

68 Igor Birman, Экономика недостач, Нью-Йорк: Chalidze Publications, 1983.

69 Vitaly Shlykov, "Nazad v budushchee, ili Ekonomicheskie uroki kholodnoi voiny," *Rossiia v Global'noi Politike*, Tom 4, No. 2, Mart-April' 2006, pp. 26–40. Shlykov, "Nevidimaia Mobilizatsii," *Forbes*, No. 3, March 2006, pp. 1–5; Shlykov, "Globalizatsiia voennoi promyshlennosti – imperativ XXI veka," *Otechestvennye zapiski*, No. 5, 2005, pp. 98–115.

70 Mikail Bulgakov, *The Master and the Margarita*, London: Vintage, 1996.

71 Harley Balzer, "Soviet Education in 1988," *Journal of Comparative Education* (1988); Murray Feshbach, "Russia's Demographic and Health Meltdowns," in John Hardt (ed.), *Russia's Uncertain Economic Future*, New York: M.E. Sharpe, 2003, 283–306. Murray Feshbach, *Ecocide in the USSR: Health and Nature Under Siege*, New York: Basic Books, 1993. Judyth Twigg, "Social Welfare: A Social Contract," in Hardt, *Russia's Uncertain Economic Future*, 300–325.

72 Richard Ericson, "The 'Second Economy' and Resource Allocation under Central Planning," *Journal of Comparative Economics*, Vol. 8, No. 1, March (1984): 1–24. Gregory Grossman, "The Second Economy in the USSR and Eastern Europe: A Bibliography" (Berkeley-Duke Occasional Papers on the Second Economy in the USSR, no. 1, University of California, Berkeley, and Duke University, updated March 1987). Aron Katsenelinboigen, "Coloured Markets in the Soviet Union," *Soviet Studies*, Vol. 29 (January 1977): 62–85.

73 Helen Muchnic, "The Literature of Nightmare," *New York Review of Books*, June 15, 1967. "It was with reference to Zamyatin that Trotsky in 1923, in his *Literature and Revolution*, coined the term 'inner émigré' to define an attitude and a quality of writing which he resented, a scornful aloofness to the Revolution, a spiritual isolation that seemed to him willful and snobbish. He was only partly right; Zamyatin was indeed aloof, but neither snobbish nor indifferent. He sensed how things were going; wrote *We*, that famous satire on totalitarianism which inspired Orwell's *1984* and Huxley's *Brave New World*, but which has never been published in Russia; and presently, finding his position in the USSR untenable – suddenly deprived of his various editorial positions, unable to publish his stories, his play taken off the boards – changed from inner to outward émigré, and ended his days in Paris, in 1937."

74 Mikhail Gorbachev, *Perestroika i Novoe Myshlenie*, Moscow: Politicheskie Literatury, 1987; Abel Aganbegyan, *Inside Perestroika: The Future of the Soviet Economy*, New York: Harper and Row, 1989; Philip Hanson, *The Rise and Fall of the Soviet Economy: An Economic History of the USSR from 1945*, London: Pearson Education, 2003; Girsh Itsykovich Khanin, *Dinamika ekonomicheskovo razvitiya*, Novosibirsk: Nauka, 1991.

75 In constructing real output indexes, it is assumed that price weights reflect marginal value added. This assumption was falsified in practice in the USSR because prices were set in accordance with the labor theory of value, not marginal utilities. The distinction is important, but the Agency never drew the problem to readers' attention. The dollar indexes the CIA compiled attempted unsuccessfully to match Soviet and American quality goods. This gave the false impression that Soviet GNP in the late 1980s was nearly two-thirds of the U.S. level.

76 The Soviet planned economy wasn't the rational scientific construct lauded by Soviet ideologists and caricatured in the West as the command economy. Central planning existed and provided a framework for enterprise factor acquisition, production, wholesaling, and retailing, but Red director micro-decisions were determined by managers' bonus incentives and legally binding inter-enterprise contracts enforceable in Soviet courts. The Soviet economy was perpetually in a state of overfull employment excess aggregate effective demand because of the state policy of guaranteed purchase. The government agreed to purchase as much as Red directors could produce, as long as products weren't defective. See Rosefielde, *Russian Economy from Lenin to Putin*.

77 "To know and not to know, to be conscious of complete truthfulness while tell-
    ing carefully constructed lies, to hold simultaneously two opinions which can-
    celled out, knowing them to be contradictory and believing in both of them, to
    use logic against logic, to repudiate morality while laying claim to it, to believe
    that democracy was impossible and that the Party was the guardian of democ-
    racy, to forget, whatever it was necessary to forget, then to draw it back into
    memory again at the moment when it was needed, and then promptly to forget it
    again, and above all, to apply the same process to the process itself – that was the
    ultimate subtlety; consciously to induce unconsciousness, and then, once again,
    to become unconscious of the act of hypnosis you had just performed. Even to
    understand the word 'doublethink' involved the use of doublethink." George
    Orwell, *Nineteen Eighty-Four*, London: Martin Secker & Warburg Ltd, London,
    part 1, chapter 3, p. 32.
78 Rosefielde, *Russia in the 21st Century*.
79 Steven Rosefielde, *False Science: Underestimating the Soviet Arms Buildup*,
    Transaction, 1982 (expanded second edition, 1987). The source for the 52,000
    nuclear weapons estimate is Vitaly Shlykov. A similar figure was published in the
    New York Times. Shlykov confirmed it with Viktor Mikhailov (head of Minatom).
80 Rosefielde, *Russia in the 21st Century*.
81 Wolf and Rowen, *The Impoverished Superpower*.
82 "In the period since 2005, the per capita GDP of Russia doubled to approximately
    $10,500 in 2010." The year 2008 is used as the endpoint in the text because Russian
    per capita GDP was lower in 2010 than 2008. World Bank, *Country Partnership
    Strategy*, p. 47. Official Russian statistics indicate a growth rate close to 3 percent per
    annum (*Rosstat*, 2014). Richard Connolly, "Troubled Times Stagnation, Sanctions
    and the Prospects for Economic Reform in Russia," *Chathamhouse*, February 2015.
    http://www.chathamhouse.org/sites/files/chathamhouse/field/field_document/
    20150224TroubledTimesRussiaConnolly.pdf.
83 This point is easily confirmed by comparing the CIA's estimate of Russian per capita
    income in 1989 of $23,546 (adjusted to a 2011 dollar price base) which should be
    more or less the same as 2011 (see Figure 7.2) because there was little or no real
    growth point to point from 1989 to 2011, with the World Bank's 2011 figure of
    $10,500. Steven Rosefielde, *Efficiency and The Economic Recovery Potential of Russia*,
    Farnham: Ashgate, 1998, Table S1, p. xxii. CIA, *Handbook of International Economic
    Statistics*, CPAS92-10005, September 1992. Obviously, the World Bank's picture of
    post-Communist Russian economic progress may be amiss. If the CIA were right
    in 1989, Russian living standards have declined substantially since 1989 using the
    World Bank's contemporary estimate. Most of the discrepancy between the $23,546
    and $10,500 figures is attributable to the CIA's exaggerated 1991 purchasing power
    parity estimates, but the point remains. Russia has not converged toward the devel-
    oped West's living standard under Yeltsin and Putin from the 1989 benchmark; it
    has diverged, falling further behind.
84 Michael Ellman, "Russia's Current Economic System: From Delusion to Glasnost,'"
    Comparative Economic Studies, 2015, 1–18.
85 http://data.worldbank.org/country/russian-federation. The WBG has also classified
    Russia as a normal middle-income country. The two concepts aren't mutually exclu-
    sive. World Bank, *Country Partnership Strategy*. The CIA's PPP estimates computed

in 2015 prices for GDP and per capita GDP respectively are: $3.718 trillion and $25,400. https://www.cia.gov/library/publications/the-world-factbook/geos/rs.html.

86 Ibid. "The country's strong economic recovery and downward poverty trends belie significant challenges of inequality and social exclusion. Since Russia began its transition from a planned economy to a market economy some 20 years ago, economic growth has been steady and GDP per capita has increased threefold. Inequality as measured by the Gini coefficient rose significantly, however, from 28.9 to 42.2 between 1992 and 2009. Social stresses have been similarly magnified. Given that federal spending on social services in 2007–2008 already accounted for about 17 percent of GDP, or half of total federal spending, and was further increased by around 1.3 percent of GDP in 2009 and 2.2 percent of GDP in 2010, effectively addressing the issues of inequality and social exclusion will require an alternative preventative approach that can tackle the root causes of these issues."

87 Ibid.

88 The "middle income trap," persistent growth retardation for middle-income countries, hypothesis recently has been ridiculed as "middle-income claptrap." See "The Middle-Income Trap," *Economist*, February 26, 2013. http://www.economist.com/blogs/freeexchange/2013/02/middle-income-trap. The hypothesis may be politically motivated.

89 Ellman, "Russia's Current Economic System."

90 Gerschenkron, *Economic Backwardness in Historical Perspective*.

91 "The narrowing in March 2011 of the list of activities of strategic importance performed by non-state-owned banks removed the need for prior government approval for foreign acquisitions in this sector. Tariffs for selected agricultural products were reduced in response to the food price shock resulting from the drought in the summer of 2011." OECD, "Economic Policy Reforms 2012: Going for Growth," 2012.

92 World Bank, *Country Partnership Strategy*. "Beyond this favorable short-term picture lie heightened vulnerabilities of the Russian budget and long-standing structural issues. First, there is the large non-oil fiscal deficit of about 11 percent of GDP, compared with the sustainable 4.5 percent level. Second, with much smaller fiscal reserves than before 2008, Russia's budget is now more vulnerable to a new, sustained drop in oil prices. Third, Russia faces major structural problems in the medium term, including the need to significantly improve the investment climate, close large infrastructure gaps, diversify its export, tax, and broader economic base, improve governance, and strengthen institutions."

93 Finally, on the structural reform front, the Russian economy is facing multiple, long-term challenges. These include, first and foremost, improving the investment climate, addressing the large infrastructure gaps, diversifying Russia's tax, export, and broader economic base, and strengthening governance and institutions. In each of these areas, Russia scores comparatively low on many measures of performance, especially for a very large middle-income country aspiring to achieve high-income status within the next decade. These challenges underpin the government's broader modernization agenda and the ongoing broad consultative discussions about the country's revised Strategy 2020. The extent to which these long-term challenges are met will determine the longer-term dynamics of the Russian economy, its catch-up with developed countries, and its ability to improve the living standards of its citizens.

94 The WBG's growth theory is another example of a Wittgenstein Tautology. It is a structuralist variant of neoclassical tauto-nomics. Ludwig Wittgenstein, "Logisch-philosophiche Abhandlung," Annalen der Naturphilosophie (Leipzig), v. 14, 1921, pp. 185–262, reprinted in English translation as *Tractatus logico-philosophicus*, New York and London, 1922.

95 Gertrude Schroeder, "The Soviet Economy on a Treadmill of Reforms," in *Soviet Economy in a Time of Change*. Washington, DC: Joint Economic Committee of Congress, 1979, 312–366.

96 Rosefielde, "Russia's Aborted Transition: 7000 Days and Counting."

97 "Russian Court Orders Seizure of Oligarch's Oil Stake," October 30, 2014. http://news.yahoo.com/russian-court-orders-seizure-oligarchs-oil-stake-131057014.html;_ylt=A0LEVvJpUahUQUMAZFUPxQt.;_ylu=X3oDMTByMG04Z2o2BHNlYwNzcgRwb3MDMQRjb2xvA2JmMQR2dGlkAw. "A judge at Moscow's Arbitration Court ordered the return to the state of the stake held by billionaire Vladimir Yevtushenkov's holding firm Sistema in oil company Bashneft." Michael O'Kane, "Russian Legislation Proposes Foreign Asset Seizures to Compensate Sanctioned Russian Nationals," October 9, 2014. http://europeansanctions.com/2014/10/09/russian-legislation-proposes-foreign-asset-seizures-to-compensate-sanctioned-russian-nationals/.

98 The Brent petroleum benchmark price on October 25, 2015 was $48 per barrel. It was $33 per barrel on January 8, 2016. It was $46 on September 7, 2016. http://www.nasdaq.com/markets/crude-oil-brent.aspx.

99 U.S. Energy Information Administration, March 2014. http://www.eia.gov/countries/cab.cfm?fips=RS.

100 Russia sells its natural resources for dollars. Plummeting dollar prices reduce the proceeds from natural resources sales. The budgetary impact, however, can be mitigated or exacerbated by fluctuations in the foreign exchange rate. Small devaluations will assure that falling dollar natural resources prices have a substantial budgetary impact. If natural resources prices and the value of the ruble drop pari passu, then the budget will be unaffected.

101 Kenneth Rapoza, "Russia Needs a 'Budget Miracle,'" *Forbes*, June 15, 2015. http://www.forbes.com/sites/kenrapoza/2016/06/15/russia-needs-a-budget-miracle/#581928974cee. Darya Korsunskaya and Elena Fabrichnaya, "As Oil Falls, Russia Choked by Military, Social Spending," Reuters, December 30, 2014. http://www.reuters.com/article/2014/12/30/russia-crisis-budget-idUSL6N0UD1AE20141230.

102 "Russian Reserves Fall below $400 Billion, First Time Since," *Reuters*, December 25, 2014. http://www.reuters.com/article/2014/12/25/us-russia-reserves-idUSKBN0K30HC20141225.

103 Nassim Taleb, *The Black Swan: Second Edition: The Impact of the Highly Improbable*, New York: Random House, 2010. Cf. "Russia 'May Face Chaos' if Extra Sanctions Imposed: Germany," AFP, January 4, 2015. "Tougher sanctions may destabilise the situation further in Russia and plunge the country into chaos, German deputy chancellor Sigmar Gabriel warned in a newspaper interview on Sunday." http://news.yahoo.com/russia-may-face-chaos-extra-sanctions-imposed-germany-140023551.html.

104 http://data.worldbank.org/country/russian-federation

105 "Russia, Iraq Supply Most Oil in Decades as 2015 Begins with Glut," MSN, January. http://www.msn.com/en-us/news/money/russia-iraq-supply-most-oil-in-decades-as-2015-begins-with-glut/ar-BBhrmyC?srcref=rss.

106 http://www.worldbank.org/en/country/russia/overview. April 2016.

107 CoCom is an acronym for Coordinating Committee for Multilateral Export Controls. CoCom was established by Western bloc powers in the first five years after the end of World War II, during the Cold War, to put an arms embargo on COMECON countries.

108 Kopf, "Russia Sanctions."

109 Richard Lipsey, "The Theory of Customs Unions: Trade Diversion and Welfare," *Economica*, Vol. 25, No. 3 (1957): 40–46.

110 Evgenia Pismennaya, "Russia's Siluanov Freed by Ruble Collapse to Slim Welfare State," *Bloomberg*, February 6, 2015. http://www.bloomberg.com/news/articles/2015-02-06/russia-s-siluanov-freed-by-ruble-collapse-to-slim-welfare-state?cmpid=yhoo. "'Dutch disease is over,' Russian Finance Minister Anton Siluanov said in an interview, referring to the fallout from a commodity boom that pushes up exchange rates and stalls competitiveness. The currency collapse is freeing the government to slim down a welfare state more generous than its Soviet predecessor, according to Siluanov."

111 Vladimir Isachenkov, "Moscow Court Rushes Verdict to Putin's Chief Foe," AP, December 29, 2014. http://abcnews.go.com/International/wireStory/moscow-court-rushes-verdict-putins-chief-foe-27878114. "Earlier this month, prosecutors asked the court to convict Alexei Navalny of defrauding a cosmetics company and to sentence him to 10 years in prison."

112 The Yukos case is a classic example. See Steven Rosefielde, "Illusion of Transition: Russia's Muscovite Future," *Eastern Economic Journal*, Vol. 31, No. 2, Spring (2005): 283–296. "The Yukos Affair: The Chase Is On: The Russian Oil Giant's Dispossessed Owners Begin the Hunt for $50 billion," *Economist*, November 15, 2014. http://www.economist.com/news/business/21632513-russian-oil-giants-dispossessed-owners-begin-hunt-50-billion-chase.

113 "Pussy Riot Activist Arrested after Pro-Alexei Navalny Protests in Moscow," *Guardian*, December 31, 2014. "Masha Alyokhina arrested with more than 100 protesters in Moscow after all-night demonstration against jailing of anti-Putin figurehead's brother." http://www.theguardian.com/world/2014/dec/31/pussy-riot-activist-masha-alyokhina-arrested-alexei-navalny-protest.

114 Aleksandr Solzhenitsyn, *The Gulag Archipelago, 1918–1956: An Experiment in Literary Investigation* (Volume One), New York: *Basic Books*, 1997; Arthur Koestler, *Darkness at Noon*, New York: Scribner, 2006.

115 Steven Rosefielde and Stephan Hedlund, *Russia since 1980: Wrestling with Westernization*, Cambridge: Cambridge University Press, 2008.

116 Elena Holodny, "The Former 'Kremlin Banker' Describes how Putin's Mind Works," *Business Insider*, July 29, 2015. http://www.businessinsider.com/ex-kremlin-banker-says-putin-isnt-evil-2015-7#ixzz3hKpu6NSZ.

117 Rosefielde and Pfouts, *Inclusive Economic Theory*.

118 Nicholas Kaldor, "Professor Chamberlin on Monopolistic and Imperfect Competition," *The Quarterly Journal of Economics*, Vol. 52, No. 3 (May 1938): 513–529.

119 Rosefielde and Mills, *Democracy and Its Elected Enemies.*

120 Mikhail Klikushin, "Russians Rage Against America Enduring Sanctions, Anger Turns to Hate: Racist Names for Obama and Putin Disses Coca-Cola," *Observer*, December 29, 2014. http://observer.com/2014/12/russians-rage-against-america/. "Anti-American sentiment has been growing slowly in Russia since the war in former Yugoslavia. But the sharp recent increase happened as a result of the US-led sanctions that were imposed on Russia after the 'Russian annexation of Crimea.' 75% of Russians do not believe that their country is responsible for the events in Ukraine. On the contrary, they blame the US."

121 East and West Germany reunited on August 31, 1990.

122 Timothy Heritage, "After 15 Years in Power, Putin Risks Running Out of Luck," *Reuters*, December 31, 2014. http://uk.reuters.com/article/2014/12/31/uk-russia-crisis-putin-idUKKBN0K81JI20141231. "The economic system of heavy state intervention, often known as 'state capitalism,' continued through the 2008–09 global financial crisis and the 2008–12 presidency of Dmitry Medvedev, an ally who stood in for Putin because of constitutional limits. During that time, Putin remained Russia's most powerful man as the dominant member of their power-sharing 'tandem' and was re-elected in March 2012 despite mass rallies against him.
"Since then, the economy has been found wanting, with recession looming, annual inflation hitting 9 percent in November and set to rise in 2015, and currency and gold reserves being depleted as the central bank tries to shore up the ruble." "Russia is going into decline. It means the model which Putin created – capitalism for friends – has already collapsed," Mikhail Kasyanov, Putin's prime minister for much of his first four-year term, said in an interview.

123 Jim Heintz, "Russians Optimistic for 2015 Despite it All," *AP*, January 1, 2015. http://finance.yahoo.com/news/russians-optimistic-2015-despite-162851094--finance.html.

124 Reality is just the other way around. Putin sees through Obama's posturing and considers him ridiculous. Robert Garver, "Obama's Slap at Putin Provokes Angry Response," *Fiscal Times*, January 21, 2015. http://finance.yahoo.com/news/obama-slap-putin-provokes-angry-173300542.html. Reporting on President Obama's State of the Union Address, January 20, 2015, Garver writes, "Last year, as we were doing the hard work of imposing sanctions along with our allies, some suggested that Mr. Putin's aggression was a masterful display of strategy and strength. Well, today, it is America that stands strong and united with our allies, while Russia is isolated, with its economy in tatters." He added, "That's how America leads – not with bluster, but with persistent, steady resolve." "Russian Foreign Minister Sergei Lavrov blasted the United States for wanting 'to dominate the world and not merely be first among equals.'"

8

Ukrainian Morass

Introduction

The viability of Putin's great power restoration campaign depends not only on Russia's capabilities, but also on the vulnerabilities of its adversaries. The weaknesses of Ukraine are integral aspects of the correlation of forces. If Ukraine were Germany, the Kremlin wouldn't have annexed Crimea or supported proxy rebellions in Novorossiya. If Ukraine were Germany, its economy would be vibrant, its government resolute, and its military counterforce credible. But Ukraine isn't Germany. It doesn't possess any of these virtues. Its economy is in shambles. Its self-serving government is corrupt, and its military ineffectual, rendering the country vulnerable to Putin's machinations. Kyiv must quickly extricate itself from this morass, putting its house in order to prevent dismemberment. Putin is betting that President Petro Poroshenko will fail, that the Kremlin will successfully dominate large portions of Novorossiya, while hypocritically paying lip service to Ukraine's sovereign autonomy.

President Poroshenko and the International Monetary Fund (IMF) acknowledge Ukraine's dismal post-Soviet performance on all these scores, but remain cautiously optimistic that it will build an efficient democratic free enterprise system soon.[1] If they are right, the correlation of forces will tilt against Moscow, and Putin's great power restoration campaign will be blunted.[2] If they are wrong, then the Kremlin will annex additional parts of Novorossiya, check further Western inroads, and expand its hegemonic sway. A great deal hinges on the battle for Novorossiya.[3]

Roving Bandits

IMF managing director Christine Lagarde is cautiously optimistic. Is her confidence justified?[4] Time will tell. However, the record is anything but reassuring. A quarter century after Ukraine became an independent, sovereign nation, it still hasn't created a governance system that enables its economy to outperform Russia's. This can be partly ascribed to the feebleness of its post-communist transition. According to the Heritage Foundation's Index of Economic Freedom, Ukraine ranks 162nd in economic freedom, just ahead of Myanmar and behind Bolivia! It is the most illiberal economy in the European region.[5] But this explanation is incomplete because some communist and former communist regimes have been able to beneficially incorporate markets and even a semblance of the rule of law into their systems.

The Chinese Communist Party successfully orchestrated post-Mao modernization without revoking the state's monopoly on freehold property, discarding intrusive economic management, or sharing political power.[6] Russia under Putin has fared well enough despite its authoritarianism, the renationalization of the military-industrial complex, and rent-granting. Ukraine's leaders, relying on similar anticompetitive methods, have persistently mismanaged possibilities. Their governance has been abysmal, not "second best."[7]

Ukraine's failure, at a high level of abstraction, is attributable to the triumph of rival regional ethnic kleptocracies over centralized authority. Oligarchs and kleptocrats in China and Russia are required to assist their authoritarian rulers' national projects. They cannot solely live off the public purse or dissipate their energies in clan turf wars as is predominantly the case in Ukraine. In Mancur Olson's terminology, Ukraine is ruled by roving bandits, in contrast to the stationary bandits in China and Russia.[8] Roving bandits destroy the incentive to invest and improve; stationary bandits under strong authoritarian direction have a vested interest in augmenting national wealth. The story of Ukraine's post-communist politics, including Poroshenko's administration, has been one of unstable, successive kleptocratic regional clan coalitions that prioritize venality over national welfare,[9] with dreadful economic results. Roving banditry doubtless isn't the only explanation for Ukraine's plight – some claim that Ukraine is a "failed state"[10] – but it provides a lucid conceptual perspective on why Kyiv has underperformed its authoritarian, post-communist peers, and why fundamental change remains implausible until there is compelling evidence that roving bandits are transforming themselves into "stationary" authoritarians or true democrats.

Post-communist Economic Performance

Ukraine's economic performance since the global financial crisis has been bleak and deteriorated further after Russia's annexation of Crimea. The data like Russia's are suspect, conflicting, and must be taken with a bucket of salt;[11] nonetheless, the consensus estimates are illuminating. According to Focus Economics,[12] a for-profit international consulting firm, Ukraine's population declined 6 percent in 2010–2015. Its GDP plummeted 15 percent in 2009,[13] another 5 percent in 2010–2015[14] before falling 17.2 percent in the first quarter of 2015,[15] and is expected to plunge 9.5 percent for the entire year.[16] The World Bank is forecasting positive GDP growth between 1 and 2 percent for 2016.[17] Consumption dropped 9.6 percent and investment 23.1 percent in 2014, while unemployment soared to 9.3 percent and inflation rose to 12.1 percent. The Ukrainian hryvnia at the end of December 2015 was 62 percent below its 2010 value.[18] Public debt skyrocketed 75 percent after 2010 from 40.1 to 70.1 percent of GDP in 2014, and 94.9 percent in 2015,[19] threatening a "Greek tragedy."[20] Ukrainian and IMF sources tell a broadly similar story.[21]

These disastrous results occurred despite substantial on-again/off-again financial assistance both from the European Union and Russia,[22] and purported progress in liberalizing its economic system.[23] While more assistance is on its way, it may well be offset by a looming debt crisis that threatens to seriously exacerbate matters.[24] As part of the Minsk II process, the IMF agreed to provide a new financial rescue package worth $17.5 billion in February 2015, bringing the international community's total bailout commitment to $40 billion.[25] This constitutes the country's fourth bailout in ten years, and comes on the heels of the April 2014 rescue program that failed to stabilize Ukraine's finances as it battled pro-Russian separatists in the east.[26]

Four months after the deal was initialed, however, it was already in tatters because it was unrealistic from the outset. The IMF rescue, which imposes austerity as a quid pro quo for liquidity without providing long-term investment support, was predicated on the implausible assumption that the "primary" budget deficit (which excludes interest repayments) would disappear entirely by 2016, "setting debt on a firm downward path."[27]

This is sheer wishful thinking. The IMF expects Ukraine to achieve a Greek level of adjustment that took four years in just one by cutting the massive deficit of Naftogaz. It assumes that Ukraine will double domestic gas prices to eliminate the losses on gas imports, but the trimming is still nowhere in sight. IMF predictions for economic growth are similarly optimistic.

The prognosis, therefore, is grim despite private creditors' acceptance of a 20 percent debt write-down on August 27, 2015.[28] The IMF is bleeding its patient to make it well, with a high probability that the cure will be worse than the disease. It is providing liquidity, but doing little to eradicate the roving banditry that makes Ukraine's economy inferior to China's and Russia's. Although this may be better than doing nothing, Poroshenko's four-year reform program and the IMF assistance do not appear to pose a serious deterrent to Putin's great power restoration campaign.[29]

Nuclear Deterrence

Ukraine also finds itself behind the eight ball because it lacks Russia's nuclear deterrent. It had a sizeable nuclear arsenal during the Soviet era, but transferred its weapons to Russia. President Leonid Kravchuk misgauged the threat of Russia's re-annexing parts of Ukraine (Novorossiya) in the early 1990s,[30] making it relatively easy for Russia, America, Britain, France, and China to coax him and his successor, Leonid Kuchma, into transferring Ukraine's nuclear weapons to the Kremlin in exchange for now apparently worthless security guarantees provided by the Budapest Memorandum on Security Assurances of 1994.[31] The result was that Russian and Ukrainian defense policies moved in opposite directions. Russia retained its nuclear superpower, preserving a credible deterrent, while Ukraine inadvertently facilitated Putin's great power restoration campaign by denuclearizing.[32]

Notes

1 "Ukraine," *IMF Country Report* 15/59, March 2015. https://www.imf.org/external/pubs/ft/scr/2015/cr1569.pdf. "In view of Ukraine's large external financing needs and the authorities' strong policy commitments, including the commitment to a debt operation to secure sustainability with high probability, and with a full appreciation of the risks, staff supports approval of Ukraine's four-year Extended Arrangement under the EFF with access equivalent to SDR12.348 billion (900 percent of quota). Staff also supports the authorities' request for approval, for a period of 12 months, of the retention of the exchange restrictions and multiple currency practices that are inconsistent with their obligations under Article VIII Sections 2 (a) and 3 on the grounds that they are non-discriminatory, imposed for balance of payments reasons, and temporary" (p. 39).

2 Eugene Rumer, letter, September 10, 2015. russiaeurasiaprogram@carnegieen dowment.org. "A year and a half into the presidency of Petro Poroshenko, Ukraine is in the midst of wide-ranging, historic reforms that promise to transform the country's political system, economy, and national security apparatus. These reforms are taking place against the backdrop of the conflict with Russian-backed separatists in eastern Ukraine, severe economic decline, and continuing divisions among political factions. The reforms are vital to Ukraine's future as an independent, sovereign country in charge of its own destiny, for Ukraine's European neighbors, and for the rest of Europe." Adrian Karatnycky and Alexander J. Motyl contend that Ukraine is recovering and draining Russia. They urge the West to seize the moment and tighten

economic sanctions. Adrian Karatnycky and Alexander J. Motyl, "How Putin's Ukrainian Dream Turned into a Nightmare," *Foreign Policy*, October 20, 2015. http://news.yahoo.com/putin-ukrainian-dream-turned-nightmare-201101741.html.

3 Anders Aslund is cautiously hopeful. See Anders Aslund, *What Went Wrong and How to Fix It*, Washington, DC: Peterson Institute, April 2015.

4 "Statement by IMF Managing Director Christine Lagarde on Ukraine," June 15, 2015. "Overall, I strongly believe that the authorities' program and the determination and boldness with which it is being implemented, despite considerable headwinds, warrant the support of the international community." Cf. The IMF's positive outlook is supported by the Carnegie Endowment for International Peace. See "Ukraine Reform Monitor," *Carnegie Endowment for International Peace*, August 2015. http://carnegieendowment.org/2015/08/19/ukraine-reform-monitor-august-2015/iewe?mkt_tok=3RkMMJWWfF9wsRogv6TNZKXonjHpfsX56OsvXqGg384 31UFwdcjKPmjr1YUATsN0aPyQAgobGp5I5FEIQ7XYTLB2t60MWA%3D%3D. Holly Ellyatt, "IMF's Lagarde on Trial: What You Need to Know," CNBC, December 18, 2015. http://finance.yahoo.com/news/imfs-lagarde-trial-know-081523718.html;_ylt=A0LEVj3OlXZWhuQA8QwnnIlQ;_ylu=X3oDMTE0MTBjbjVmBGNvbG8DYmYxBHBvcwMxBHZ0aWQDUTRDVFJMMV8xBHNlYwNzYw--https://www.imf.org/external/np/sec/pr/2015/pr15285.htm. "A French court has ordered Christine Lagarde, the head of the International Monetary Fund (IMF), to face trial over her alleged role in a payout to a French tycoon in 2008. If convicted of 'negligence' in a public office, the charge against her, she could face up to a year in prison. Lagarde has been called to face trial in court over her alleged role in a 404 million euros ($438.5 million) payout to French businessman and one-time politician Bernard Tapie."

5 Heritage Foundation 2015 Index of Economic Freedom. http://www.heritage.org/index/country/ukraine.

6 Steven Rosefielde, "The Illusion of Westernization in Russia and China," *Comparative Economic Studies*, Vol. 49 (2007): 495–513. Yoji Koyama, *EU's Eastward Enlargement: Central and Eastern Europe's Strategies for Development*, Singapore: World Scientific Publishers, 2015.

7 Steven Rosefielde, "Economic Theory of the Second Worst," *Higher School of Economics Journal* (HSE) (Moscow) (2015): 30–44.

8 Mancur Olson, "Dictatorship, Democracy, and Development," *The American Political Science Review*, Vol. 87, No. 3 (September 1993): 567–576. "Under anarchy, uncoordinated competitive theft by 'roving bandits' destroys the incentive to invest and produce, leaving little for either the population or the bandits. Both can be better off if a bandit sets himself up as a dictator–a 'stationary bandit' who monopolizes and rationalizes theft in the form of taxes. A secure autocrat has an encompassing interest in his domain that leads him to provide a peaceful order and other public goods that increase productivity. Whenever an autocrat expects a brief tenure, it pays him to confiscate those assets whose tax yield over his tenure is less than their total value. This incentive plus the inherent uncertainty of succession in dictatorships imply that autocracies will rarely have good economic performance for more than a generation. The conditions necessary for a lasting democracy are the same necessary for the security of property and contract rights that generates economic growth."

9 Steven Rosefielde and Bruno Dallago, *Transformation and Crisis in Central and Eastern Europe: Challenges and Prospects*, London: Routledge, 2016.

10 "Ukraine is 'a failed state' unable to guarantee the physical safety of the business," *RT*, June 2014. http://rt.com/op-edge/166812-gas-pipeline-blast-ukraine-russia/. "Ukraine does not control its territory and is unable to guarantee not only the lives of its own citizens but also the economic safety of the pipeline operation, or the businesses on its territory, political scientist Mateusz Piskorsky told RT." Rostislav Ishchenko, "Ukraine: A Miserably Failed State," *Global Review*, May 5, 2015. https://globrev.wordpress.com/2015/05/25/ukraine-a-miserably-failed-state/. The author argues that there is no need for Novorossiya. Ukraine's failed state will compel it to once again become a Russian federal republic.

11 https://www.cia.gov/library/publications/the-world-factbook/geos/up.html

12 Focus Economics is a private service company that provides economic analysis and compiles more than 1,600 macroeconomic forecasts for more than 105 countries. It is supported by an extensive global network of analysts, and its research is derived from projections by international banks, national financial institutions, consultancies, and other economic think tanks.

13 https://www.cia.gov/library/publications/the-world-factbook/geos/up.html

14 Focus Economics, *Ukraine Economic Outlook*, June 9, 2015. http://www.focus-economics.com/countries/ukraine

15 Focus Economics, Ukraine Consumption, June 19, 2015. http://www.focus-economics.com/country-indicator/ukraine/consumption. "According to official data released by State Statistics Service Ukraine, GDP contracted 17.2% in Q1 over the same period of the previous year, which was less than the previously released estimate of a 17.6% decrease. In addition, the contraction still represented a notable deterioration from Q4's 14.8% decrease and represents the worst result since Q2 2009. Ukraine has entered a downward economic spiral as a result of the military conflict and political instability in the east of the country. The large contraction was driven by a worsening of the external sector combined with shrinking domestic demand. Private consumption fell 20.7% annually in Q1, which was a larger contraction than Q4's 13.6% decline. Fixed investment plummeted 25.1%, which followed Q4's 26.2% decrease. In contrast, government consumption recorded the only expansion, growing 5.0% in Q1, which was up from the 3.5% increase in Q4. On the external front, exports tumbled 26.2% in the first quarter (Q4: −31.0% yoy) and imports plummeted 20.1% (Q4: −29.0% yoy). As a result, the net contribution of the external sector to GDP growth swung from plus 4.9 percentage points in Q4 to minus 0.6 percentage points in Q1. Focus Economics participants see the economy contracting 7.4% in 2015, which is down 1.1 percentage points from last month's forecast. For 2016, panelists expect that the economy will rebound to grow 1.8%." The CIA estimates Ukraine's 2015 GDP contraction at 9.9 percent. https://www.cia.gov/library/publications/the-world-factbook/geos/up.html.

16 Jeremy Tordjman, "IMF Approves Loan to Ukraine Despite Debt Concerns," *AFP*, July 31, 2015.

17 http://www.worldbank.org/en/country/ukraine/overview

18 http://finance.yahoo.com/currency-investing. A dollar bought eight hryvnia in 2010 and twenty-one in 2015.

19 https://www.cia.gov/library/publications/the-world-factbook/geos/up.html

20 Focus Economics, *Ukraine Economic Outlook*, June 9, 2015. http://www.focus-economics.com/countries/ukraine. On Ukraine's economy, see "The New Greece in the East," *Economist*, March 12, 2015. http://www.economist.com/blogs/freeex-change/2015/03/ukraine-s-economy.

21 Ukraine GDP Growth Rate 2010–2015, *Trading Economics*, June 28, 2015. http://www.tradingeconomics.com/ukraine/gdp-growth. "Ukraine," IMF Country Report 15/59, March 2015. https://www.imf.org/external/pubs/ft/scr/2015/cr1569.pdf.

22 https://www.cia.gov/library/publications/the-world-factbook/geos/up.html. Updated June 28, 2015. The CIA reports: "In April 2010, Ukraine negotiated a price discount on Russian gas imports in exchange for extending Russia's lease on its naval base in Crimea. Movement toward an Association Agreement with the European Union, which would commit Ukraine to economic and financial reforms in exchange for preferential access to EU markets, was curtailed by the November 2013 decision of President Yanukovych against signing this treaty. In response, on 17 December 2013 President Yanukovych and President Putin concluded a financial assistance package containing $15 billion in loans and lower gas prices. However, the end of the Yanukovych government in February 2014 caused Russia to halt further funding. With the formation of an interim government in late February 2014, the international community began efforts to stabilize the Ukrainian economy, including a 27 March 2014 IMF assistance package of $14–18 billion. Russia's seizure of the Crimean Peninsula has created uncertainty as to the annual rate of growth of the Ukrainian economy in 2014."

23 "David Lipton, the IMF's first deputy managing director, said that the Ukrainian authorities had made a 'strong start' in implementing their economic program." Tordjman, "IMF Approves Loan to Ukraine."
    "The momentum needs to be sustained, as significant structural and institutional reforms are still needed to address economic imbalances that held Ukraine back in the past," Lipton said in a separate statement.

24 Russia's willingness to lend to Ukraine was contingent on an IMF provision preventing the IMF from lending to Ukraine if it defaulted on its sovereign debt to any nation. Anticipating the Ukraine would do just that – default on a $3 billion sovereign debt to Russia due on December 20, 2015 – the IMF dropped its internally imposed lending prohibition in December 2015. This allows it to continue lending to Ukraine after Kyiv defaults on its debt to Russia, but obviously will deter future lending from non-IMF sources. See "Michael Hudson: The IMF Changes Its Rules to Isolate China and Russia," *Naked Capitalism*, December 12, 2015. http://www.nakedcapitalism.com/2015/12/michael-hudson-the-imf-changes-its-rules-to-isolate-china-and-russia.html.

25 "IMF: Ukraine to Get $40 Billion Bailout," *DW*, February 12, 2015. http://www.dw.com/en/imf-ukraine-to-get-40-billion-bailout/a-18250993.

26 It is said to include an in-depth restructuring of Naftogaz, Ukraine's state-owned natural gas firm, and to be a realistic program that can represent a turning point for Ukraine. "IMF: Ukraine to Get $40 billion bailout."

27 "The New Greece in the East," *Economist*, March 12, 2015. http://www.economist.com/blogs/freeexchange/2015/03/ukraine-s-economy.

28 "Ukraine Secures Debt-Relief Deal, Finance Ministry Says Private Creditors Accept 20% Write-Down on the Face Value of Their Ukrainian Bonds," *Wall*

Street Journal, August 27, 2015. http://www.wsj.com/articles/ukraine-secures-debt-relief-deal-finance-ministry-says-1440668275. Evgenia Pismennaya, "Russia Has Excluded Itself from this Settlement," *Bloomberg Business*, August 27, 2015. http://www.bloomberg.com/news/articles/2015-08-27/russia-says-it-won-t-participate-in-ukraine-restructuring?cmpid=yhoo.

29 CSIS, The Ukrainian Crisis Timeline, December 18, 2015. http://csis.org/ukraine/index.htm. "Ukraine Places Moratorium on Russia Debt Repayment."

"IMF officials stated today that Ukraine's bailout program may be in threat, though not because of the decision to default on the $3 billion debt to Russia. Instead, IMF first deputy director David Lipton stated that the possible failure of the Rada to pass a proposed tax code and budget for 2016 that are consistent with the terms of the bailout program may 'interrupt the program and inevitably disrupt the associated international financing.'"

30 U.S. Congress, The December 1, 1991 Referendum/Presidential Election in Ukraine (A Report Prepared by the Staff of the Commission on Security and Cooperation in Europe), 1992, p. 9. http://www.google.com/url?sa=t&rct=j&q=&esrc=s&source=web&cd=13&ved=0CG8QFjAM&url=http%3A%2F%2Fcsce.gov%2Findex.cfm%3FFuseAction%3DFiles.Download%26FileStore_id%3D297&ei=jxlRU6LYMMmnsQS-sIHgBw&usg=AFQjCNHx62W05zpwiYDWmrDK9DDDBLiYzQ&bvm=bv.65058239,d.cWc. Kravchuk's secessionist party had endorsed denuclearization before Ukrainian independence, but this needed not to have been any more binding than his commitment to privatization and democracy.

31 Ukraine had the world's third largest nuclear arsenal, larger than Britain's, France's, and China's combined. On June 1, 1996, Ukraine became a non-nuclear nation when it sent the last of its 1,900 strategic nuclear warheads to Russia for dismantling. In return for giving up its nuclear weapons, Ukraine, the United States of America, Russia, and the United Kingdom signed the 1994 Budapest Memorandum on Security Assurances, pledging to respect Ukraine's territorial integrity, a pledge broken by Russia's 2014 invasion of Crimea. Belarus and Kazakhstan also transferred their nuclear weapons to Russia. Belarus had eighty-one single warhead missiles stationed on its territory after the Soviet Union collapsed in 1991. They were all transferred to Russia by 1996. In May 1992, Belarus acceded to the Nuclear Non-Proliferation Treaty. Kazakhstan inherited 1,400 nuclear weapons from the Soviet Union and transferred them all to Russia by 1995. Kazakhstan has since acceded to the Nuclear Non-Proliferation Treaty. Strobe Talbott was a key player in America's effort to make Ukraine a non-nuclear state. See Sarah Mend, "The View from Above: An Insider's Take on Clinton's Russia Policy," *Foreign Affairs*, July/August 2002. Rose Gottemoeller former U.S. assistant secretary of state and New START negotiator, insists the United States wisely counseled Ukraine to denuclearize, and has honored its Budapest Memorandum. See "US Rejects Criticism of Historic Ukraine Nuclear Deal," *AFP*, December 5, 2014. http://news.yahoo.com/us-rejects-criticism-historic-ukraine-nuclear-deal-213809874.html. "Rose Gottemoeller, head of arms control and international security for the US government, said her country 'has gone every step towards continuing to defend and develop a means of bolstering Ukraine.' Gottemoeller, who was

a negotiator at the Budapest talks 20 years ago, sidestepped questions from reporters on whether Ukraine would have been spared a Russian invasion if it still had nuclear weapons."

32 Olexiy Haran, "Disintegration of the Soviet Union and the US Position on the Independence of Ukraine," *Belfer Center*, Discussion Paper 95-09, 1995.

9

Western Secular Stagnation

The credibility of Western leaders' supposition that "this time will be the same" rests in part on the premise that America's and the European Union's economic performance will surpass Russia's. It is widely supposed that both the level and trend in the economic correlation of forces assures Western supremacy. The economy has long been the Kremlin's albatross,[1] and it is reasonable to suppose that it will be so again, unless Western economic performance falls substantially short of its historical norm in the years immediately ahead. However, there are grounds for concern. America's and the European Union's economic performance after the financial crisis of 2008 has been subpar and worse than Russia's, a trend that may persist after 2016 due to a phenomenon called secular stagnation. Today's clash of civilizations consequently may turn not just on Russia's economic dyspepsia, but on the West's ability to overcome its own economic malaise.

Secular stagnation is a state of perpetual arrested economic motion. The term implies chronic glacial or zero per capita GDP growth that may be attributable either to high time preference[2] or to systemic dysfunction. A healthy economy could remain in no growth steady state equilibrium if the labor force and the capital stock net of repair, maintenance, and replacement are constant, and there is no innovation.[3] This kind of secular stagnation may be optimal even though living standards are frozen because consumers could consider the level of goods and services provided across time to be best. If, however, consumers prefer continuously improving living standards and fail to obtain them because economic efficiency has declined, technological progress has been obstructed, and macroeconomic dysfunction persists, then secular stagnation is a malady, not a blessing.

Paul Krugman, Larry Summers, and Joseph Stiglitz claim that America and the European Union have fallen into pathological secular stagnation.[4] Medium American household income is down since 2007 and hasn't grown

in real terms for two decades.[5] They contend that consumers in both systems desire steady growth, are willing to pay for it, and that supply side
advances in science, technology, skills, and learning should make their
dreams come true, but secular stagnation has taken hold instead because
the West's economies are chronically malfunctioning.[6] They insist that
the malady has become endemic and America's and the European Union's
economies will continue to languish until their governments administer
extra-strength stimulants.[7]

Their diagnosis bears directly on the correlation of forces. If they are
right,[8] even for the wrong reasons, secular stagnation in the West may neu-
tralize one of America's and the European Union's strongest geopolitical
advantages.[9] Their view has been challenged on diverse grounds, but they
are sticking to their guns.

Symptoms of Western Secular Stagnation

The fundamentals supporting their secular stagnation hypothesis are
cogently detailed by the Economic Policy Institute (EPI).[10] Its data confirm
that the United States is not providing enough positions for jobseekers,
despite the appearance of full employment (5.1 percent in July 2015) because
labor force participation is shrinking (some are discouraged workers who
never found jobs in the first place and so are not counted by the EPI).[11] The
2008 financial crisis and its aftermath cost America 7.9 million jobs as of
November 2013. The figure for November 2014 was 7.4 million, despite the
gain of 1.7 million jobs in 2014.[12] The share of twenty-five- to fifty-four-
year-olds with a job has barely budged from the 2009 recession trough. If
workers who left the labor force because they were discouraged by the 2008
crisis were classified as involuntarily unemployed, the unemployment rate
would be grimly higher.[13] The EPI estimates that America's weak economy
has sidelined 5.7 million workers.[14] This weakness cannot be explained in
conventional Keynesian macroeconomic terms by resistance to wage cuts
("sticky wages").[15] The real inflation-adjusted wages of the bottom 70 percent of American workers have been flat or falling since 2002, in stark
contrast to soaring labor productivity. While the inflation-adjusted benefit to employers from hiring workers has steadily increased, demand for
labor has plummeted. Neoclassical economic theory teaches that rational
employers should hire workers whenever marginal (additional) revenue
exceeds marginal cost (there are untapped profits), but this is not happen-
ing. Something clearly is amiss. Either the rationality axiom (rational suppliers maximize profits) is wrong, and/or countervailing factors are at play.

This deduction is underscored by data on corporate profits and executive compensation. Corporate profit rates (capital's share of income) in 2013 were at a forty-four-year peak. Executive compensation has followed suit, bolstering long-established disparities between executive and worker compensation. These trends are apt to persist, other things equal, because wages and salaries of young new market entrants are deteriorating, in part due to the emerging "internship" practices compelling jobseekers to gratuitously work long periods before being treated as regular employees. The situation for technical workers is not substantially better.

The present danger – as the EPI perceives it – therefore is a blighted future of substandard economic growth, stagnation, or worse, exacerbated by abnormally high unemployment and underemployment, widening income, and wealth disparities between corporate executives and workers (including the middle class), and deteriorating conditions for black and Hispanic retirees.[16] This portrayal of secular stagnation is gaining currency across the political spectrum as Democrats and Republicans tussle over who owns the social justice issue in future elections.[17]

The EPI's data are convincing. They support Summers and Krugman's contention that the United States is now in a period of secular stagnation. Even using official GDP statistics, which are biased upward by hidden inflation, economic growth has been disappointing almost everywhere in the world since 2008. Given the anticipated stimulatory effects of internal devaluations (reduced costs of labor, capital, and materials), huge government deficit spending (in absolute and relative terms), monetary expansion, cheap money and external currency devaluations, economic growth and the rebound in employment should have been more vigorous.[18]

The correspondence between the facts and the Summers-Krugman story, however, does not mean that their analysis is complete.[19] They have correctly stated the symptoms, but neither their diagnosis (that government spending is inadequate, which they call "austerity") nor their prescriptions (perpetual high-deficit spending, easy money, and doubling the minimum wage) is sound.[20] The model underlying their diagnosis is a Wittgenstein tautology, not a scientifically valid behavioral theory. It is a logically consistent model, but its specification is a causal daisy chain of ambiguous linkages, unsubstantiated assumptions, and omitted variables, and as such non-definitively falsifiable. There is no reason to believe that full employment and economic growth depend primarily and positively on deficit spending, inflation, egalitarianism, and social justice. Inegalitarian and unjust economies may perform as well as or better than their just egalitarian twins in terms of employment and growth.

Competitive labor market efficiency is more likely to determine employment than deficit spending and excess money emission. Overheated economies may temporarily spur employment and growth, but just as easily could reduce labor demand by increasing liquidity preference.[21] Nonetheless, we know with certainty that more than $6 trillion of deficit spending and the quadrupling of the money supply since 2008 have not rejuvenated American economic growth back to its historic norm,[22] and that the European Union and Japan, relying on the same stimulants, fared even worse. The European Union in desperation decided to increase monetary stimulus by $1.25 trillion in 2015 and 2016,[23] which some believe will have dire ramifications.[24] The West's economic malaise, it seems, is due to more than austerity. It appears to be deeply rooted in its private sector's anti-competitiveness, and the stultifying effects of government miss taxation and microeconomic miss regulation.[25]

Unscrupulous Private Agents and Public Policy Makers

The secular stagnation that Summers, Krugman, and Stiglitz perceive in the data is most likely caused by collusive state-private "partnership" where big government, big business, and big social advocacy jointly supervene democratic free enterprise.[26] The result is over-taxation of the productive middle class (new working class);[27] anticompetitive coddling of big business with privileged contracts, rents, roundabout subsidies, price-fixing schemes, insurance guarantees and bailouts; the regulatory overburdening of small businesses; the proliferation of profit-impairing mandates; the miss administration of entrepreneurial innovation; anticompetitive executive orders; and the discouragement of initiative with lavish entitlements to the undeserving. The American government abuses presidential executive orders,[28] miss regulates, excessively mandates, over-taxes, stealthily taxes, abets private sector speculation, miss entitles, miss transfers, incentivizes welfare dependency and feigned disability over employment,[29] and politicizes science and education.

Collusive state-private "partnership" (a euphemism for "politocracy")[30] and anticompetitive, pro-speculative regulation most likely are the principal causes of the West's economic lethargy, not Keynesian under-consumption[31] or inequality,[32] and augur badly for America and the European Union's geopolitical clout moving forward because these inefficiencies cannot be quickly eradicated. They are embedded in the mega-"welfare" state. In the Krugman-Summers world, secular stagnation purportedly is readily cured by printing money, unbridled deficit spending, and ever-mounting national debt. Government doesn't seem to have any qualms about spending other people's money. The opposite, however, is true when the root problem is private sector anti-competitiveness, stultifying state over-taxation and miss regulation, and collusive state-private partnership. Big government has intense qualms about retracting its overreach and slenderizing because while that nation is apt to benefit, insiders must relinquish profits from the sale of public service (disservices) and accept reductions in personal power. There is no evidence that they are willing to do either,[33] and consequently secular stagnation is unlikely to vanish quietly into the night.

Few Western leaders are willing to accept that their policies are stultifying economic potential. They are aware that secular stagnation could thwart their ambitions, but refuse to take the threat seriously. They rely on "strategic patience" to bail out the economy in precisely the same way they confidently anticipate that it assures that the outcome of Cold War II will be the same as Cold War I.

Economic miracles sometimes happen. America and the European Union's economies are remarkably adaptive, and their performance could improve despite all the negatives,[34] but if they don't, the prospect that this time will be the same is significantly diminished. It will be extremely difficult for the West to defeat Putin if its economies are ossified in secular stagnation.

Notes

1 Alexander Gerschenkron, "The Rate of Industrial Growth in Russia since 1885," *Journal of Economic History* 7-S (1947): 144–174.

2 Irving Fisher, *The Theory of Interest*, Clifton, NJ: Augustus M. Kelley, 1974 (originally published in 1930).

3 Robert M. Solow, "Technical Change and the Aggregate Production Function," *Review of Economics and Statistics* Vol. 39, No. 3 (1957): 312–320; Trevor W. Swan, "Economic Growth and Capital Accumulation," *Economic Record* (John Wiley & Sons) Vol. 32, No. 2 (November 1956): 334–361.

4 Paul Krugman, *The Return of Depression Economics and the Crisis of 2008*, New York: W. W. Norton Company, 2009; Lawrence Summers, "Washington Must Not Settle for Secular Stagnation," *Financial Times* (December 5, 2013). Retrieved from http://www.ft.com/cms/s/2/ba0f1386-7169-11e3-8f92-00144feabdc0.html# ixzz2pi6xfiEe. James Pethokoukis, "The Slump that Never Ends: Does the US Face 'Secular Stagnation'?" AEI (November 19, 2013; Henry Blodget, "Has the US Entered a 'Permanent Slump'?" *Daily Ticker* (November 18, 2013). Retrieved from http:// finance.yahoo.com/blogs/daily-ticker/u-economy-entered-permanent-slump-165120719.html. "Summers speculates that the natural interest rate 'consistent with full employment'" fell "to negative 2% or negative 3% sometime in the middle of the last decade." But conventional monetary policy cannot push rates that low, the

dreaded Zero Lower Bound. Thus, Summers concludes, "We may well need, in the years ahead, to think about how we manage an economy in which the zero nominal interest rate is a chronic and systemic inhibitor of economic activity, holding our economies back, below their potential." Alan Greenspan, "Never Saw it Coming," *Foreign Affairs* (November/December 2013). Retrieved from http://www.foreignaffairs .com/articles/140161/alan-greenspan/. Dan Weil, "Larry Summers: Europe, US on Brink of Deflationary Spiral for Next Decade," *MoneyNews*, January 25, 2015. http://www.Newsmax.com/Finance/Summers-deflation-Europe-economy/2015/ 01/23/id/620340/#ixzz3Psz9uvhO. Joseph Stiglitz, "Economic Stagnation by Design," *Social Europe*, February 6, 2014. http://www.socialeurope.eu/2014/02/ economic-stagnation/. "The basic point that I raised a half-decade ago was that, in a fundamental sense, the US economy was sick even before the crisis: it was only an asset-price bubble, created through lax regulation and low interest rates, that had made the economy seem robust. Beneath the surface, numerous problems were festering: growing inequality; an unmet need for structural reform (moving from a manufacturing-based economy to services and adapting to changing global comparative advantages); persistent global imbalances; and a financial system more attuned to speculating than to making investments that would create jobs, increase productivity, and redeploy surpluses to maximize social returns." "Instead, our current difficulties are the result of flawed policies. There are alternatives. But we will not find them in the self-satisfied complacency of the elites, whose incomes and stock portfolios are once again soaring. Only some people, it seems, must adjust to a permanently lower standard of living. Unfortunately, those people happen to be most people." Joseph Stiglitz, "The Politics of Economic Stupidity," *Project Syndicate*, January 23, 2015. http://www.project-syndicate.org/ commentary/politics-of-economic-stupidity-by-joseph-e-stiglitz.

5   "Obama's Economy in 10 Charts," *CNN Money*, October 28, 2015. http://money.cnn .com/gallery/news/economy/2015/10/28/obama-economy-10-charts/index.html.

6   James Pethokoukis, "Is America's Entrepreneurial Engine Roaring or Sputtering?" *AEI*, January 16, 2015. http://www.aei.org/publication/americas-entrepreneurial- engine-roaring-sputtering/?utm_source=today&utm_medium=paramount&utm_ campaign=012015.

7   Michael Spense, "How to Fight Secular Stagnation," Project Syndicate, August 29, 2016. https://www.project-syndicate.org/commentary/how-to-fight-secular- stagnation-by-michael-spence-2016-08?utm_source=Temporary+signups+on +site&utm_campaign=e1c904d46e-Leonard_Playing_Defense_Europe_temps_ 4_9_2016&utm_medium=email&utm_term=0_85daf1562e-e1c904d46e- 104851053. "Much of the world, especially the advanced economies, has been mired in a pattern of slow and declining GDP growth in recent years, causing many to wonder whether this is becoming a semi-permanent condition – so- called 'secular stagnation.' The answer is probably yes."

8   John Taylor has dismissed the Summers-Krugman secular stagnation crisis as hokum because he believes that free markets assure a robust American economic recovery. However, while he is justified in challenging Krugman's liquidity trap framework, his own critique of abusive American government points to a plau- sible alternative explanation for the United States' economic dyspepsia. See John Taylor, "Economic Hokum of 'Secular Stagnation': Blaming the Market for the

Failure of Bad Government Policies Is no More Persuasive Now than It Was in the 1930s," *The Wall Street Journal*, January 1, 2014. Retrieved from http://online. wsj.com/news/article_email/SB10001424052702304858104579263953449606842-lMyQjAxMTA0MDAwMjEwNDIyWj.

9 James Pethokoukis, "Is America Really Suffering a 'Great Stagnation'? Why Goldman Sachs Is Skeptical." AEI, May 26, 2015. http://www.aei.org/publication/is-america-really-suffering-a-great-stagnation-why-goldman-sachs-is-skeptical/?utm_source=paramount&utm_medium=email&utm_content=AEITODAY&utm_campaign=052715. "Mismeasurement of inflation has probably for years understated real GDP and income growth. But the IT revolution has likely made that understatement a worse and growing problem. (Goldman's conclusion is also very much in sync with the innovation and productivity research of AEI's Stephen Oliner.) Goldman Sachs disregards offsetting hidden inflation."

10 www.stateofworkingamerica.org. The EPI is a Washington DC think tank founded in 1986 by left-liberal economists Jeff Faux, Lester Thurow, Ray Marshall, Barry Bluestone, Robert Reich, and Robert Kuttner. Thurow, for example, is a longtime advocate of a political and economic system of the Japanese and European type, in which governmental involvement in the direction of the economy is far more extensive than is presently the case in the United States – a model that has come to be known as the "Third Way." See Lester Thurow, *Zero Sum Society*, New York: Basic Books, 1980.

11 Former chief economist to Vice President Joseph Biden Jr. Jared Bernstein reports that American unemployment, counting all missing workers, in January 2014 was 10.2 percent. He contends that the official 6.7 percent instantaneous rate is misleading. See Jared Bernstein, "The Wrong Guidepost on Unemployment," Yahoo News! January 15, 2014. Retrieved from http://economix.blogs.nytimes.com/2014/01/15/the-wrong-guidepost-on-unemployment/?partner=yahoofinance.

12 In November 2013, the labor market had 1.3 million fewer jobs than when the recession began in December 2007. Further, because the potential labor force grows every month, the economy would have had to add 6.6 million jobs just to preserve the labor market health that prevailed in December 2007. Counting jobs lost plus jobs that should have been gained to absorb potential new labor market entrants, the U.S. economy had a jobs shortfall of 7.9 million in November 2013. The number of potential jobseekers increased 1.3 million using EPI's estimator, while the number of new jobs created was 1.7 million. See http://www.ncsl.org/research/labor-and-employment/national-employment-monthly-update.aspx.

13 Nicholas Eberstadt, "The Idle Army: America's Unworking Men: Millions of Young Males Have Left the Workforce and Civic Life. Full Employment? The U.S. Isn't Even Close." *Wall Street Journal*, September 2, 2016. http://www.wsj.com/articles/the-idle-army-americas-unworking-men-1472769641. "Near-full employment? In 2015 the work rate (the ratio of employment to population) for American males age 25 to 54 was 84.4%. That's slightly lower than it had been in 1940, 86.4%, at the tail end of the Great Depression."

14 The 5.7 million figure excludes normal Keynesian transitory unemployment. This is why it is lower than the 7.4 million lost jobs estimate. Rodney Johnson, "The Sun Always Shines at the BLS," *Economy & Markets*, June 18, 2014.

15 John Maynard Keynes is the founder of modern macroeconomic theory. He argued that wage and price rigidities prevented economies from adjusting

to negative shocks that caused depressions and advocated deficit spending as the antidote. See John Maynard Keynes, *The General Theory of Employment, Interest and Money*, London: Macmillan Cambridge University Press, for Royal Economic Society, 1936.

16　http://news.yahoo.com/why-racial-wealth-gap-could-spell-doom-americas-183454552.html. Global Policy Solutions argues that ignoring our escalating racial wealth disparities will lead to "national peril." "Beyond Broke: Why Closing the Racial Wealth Gap Is a Priority for National Economic Security." According to the report, between 2005 and 2011, the median net worth of minority households remained at recession-era levels, "reflecting a drop of 58% for Latinos, 48% for Asians, [and] 45% for African Americans," compared to just 21 percent for whites. Moreover, the differences in both net worth and cash on hand are even more striking. Beyond Broke researchers found the median liquid wealth for Latinos is a mere $340, while African Americans have just $200 in liquid assets. On the other hand, Asians hold $19,500 in median liquid wealth, compared to $23,000 for whites. Furthermore, blacks and Latinos are twice as likely as whites to have no financial assets.

17　Brooks, "A Conservative Social Justice Agenda." "The Obama administration's 'progressive' agenda has left the poor behind. Years after the Great Recession, real need persists. The left's misguided policies and materialistic culture only exacerbate the problem. It is conservatives and libertarians who must be struggling, Americans' true champions." "The number of citizens who rely on 'food stamps' has soared by 50% since early 2009. Just 63% of Americans are working or seeking work, the lowest rate since the 1970s. Crisis-level unemployment persists in vulnerable communities – 36% for African-American teens." "Vulnerable people need three things: Personal moral transformation, material relief, and the opportunity to rise."

18　J. Bradford DeLong, "The Tragedy of Ben Bernanke," *Project Syndicate*, October 29, 2015. https://www.project-syndicate.org/commentary/bernanke-memoir-monetary-policy-lessons-by-j--bradford-delong-2015-10?utm_source=Project+Syndicate+Newsletter&utm_campaign=ba54bcb110-Brad_DeLong_The_Tragedy_of_Ben_Bernanke10_31_2015&utm_medium=email&utm_term=0_73bad5b7d8-ba54bcb110-93559677. DeLong reports that all leading economists, including Kenneth Rogoff and himself, agree that post-crisis American economic growth has been anemic and macroeconomic theorists cannot convincingly explain why.

19　Steven Rosefielde and Ralph W. Pfouts, *Inclusive Economic Theory*, Singapore: World Scientific Publishers, 2014.

20　Summers has moved away from advocating "easy money" and now stresses intensified deficit spending. "The third approach – and the one that holds most promise – is a commitment to raising the level of demand at any given level of interest rates, through policies that restore a situation where reasonable growth and reasonable interest rates can coincide. This means ending the disastrous trend towards ever less government spending and employment each year – and taking advantage of the current period of economic slack to renew and build up our infrastructure. If the government had invested more over the past five years, our debt burden relative to our incomes would be lower: allowing slackening in the economy has hurt its potential in the long run." Summers, "Washington Must Not Settle for Secular Stagnation."

21 Paul R. Krugman, "It's Baack: Japan's Slump and the Return of the Liquidity Trap," *Brookings*, 2008. http://www.brookings.edu/~/media/projects/bpea/1998%202/ 1998b_bpea_krugman_dominquez_rogoff.pdf

22 "Obama's 2014 State of the Union Address: Full Text," January 28, 2014. Retrieved from http://www.cbsnews.com/news/obamas-2014-state-of-the-union-address-full-text/.

23 "ECB Unveils Massive QE Boost for Eurozone," *BBC*, January 22, 2015. http://www .bbc.com/news/business-30933515. "The European Central Bank (ECB) will inject at least €1.1 trillion (£834bn) into the ailing eurozone economy. The ECB will buy €60bn bonds each month from banks until the end of September 2016, or even longer, in what is called quantitative easing (QE)."

24 Yanis Varoufakis, "Schäuble's Gathering Storm," Project Syndicate, October 23, 2015. https://www.project-syndicate.org/commentary/germany-versus-france-italy-by-yanis-varoufakis-2015-10?utm_source=Project+Syndicate+Newsletter&utm_ campaign=94ec6c2dde-Varoufakis_Schauble%27s_Gathering_Storm_10_25_ 2015&utm_medium=email&utm_term=0_73bad5b7d8-94ec6c2dde-93559677. "Europe's crisis is poised to enter its most dangerous phase. After forcing Greece to accept another 'extend-and-pretend' bailout agreement, fresh battle lines are being drawn. And, with the refugee influx exposing the damage caused by divergent economic prospects and sky-high youth unemployment in Europe's periphery, the ramifications are ominous, as recent statements by three European politicians – Italian Prime Minister Matteo Renzi, French Economy Minister Emmanuel Macron, and German Finance Minister Wolfgang Schäuble – have made clear. Renzi has come close to demolishing, at least rhetorically, the fiscal rules that Germany has defended for so long. In a remarkable act of defiance, he threatened that if the European Commission rejected Italy's national budget, he would re-submit it without change. This was not the first time Renzi had alienated Germany's leaders. And it was no accident that his statement followed a months-long effort by his own finance minister, Pier Carlo Padoan, to demonstrate Italy's commitment to the eurozone's German-backed 'rules.' Renzi understands that adherence to German-inspired parsimony is leading Italy's economy and public finances into deeper stagnation, accompanied by further deterioration of the debt-to-GDP ratio. A consummate politician, Renzi knows that this is a short path to electoral disaster. Macron is very different from Renzi in both style and substance. A banker-turned-politician, he is President François Hollande's only minister who combines a serious understanding of France's and Europe's macroeconomic challenges with a reputation in Germany as a reformer and skillful interlocutor. So when he speaks of an impending religious war in Europe, between the Calvinist German-dominated northeast and the largely Catholic periphery, it is time to take notice."

25 Klaus Schwab, "The Global Economy 2014," Project Syndicate, January 22, 2014. Retrieved from digital@project-syndicate.org. Schwab is executive chairman of the World Economic Forum. He writes "The Fed's QE policy, and variants of it elsewhere, have caused the major central banks' balance sheets to expand dramatically (from $5–6 trillion prior to the crisis to almost $20 trillion now), causing financial markets to become addicted to easy money. This has led, in turn, to a global search for yield, artificial asset-price inflation, and misallocation of capital. As a result, the longer QE lasts, the greater the collateral damage to the real economy.

The concern now is that when the Fed begins to taper QE and dollar liquidity drains from global markets, structural problems and imbalances will resurface. After all, competitiveness-enhancing reforms in many advanced economies remain far from complete, while the ratio of these countries' total public and private debt to GDP is now 30% higher than before the crisis."

26 Steven Rosefielde and Quinn Mills, *Democracy and Its Elected Enemies: American Political Capture and Economic Decline*, Cambridge: Cambridge University Press, 2013.

27 Steven Rosefielde and Quinn Mill, *Global Economic Turmoil and the Public Good*, Singapore: World Scientific Publishers, 2015.

28 Jeff Mason, "Obama Signs Order to Raise Minimum Wage for Federal Contractors," *Reuters*, February 12, 2014. Retrieved from http://news.yahoo.com/obama- sign-order-federal-minimum-wage-hike-wednesday-110247693--business.html. Obama's action is an usurpation of congressional authority and an arbitrary tax on the public because the expense must be funded with taxes or borrowed funds.

29 Annie Lowrey, "States Cutting Weeks of Aid to Jobless," *Wall Street Journal*, January 22, 2014. Cutting the maximum number of weeks of unemployment has stimulated employment. Cf. Dennis Maki and Z. A. Spindler, "The Effect of Unemployment Compensation on the Rate of Unemployment in Great Britain," *Oxford Economic Papers*, New Series, Vol. 27, No. 3 (1975): 440–454.

30 Rosefielde and Mills, *Democracy and Its Elected Enemies*.

31 Keynes claimed that aggregate demand is deficient during depressions because unemployed workers cannot afford to consume as much as they did when they were working. This is often referred to under consumptionism. There are pre-Keynesian and Marxist versions of the same basic idea. Cf. Robert Record, "How the War on Poverty Was Lost: Fifty Years and $20 Trillion Later, LBJ's Goal to Help the Poor Become Self-Supporting has Failed," *Wall Street Journal*, January 7, 2014. Retrieved from http://online.wsj.com/news/article_email/SB10001424052702303345104579282760272285556-lMyQjAx MTA0MDAwODEwNDgyWj. Cf. Jonathan Leightner, *The Limits of Monetary, Fiscal, and Trade Policies: International Comparisons and a Solution*, Singapore: World Scientific Publishers, 2014.

32 Thomas Piketty, *Capital in the Twenty-First Century*, Cambridge MA: Harvard University Press, 2014. Piketty recommends a global wealth tax to redress the planet's economic woes. Cf. Tim Worstall, "Why Thomas Piketty's Global Wealth Tax Won't Work," *Forbes*, March 30, 2014. Retrieved from http://www.forbes.com/sites/timworstall/2014/03/30/why-thomas-pikettys-global-wealth-tax-wont-work/. "The Super Rich Are Richer than We Thought, Hiding Huge Sums, New Reports Find," *Huffington Post*, April 12, 2014. Retrieved from http://www.huffingtonpost.com/2014/04/12/super-rich-richer_n_5138753.html?.

33 Rosefielde and Mills, *Democracy and Its Elected Enemies*.

34 Brad DeLong, "The Economic Trend Is Our Friend," Project Syndicate, August 31, 2016. https://www.project-syndicate.org/commentary/economic-growth-long-term-trends-by-j--bradford-delong-2016-08 "Pessimism understandably comes easy these days – perhaps too easy. In fact, enthusiastic and positive contrarianism is in order: if we look at global economic growth not just five years out, but over the next 30–60 years, the picture looks much brighter.

"The reason is simple: the large-scale trends that have fueled global growth since World War II have not stopped. More people are gaining access to new, productivity enhancing technologies, more people are engaging in mutually beneficial trade, and fewer people are being born, thus allaying any continued fears of a so-called population bomb."

10

Military Cross-Currents

The likelihood that Cold War II will mimic Cold War I depends not only on the economic factors considered in the preceding three chapters, but on the comparative prowess of Russia's, Ukraine's and the West's military-industrial complexes, weapons technologies, deployable forces to critical theaters of military operations, readiness, strategies, tactics, geography, and, most important of all, a political commitment to deter, expand, and fight in key zones of conflict. These are the military dimensions of the correlation of forces. Russia's military-industrial and defense-spending statistics suggest that it is rapidly building up its forces, while the West builds its forces down. NATO has sufficient military power to stop the Kremlin, but appears reluctant to employ these assets in Ukraine, and perhaps even the Baltic states, while pressing color revolutions, regime change, and NATO accession in Russia's environs. The divergence in Russia and the West's arms procurement and defense-spending trajectories together with the West's aversion to combat in Ukraine and perhaps the Baltic states is turning the military component of the correlation of forces strongly against NATO, and seriously calling into question the West's confidence that this time will be the same.[1]

Russia

There is broad agreement across the political spectrum that the Soviet Union was a military superpower. Some claimed that America and the USSR had strategic nuclear parity, others that the Kremlin's atomic arsenal greatly surpassed Washington's. The consensus view about conventional forces was even more favorable to the Soviet side. The USSR's non-nuclear armaments (including tank armies, combat aircraft, ballistic missiles, biological and chemical weapons of mass destruction) and uniformed military manpower exceeded the West's by wide margins, leading some to infer that nuclear deterrence not only diminished the risk of Western aggression in the Kremlin's eyes, but freed the USSR to wage conventional war. The Soviet Union was seen as a threat during Cold War I because the Kremlin had the capability to expand the USSR's sphere of influence through lethal and nonlethal coercion and the judicious use of armed force if its Machiavellian rational actors chose to do so.[2]

Then, suddenly, with little warning, Kremlin military power crumbled in the early 1990s.[3] The USSR's dissolution shrank its empire by almost 30 percent (50 percent in terms of population) and sharply degraded strategic nuclear capabilities. Russia nearly halted new weapons production, decommissioned deployed weapons, mothballed armaments, scrapped weapons, depleted prolonged warfighting reserves, destroyed human and defense institutional capital, decimated military RDT&E, degraded readiness, and rendered its arsenal obsolete, but preserved its military-industrial production capabilities. The CIA estimates that Soviet and Russian military procurement fell 90 percent in the early 1990s, a dramatic statistic that epitomizes both the sharp deterioration in Russia's absolute military might and correlation of forces immediately after communism's demise. Its nuclear arsenal protected the homeland from Chinese and Western incursions, but Moscow found it difficult to preserve and defend spheres of interest in its neighborhood and the more distant abroad. The Kremlin lost fourteen Soviet republics, the former Soviet Union's satellites in Eastern and Central Europe and, its global influence, and was treated as a token "partner" in a new West-imposed global order.

Boris Yeltsin passively accepted this "new normal," but Vladimir Putin didn't. He immediately commissioned a military recovery plan that established the foundations for a reversal of fortune after his first two presidential terms.[4] The success of his endeavor, despite immense skepticism,[5] is reflected in the West's current perception of the Kremlin's military capabilities. The correlation of military forces favoring the West has deteriorated enough that America and the European Union believe that Russia poses a credible military threat to Mariupol and other parts of Ukraine (eastern, southeastern, and Donbas) in Novorossiya that Putin claims belong historically to Russia. Estonia is building a fence to keep Russian infiltrators out,[6] the Finnish president openly questions his nation's ability to defend the Baltic states against Russia,[7] and Poland is sufficiently concerned that it is acquiring heavy weapons from the United States.[8]

The credibility of these threats is confirmed by an authoritative inventory of Russia's military-industrial accomplishments (budgetary expenditures and weapons procurement) that recently has been compiled by Julian Cooper for FOI (Swedish Defense Research Agency) and serves as a baseline.[9] Cooper's appendix contains a complete line item inventory of Russian weapons acquisitions 2010–2015 for those desiring further documentation.

Armament Programme for Russia for the Years 2011 to 2020

Putin's goal of restoring Russia's great power – reflected in Crimea's annexation – depends critically on the past success of the VPK's military-industrial R&D 2002–2010 initiative achieved under The Reform and Development of the Defense Industrial Complex Program 2002–2006 signed by Prime Minister Mikhail Kasyanov in October 2001,[10] and the State Armament Programme for Russia for the years 2011 to 2020 signed by President Dmitri Medvedev at the end of 2010. Cooper summarizes the program and its accomplishment through 2015 as follows:

This was a highly ambitious document setting out plans for the procurement of weapons and other military equipment, plus research and development for the creation of new systems, to a total value of over 20 trillion rubles, or US$680 billion at the exchange rate of the day. The aim of the programme was to increase the share of modern armaments held by the armed forces from 15 per cent in 2010 to 30 percent in 2015 and 70 per cent in 2020. The programme has been implemented through the budget-funded annual state defence order supplemented by state guaranteed credits. By 2014 the military output of the defence industry was growing at an annual rate of over 20 percent, compared with 6 percent three years earlier. The volume of new weapons procured steadily increased, the rate of renewal being particularly strong in the strategic missile forces and the air force, but not as impressive in the navy and ground forces. In 2014 the work of the defence industry began to be affected by the Ukraine crisis, with a breakdown of military-related deliveries from Ukraine and the imposition of sanctions by NATO and European Union member countries. The performance of the economy began to deteriorate, putting pressure on state finances. It was decided to postpone for three years the approval of the successor state armament programme, 2016–2025. Nevertheless, the implementation of the programme to date has secured a meaningful modernisation of the hardware of the Russian armed forces for the first time since the final years of the USSR.

Insofar as Cooper is correct,[11] despite the adverse consequences of the global financial crisis of 2008, Russia has not only succeeded in augmenting the size of its arsenal, but has also significantly modernized its armed forces.[12] Eugene Kogan concurs.[13] The quantitative improvement may be partly attributable to restarting existing weapon production lines with negligible systemic implications (economic recovery), but modernization is another story. It demonstrates that Russia's post-communist economy, like its Soviet predecessor, is capable of manufacturing large quantities of technologically improved weapons systems.

Sources of Quantitative Growth and Modernization

Quantitative weapons growth and modernization depend on engineering prowess and economic efficiency. Engineers design weapons and the factories needed to produce them. Russian military specifications, like their counterparts in the West, are determined by military professionals, not private consumer preferences. The volumes of weapons produced, given prevailing technologies depend formally on each good's production function, factor supplies, and allocative efficiency.[14] Output can be increased by building additional factories, employing more variable capital and labor, allocating factors to better use, and improving technology,[15] even if factor and product prices in multiproduct firms aren't generally competitive.[16] Just as in the West, optimization (maximal efficiency) cannot be fully achieved if prices are distorted by anticompetitive influences. This means that the Kremlin can increase weapons production from the achieved level to the extent that Putin desires within conventional "bounded rationality constraints,"[17] and in accordance with his willingness to divert resources from the civilian sector to military production. Even more can be achieved by improving production technologies and "second worst" allocative efficiency.[18] The claim that Russia's economy cannot support the creation and maintenance of formidable armed forces is fundamentally misguided on engineering and microeconomic grounds, an assertion the Soviet experience confirms. The same argument holds for improved weapons design, the development of new weapons systems, and the modernization of productive capacities. The Kremlin can and historically has continuously enhanced the technological proficiency of its weapons and modernized its armament production facilities and inter-industrial material supplies networks. There are two highly classified programs (*federalnye tselevye progammy-FTsP*) in place today approved by President Dmitrii Medvedev on December 31, 2010 facilitating the implementation of the Russian state armament programme, 2011–2020 (*gosudarstvennaia programma vooruzhenii*) by funding the modernization of the industrial base of the defense sector (FTsP Development of the defense-industrial complex, 2011–2020) and inter-industrial supply (FTsP Development, restoration and organization of the production of strategic scarce and import substituting materials and small-scale chemistry for armaments, military, and special technology in 2009–2011 and to 2015).[19]

VPK Policy, Institutional and Incentive Reform

The performance and potentials of Russia's military-industrial system and economy took a quantum leap after the 2008 global financial crisis. These changes were planned as early as 2002, but materialized a few years later than originally envisioned in the Reform and Development of the Defense Industrial Complex Program 2002–2006. Military spending in Kasyanov's document focused on designing and developing fifth-generation weapons rather than augmenting inventories of standard equipment. Military R&D temporarily took pride of place over procurement until new technologies came on stream and manufacturing facilities were installed for the mass production of advanced armaments. During this period and a few years beyond, it seemed as if the directors of the VPK and enterprise managers were content to throw money down an R&D black hole.[20] There was no credible evidence of success while reports indicated that key officials managed to live comfortably by diverting funds to personal use while feigning bold R&D ventures. The Russian defense budgetary and weapons procurement data compiled by Cooper,[21] confirmed by multiple sources, reveal that the VPK has moved beyond the R&D phase of its military restoration project to rapid rearmament.[22] He contends that a meaningful modernization of the hardware of the Russian armed forces occurred 2010–2015 for the first time since the final years of the USSR, driven by the rapid procurement of new advanced weapons.[23]

This means not only that Putin has adhered to the policy laid out in in the Reform and Development of the Defense Industrial Complex Program 2002–2006, albeit with a delay, but the companion institutional and incentive reforms required for success were implemented, especially during the FTsP Development of the defense-industrial complex 2011–2020 program. The surge in Russian weapons cannot be explained by revving up idled production lines for fourth-generation equipment. It reflects modernization of weapon characteristics, updating old production lines, building new modern production facilities, and switching from managerial regimes rewarding executives for mass production rather than military R&D.

The literature on these subjects provides a clear, if incomplete picture of what has transpired. First, after Yeltsin's experiment with privatization, the VPK and closely associated "strategic enterprises" like Transneft, Gazprom, Rosneftegaz, and Alrosa were renationalized in 2004. Initially, state ownership included private shareholding participation, but now 100 percent state proprietorship is more frequently the norm.[24] However, unlike Soviet arrangements, state ownership doesn't bar VPK enterprises or public-private partnerships (PPP) from competing among each other.[25] Military-industrial firms (including holding companies) are permitted to operate on a for-profit basis. They compete for state orders and export sales (contracts) and can outsource. Shareholders and/

or manages are variously incentivized to profit-seek and incompletely profit-maximize rather than comply with MOD commands and/or rent-seek. They have fewer degrees of freedom than private Western defense corporations like Boeing, but are self-motivated to efficiently produce in accordance with Herbert Simon's bounded rationality framework and William Baumol's satisficing concept.[26] This bolstered VPK initiative when the MOD stopped prioritizing military R&D. Weapon producers could pretend to increase output, continue rent-seeking, and live passively off state funds. This may well have been the most likely outcome, but judging from Cooper's evidence Putin beat the odds by imposing firm discipline and containing rent-seeking, buttressed with competitive reforms and sufficient material incentives. No one denies that kleptocratic rent-seeking persists, nor the latent threat it poses to Russia's military-industrial revival. The system could relapse into indolence when Putin retires, but it now needs to be recognized that sustainable Russian military modernization is also a distinct possibility.

Escalation Dominance

The Kremlin's drive to restore Russia's great power status has much in common with Soviet precedent, but differs on several important scores. The *genstab* (Soviet General Staff) strove to achieve full spectrum strategic and tactical battlefield dominance. It maintained the world's largest tank armies for blitzkrieg attack against NATO and was prepared to use tactical nuclear and biological weapons in its order of battle. The USSR maintained vast strategic nuclear forces (including reloads) for disarming first strikes and second-strike retaliation. It constructed antiballistic missile defences to reinforce strategic nuclear deterrence and sought to achieve escalation domination at all combat intensities across the globe and planned for prolonged warfighting engagements.

Russia's 2010 military doctrine retains these essentials,[27] but scales down the defense mission, concentrating forces on its Western periphery, foregoing a Pacific blue water navy, and prolonged warfighting reserves. The goal is an economically cost-effective military capable of quick victories in key theaters of military operation (TVD) through the rapid deployment of superior battlefield forces, buttressed by strategic nuclear deterrence.[28] Instead of doing everything poorly, the new doctrine strives to do the essentials well.[29]

This means in practice that NATO cannot tactically deter Russia in the Baltics or Ukraine. The Kremlin has operational weapons fitted with tactical nuclear ordnance ready for employment on Europe's battlefields. Western leaders might be chastened by the methodical and rapid manner in which Moscow has transformed the military correlation of forces on Russia's western periphery, but are unfazed. They insist that tactical escalation dominance and rapid war-winning capabilities are moot because mutually assured strategic nuclear deterrence (MAD) means that the tactical escalation dominance and quick victories cannot be exploited.[30] Moscow cannot employ its tactical escalation dominance because it fears America's strategic nuclear retaliation, and quick victories on periphery would lead to prolonged war with the West that Russia could not win. This reasoning is hardly failsafe, but Washington and Berlin are prepared to rely on it until something far more catastrophic than Crimea's annexation alters their outlook.

No one is suggesting that Russia's military can easily defeat the West in World War III or that the Kremlin's arms buildup will soon empower it to invade and conquer the NATO heartland, but many legitimately fret that Moscow can fight and win territory against two candidates for NATO membership – Ukraine and Georgia – and perhaps non-NATO Finland and the NATO Baltic states.[31] Needless to say, the military component of the correlation of forces is only one of many factors shaping Putin's actions; nonetheless, it merits close attention.

Defense experts know that public statistics on arsenals, decommissioned armaments including nuclear warheads, ballistic missile reloads, dual-use capabilities, prolonged warfighting reserves, weapons production, deployments, military manpower, and readiness, as well as judgments about combat effectiveness, can be seriously misleading. There is a façade of transparency provided by various "authoritative" sources like the International Institute for Strategic Studies' Military Balance that serves sundry purposes, but there are also many deep secrets and conflicts of opinion. However, there is no dispute about the shift in correlation of forces under Putin's watch appraised from the standpoint of rising Kremlin military power. Moscow's military modernization and rearmament programs, as well as improved readiness, have been successful enough for Russia to credibly employ nonlethal and lethal coercion against it neighbors and to capture strategically significant territorial assets through the deft use of hybrid warfare.[32] This would have been impossible under Yeltsin. The Kremlin has limited itself thus far mostly to proxy warfare,[33] but could have just as easily seized Crimea with its own forces accepting the risk of a Western counterstrike.[34]

Europe

This success has been primarily the Kremlin's doing, facilitated by a huge contraction in Western defense spending, particularly in the development, deployment, and maintenance of forces needed to counter Russia's challenge.[35] Official statistics on Europe's defense spending undistorted by America's out-of-theater military activities declined from $314 billion to $227 billion between 1990 and 2015, computed in constant 2010 dollars,[36] even though NATO membership has nearly doubled. According to the International Institute for Strategic Studies, Germany's defense spending has fallen by 4.3 percent since 2008. In the same period, the United Kingdom has reduced its defense spending by 9.1 percent and Italy by 21 percent. This has led to a sharp drop in military capabilities in bigger and more exposed NATO member states, and it has made the already uneven burden sharing in the alliance more lopsided. Jan Techau contends that the reduction together with America's diminished security footprint in Europe (the permanent U.S. troop presence in Europe has been very substantially reduced since the 1990s) has created a security vacuum with scant prospects for swift reversal. Europe spends less than 2 percent of its GDP on defense, which is less than a quarter of the author's estimate of Russia's contemporary defense burden (CIA building block method). Its declaratory goal is to increase the defense spending to 2 percent, but the Europeans have yet to reallocate funds from civilian to military purposes. The glaring discrepancy between NATO's rhetorical posture and its budgetary actions has not been overlooked in Moscow and must surely fortify Putin's resolve.

NATO hasn't been feckless. It has adopted a Readiness Action Plan (RAP) that encompasses a full array of military steps designed to enhance the deterrent value of NATO's military posture on its Eastern border. NATO has reassured the populations of Central and Eastern Europe that it will come to their aid under Article 5, if Russia attacks them. The pledge has been reinforced by land, sea, and air exercises focused on collective defense and crisis management on NATO's eastern flank. RAP has initiated "adaptation measures"; that is, longer-term changes to NATO's forces and command structures, including tripling the strength of the NATO Response Force (NRF), creating a Very High Readiness Joint Task Force (VJTF) deployable on short notice, and enhancing standing naval forces. Toward this end, six NATO Force Integration Units (NFIUs) – small headquarters – are being established in Central and Eastern Europe, along with a headquarters for the Multinational Corps Northeast in Szczecin, Poland, and a standing joint logistics support group headquarters.[37] All these actions have real deterrent value, but will soon be overwhelmed by Russia's fast-paced arms buildup because readiness in the intermediate term is an inadequate substitute for large-scale, fifth-generation, conventional forces deployed on the periphery, including Novorossiya.

Moreover, bold talk and a willingness to employ force are two very different things. European governments find it difficult to maintain political support, not only for defense spending, but also, and more fundamentally, for conceptualizing security as both territorial defense and expeditionary interventionism. Germany for one has made it clear enough that it won't fight in Novorossiya to reverse Crimea's annexation. The United Kingdom, France, and Italy won't participate in air, sea, or land assaults on Russian soil or the Luhansk People's Republic either.[38] NATO isn't a paper tiger, but neither is it a daunting foe, if Putin is patient enough to expand the Kremlin's sphere of influence, gradually allowing the creation of a succession of "new normal" status quos that increase Russia's reach while the West persistently temporizes. This is the strategy Stalin used to build his postwar Eastern and Central European satellite system in the early postwar era, and there seems little to prevent the ploy from succeeding today. Indeed, the opportunity for Putin is better than it was for Stalin because the strategic vacuum created by Europe's unwillingness to adequately defend itself and America's gradual withdrawal from the continent invites the Kremlin to fill the void. The West from a military perspective is in retreat precisely at the moment Putin has chosen to launch his project for the restoration of Russia's great power, suggesting that Moscow's pressure won't evaporate of its own accord.

Theaters of Military Operation

Russia and the West both desire to expand their spheres of influence on each other's turf. The West's preferred tactic is pressing color revolutions, regime change ("Putin must go"),[39] accession to the European Union and NATO, and foreign direct investment. Russia employs analogous methods plus hybrid warfare and in the Crimean case added annexation. How might shifts in the military correlation of forces given recent trends affect the outcomes of spheres of influence tussles during the remainder of Putin's years in power? Consider two carefully crafted and illuminating hypothetical cases that could occur just prior to his likely fourth presidential term in 2018 that leave ample time for the Kremlin to conquer, annex, and consolidate gains before Russia's legislative elections in 2020.[40] Both are concordant with Russia National Security Strategy and the latest version of its military doctrine.[41] In the first scenario, the West is the transgressor. It manages to entice a country in Russia's neighborhood (Finland, Ukraine, Moldova, Transdnistria, Armenia, Georgia, South Ossetia, Azerbaijan, or Belarus) to join NATO, provoking the Kremlin to retaliate by seizing and/ or annexing territory. Call this the "West's Greater Europe gambit." In the second scenario, Russia is a blue skies aggressor. It uses uniformed Russian troops to wrest territory without provocation from a neighboring sovereign state (Finland, Estonia, Latvia, Lithuania, Ukraine, Moldova, Armenia, or Georgia) that is a neutral, an EU accession candidate, or an EU-NATO member. Classify this as a "Greater Russia re-conquest initiative." Will a pattern of gradual NATO diminishment and rapid Russian weapons growth allow the Kremlin to prevail in one or both scenarios, holding other aspects of the correlation of forces constant?

The West's Greater Europe Gambit

The Greater Europe gambit (scenario one) assumes that the Kremlin continues modernizing its strategic and tactical nuclear forces, opts to reintroduce nuclear armed intermediate range ballistic missiles,[42] and continues to gradually escalate its nuclear saber rattling, making it relatively safe for Russia to wage conventional war in NATO's European periphery. This is a fundamental aspect of assured nuclear deterrence – making the world free for conventional warfighting. Assume further that Moscow substantially increases the share of combat-effective fifth-generation weapons in its conventional forces (sixth-generation jet fighter technology won't be available in America until the 2025–2030 time frame),[43] improves its rapid deployment capabilities, and increases the readiness both of its active troops and prolonged warfighting reserves.[44] Finally, assume too that NATO, in an environment of shrinking European military budgets, fails to develop credible rapid-reaction air, sea (operating in the Black Sea), and ground forces capable of defeating Russia in a sustained war in the territories of Ukraine, Moldova, Transdnistria, Armenia, Georgia, South Ossetia, Azerbaijan, or Belarus. What would NATO do in this realistic environment if Putin responded to a Greater Europe gambit by swiftly conquering part or all of a target country?[45] Would NATO's members, including Germany, France, Italy, and Turkey, commit themselves to a full-scale war in Russia's backyard over the organization's "right" to attract new recruits from the Kremlin's sphere of influence?

Polls show that Germany's electorate today opposes any kind of armed intervention in Ukraine. No information is available regarding the attitude of Germans toward high-intensity "boots on the ground" operations in Moldova, Transdnistria, Armenia, Georgia, South Ossetia, Azerbaijan, or Belarus, but there are no reasons to suppose there would be a groundswell for war. It therefore can be plausibly inferred that Russia's arms buildup is not only improving the military correlation of forces from Moscow's perspective. It is providing Russia with a credible defense of its realms from what it considers Western provocations, even if American and EU leaders believe that the Kremlin is unjustified in feeling provoked by color revolutions, regime change, and accession to the European Union and NATO. Faith in the righteousness of its cause cannot shield the West from being forced to stand down or incur a humiliating defeat in scenario one.

Greater Russia Re-conquest Initiative

Now suppose alternatively, given the same core assumptions that applied in the first scenario, that Putin decides to wrest territory from a neighboring sovereign state (Finland, Estonia, Latvia, Lithuania, Ukraine, Moldova, Armenia, or Georgia), a neutral, EU-NATO member, or an EU accession candidate. He is nakedly aggressive. There is no Western provocation. What would be the prospects for the Kremlin's success in the period of high vulnerability, 2018–2020?

The answer is great. The Kremlin will have a distinct advantage because of asymmetries in the deployment, command, control, and communications in theaters of military operation under consideration in scenario 2, even if Russia fails to cultivate fifth columns in the victim's territory. Putin has ample time to prepare limited "shock-and-awe" wars by 2018 that would simultaneously achieve valuable objectives and discourage the onset of World War III by encouraging Western leaders to place their faith in strategic patience.[46] He could wager on strategic surprise, confronting Washington and Berlin with a fait accompli like his Crimean annexation by prepositioning, rapidly deploying massive combined armed forces, and striking quickly, while simultaneously threatening out-of-theater targets to stretch NATO's retaliatory assets. The ploy should be effective because, by assumption, the West won't pay for the readiness needed to credibly retaliate and NATO wasn't designed for swift responses to Greater Russian re-conquest initiatives. It was created to close the barn door after Stalin seized his Eastern and Central European empires in 1947; not to dislodge a nuclear superpower arguably on its own turf.

Surgical shock-and-awe tactics are apt to work better in some countries than others. They can be employed in Moldova, Armenia, or Georgia, but this would be overkill. There doesn't appear to be any pressing reason to conquer Finland, and attacking Estonia, Latvia, or Lithuania would invoke article 5 of the founding 1949 NATO treaty, although this paper pledge isn't the ironclad guarantee many suppose. Insiders know that article 5 is more a hope and prayer than a promise for the Baltics.

The Washington Treaty clearly states that an attack on any member shall be deemed an attack on the collective, but the assistance entailed is vague, allowing members broad wiggle room to decide whether and to what extent to fight.[47] The political calculation would necessarily require delicate judgment, but it would hardly be unreasonable for Putin to conclude that he could launch an invasion from Narva or Kaliningrad to seize and annex a large chunk of Estonia, Latvia, and Lithuania, and then gull the West gradually into accommodating the new normal.

The most lucrative target of opportunity from multiple perspectives, however, continues to be the eastern, southeastern, and Donbas regions of tsarist Novorossiya. There are considerable strategic military and economic advantages to annexing the northern coast of the Black Sea, including Mariupol and Odessa, as a gateway to Moldova and beyond. Russia would not only gain valuable natural resources, but could more effectively project forces against Ukraine, Turkey, and the Middle East. The West would be enraged, but also toothless in the face of the carefully planned 2018 strike hypothesized in scenario 2 that overcame existing obstacles to conquest. The presence of superior, entrenched Russian military forces and the exorbitant military costs of physically dislodging Kremlin armies might well daunt Western leaders.

Scenarios 1 and 2 do not preclude alternatives or serve as reliable predictors of the shape of things to come because military power is only one component of the correlation of forces. Nonetheless, both scenarios illustrate that the Kremlin's investment in military strength can be construed as a strategically opportunistic, rational response to the drift in Western security policy, and that Russia's drive to restore its great power is unlikely to fade quietly into the night under Putin's watch.

Revolution in Military Affairs

The shock-and-awe strategies available to Putin in 2018 are fully compatible with Soviet military thinking, including Marshal of the Soviet Union Nikolai Ogarkov's concept of the revolution in military affairs (RMA).[48] The doctrine has been variously interpreted, but the core idea stresses the decisive role of advanced weapons technology, information technology, military organization, and military doctrine in dominating the modern battlefield through intelligence, surveillance and reconnaissance, command, control, communications, intelligence processing, and precision force. Ogarkov understood by the end of the 1970s that the West was outpacing the USSR in all these regards, and Russia doubtlessly remains disadvantaged. Putin's options looking toward 2018 therefore must be appropriately hedged in two ways. He must choose his targets, carefully avoiding engagements where the West's RMA advantage is likely to be decisive,[49] and keep a sharp eye out for the emergence of revolutionary weapons.

Scenarios 1 and 2 were crafted to minimize the possibilities of Russia being defeated by the West's superior RMA capabilities. Putin should be reassured on this score. Nonetheless, should he be chastened by the danger of sixth-generation Western military technologies already on the horizon?[50] Recent headlines might give him pause. Sensational stories about breakthrough weapons periodically grab media attention. However, Putin should not be unduly alarmed. The IISS and most informed observers contend that while a host of exotic weapons is currently being developed across the globe, any war fought before 2020 will almost certainly be waged with fourth- and fifth-generation arms.[51]

Directed Energy Weapons

There are two types of revolutionary weapons technologies that some believe might drastically alter the military correlation of forces in the foreseeable future: laser and radio-frequency weapons. Both have been actively under development for at least forty years, and are viewed as disruptive technologies applicable primarily to tactical rather than strategic missions. Laser systems as currently envisioned are intended to supplement, not replace existing weapons. One option on the table is using lasers against fast-attack naval craft or unmanned aerial vehicles without having to employ costlier anti-ship missiles. More powerful laser systems are being tested, but progress has been incremental and no monopolies exist yet on these technologies.

Radio-frequency weapons, commonly called high-power microwave systems, have the potential to temporarily or permanently disable systems that rely on computers or electronics by emitting very high-output, short-duration, electromagnetic bursts. They have been successfully applied in niche applications like counter-personnel, counter-vehicle, and counter-improvised-explosive-device systems, but the development of effective stand-off weapons has proven more challenging. Development is proceeding with lowered expectations, and it is unlikely that directed energy weapons will transformation battlefields in Novorossiya or the Baltic states to Russia's disadvantage in years immediately ahead.[52]

Hybrid Warfare

Emergent sixth-generation technologies don't seem likely to put scenarios 1 and 2 at risk, but another squiggle favoring Russia requires consideration. The Kremlin can adopt a dual-strategic approach. Russia's RMA operations in scenarios 1 and 2 can be leveraged by marrying them with hybrid warfare;[53] a military strategy that blends conventional warfare, irregular warfare (guerrilla warfare), and cyberwarfare.[54] The tactic effectively applied by the Kremlin in Crimea, Luhansk, and Donetsk allows aggressors to mask and plausibly deny involvement, while carrying out kinetic, covert subversive and dis-informational operations.[55] The approach is flexible, dynamic, and difficult to defend. It can be employed to soften targets prior to RMA attack, and/or deter retaliation after targets have been seized and/or annexed. The IISS considers Russia's use of hybrid war in Crimea, Luhansk, and Donetsk "sophisticated," urging policy makers to take the threat seriously when "crafting new concepts and re-examining existing strategies" precisely because they serve as a potent device for circumventing Article 5 of the NATO treaty,[56] and sowing Western discord.

Finally, another word is needed about asymmetric warfare. The enemy can be engaged and depleted in a third theater. Russia's Syrian intervention on Bashar al-Assad's behalf and indirectly against Western forces battling IS not only diverts attention from Ukraine, demonstrates the Kremlin's military prowess (attacking Syrian targets with cruise missiles launched from the Caspian Sea),[57] and circumvents Obama's policy of diplomatically isolating Russia, but further strains NATO's dwindling budgetary resources dedicated to countering Kremlin challenges in Europe. The West is wealthy enough to fight wars on multiple fronts, but Putin seems to believe he can outfox NATO in both TVDs.[58]

Conclusion

Western leaders appear to want to change the subject. They don't want Crimea's annexation, hybrid warfare in Novorossiya, across Russia's periphery and Syria,[59] and the expansion of the Kremlin's sphere of influence to crowd out other domestic and foreign agendas (including the Middle East). They are hoping that Putin will go away (democratic revolution), or that punitive economic sanctions, high occupation costs in Crimea, Luhansk, and Donetsk, and plummeting natural resources prices will deflate Moscow's aspirations. These hopes don't constitute an adequate response to the Kremlin's challenge. Putin has been assiduously pursuing the restoration of Russia's great power since he came to office in 2000. He is constructing the forces and strategies to achieve his goals,[60] and is unlikely to be deterred by NATO's build down.

The message for Western policy makers is simple. Wake up and shoulder the costs of deterring Putin in key TVDs. This means matching the scale, quality, and readiness of Russia's conventional armed forces. The goal can be partially accomplished by ramping up exercises in frequency and scale, and by adequately supplying NATO troops with armor. A clear signal also should be given to Russia that sub-strategic nuclear weapons are impermissible, even though NATO is unlikely to retaliate under the threat of mutually assured destruction.[61]

Notes

1 Roger Zakheim, "Clinton and Trump Both Offer More of the Same for the Military," *AEI*, September 2, 2016. http://www.aei.org/publication/clinton-and-trump-both-offer-more-of-the-same-for-the-military/?utm_source=paramount&utm_medium=email&utm_content=AEITODAY&utm_campaign=090616. "Those challenges can be broken down into three areas: modernizing and growing our military capability to deter revisionist powers like China and Russia; rebuilding and restoring the readiness of our forces to sustain operations in a low-end terrorism fight as well as high-end warfare; and resourcing a strategy to truly defeat ISIS. In other words, we lack a military capable of deterring adversaries and assuring allies in three key regions of the world. Despite a public record chock full of testimony from military leaders pleading for relief and warning of dire consequences if unaddressed, the administration response to all three challenges has been anemic. It ranges from outright denial, in the case of the readiness crisis, to inadequate, in the case of military modernization."

2 Steven Rosefielde, *False Science: Underestimating the Soviet Arms Buildup*, New Brunswick, NJ: Transaction Press, 1987; Rosefielde, *Russia in the 21st Century: The Prodigal Superpower*, Cambridge: Cambridge University Press, 2005; Steven Rosefielde and Stefan Hedlund, *Russia since 1980*, Cambridge: Cambridge University Press, 2008.

3 Steven Rosefielde, *Russia since 1980: Wrestling with Westernization*, Cambridge: Cambridge University Press, 2009.

4 A five-volume, top-secret military modernization plan was signed by Russian prime minister Mikhail Kasyanov in 2002. It laid out a two-stage program focusing on developing fifth-generation weapons from 2002 to 2008, followed by their mass production. The R&D outlays were made, but Russia's latest arms buildup was delayed until 2010. Thereafter, weapons production surged.

5 Steven Rosefielde," Russian Military, Political and Economic Reform: Can the Kremlin Placate Washington?" U.S. Army War College, Carlisle Barracks, May 14–15, 2014. Rosefielde, "Turmoil in the Kremlin: Sputtering Toward Fortress Russia," *Problems of Post-Communism*, Vol. 53, No. 5, September/October (2006): 3–10; Rosefielde, "Russian Rearmament: Motives Options and Prospects," in Jan Leijonhielm and Fredrik Westerlund, eds., *Russian Power Structures: Present and Future Roles in Russian Politics*, FOI-R-2437-SE, Stockholm, December 2007, pp. 71–96; Rosefielde, "Postcrisis Russia: Counting on Miracles in Uncertain Times," in Carolina Vendil Pallin and Bertil Nygren, eds., *Russian Defense Prospects*, New York: Routledge, 2012, 134–150; Rosefielde, "Economics of the Military-Industrial Complex," in Michael Alexeev and Shlomo Weber, eds., *The Oxford Handbook of Russian Economy*, Oxford: Oxford University Press, 2012; Rosefielde, "The Impossibility of Russian Economic Reform: Waiting for Godot." US Army War College, Carlisle Barracks, 2012.

6 "Estonia to Build Fence at Russian Border," *SNEWSi*, August 25, 2015. http://snewsi .com/id/15318965440/ "Russia Mocks Estonian Plans to Fence Border," *Baltic Times*, August 26, 2015. http://www.baltictimes.com/russia_mocks_estonian_plans_to_ fence_border/.

7 "President: Finland 'In No Position' to Defend Baltic States," Agence France-Presse, August 25, 2015. http://www.defensenews.com/story/defense/international/ europe/2015/08/25/president-finland-position-defend-baltic-states/32367549/. " 'Finland is not in a position where it could offer others security guarantees which we ourselves don't even have.'" The Finns didn't publish this story in English, and the French version may derive from Russian sources.

8 "U.S. to Deploy Heavy Weapons to Poland in 2016," *AFP*, August 27, 2015. http:// hotair.com/headlines/archives/2015/08/27/u-s-to-deploy-heavy-weapons-to-poland-in-2016/.

9 Julian Cooper, *Russia's State Armament Programme to 2020: A Quantitative Assessment of Implementation 2011–2015*, FOI, FOI-R--4239—SE, March 2016. "This report provides an overview of the implementation of the Russian state armament programme to 2020 as the end of its first five year approaches. It is an empirical study designed to present data that is not readily accessible to analysts." Cf. Eugene Kogan, *Russian Military Capabilities*, Tiblisi, Georgia: Georgian Foundation for Strategic and International Studies, 2016.

Mikhail Barabanov, "Testing a 'New Look,' The Ukrainian Conflict and Military Reform in Russia," in Centre for Analysis of Strategies and Technologies (CAST) online at: www.cast.ru/eng/?id=578 – online on December 18, 2014. Bettina Renz, "Russian Military Capabilities after 20 Years of Reform," in *Survival*, Vol. 56, No. 3 (June–July 2014): 61–84.

10 The author possesses a signed copy of the unpublished program summary. The document reveals that the Kremlin intended to move toward reconsolidation of state authority, driven in part by the aging of the OPK's capital stock, underemployment, low pay, and poor enterprise finances. Cf. Vitaly Shlykov, "Russian Defense Industrial Complex after 9-11," paper presented at Russian Security Policy and the War on Terrorism, U.S. Naval Postgraduate School, Monterey, CA, June 4–5, 2002. For a discussion of earlier reforms, see Alexei Izyumov, Leonid Kosals, and Rosalina Ryvkina "Privatisation of the Russian Defense Industry: Ownership and Control

Issues," *Post-communist Economies* Vol. 12, No. 4 (2001): 485–496; idem, "Defense Industrial Transformation in Russia: Evidence from a Longitudinal Survey," *Post-communist Economies* Vol. 12, No.2 (2001): 215–227.

11   Steven Rosefielde, *Kremlin Strikes Back: Russia and the West after Crimea's Annexation*, Cambridge: Cambridge University Press, 2016; Michael Ellman, "Russia's Current Economic System: From Delusion to Glasnost,'" *Comparative Economic Studies*, 2015, 1–18. But cf. Gustav Gressel, "Russia's Quiet Military Revolution, and What it Means for Europe," *European Council on Foreign Relations (ECFR)*, December 31, 2015. http://www.isn.ethz.ch/Digital-Library/Articles/Detail/?id=195415. "The West has underestimated the significance of Russia's military reforms. Western – especially US – analysts have exclusively focused on the third phase of reform: the phasing in of new equipment. Numerous Russian and Western articles have stated that the Russian armed forces were still using legacy equipment from the Soviet Union and that its replacement was occurring more slowly than planned by the Kremlin [ix]. However, this is a misunderstanding of the nature of the reforms. The initial stages were not designed to create a new army in terms of equipment, but to ensure that existing equipment was ready to use, and to make the organisation that uses it more effective and professional. Indeed, to successfully intervene in Russia's neighbourhood, Moscow does not necessarily need the latest cutting-edge defence technology. Rather, such interventions would have to be precisely targeted and quickly executed to pre-empt a proper Western reaction."

12   Bryan Bender, "The Secret U.S. Army Study that Targets Moscow," *Politico*, April 14, 2016. http://www.politico.com/magazine/story/2016/04/moscow-pentagon-us-secret-study-213811. "Lieutenant General H. R. McMaster told the Senate Armed Services committee last week that 'in Ukraine, the combination of unmanned aerial systems and offensive cyber and advanced electronic warfare capabilities depict a high degree of technological sophistication.'"

13   Eugene Kogan, *Russian Military Capabilities*, Tiblisi Georgia: Georgian Foundation for Strategic and International Studies, 2016. "It can be said that the Russian military has indeed learnt their lessons from the Russia–Georgia war of August 2008. The manner that the military operated in Crimea, and most recently, in Syria demonstrated that military operations combined three most important components: surprise, mobility and swiftness (SMS). Whether or not the same lethal combination would be successfully replicated elsewhere remains to be seen. On the other hand, to state unequivocally that the Russian military is not capable of competing in conventional warfare beyond the post-Soviet space or in confrontation with NATO would be short-sighted and inaccurate. Such an assumption is no longer far-fetched but rather realistic even though experts in the field may disagree with the author. The Western perception of the current Russian military is undergoing a sea of change. It is evident that the agility and the rapidness of the military to perform before other actors intervene took the West at large by surprise. As a result, there is more and more talk about Russian military operations against the Baltic States even though they are NATO members and NATO's famous dictum, an attack on one is an attack on all, appears to no longer be deterring Russia. In other words, the West at large can no longer take for granted that the Russian military will not seize the opportunity to intervene if they see fit. After all, President Vladimir Putin showed repeatedly his flair

for being an opportunist and not being shy of military adventurism. Although the 2008–2012 military reform degraded Russia's combat capabilities in its western regions, Moscow's shift towards operations in *limited conflicts* [author's italics] riveted more attention to mobile and special operations forces. As a result, not only did the Airborne Forces avoid manpower cuts but they also kept their divisions and amplified their strength. Special Operations Forces (SOFs), too, began their buildup and increased combat readiness. The modernisation of Army Aviation units began swiftly and was accompanied by the procurement of a large number of new helicopters and a substantial number of new combat aircraft. As Barabanov continues, the procurement of a large number of new but not modernised helicopters accentuated mobility. In addition to mobility, large investments in human resources and combat training paid off generously in 2014 with a better army and more skilful personnel, especially among officers. Another positive factor is a large number of officers with real combat experience acquired in the Chechen wars, counter-terrorism operations in the North Caucasus and various local conflicts in the post-Soviet states. Additionally, numerous exercises have been held at all levels, including regular strategic manoeuvres, new education and combat training methods introduced and more professional soldiers recruited. New arms and hardware supplies since 2007 have considerably improved the army's material status and equipage, primarily in the Air Force and Army Aviation units. A major breakthrough was also made in logistics. After the Georgian campaign, the Russian army has been enhancing its strategic manoeuvre capabilities for years and practicing deployment over great distances which proved highly instrumental during the Ukrainian crisis. However, the Ukrainian crisis showed once again that the Russian army's weak spot was the dominating number of conscripts, the reduced length of military service (one year) and the lack of a sufficient number of contract servicemen. Although Russia had declared the goal of creating a permanent readiness army, many military units and formations were not used in full in 2014 due to both the shortage of personnel in the majority of units and the cyclic nature of conscript training. As a result, 'permanent readiness' formations could send no more than two-thirds of their personnel to the operational area, leaving behind untrained soldiers drafted in the fall. Another serious issue is the reserve. No optimal reserve model has so far been worked out for the 'new look.' Additionally, there are still no clear-cut mechanisms for deploying additional units and formations and replacing lost personnel during wartime. Despite the abovementioned shortcomings, the efficiency with which Russian forces have assumed control over Crimea is hard to reconcile with the image of an inadequate military close to collapse. Despite claims to the contrary, Russia is much closer to having the military it needs that has often been suggested. In other words, the Western perception of the not sufficiently prepared Russian military was deeply mistaken. The 2008–2012 military reform prepared the military for the year 2013. The Kremlin began to set up a pool of rapid deployment forces in 2013 in order to be able to intervene in its neighbourhood. These well-equipped, well-trained, modern forces consist of Airborne Forces (four divisions, five brigades), Marines (four brigades, eight separate regiments), GRU Intelligence Forces (GRU Spetsnaz) brigades and three or four elite Ground Forces units as well as air and naval support. The MoD planned that, in the coming years, all of these units would be made up of professionals. On this basis, the Airborne Forces already count up to 20 battalions. There is every reason to believe that the 30,000 to 40,000 troops transferred to the south-eastern border of Ukraine in February 2014 were the backbone of these rapid deployment forces that realistically may have 100,000 and more troops ready for rapid deployment. The GRU Spetsnaz forces, in particular, have both expanded – with two new brigades: the 100th and the 25th – and developed. Most of the 15,000 to 17,000 Spetsnaz are essentially very well-trained light infantry and intervention forces. However, a growing awareness of the need for truly 'tier one' special forces able to operate in small teams and complex political environment led to the decision to create the Special Operations Command (or KSO in Russian) in 2010. Becoming operational in 2013, the KSO first saw action in the seizure of Crimea in 2014. Numbering about 500 operators with integral airlift and close air support assets, the KSO represents a genuine enhancement of Russian capabilities and one designed for precisely the kind of military political operations described for the first time in the 2014 doctrine. On the other hand, attempts to increase the proportion of the Armed Forces staffed on a professional, volunteer basis continue to lag behind plans. As of December 2014 the total such kontraktniki in the military numbered 295,000: a solid increase from 2013's 186,000 but still well short of the 499,000 meant to be in the ranks by 2017. As of December 2015 the total of such kontraktniki in the military numbered 352,000 while their number should reach 384,000 in 2016.8 It can be assumed that the number of professional soldiers is likely to increase until 2017. Thus, the term lagging behind will become obsolete.

"General Yuri Borisov, Deputy Minister of Defence for Procurement (hereafter cited as General Borisov), said in late January 2015 that: 'The segment of modern equipment in the Aerospace Defence Forces (or VKO in Russian), the Navy and the Strategic Missile Forces (or RVSN in Russian) is at the rate of more than 40%.' Currently, only 28% of the Russian Air Force inventory consists of modern equipment while the figure stands at 26% for the Ground Forces and the rest of the Russian military. RIA Novosti reported in early October 2015 by citing General Borisov that: 'Modern hardware now makes up 45.8% of the Aerospace Forces (or VKS in Russian).' Finally, in early February 2016 General Sergei Shoigu, Minister of Defence, said that: 'Forty seven percent of the country's arms and equipment inventory is now considered "modern."' The most modern area is its nuclear deterrent which between the three elements of its nuclear triad are reported to be 55% modernised. The Aerospace Forces are at 52% with the Navy sitting at 39% and the Ground Forces at 35% at the close of 2015. The further increase in modern equipment requires substantial funds that, despite the current economic crisis, President Vladimir Putin and his administration are ready to shoulder. Therefore, the pronounced target for the Armed Forces to have 70% of modern equipment by 2020 is no longer a far-fetched scenario but a fact that the West at large need to acknowledge, carefully monitor and think through as to what it can do about it. The author's assertion may be dismissed out of hand by the expert community but facts presented above reinforce the author's assertion. Furthermore, the section below, entitled Defence Spending, reinforces the author's view that the reshaping of the Russian military and equipping it with modern weapons is on the right track."

14 Steven Rosefielde and Ralph W. Pfouts, *Inclusive Economic Theory*, Singapore: World Scientific Publishers, 2013. Mathematical and geometric proofs are provided in this volume.

15 Robert Solow, "A Contribution to the Theory of Economic Growth," *Quarterly Journal of Economics* 70 (February 1956): 65–94; Solow "Technical Change and the Aggregate Production Function," *Review of Economics and Statistics* 39 (August 1957): 312–320; Trevor Swan, "Economic Growth and Capital Accumulation," *Economic Record* 32 (November 1956): 334–61.

16 Steven Rosefielde, *Russian Economy from Lenin to Putin*, New York: Wiley, 2007.

17 Igor Birman, "From the Achieved Level," *Soviet Studies* Vol. 30, No. 2 (1978): 153–172; Herbert Simon, "Bounded Rationality and Organizational Learning," *Organization Science*, Vol. 2, No. 1 (1991): 125–134. Reinhard Selten, "What Is Bounded Rationality?" in Gerd Gigerenzer and Reinhard Selten, eds., *Bounded Rationality: The Adaptive Toolbox*, Cambridge, MA, 2002; Herbert Simon, *Models of Bounded Rationality*, Cambridge, MA: 1982.

18 The term "second worst" emphasizes the magnitude of observable deviations from optimality. It is a word play on the more familiar term "second best." There is a tendency to downplay the consequences of Western anti-competitiveness in the neoclassical economic theory literature by describing suboptimal outcomes as "second best." Second worst cautions scholars that the Western economic performance typically is substantially inferior to the ideal. Steven Rosefielde, "Economic Theory of the Second Worst," *Higher School of Economics Journal* (HSE) (Moscow) (2015): 30–44. Cf. Richard Lipsey and Kelvin Lancaster, "The General Theory of Second Best," *Review of Economic Studies* Vol. 24, No 1 (1956): 11–32. The term was first coined by James Meade. See James Meade, *Trade and Welfare*, London: Oxford University Press, 1955.

19 Cooper, *Russia's State Armament Programme to 2020*. "It is a highly classified document in twelve sections. Ten are devoted to particular services of the MOD – ground forces, navy, air force, etc. – one to all other forces and one (the tenth) to R&D relating to the development of armaments – fundamental, exploratory and Applied." "Total funding is usually given as 20.7 trillion rubles".

20 Steven Rosefielde, "Russian Rearmament: Motives Options and Prospects," in Jan Leijonhielm and Fredrik Westerlund, eds., *Russian Power Structures: Present and Future Roles in Russian Politics*, FOI-R-2437-SE, Stockholm, December 2007, 71–96.

21 Cooper, *Russia's State Armament Programme to 2020*.

22 Cooper, *Russia's State Armament Programme to 2020*.

23 Cooper, *Russia's State Armament Programme to 2020*.

24 Carsten Sprenger, "State-Owned Enterprises in Russia." Presentation at the OECD Roundtable on Corporate Governance of SOEs, Moscow, October 27, 2008. https://www.oecd.org/corporate/ca/corporategovernanceprinciples/42576825.pdf.

25 Yiyi Liu and Steven Rosefielde, "Public Private Partnerships: Antidote for Secular Stagnation?" in Steven Rosefielde, Masaaki Kuboniwa, Satoshi Mizobata, and Kumiko Haba, eds., *EU Economic Stagnation and Political Strife: Lessons for Asia*, Singapore: World Scientific Publishers, 2016.

26 William Baumol, *Business Behavior, Value and Growth* (rev. ed.), New York: Macmillan, 1959.

27 *Voyennaya doktrina Rossiyskoy Federatsii Военная доктрина Российской Федерации* [*Military doctrine of the Russian Federation*]. scrf.gov.ru (in Russian). Moscow: Security Council of the Russian Federation. 2010-06-25 [presidential decree 2010-06-25]. Cf. Sinovets, Polina; Renz, Bettina (July 2015). "Russia's 2014 Military Doctrine and Beyond: Threat Perceptions, Capabilities and Ambitions." Research Paper (Rome: NATO Defense College, Research Division).

28 The Kremlin's arms buildup has multiple purposes, including the achievement of battlefield escalation dominance with conventional and nuclear ordnance up to the strategic nuclear threshold (a global reconnaissance/strike capability to wage intercontinental conventional war against the United States/allies and other adversaries in support of Russian national interests). See James Howe, "Future Russian Strategic Nuclear and Non-nuclear Forces: 2022", paper presented to the American Foreign Policy Council Conference on "The Russian Military in the Contemporary Perspective" held May 9–10, 2016, in Washington, DC. Cf. Dima Adamsky, "The Current State of Russian Strategic Thought in the Nuclear Realm," paper presented to the American Foreign Policy Council Conference on "The Russian Military in the Contemporary Perspective." Mark B. Schneider, "Russian Nuclear Weapons Policy and Programs, the European Security Crisis, and the Threat to NATO," paper presented to the American Foreign Policy Council Conference on "The Russian Military in the Contemporary Perspective."

29 Keir Giles, *Russia's "New" Tools for Confronting the West: Continuity and Innovation in Moscow's Exercise of Power*, Chatham House, The Royal Institute of International Affairs, March 2016.

30 The doctrine of MAD is usually associated with U.S. Defense Secretary Robert McNamara and has various counter-value and counter-force interpretations. It can be claimed that MAD never was America's sole deterrent strategy. See National Archives and Records Administration, RG 200, Defense Programs and Operations, LeMay's Memo to President and JCS Views, Box 83. Secret.

31 Estonia, Latvia, and Lithuania.

32 *Military Balance*, International Institute for Strategic Studies, Volume 115, Issue 12015. Hybrid warfare is a military strategy that blends conventional warfare, irregular warfare (guerrilla warfare), and cyberwarfare. This is a Western definition. The Russians only use the term *gibridnaia voina* when they refer to the Western debate. For a discussion of the nature of Russian military strategy in Ukraine and against NATO more generally, see Samuel Charap, "The Ghost of Hybrid War," *Survival*, December 2015–January 2016.

33 Stephen Blank contends that 9,000 people have been killed in Ukraine, including many by Russian forces. Personal correspondence, January 4, 2016.

34 Jacob Kipp, "Putin's Ukrainian Gambit," Conference on Challenges to the European Union, University of North Carolina, Chapel Hill, September 18–20, 2014.

35 Jan Techau, "The Politics of 2 Percent: NATO and the Security Vacuum in Europe," *Carnegie Europe*, September 2, 2015. http://carnegieeurope.eu/2015/08/31/politics-of-2-percent-nato-and-security-vacuum-in-europe/ifig?mkt_tok=3RkMMJWWf F9wsRogva3BZKXonjHpfsX56OsvXqGg38431UFwdcjKPmjr1YUDTcZ0aPyQAg obGp5I5FEIQ7XYTLB2t60MWA%3D%3D. "The members of the North Atlantic Treaty Organization (NATO) pledged in 2014 to increase their defense spending to 2 percent of their gross domestic products by 2024. It is unrealistic to assume

that this goal will ever be reached by all 28 allies, and yet the 2 percent metric persists – and it has assumed a significance beyond its face value. It is about addressing Europe's growing security vacuum and defining who will be in charge of European security. The reduction of the U.S. security footprint in Europe and Europeans' dramatic loss of military capability since the 1990s have created a security vacuum in Europe. NATO's 2 percent metric is one instrument to address that. As a way to measure an increase in military capability, the 2 percent metric is barely useful. It does not measure spending in real terms or actual output. The target has had some success in stimulating debate on European security. It has become an important gauge of who is and who is not politically committed to NATO's core task: Europe's security.

"Europeans underestimate the political significance of 2 percent in the U.S. debate over security commitments to Europe. Americans overestimate the political significance of 2 percent among Europeans struggling with austerity and divergent threat perceptions, which make it difficult to increase their defense commitments."

36 NATO, "Defense Expenditures Data for 2014 and Estimates for 2015," press release, June 22, 2015. www.nato.int/cps/en/natohq/news_120866.htm.

37 The Readiness Action Plan, NATO, September 2015. http://www.nato.int/cps/en/natohq/topics_119.

38 "Eastern Europe Fears Closer French-Russian Ties Amid Ukraine Crisis," *Economic Times*, November 23, 2015. http://economictimes.indiatimes.com/articleshow/49888340.cms?utm_source=contentofinterest&utm_medium=text&utm_campaign=cppst.

39 Michael McFaul and Anders Aslund have publicly expressed this view. Anders Aslund, group e-mail, December 12, 2011. "Has Putin Come to the End of His Regime?" "On Saturday, December 10, the spell of the Vladimir Putin regime was broken. Today, the key questions that many are asking are how fast he will lose power and what will come in his place. Peaceful mass demonstrations took place all over Russia. In Moscow, probably 80,000 gathered on Bolotnaya Ploshchad near the Kremlin to protest against Putin and what they and most observers say were the stolen elections of December 4. I had argued before these protests that if more than 50,000 came, the regime would be seen as finished. This was the biggest and most important demonstration in Russia since August 1991. Demonstrations took place in at least 15 Russian cities throughout the country, so this is a national phenomenon and not limited to Moscow."

40 Russia switched from a four-year to a six-year presidential cycle in 2012.

41 Pynnoniemi Katri, "Analysis of the Signals and Assumptions Embedded in Russia's Adjusted Security Doctrines," *Russian Analytical Digest*, No. 173, October 12, 2015. http://www.css.ethz.ch/publications/pdfs/Russian_Analytical_Digest_175.pdf.

42 Gudrun Persson, "Russian Strategic Deterrence – Beyond the Brinkmanship?" FOI, *RUES Briefing* 29, September 17, 2015. "Makhmut Gareev, influential military theorist and a veteran of the Second World War, stated in July 2013 that the destruction of the intermediate-range ballistic missiles in the late 1980s and 1990s was a mistake. 'Now also the highest leadership of the Russian Federation recognizes this mistake,' he wrote."

43 Military theorists often conceptualize weapons technologies and styles of warfighting in terms of generation. William Lind introduced the idea in 1989. See Antulio

Echevarria, "Fourth-Generation War and Other Myths," Strategic Studies Institute (United States Army War College), November 2005. First-generation warfare refers to battles fought with massed manpower, using line and column tactics with uniformed soldiers governed by the state. Second-generation warfare is the tactics used after the invention of the rifled musket and breech-loading weapons and continuing through the development of the machine gun and indirect fire. Third-generation warfare focuses on using speed and surprise to bypass the enemy's lines and collapse its forces from the rear. Essentially, this was the end of linear warfare on a tactical level, with units seeking not simply to meet each other face to face, but to outmaneuver each other to gain the greatest advantage. Fourth-generation warfare is characterized by a return to decentralized forms of warfare, blurring of the lines between war and politics, combatants and civilians due to nation-states' loss of their near-monopoly on combat forces, returning to modes of conflict common in premodern times. Fifth-generation warfare emphasizes the impact of precision-guided weapons and advanced electronic technologies on all prior forms of warfighting.

44 For a knowledgeable discussion of the difficulties the Kremlin faces in achieving its military modernization goals, see Pavel Baev, "Russian Air Power Is too Brittle for Brinksmanship", *Ponars*, Policy Memo 398, November 2015. Cf. Dmitry Gorenburg, "Russia's State Armaments Program 2020: Is the Third Time the Charm for Military Modernization?" *PONARS Eurasia* Policy Memo No. 125, October 2010. Dmitry Gorenburg, "Russian Naval Shipbuilding: Is It Possible to Fulfill the Kremlin's Grand Expectations?" *PONARS Eurasia* Policy Memo No. 395, October 2015. Johan Norberg, Training to Fight – Russia's Major Military Exercises 2011–2014, FOI-R– 4128 – SE, December 2015. "Russia's Armed Forces in the four years 2011–2014 trained to launch and fight largescale joint inter-service operations, i.e. launching and waging interstate wars." "Russian Armed Forces carried out at least one joint inter-service exercise each year in the three years 2011–2013. This enabled senior Russian military and political decision makers to exercise in a scenario where Russia was fighting two operations at the same time. In 2011 and 2012, smaller parallel joint inter-service exercises took place simultaneously. In 2013, the parallel exercise was a Navy exercise, but probably coordinated with the annual strategic exercise. In 2014, the size of the annual strategic exercise, 155,000 men, made parallel exercises redundant. In 2013 and 2014, the Russian Armed Forces also carried out surprise inspections to check and develop combat readiness, both in separate functions in the Armed Forces and in systemic tests in entire military districts. Altogether, these exercises related to Russia's collective ability to launch and wage interstate wars in all of Russia's strategic directions." www.foi.se/russia.

45 It is difficult to ascertain what Putin deems a casus belli. He appeared to tolerate Ukraine's democratization, its aspiration to join the European Union, and the more remote prospect of NATO accession before striking Crimea. His judgment about red lines should be expected to be on a case-by-case basis.

46 Harlan Ullman and James Wade, *Shock and Awe: Achieving Rapid Dominance*, National Defense University, 1996.

47 *Washington Treaty*, Article 5, August 24, 1949. www.nato.int/cps/en/natolive/official _texts_17120.htm. "The Parties agree that an armed attack against one or more of them in Europe or North America shall be considered an attack against them all

and consequently they agree that, if such an armed attack occurs, each of them, in exercise of the right of individual or collective self-defence recognised by Article 51 of the Charter of the United Nations, will assist the Party or Parties so attacked by taking forthwith, individually and in concert with the other Parties, such action as it deems necessary, including the use of armed force, to restore and maintain the security of the North Atlantic area.

"Any such armed attack and all measures taken as a result thereof shall immediately be reported to the Security Council. Such measures shall be terminated when the Security Council has taken the measures necessary to restore and maintain international peace and security."

48 N.V. Ogarkov, *Vsegda v golovnosti k zashchite Otechestva*, Moskva 1982, 31; N. V. Ogarkov, *Istoriya Uchit vditel'nosti*, Moskva 1985, 41; Steven Metz and James Kievit, *Strategy and the Revolution in Military Affairs: From Theory to Policy*, US Army War College, June 27, 1995. http://www.strategicstudiesinstitute.army.mil/pubs/summary .cfm?q=236.

Stephen Biddle, *Military Power: Explaining Victory and Defeat in Modern Battle*, Princeton, NJ: Princeton University Press, 2006; Donald Rumsfeld, "Transforming the Military," *Foreign Affairs*, Vol. 81, No. 3, May/June (2002): 20–32; Mary FitzGerald, "Marshal Ogarkov and the New Revolution in Soviet Military Affairs," *Defense Analysis*, Vol. 3, No. 1 (1987): 13–19 (Center for Naval Analyses, Alexandria, Virginia, CRM 87-2/ January 1987). http://www.tandfonline.com/doi/pdf/10.1080/ 07430178708405274.

49 Donald Rumsfeld, "Transforming the Military," *Foreign Affairs*, Vol. 81, No. 3, May/ June (2002): 20–32.

50 Staff Writers, "All I Want for Christmas Is a Laser Gunship: US Air Force," *Space Daily*, September 22, 2015. http://www.spacedaily.com/reports/All_I_Want_for_ Christmas_is_a_Laser_Gunship_US_Air_Force_General_999.html.

"The head of US Air Force Special Operations Command has told manufacturers of military aeronautics that he wants to see airborne laser weapon capability by the end of the decade.

"The head of US Air Force Special Operations Command has shared his vision for his dream warship, which will boast a laser weapon capable of disabling moving targets such as missiles and drones, and able to 'burn a beer-can sized hole' in stationary targets such as communications towers, and boats."

51 *Military Balance*, International Institute for Strategic Studies, Volume 115, Issue 12015.

52 Ibid.

53 Russian military experts consider the term *hybrid warfare* a Western concept, and don't include it in their doctrine. The term is employed here to stress the inclusiveness of Russian military tactics.

54 Frank Hoffman, *Conflict in the 21st Century: The Rise of Hybrid War*, Arlington: Potomac Institute for Policy Studies, 2007; Brian P. Fleming. "Hybrid Threat Concept: Contemporary War, Military Planning and the Advent of Unrestricted Operational Art," Washington, DC: *United States Army Command and General Staff College*, May 19, 2011.

55 Frank Hoffman, "Hybrid Warfare and Challenges," *JFQ: Joint Force Quarterly* (2009): 34–48.

56 *Military Balance*, International Institute for Strategic Studies, Volume 115, Issue 12015, p. 17. The challenge was a central topic of discussion at the September 2014 NATO Summit in Wales.

57 Dmitri Trenin, "Putin's Syria Gambit Aims at Something Bigger than Syria," Carnegie Moscow Center, October 13, 2015. http://carnegie.ru/2015/10/13/putin-s-syria-gambit-aims-at-something-bigger-than-syria/ij2j.

58 Robin Emmott, "Upstaged NATO Searches for '360-Degree' Response to Russia," *Yahoo News*, October 22, 2015. http://news.yahoo.com/upstaged-nato-searches-360-degree-response-russia-141547940.html.

59 Anthony Cordesman, "Russia in Syria: Hybrid Political Warfare," *CSIS*, September 23, 2015. http://csis.org/publication/russia-syria-hybrid-political-warfare.

60 Roger McDermott, "Russia's Strategic Mobility and Its Military Deployment in Syria," *RUFS Briefing*, No. 31, November 12, 2015. foi@nyhetsbrev.foi.se "Russia's ability to project power beyond its immediate border has been questioned since the dissolution of the Soviet Union. On 30 September 2015, Russia launched its first out-of-area military operation since the Soviet-Afghanistan War. It witnessed remarkable speed and sophisticated planning advances to support the reinforcement of the Tartus naval depot and form a de facto forward operating airbase in Latakia. Such movements of air assets and military hardware and weapons also aimed at boosting military-technical aid to the Syrian government and sustaining Russia's air campaign was made possible by recent advances in Russia's combat service support system. The pre-existing logistics and supply system was reformed in 2010 into Materiel-Technical Support (materialno-tekhnicheskogo obespechniia – MTO); additional improvements resulted from testing the MTO during strategic-operational military exercises and in conducting service level exercises. In this case, Moscow has overcome traditional reliance upon railway infrastructure, geographically impossible in its Syria intervention, and greatly enhanced its use of sea lines of communication (SLOCs) and air lines of communication (ALOCs).

61 Johan Norberg suggested these policy prescriptions.

11

X-Factors

The ability of Russia and the West to effectively cope with the repercussions of the Kremlin's annexation of Crimea depends significantly on three additional x-factors: leadership, ideology, and the natural resources supercycle. These aspects of the correlation of forces are all difficult to judge, but nonetheless deserve explicit mention.

There is little to be said about the competence and quality of Putin's, Poroshenko's, Obama's, and Merkel's leadership beyond the obvious. Putin and Merkel are shrewd and competent politicians; Poroshenko and Obama often seem out of their depth.[1] Neither Hillary Clinton nor Donald Trump are likely to outmatch Putin. Consequently, while it can be plausibly supposed that personal leadership could tip the scales of Cold War II, the prudent course is to anticipate a wash. We cannot tell from the data at hand whether the leadership factor will be decisive, and therefore should infer that, if one side or the other wins, the victory likely will be attributable to other aspects of the correlation of forces and, perhaps, to serendipity.

The same judgment holds for ideology. Russia's repudiation of communism deprived the Kremlin of a powerful tool for mobilizing domestic resolve and limiting the West's political room for maneuver. Moscow had many advocates abroad. Moreover, communism's defeat was trumpeted in the West as capitalism's triumph. This, coupled with the short-lived economic boom triggered by the inauguration of the Eurozone in 1999, gave the West an aura of success that made it seem invincible. The correlation of ideological forces strongly favored America and Europe until 2008, when the attractions of the debt-ridden welfare state, affirmative action, restorative justice, and multiculturalism were called into question by the global financial crisis, and Putin's efforts at sparking neo-nationalism started bearing fruit. This drift continues and aids the Kremlin's cause, but Russian nationalism has little attraction for non-Russians and is a very weak substitute for proletarian internationalism. On balance the West still has the ideological upper hand.

Everyone knows that one of the most decisive factors governing the correlation of forces and the outcome of Cold War II could be natural resources prices. They are a wild card that profoundly affects Russia's economic power, but lies largely beyond the Kremlin's control. The issue was touched on in Chapter 7; however, a few words about long term trends in natural resources supplies, and prices may be illuminating.

Russia's wealth and income are strongly tied to its natural resources. The Federation is estimated to hold more than 20 percent of the world's mineral and fuel reserves. Natural resources account for 95.7 percent of national economic wealth. Russia ranks first in the world in gas reserves (32 percent of the world's reserves, 30 percent of global production), second in oil production (10 percent share of world production), third in coal reserves (22 coal basins; 115 fields, including about 15.6 percent in European Russia, about 66.8 percent in Siberia, about 12.9 percent in the Far East, and about 4.3 percent in the Urals). Russia has the world's largest iron ore reserves, is second in tin, is third in lead, and is a leader in timber assets.[2]

These endowments are blessings, but their value fluctuates with market demand. High prices increase wealth and often trigger booms. Low prices diminish wealth and sometimes precipitate busts. These gains and losses aren't always unidirectional. Offsetting side effects occasionally occur. Natural resources price–driven economic booms may hollow out industry ("resource curse"/Dutch disease);[3] busts may stimulate re-industrialization. Broadly speaking, high natural resources prices enhance prospects for the success of Putin's great power restoration project; low prices diminish them. If natural resources prices continue to decline, then Western leaders' faith that this time will be the same becomes more compelling.

Natural resources price fluctuations often are violent. A barrel of oil fetched $147 in 2008, and then plunged to $32 in a matter of months before recovering to $115 in 2013.[4] Prices began crashing again in June 2014 and for the moment petroleum prices seem to be stabilizing between $45 and $50 per barrel. One analyst is predicting that the price of a barrel of oil will ultimately bottom in a range between $10 and $20 per barrel.[5] This obviously is bad news for Putin. However, some specialists who acknowledge the possibility that natural resources prices will remain at low levels for the foreseeable future insist that today's cheap natural resources are best viewed as a blip in a "bull" super-cycle; Russia's intermediate-term prospects are bright.

This outlook is driven by a variety of plausible assumptions about natural resources markets detached from concerns about Cold War II. Natural resources super-cycle proponents foresee a future of intensifying nonrenewable natural resources shortages propelled by depleting energy and mineral supplies and surging demand from newly developing nations that they predict will catapult resources prices into the stratosphere, abetted by oligopoly power, loose monetary, credit policy, and financial speculation. The historical record can be debated, but the megatrend forecast cannot be ruled out. There is no shortage of experts who believe that the long-wave inflation-adjusted trend line for natural resources prices is up.[6]

Natural resources super-cycle theory borders on the occult. There are too many imponderables to rule it in or out. Nonetheless, it is easy to envision circumstances outside of Russia's control that will propel natural resources prices to record heights. OPEC could put its house in order, Third World development could be reinvigorated, war in the Middle East could drastically reduce petroleum supplies, and so forth. National security analysts therefore should keep an open mind on this matter, and be alert to the changing tides of expectation.[7]

Notes

1 For a backhanded defense of Obama, see Janet Maslin, "If You Were So Inclined, You Could Stick It on a Bumper: Edward Klein's Invective-Laden Obama Book," *New York Times,* May 16, 2012. http://www.nytimes.com/2012/05/17/books/edward-kleins -invective-laden-obama-book.html?_r=0 Cf. Edward Klein, *Amateur: Barack Obama in the White House.* New York: Regnery, 2012.

2 http://www.advantour.com/russia/economy/natural-resources.htm Cf. *CIA World Factbook: Russia,* 2015.

3 Jeffrey Sachs and Andrew Warner, "The Curse of Natural Resources," *European Economic Review* 45 (4–6) (2001): 827–838. Paul Stevens, "Resource Impact: Curse or Blessing? A Literature Survey," *Journal of Energy Literature* 9 (1) (2003): 3–42. Jeffrey A. Frankel, *The Natural Resource Curse: A Survey,* NBER Working Paper No. 15836, March 2010. Warner Max Corden, "Boom Sector and Dutch Disease Economics: Survey and Consolidation," *Oxford Economic Papers* 36, 1984, p. 362.

4 Harry Dent Jr., "Oil Will Fall to '$10 or $20,'" *Business Insider,* June 23, 2015. http:// www.businessinsider.com/oil-prices-are-headed-lower-2015-6.

5 Ibid. Cf. Vladimir Popov, Viktor Polterovich, and Alexander Tonis, "Resource Abundance: A Curse or Blessing?" DESA Working Paper No. 93, June 2010. Vladimir Popov, Viktor Polterovich, and Alexander Tonis, "Mechanisms of Resource Curse, Economic Policy and Growth," NES Working Paper # WP/2008/082.

6 Octaviano Canuto, "The Commodity Super Cycle: Is This Time Different?" *World Bank,* Number 150, June 2014. http://siteresources.worldbank.org/EXTPREMNET/ Resources/EP150.pdf.

7   Kenneth Rogoff, "Oil Prices and Global Growth," *Project Syndicate*, December 14, 2015. https://www.project-syndicate.org/commentary/oil-prices-global-growth-by-kenneth-rogoff-2015-12?utm_source=Project+Syndicate+Newsletter&utm_campaign=c9ff3f432f-Rogoff_Oil_Prices_and_Global_Growth_12_20_2015&utm_medium=email&utm_term=0_73bad5b7d8-c9ff3f432f-93559677. "One of the biggest economic surprises of 2015 is that the stunning drop in global oil prices did not deliver a bigger boost to global growth. Despite the collapse in prices, from over $115 per barrel in June 2014 to $45 at the end of November 2015, most macroeconomic models suggest that the impact on global growth has been less than expected – perhaps 0.5% of global GDP." "In short, oil prices were not quite as consequential for global growth in 2015 as seemed likely at the beginning of the year. And strong reserve positions and relatively conservative macroeconomic policies have enabled most major producers to weather enormous fiscal stress so far, without falling into crisis. But next year could be different, and not in a good way – especially for producers."

PART IV

DUTY TO PREVAIL

12

Strategies

The Kremlin and the West both intend to resolve Cold War II in their own favor. They are motivated by a duty to prevail. Both are trying to capitalize on positive twists in the correlation of forces, and will persevere if the tide moves against them, but have adopted different strategies that could have a bearing on outcomes. The West inclines toward strategic patience to accommodate diverse constituencies, while the Kremlin tends to prioritize the preservation and expansion of its spheres of influence above domestic concerns in accordance with Muscovite tradition.

Russia's attachment to authoritarianism and imperial power is embedded in its culture and needs to be appreciated in gauging Putin's approach to Cold War II. It cannot be grasped by assuming that the Kremlin secretly wants to be "normal" like the West. Washington and Berlin's faith in the mantra of deterrence, engagement, and transformation is misplaced because Russian leaders don't want to change.

The term *Muscovite* refers to a system of rule associated with Ivan III Vasilyevich (the Great), Grand Prince of Moscow and all Rus (1440–1505), who laid the foundations for the Russian state, and his successors, including Ivan IV (Grozny). It links Russia's state governance to its pre-communist past.

State policy in this paradigm is primarily driven by authoritarian power-seeking, the need for dependable internal regime support, control and security, insider enrichment, rent-granting (gifting management privileges to supporters in return for loyalty and a share of the proceeds),[1] satisficing (acceptance of adequate results without exhaustively searching for better outcomes),[2] strategic opportunism (preparing to seize windfall opportunities),[3] and imperial expansion rather than rational and just utility maximizing by individuals and the state. It may contain elements of rational choice and virtuous utility maximizing, but these motives are subsidiary.

The paradigm in its current "sovereign democratic" version concentrates national priority-setting in the hands of Putin, the power services, and oligarchs,[4] instead of dispersing it across society. They control the supply side of the "commanding heights" where state ownership continues to hold sway (natural resources sector, communications, and the military-industrial complex), including production and distribution. They determine what is produced in these spheres and allocate output to alternative use. It is their demand, not rationally guided competitive individual utility-seeking, that governs the broad contours of the production-commanding heights. Outside the commanding heights, Russians are permitted weak consumer sovereignty (the right to buy goods at semi-competitive prices, given oligarchy and Putin's control over public spending).

Putin's regime first and foremost promotes authoritarian power-seeking. It doesn't serve the people according to the precepts of the Enlightenment, and it is intrinsically inefficient. Muscovite governance partially compensates for this inefficiency with resource mobilization. It concentrates authority to an exceptional degree in the hands of Russia's supreme leaders (*vozhds*), inclining them to prize national power, military might, and strategic opportunism where the system permits them to excel.[5] The Kremlin is wedded to the resource mobilization approach to strategic engagement because it has no viable alternative and *vozhds* have the authority to bend subordinates to their will. They cannot and don't rely on superior economic, political, social, and civic factors to keep rival powers at bay.

Russia's *vozhds* can wager on the resource mobilization approach to strategic engagement because they are far more powerful than Western presidents, allowing them to operate with a narrower stakeholder base of support. The secret police (FSB) is the *vozhds*' ultimate political enforcement mechanism. It is more powerful than the legislature, the bureaucracy, and the military in imposing the *vozhds*' will. The *vozhds*' power is further enhanced by the absence of the rule of law in politics, business, and civil society.

Being above the law enables Kremlin *vozhds* to gather power like masters of positional chess, so that they can pounce when opportunity knocks. They are apt to act like despots, even though this is strenuously denied. Stalin, the faithful still tell us, killed no one unjustly, and should be regarded with deep reverence.[6]

The Muscovite system makes its *vozhds* predictable. They don't count on economic, political, social, and civic superiority to carry the day,[7] and don't feel obliged to accommodate popular demands in the distribution of public resources. They mobilize instead to preserve and expand national power.

Western leaders operate the other way around. They are reluctant to mobilize national resources and alter economic policies to preserve and expand national power whenever this diverts public spending from civilian purposes because of the powerful opposition of diverse domestic constituencies. This induces America and the European Union to count on the West's economic, cultural, and political superiority to prevail. Western leaders can adjust to circumstances, but democratic political rigidities often inhibit them from responding effectively when the correlation of forces adversely shifts against them.

The West's Cold War II strategy is superior when long-term efficiency is decisive. The Muscovite approach is better when the West mistakenly takes its efficiency for granted and fails to adequately defend itself. Claiming to do the right thing while failing to do so invites aggression.

Notes

1   Steven Rosefielde, *Russian Economy from Lenin to Putin*, New York: Wiley, 2007.
2   Herbert Simon, "A Behavioral Model of Rational Choice," in Simon, *Models of Man: Social and Rational – Mathematical Essays on Rational Human Behavior in a Social Setting*, New York: Wiley, 1957, 241–260.
3   Rosefielde, *Russian Economy from Lenin to Putin*.
4   Gregory Grossman, "Notes for a Theory of the Command Economy," *Soviet Studies*, 15(2) (1963): 101–123. Grossman's command theory can be viewed as a constrained variant of Bergson's neoclassical approach where planners are incapable of devising optimal directives. Alec Nove's analysis is similar. See Alec Nove, *The Soviet Economic System*, London: George Allen & Unwin, 1977. Both approaches focus on the supply side and fail to endogenize ideocratic motivation, tacitly accepting the Communist Party's claim that everything it did was to maximize the proletariat's welfare.
5   Steven Rosefielde and Stefan Hedlund, *Russia since 1980: Wrestling with Westernization*, Cambridge: Cambridge University Press, 2007.
6   Grover Furr, *Khrushchev Lied: The Evidence that Every "Revelation" of Stalin's (and Beria's) Crimes in Nikita Khrushchev's Infamous "Secret Speech" to the 20th Party Congress of the Communist Party of the Soviet Union on February 25, 1956, Is Provably False*, Kettering, OH: Erythros Press & Media, 2011; Furr, *The Murder of Sergei Kirov: History, Scholarship and the Anti-Stalin Paradigm*, Kettering, OH: Erythros Press & Media, 2013. Cf. Robert Service, *Stalin*, Cambridge, MA: Belknap/Harvard University Press, 2005; *Stalin and His Hangmen: The Tyrant and Those Who Killed for Him*, New York: Random House, 2005; Oleg Khlevniuk and Nora Favorov, *Stalin: New Biography of a Dictator*, New Haven, CT: Yale University Press, 2015; and Stephen Kotkin, *Stalin Volume 1: Paradoxes of Power, 1878–1928*, New York: Penguin, 2014.
7   This was true even under Soviet communism, where communism's economic and social superiority were ardently proclaimed. See Steven Rosefielde, *False Science: Underestimating the Soviet Arms Buildup*, Rutgers NJ: Transaction Press, 1982 (Expanded Second Edition, 1987).

13

Double Gaming

Russia's and the West's strategies encourage them to shun compromise and to perpetuate Cold War II using all means fair and foul within self-imposed cultural guidelines. Their leaders double-speak and double-think,[1] endeavoring to manage their adversaries' and their own publics' perceptions.[2] Both sides seek to persuade anyone who will listen that they are righteous, reasonable, and invincible to weaken their opponents' resolve and to muster domestic support. Their deceptions may sometimes facilitate capitulation or speedy compromise, but also may prove counterproductive, and even verge on the catastrophic when leaders conflate their own lies with the truth.[3] If double gaming induces cognitive dissonance,[4] and "motivated reason"[5] beguiles leaders into wishful thinking about economic prospects and defense sufficiency, their actions may invite rather than deter aggression.

There are three aspects to double gaming: misrepresentation, manipulation, and concealment. First, both sides throughout their hierarchies[6] and their advocates burnish their images with lofty official mischaracterizations of purpose and by impugning the motives of adversaries to cultivate support for their policies. Second, they buttress their misrepresentation by actively disseminating disinformation through seemingly unbiased channels. And third, they conceal ulterior motives inconsistent with the national interest to retain a free hand in pursuing partisan and personal objectives.

Russians and Westerners know that leaders exaggerate the virtues of their policies and vilify their adversaries. Both sides strongly distrust each other's claims, and their publics are suspicious about their own leaders. Nonetheless, all players can be gulled, which is why double gaming is pervasive – a danger increased by high-tech methods and media filtering. Russia and the West today enhance the effectiveness of their double games by using ostensibly neutral third parties to espouse official views, while simultaneously reducing public access to pertinent information.

Adrian Chen has recently provided insight into Putin's covert high-tech disinformation factories targeting public opinion in Ukraine and other contested areas. He reports that the Kremlin has established an elaborate cyber-trolling media disinformation operation under the auspices of the Saint Petersburg "Internet Research Agency."[7] Its job is to create content for every popular social network: LiveJournal, VKontakte, Facebook, Twitter, Instagram, and the comment sections of Russian news outlets.

Workers received a constant stream of 'technical tasks' – point-by-point exegeses of the themes they were to address, all pegged to the latest news. Ukraine was always a major topic, because of the civil war there between Russian-backed separatists and the Ukrainian Army; Savchuk and her co-workers would post comments that disparaged the Ukrainian president, Petro Poroshenko, and highlighted Ukrainian Army atrocities. Russian domestic affairs were also a major topic. Last year, after a financial crisis hit Russia and the ruble collapsed, the professional trolls left optimistic posts about the pace of recovery. Savchuk also says that in March, after the opposition leader Boris Nemtsov was murdered, she and her entire team were moved to the department that left comments on the websites of Russian news outlets and ordered to suggest that the opposition itself had set up the murder.[8]

U.S intelligence agencies and the FBI reported in September 2016 that they were investigating a covert Russian plot to disrupt the November American presidential election with cyber disinformation.[9]

Covert actions, including disinformative propaganda campaigns, always have been part of diplomacy, but contemporary variants are more potent, making it especially difficult for the public to obtain a clear perception of Cold War II and the possibilities for its resolution. Double-gamed cyber-trolling and media management, including suppression of evidence and scanty coverage, warp and disempower rational popular control over public policy.[10] They allow Putin and the West to manipulate each other and act capriciously with scant regard for national interest.

The effectiveness of these efforts depends partly on disinformation. Rational actors who would normally make sound judgment often are unwittingly misled by erroneous information, a problem compounded by cognitive dissonance and motivated reason, which disorient rational faculties and empower rationalization. Cyber-trolling and media management bombard publics and decision makers with a welter of contradictory "facts" and claims that they have neither the time nor the training to sort out, leading them either to shut down or act uncritically. They cannot make wise choices, lose sight of their duty, and fall prey to platitudes, slogans, emotion, prejudice, and opportunism.

The problem can be mitigated by acknowledging the dangers of cognitive dissonance and motivated reason attributable to double gaming, focusing on the core problematic and exposing the lies, half-truths, and evasions used to deceive rivals and manipulate public opinion.

Cold War II's core problematic isn't difficult to deconstruct. Russia has annexed Crimea, and is using proxies to occupy Luhansk and Donbas. It has declared its ambition to reclaim Novorossiya and has made menacing gestures toward the Baltic states. These events, actions, and declarations are facts that pose straightforward challenges. What would it take to return Crimea to Kyiv's control? What would it take to dislodge Russian proxies from Donbas? What would it take to halt further incursions into Novorossiya? Objective answers can be obtained by applying the LeChatelier Principle,[11] loosely interpreted for our purposes to mean considering responses that directly restore the status quo ante equilibrium. The principle allows us to ask what would be the military cost in blood and treasure of returning Crimea to Kyiv's control, dislodging Russian proxies from Luhansk and Donbas, and halting further incursions into Novorossiya.

Whatever the answers may be, inclusive analysis requires that they be refined by taking account of trends in the correlation of forces to ascertain the dollar cost of achieving the same objectives with nonviolent methods (economic, diplomatic, legal, political, etc.), providing decision makers with a complete, albeit contestable menu of options.

This comprehensive inventory of remedies and palliatives must then be evaluated normatively, and debated in its entirety to determine what ought to be done. The approach is inclusively scientific because it separates objective possibilities from normative considerations before integrating them to obtain morally guided rational and wise responses to the Kremlin's military challenges.

Russia's annexation of Crimea, proxy occupation of Donbas, and threats against the rest of Novorossiya don't have to be haphazardly countered because simple analytic methods, if scrupulously applied, are sufficient to grasp the fundamentals despite the obscuring effect of double gaming. If leaders discipline themselves in all regards, double gaming shouldn't prevent them from doing the right thing.

The main lessons of this sort of analytic exercise are readily deduced and don't require elaborate calculations. The costs in blood and treasure of any Western attempt to dislodge Russia militarily from Crimea are prohibitive. The Kremlin's armed forces are too powerful to be routed (with or without factoring in the risk of nuclear war) at an acceptable price. American and

European electorates won't countenance the body bags. The same assessment applies to dislodging proxies from Luhansk and Donbas. The military cost of deterring Russian aggression beyond Luhansk and Donbas in Novorossiya might be tolerable, but even this less ambitious mission hasn't mustered any enthusiasm in the West. Europe and America were unwilling to fight World War III with Stalin over Czechoslovakia or Yugoslavia in the early 1950s, and they won't do so now over Ukraine. The West doesn't have a viable military option for expanding its sphere of influence.

America's and the European Union's default option is soft power. It worked well when the Soviet leaders faced a "realization crisis" and Russia was prostrate, but it will be extremely costly today as a surrogate for military force. A complete economic blockade, including Russia's expulsion from the World Trade Organization (WTO), that prevented the Kremlin from doing business with third parties like China would severely disrupt global economic commerce and roil international relations. The same prospect holds for noneconomic soft power initiatives. The stronger the medicine, the higher the cost, including collateral damage. Soft power is an unreliable tool for chastening an implacable adversary. It won't induce Putin to revoke Russia's annexation of Crimea, or to abandon his proxy occupation of Luhansk and Donbas and threats against the rest of Novorossiya, unless he has a change of heart. This makes clear that the West has only two viable options. It can negotiate a deal on spheres of influence, color revolutions, and regime change, or it can persist in its present Cold War II course, pretending that it knows "this time will be the same," concentrating its energies on other business, and accepting high risk for improbable geopolitical gain.

Putin's calculus is similar. His Muscovite-driven great power restoration project impels him to continue rolling back the West's post-Soviet sphere of influence gains, but military conquest in Europe beyond Novorossiya and the Baltics is prohibitively costly. He can use military force outside Europe for diverse purposes, but is checked in the heartland. His default option, like the West's, is soft power, including disinformation and covert operations. He knows that this is a weak reed, but hopes for internal and external gains while insisting that "this time will be different."

It follows directly that, double gaming notwithstanding, the expected gains of postponing a compromise solution for both sides are small and don't warrant taking catastrophic risks. If leaders pierce the veil of double gaming, overcome their cognitive dissonance, discard their motivated reason, and objectively analyze the fundamentals, they should be more amenable to negotiating settlement sooner rather than later.

Staying the double gaming course makes more sense for Putin than the West because he is prepared to expand the Kremlin's sphere of influence along and within Russia's periphery with massive force if conditions are propitious. The prospect adds a grain of rationality to the Kremlin's massive disinformation initiatives, but he too should be able to appreciate the benefits of compromise if the West decides to move toward sustained Cold Peace or durable condominium.

Notes

1 "To know and not to know, to be conscious of complete truthfulness while telling carefully constructed lies (double-speaking), to hold simultaneously two opinions which cancelled out, knowing them to be contradictory and believing in both of them (double-thinking), to use logic against logic, to repudiate morality while laying claim to it (double-standards), to believe that democracy was impossible and that the Party was the guardian of democracy, to forget, whatever it was necessary to forget, then to draw it back into memory again at the moment when it was needed, and then promptly to forget it again, and above all, to apply the same process to the process itself – that was the ultimate subtlety; consciously to induce unconsciousness, and then, once again, to become unconscious of the act of hypnosis you had just performed(double-consciousness and unconsciousness). Even to understand the word 'doublethink' involved the use of doublethink." George Orwell, *Nineteen Eighty-Four*, London: Martin Secker & Warburg Ltd, 1949, part 1, chapter 3, p. 32. Ingsoc's (English socialism) credo: War is Peace, Freedom is Slavery, and Ignorance is Strength.

2 Cf. Leon Aron, "Russian Propaganda: Ways and Means," Testimony before the Senate Foreign Relations Committee, Subcommittee on Europe and Regional Security Cooperation on "Putin's Invasion of Ukraine and the Propaganda that Threatens Europe, *AEI*, November 3, 2015. https://www.aei.org/publication/russian-propaganda-ways-and-means/?utm_source=paramount&utm_medium=email&utm_content=AEITODAY&utm_campaign=110415.

3 Armin Rosen, "This Declassified US Intelligence Report from 1990 Is One of the Most Terrifying Things You'll ever Read," *Business Insider*, October 28, 2015. http://finance.yahoo.com/news/declassified-us-intelligence-report-1990-192052241.html.

"The 1983 US-Soviet 'war scare' is one of the most controversial episodes of the Cold War.

Now we finally know it was also one of the most dangerous, thanks to a February 1990 report published by the National Security Archive at George Washington University this week after a 12-year Freedom of Information Act battle.

The US and Soviets were dangerously close to going to war in November 1983, the bombshell report found, and the Cold War-era US national-security apparatus missed many warning signs.

That 1983 'war scare' was spurred by a large-scale US military exercise in Eastern Europe called Able Archer that the Soviets apparently believed was part of allied preparation for a real war." Cf. Steven Rosefielde and Quinn Mills, *Master of Illusion*, Cambridge: Cambridge University Press, 2007.

4 Cognitive dissonance is the perplexity caused when individuals are confronted with a paradox; that is, two or more contradictory beliefs, ideas, or values. Leon Festinger, *A Theory of Cognitive Dissonance*, Palo Alto, CA: Stanford University Press, 1957.

5 "Motivated reasoning leads people to confirm what they already believe, while ignoring contrary data. But it also drives people to develop elaborate rationalizations to justify holding beliefs that logic and evidence have shown to be wrong. Motivated reasoning responds defensively to contrary evidence, actively discrediting such evidence or its source without logical or evidentiary justification. Clearly, motivated reasoning is emotion driven. It seems to be assumed by social scientists that motivated reasoning is driven by a desire to avoid cognitive dissonance. Self-delusion, in other words, feels good, and that's what motivates people to vehemently defend obvious falsehoods." *The Skeptic's Dictionary.* http://skepdic.com/motivatedreasoning.html; Milton Lodge and Charles Taber, "Three Steps toward a Theory of Motivated Political Reasoning," in Arthur Lupia, ed., *Elements of Reason: Cognition, Choice and Bounds of Rationality*, Cambridge University Press, 2000; Charles Taber, "The Interpretation of Foreign Policy Events: A Cognitive Process Theory," in D. A. Sylvan and J. F. Voss, eds., *Problem Representation in Political Decision Making*, London: Cambridge University Press, 1998.

6 Timothy Carney, "The Export-Import Bank Is the International Bank of Clinton," *AEI*, June 11, 2015. http://www.aei.org/publication/the-export-import-bank-is-the-international-bank-of-clinton/?utm_source=paramount&utm_medium=email&utm_content=AEITODAY&utm_campaign=061115; "It makes perfect sense, then, for Hillary Clinton to support Ex-Im. Jeb Hensarling, chairman of the House Financial Services Committee, put it well: "Hillary Clinton is a natural cheerleader for the Export-Import Bank. After all, Ex-Im's biggest beneficiaries are foreign governments and giant corporations. Conveniently, these just happen to be among the biggest donors to the Clinton Foundation as well as major underwriters of the speaking fees that added millions of dollars to the Clinton bank account."

7 Adrian Chen, "The Agency." *New York Times Magazine*, June 2, 2015. http://www.nytimes.com/2015/06/07/magazine/the-agency.html?_r=1.

8 Ibid.

9 Dana Priest, Ellen Nakashima, and Tom Hamburger, "U.S. Investigating Potential Covert Russian Plan to Disrupt November Elections," *Washington Post*, September 5, 2016. https://www.washingtonpost.com/world/national-security/intelligence-community-investigating-covert-russian-influence-operations-in-the-united-states/2016/09/04/aec27fa0-7156-11e6-8533-6b0b0ded0253_story.html. "U.S. intelligence officials described the covert influence campaign here as 'ambitious' and said it is also designed to counter U.S. leadership and influence in international affairs." "The Russian government hack of the Democratic National Committee, disclosed by the DNC in June but not yet officially ascribed by the U.S. government to Russia, and the subsequent release of 20,000 hacked DNC emails by WikiLeaks, shocked officials. Cyber-analysts traced its digital markings to known Russian government hacking groups."

10 David Greenberg, *Republic of Spin: An Inside History of the American Presidency*, New York: W.W. Norton, 2016.

11 Paul Milgrom and John Roberts, "The LeChatelier Principle," *American Economic Review*, 86, 1 (1996): 173–179; Paul Samuelson, "The Lechatelier Principle in Linear Programming," Santa Monica. CA: Rand Corporation, 1949; Paul Samuelson, "An Extension of the Lechatelier Principle," *Econometrica*, 28 (1960): 368–379.

PART V

WHAT IS TO BE DONE?

14

Coexistence

Russia's annexation of Crimea and its ensuing surrogacy war against Ukraine has shredded the West's vision of the post-Soviet world order.[1] The Kremlin's claim of hegemonic rights violates the fundamental axioms of America and the European Union's progressive rules-based world order.[2] Hegemony in contemporary Western doctrine is illegitimate.[3] No nation should be made vassal to another. Progress requires that all nations embrace true democracy and economic liberalization, subject to enlightened minority rights guarantees (ethnic, gender, religious, social) and egalitarian economic transfers.[4]

Putin's rejection of the West's rules and values combined with his arm twisting and aggression mean that coexistence has replaced the world order (one set of principles governing every nation's internal and external affairs), and that pragmatic terms of engagement that fall short of the comprehensive ideal are needed to reduce the perils of East-West armed conflict. In general, any violation of America and the European Union's ideal world order substitutes alternative values and rules or opens the door to conflicts that can only be resolved by coercion, accommodation, appeasement, and capitulation between and among rivals. Every violation creates a conceptual space diluting, partitioning, or contravening the West's ideal world order, and may also entail complex interactive effects within and outside the system. What should be done?

Compromise

A scheme for a universal world order that is unacceptable to Russia and/or other great powers isn't a viable world order at all. It is a recipe for conflict rather than a basis for mutual accommodation and conflict adjudication. At this juncture, the West is sticking to its guns. It is uninterested in crafting new rules that restrict its global aspirations. It has no intention of being drawn into Putin's twin advocacy of his Greater Europe Plan and Yalta II, or bolstering its authority by engaging in an arms race with the Kremlin (and China) and substantially intensifying its soft power countermeasures to pressure Kremlin compliance. It is leaving the future to fate, confident that this time will be the same.

The strategy could work. However, tenacity isn't the only game in town. There are alternatives. The West could mobilize for victory. It could assemble military forces to hold the line in Novorossiya, and potentially dislodge the Kremlin from Luhansk, Donbas and Crimea. It could eradicate secular stagnation by weening itself from excessive government deficit spending, money emission, and support for financial speculation. It can tame insider self-seeking, curtail big government, discourage dependency, eradicate transfers to the privileged, and promote economic freedom (liberalization and competitiveness). In short, if the West creates a robust defense and transforms itself into the ideal social system it claims to be, it will weaken resistance to the global rule of law. The result would be Western victory, not interim Cold Peace or durable coexistence. This is the best solution.

If the West cannot discipline itself to achieve the best, then it can wager on accommodation in varying degrees to nudge the Kremlin toward ultimately accepting its version of the universal rule of law. It can modify its strategy by tempering its support for color revolutions and regime change, shifting conceptually from Cold War II to interim Cold Peace, a tactical adjustment that should be acceptable if Western leaders are really confident that this time will be the same. The approach sacrifices principle for the sake of reducing the likelihood of armed combat, without accepting permanent condominium.

The West has a bolder option too. It can accept permanent condominium. This would mark a return to Khrushchev's peaceful coexistence, and to pre–World War I concepts of spheres of great power influence. Condominium (or multi-dominium) could be informally negotiated, or codified in a formal conference establishing a multipolar world order (Yalta II) with well-defined spheres of influence.

No approach is failsafe, including the West's quest to globalize its rule of law. All are reversible. This means that the best choices are contextual. How should the West proceed given existing cultural and political constraints?

The options are limited because Western policy makers aren't ready to abandon color revolutions and regime change. American and EU policy makers will avoid committing themselves to any doctrinal change like disavowing its policy of regime change that prevents them from expanding the West's sphere of influence in Eurasia, but they may be willing to settle for interim Cold Peace II without abandoning hope for a better ultimate outcome. This requires the West to dial down color revolutions and regime change, dial up democratic dialogue, and tactically concede Russian authority in its sphere of influence. It is tantamount to de facto recognition of the possibility of durable coexistence of democratic and authoritarian states, and paves the way toward "normalization" on Western terms, if, and only if Washington and Brussels are competent enough to outwit Putin. If Putin outwits them, durable condominium (or multi-dominium) will concede more to authoritarianism than it should.

Either way, if Cold Peace II suffices to halt Kremlin aggression in Novorossiya and/or the Baltic states, the West can continue doing business as usual, counting on strategic patience. If this proves insufficient, the West can roll back its concessions and reassess whether it is willing to abandon its faith that this time will be the same. It doesn't have to abandon Cold Peace. Much can be accomplished merely by building a military capacity to dislodge the Kremlin from Crimea, Luhansk and the Donbas. The West doesn't have to fight. A credible deterrent may suffice.

The evidence assembled in this volume suggests that Putin has the will and the room to push the envelope whether or not the West tries to normalize relations (beyond tactically partnering in Syria) by conceding coexistence on a temporary or permanent basis. He can devour chunks of Novorossiya and the Baltic states in small bits and sow the seeds of dissension in Europe without provoking the West to change its strategic vision. The Minsk process is an effort to dissuade piecemeal Kremlin aggression in Novorossiya and elsewhere in Russia's neighborhood. It may succeed, and if it does, prospects for an era of Cold Peace will be auspicious. If it or any follow-on Minsk III initiative fails, Cold War II will persist until one side or the other prevails; or the conflict escalates into a conflagration.

The denouement is less certain than Western politicians believe because they have a warped impression of the correlation of forces and are bemused by cognitive dissonance and motivated reason. Russia's position is better than the American and European policy-making community warrants and could improve further if natural resources prices rebound in 2017.

Common Ground

Avoiding a conflagration and shifting from Cold War II to Cold Peace without conceding durable condominium today should not be difficult. Although tattered, many elements of the West's idealist world order remain intact. Putin's Russia has withdrawn from the Treaty on Conventional Armed Forces in Europe (CFE),[5] and the West has barred the Kremlin from the G8,[6] but Russia participates in the United Nations (including the International Court of Justice), International Criminal Court (crimes against humanity), World Trade Organization (WTO), International Labor Organization (ILO), International Monetary Fund (IMF), World Bank (WB), Asian Infrastructure Investment Bank (AIIB), Shanghai Cooperation Agreement (SCO), "Silk Road Economic Belt,"[7] New Strategic Arms Reduction Treaty (START), International Atomic Energy Treaty (IAE), Antarctic Treaty System, Single Convention on Narcotic Drugs, Outer Space Treaty, Treaty on the Non-Proliferation of Nuclear Weapons, Convention on the Prohibition of the Development, Production and Stockpiling of Bacteriological (Biological) and Toxin Weapons and on their Destruction, Intermediate-Range Nuclear Forces Treaty (INF), Montreal Protocol on Substances that Deplete the Ozone Layer, Treaty on the Final Settlement with Respect to Germany, International Covenant on Civil and Political Rights (ICCPR), Chemical Weapons Convention (CWC), and the Kremlin Accords (which stopped the preprogrammed aiming of nuclear missiles at targets on any nation and provided for the dismantling of the Russian nuclear arsenal positioned in Ukraine). Russia is also an integral member of global financial networks,[8] and abides by the commercial laws of host states. Obviously, annexing Crimea isn't tantamount to Moscow's complete repudiation of Western values and the West's aspirations for a rules-based world order. The Kremlin's withdrawal from globalist institutions and prior accords is limited and reversible.

Accommodation

Room exists for exiting Cold War II, moreover, because the Kremlin's great power restoration project is narrowly conceived. The Kremlin isn't demanding the eradication of the global institutions in which it participates, nor does it insist that Western nations outside Moscow's spheres of influence embrace Russia's values. Putin isn't proselytizing Muscovite utopia. American and EU leaders aren't being pressed to abandon democracy, equality, personal liberty, free enterprise, religious conscience, social justice, or minority, feminist and homosexual, or transgender affirmative action. Putin intermittently pays lip service to most of these causes.

The Kremlin seeks instead more narrowly to amend prevailing Western international rules and values in order to push back against America and the European Union, and expand its own hegemonic reach. This clearly places the two sides on a collision course, but doesn't necessitate the torpedoing of one or both ships because the discord isn't comprehensive. The damage can be contained by building on common ground and nimbly navigating perils.

Mutual accommodation within a Cold Peace framework should be achievable if both sides are willing and pragmatic. This will infringe some idealist principles and notions of honor (duty to prevail),[9] but under the circumstances, it may be wiser to resist cutting off one's nose to spite one's face because the material and human cost of intransigence could be catastrophic. Putin, Obama, and Merkel have already gotten the ball rolling by toning down their rhetoric and normalizing aspects of their relationship without jeopardizing their grip on domestic political power.

Pragmatic World Order

The spirit of compromise can be fostered by recognizing that the concept of world order serves both as an ideal and a means to pragmatic ends. In an imperfect universe, institutions, rules, and values alone cannot assure harmony and justice. They can only serve as tools for adjudicating, resolving, freezing, or dissipating conflicts. It is essential, therefore, to avoid conflating the quixotic quest for a harmonious world order with the task of adaptively renegotiating pragmatic rules of international engagement. The best here is the enemy of the good.[10] Sublime world order isn't a *sine qua non*. What is needed are adaptable rules, institutions, and values that establish Cold Peace as a platform for non-belligerently advancing the causes of democracy, equality, personal liberty, free enterprise, religious conscience, social justice, and affirmative action. If the West is confident that its ideals are superior, it can afford to be strategically patient.[11]

America and the European can facilitate Cold Peace and move forward toward a less conflicted rules and values-based world order by:

1. Tacitly acknowledging the limited practicality of their military options
2. Tacitly recognizing the ineffectuality of their economic and diplomatic sanctions
3. Tempering Putin's ambitions by putting their own military, economic, and political houses in order
4. Making symbolic goodwill gestures, including:
   a. Curbing color revolutionary rhetoric
   b. Shelving Ukrainian accession to the European Union and NATO
   c. Limiting military assistance to Ukraine
   d. Disengaging and normalizing relations with Russia
   e. Initiating Track II (back track) negotiations on condominium.[12]

Track II serves as a reminder that precedents exist for crafting acceptable rules and values-based engagement for contemporary rival civilizations as a prelude to Yalta II informal diplomatic conversations. Neither side has to send a "costly signal."[13] The aim of Track II talks should be Cold Peace or peaceful coexistence as may have been intended at Yalta I.

Low-intensity cold war akin to the early Gorbachev period would be acceptable. Moreover, reflection shows that there are ample grounds for expecting better results now than those realized under Cold War I disengagement. The Kremlin is no longer autarkic or ideologically motivated to destroy Western capitalism. It appreciates the benefits of East-West commerce, finance, travel, and labor mobility, allowing Putin wider scope for comprise than Joseph Stalin. The challenge won't be in getting started, but in identifying and negotiating defensible red lines.

The West today probably can settle the Ukrainian imbroglio without sacrificing most of its post-Soviet geopolitical gains.[14] It merely has to accept that America and the European Union don't have a monopoly on spheres of influence and cannot prevent the Kremlin from acquiring everything Moscow covets. Nonetheless, America and the European Union resist compromise.[15]

Strategic Incoherence

This reluctance partly reflects the West's larger strategic ineptitude.[16] Commenting on the Obama administration's decision to trade permanent "relief from sanctions in exchange for temporary restraints on Iranian conduct," Henry Kissinger and George Schultz recently asserted that "Until clarity on an American strategic political concept is reached, the projected nuclear agreement will reinforce, not resolve, the world's challenges in the region."[17] Both former American Secretaries of State fault contemporary Western leaders for being strategically befuddled.[18]

The complaint isn't that they are uninformed, ill-informed, unprofessional, or unable to formulate priorities. It is that the priorities they champion are inimical to the West's best interests. Treaty drafters contend that eliminating sanctions against Iran becoming a nuclear weapons state alongside America, Russia, the United Kingdom, France, and China will advance the cause of reconciliation and stability in the Middle East. Kissinger and Schultz, however, show this outcome is improbable because the Obama administration hasn't devised a feasible program for coping with regional conventional arms and nuclear competition that the treaty is sure to unleash.[19] Anthony Cordesman describes the phenomenon

more grandiosely as a "failed approach to chaos theory."[20] The same sort
of half-baked strategy lies at the root of the West's muddled management
of the Crimean annexation crisis.[21] America and the European Union are
stiff-necked. They know what they want, know that they cannot get it, have
no practical strategy for reconciling the contradiction, and don't care, confident that "this time will be the same."

Rivalry

Avoiding war and establishing Cold Peace based on patchwork Wilsonian
ideals won't stop the march of history. Even if Russia and the West successfully negotiate condominium under conditions of Cold War or Cold Peace,
they will continue jousting with nonlethal means.[22] Russia's annexation of
Crimea isn't an aberration. It's the starting shot of the Kremlin's drive back
to the future, an attempt to revive and expand the Muscovite empire, including contested areas of the Arctic.[23] Both camps will cultivate grand illusions.
They will put their best foot forward to shake their rival's confidence and
promote their own cause. Each will tout its comparative economic, political, and civic merit by all means fair and foul, including media manipulation, cyber warfare, espionage, covert action, and co-option. Russians will
portray the West as a failing civilization,[24] and the West will reciprocate,
occasionally relieved by ephemeral bouts of cordiality (Détente, new thinking, resets, etc.). This skirmishing is unavoidable as long as both sides insist
on their independent spheres of influence; however, it is unlikely to significantly advance either cause unless claims and counterclaims are valid.

If Russia's economy is moribund, its civil society restive, and its government teetering on the brink of regime change, then revived prosperity,
social justice, and democratic rectitude in the West may bring the Kremlin
back into the Wilsonian fold. Vice versa, if the shoe is on the other foot,
Moscow may well expand its sphere of influence.

Stumbling to War

Graham Allison and Dimitri Simes have recently lent their voices to the cho-
rus advocating Cold Peace by affirming their faith in strategic patience and
stressing the dangers of conventional and nuclear war with Russia.[25] Their
concerns are plausible, but also provide insight into why Putin believes that
he can outplay the West after Russia's Crimean annexation not just over the
terms of Cold Peace, but after its implementation. In a nutshell, they argue
that Russia's confrontation with the West is combustible because America

and the European Union, underestimating Putin's resolve, may not take the steps necessary to prevent catastrophic escalation.[26]

The starting point for Allison's and Simes's alert is Christopher Clark's *Sleepwalkers*, a sober analysis of how Europe and Russia blundered into the First World War.[27] They, like Barbara Tuchman before them, assert the conflagration was the unintended consequence of a reactive process driven by arrogance, fear, and opportunism that swept reason and common sense aside.[28]

Allison, as a student of the Cuban Missile Crisis and bureaucratic decision making,[29] reminds us in the current context that Western policy makers shouldn't suppose that Putin and his entourage will rationally interpret and prudently respond to the West's defense of Kyiv.[30] Washington and Brussels should not expect Moscow to passively accept Ukraine's accession to the European Union and NATO.[31] Simes, a knowledgeable Kremlinologist,[32] drives the point home by detailing Kremlin fears and complexes, buttressing his case by portraying Putin as a pragmatist harried by hardline "hotheads."[33]

Given these premises, Allison and Simes pose the crucial rhetorical question: "Could a U.S. response to Russia's actions in Ukraine provoke a confrontation that leads to a U.S.-Russian war?"[34] Allison answers affirmatively, invoking the "Thucydides Trap" to suggest that America's own empire building could prove its undoing with respect to both Russia and China.[35] "In a timeless passage in his history of the Peloponnesian War, Thucydides recounts the Athenian response to a troubled Sparta: "'We did not gain this empire by force. … Our allies came to us of their own accord and begged us to lead them.'" Needless to say, Sparta did not find that explanation reassuring – and that excuse did not prevent thirty years of war that ended with defeat for Athens, but at a price far beyond any benefits that accrued to the victor."[36]

Simes reinforces Allison's analogy with a wide array of examples ranging from America's misreading of Japanese resolve in 1941 to its misadventures in Kosovo, Iran, and the Middle East,[37] peppered with asides about the West's transgressions against Russia that incense Kremlin "hotheads,"[38] before concluding with a short list of redlines that are apt to culminate in war. These triggers are ratcheted economic sanctions (including barring Russia from participating in SWIFT bank clearing operations),[39] the prospect of military defeat of the separatists,[40] and NATO membership for Ukraine.[41]

Allison and Simes don't advise Western leaders to acquiesce to all Putin's demands,[42] urging shrewd concessions instead to avert Armageddon, but the redlines that they attribute to Putin, especially the second, will encourage the Kremlin to drive a very hard bargain because Moscow is adept at manufacturing "separatists." Allison and Simes are right to call the West's attention to the catastrophic strategic nuclear risks posed by Russia's annexation of Crimea and its irredentist claims in Novorossiya. Their fears are probably overdrawn. Nonetheless, their analysis adds weight to the proposition that the benefits of transitioning swiftly from Cold War II to Cold Peace outweigh the risks.[43]

Notes

1 David M. Kennedy, "What 'W' Owes to 'WW': President Bush May Not Even Know It, but He Can Trace His View of the World to Woodrow Wilson, Who Defined a Diplomatic Destiny for America That We Can't Escape," *The Atlantic Monthly*, Vol. 295, No 2 (March 2005): 36ff.; David Steigerwald, *Wilsonian Idealism in America*, Ithaca, NY: Cornell University Press, 1994; G. John Ikenberry, *Liberal Leviathan: The Origins, Crisis, and Transformation of the American World Order*, Princeton, NJ: Princeton University Press, 2011; Beate Jahn, *Liberal Internationalism: Theory, History, Practice*, London: Palgrave Macmillan, 2013; Amitav Acharya, *The End of American World Order*, New York: Polity, 2014.
2 This holds even if the West's advocacy of its New World Order is motivated by a hidden agenda. On American insincerity, see Strobe Talbott, *The Russia Hand: A Memoir of Presidential Diplomacy*, New York: Random House, 2003.
3 Patrick Smith and Stephen Cohen, "The *New York Times* 'Basically Rewrites Whatever the Kiev Authorities Say': Stephen F. Cohen on the U.S./Russia/Ukraine History the Media Won't Tell You," *Salon*, April 16, 2015. http://www.salon.com/2015/04/16/the_new_york_times_basically_rewrites_whatever_the_kiev_authorities_say_stephen_f_cohen_on_the_u_s_russiaukraine_history_the_media_wont_tell_you/. "Our position is that nobody is entitled to a sphere of influence in the 21st century. Russia wants a sphere of influence in the sense that it doesn't want American military bases in Ukraine or in the Baltics or in Georgia. But what is the expansion of NATO other than the expansion of the American zone or sphere of influence? It's not just military. It's financial, it's economic, it's cultural, it's intermarriage – soldiers, infrastructure. It's probably the most dramatic expansion of a great sphere of influence in such a short time and in peacetime in the history of the world. So you have Vice President Biden constantly saying, 'Russia wants a sphere of influence and we won't allow it.' Well, we are shoving our sphere of influence down Russia's throat, on the assumption that it won't push back. Obviously, the discussion might well begin: 'Is Russia entitled to a zone or sphere in its neighborhood free of foreign military bases?' Just that, nothing more. If the answer is yes, NATO expansion should've ended in Eastern Germany, as the Russians were promised. But we've crept closer and closer. Ukraine is about NATO-expansion-no-matter-what. Washington can go on about democracy and sovereignty and all the rest, but it's about that. And we can't re-open this question. ... The hypocrisy, or the inability to connect the dots in America, is astonishing."
4 Thomas Piketty, *Capital in the Twenty-First Century*, Cambridge, MA: Harvard University Press, 2014.

5 "Russia's Withdrawal from CFE Treaty Work a 'Dangerous Move,' Says OSCE PA Security Chair," March 13, 2015. http://www.osce.org/pa/144946.

6 Alison Smale and Michael Shear, "Russia Is Ousted from Group of 8 by U.S. and Allies," *New York Times*, March 24, 2014. http://www.nytimes.com/2014/03/25/world/europe/obama-russia-crimea.html?_r=0. Birgit Bennen, "Merkel Says Russia Can't Return to G-7 as Ukraine Festers," Bloomberg, May 21, 2015. http://www.bloomberg.com/news/articles/2015-05-21/merkel-says-russia-must-respect-international-law-to-rejoin-g-7?cmpid=yhoo. "German Chancellor Angela Merkel said Russia can't rejoin Group of Seven meetings unless it respects international law, underscoring President Vladimir Putin's exclusion from the G-7 summit she's hosting next month. Addressing Germany's lower house of parliament in Berlin on her summit agenda, Merkel said Putin's encroachment on Ukraine signals that Russia isn't part of the group of advanced economies' 'community of values.' Resolving the Ukraine conflict will require 'patience and staying power,' she said."

7 Valdai Discussion Club Analyzed Prospects of the "Silk Road Economic Belt," *Valdai*, April 17, 2015. Project http://valdaiclub.com/event/76800.html.

8 Sergei Dubinin, "Russian Economy: Overcoming Crisis in the Finance Sector," *Valdai*, April 10, 2015. http://valdaiclub.com/economy/76620.html. "Sergei Dubinin, former Chairman of Russia's Central Bank, asserts that 'Russia's Central Bank has become a genuine mega-regulator that coordinates not only the country's banking system, but also all its financial markets and their institutions, including non-public pension funds, insurance companies and stock exchanges.'" "It has become an integral part of the global financial architecture in most countries."

9 Idealist arguments are couched in terms of reason; honor (Eleftheria i thanatos: freedom or death) is a claim to obligation that trumps reason and consequentialism. Neither takes precedence over wisdom. "Discretion is the better part of valor" (Shakespeare's *Henry IV*).

10 Voltaire, "La Bégueule" (Contes, 1772).

11 José Ignacio Torreblanca, "Strategic Patience with Russia Will Pay Off," *European Council on Foreign Relations*, December 10, 2014. http://www.ecfr.eu/article/commentary_strategic_patience_with_russia_will_pay_off378.

12 Joseph Montville, "Track Two Diplomacy: The Work of Healing History." *Whitehead Journal of Diplomacy and International Relations*, Vol. 7, No. 15 (2006). http://blogs.shu.edu/diplomacy/files/archives/03Montville.pdf. Track Two diplomacy referred to conflict resolution efforts by professional nongovernmental conflict resolution practitioners and theorists.

13 Elena Alekseenkova, "Chaos and Play without Rules: On the Current Crisis of Confidence in Trust in Relations between Russia and the West," *Valdai*, April 15, 2015. http://russiancouncil.ru/en/inner/?id_4=5686#top. Andrew Kydd, *Trust and Mistrust in International Relations*, Princeton, NJ: Princeton University Press, 2005.

Greg Botelho and Lindsay Isaac, "Russian Convoy Rolls into Ukraine: 'Humanitarian' Aid or 'Direct Invasion'?" // CNN. Edition: International, August 28, 2014. (http://edition.cnn.com/2014/08/22/world/europe/ukraine-crisis/).

14 Henry Kissinger, "Henry Kissinger: To Settle the Ukraine Crisis, Start at the End," *Washington Post*, March 5, 2014. http://www.washingtonpost.com/opinions/henry-kissinger-to-settle-the-ukraine-crisis-start-at-the-end/2014/03/05/46dad868-a496-11e3-8466-d34c451760b9_story.html. Terry Atlas, "Brzezinski

Sees Finlandization of Ukraine as Deal Maker," *Bloomberg*, April 12, 2014. http://www.bloomberg.com/news/articles/2014-04-11/brzezinski-sees-finlandization-of-ukraine-as-deal-maker. Clifford G. Gaddy, "Finlandization for Ukraine: Realistic or Utopian?" *Brookings*, March 6, 2014. http://www.brookings.edu/blogs/up-front/posts/2014/03/06-finlandization-ukraine-realistic-utopian-gaddy. James Kirchick, "Finlandization Is Not a Solution for Ukraine," *American Interest*, July 2014. http://www.the-american-interest.com/2014/07/27/finlandization-is-not-a-solution-for-ukraine/. "The term 'Finlandization' is making a comeback as a proposed remedy for Ukraine's delicate position between East and West. A look back at Finland's postwar experience shows us why this is a bad idea." Henry Meyer, Daryna Krasnolutska, and Volodymyr Verbyany, "Russia Says Ukraine Must Be 'Neutral' as It Accuses U.S., NATO," Bloomberg, April 21, 2015. http://www.bloomberg.com/news/articles/2015-04-21/ukraine-pushes-for-un-peacekeepers-as-rockets-disrupt-cease-fire?cmpid=yhoo. "Minister Sergei Lavrov said in an interview with three Moscow radio stations on Wednesday, 'It's in our interests not to divide Ukraine, it's in our interests to keep it neutral in military terms,' Lavrov said. 'We want Ukraine to be peaceful and quiet. To achieve that, it's necessary to keep Ukraine unified and not allow it to be torn into pieces.'"

15 Vikas Shukla, "Russia, China Challenge U.S. Hegemony; Nuclear War 'Likely Future,'" *Value Walk*, May 13, 2015. http://www.valuewalk.com/2015/05/russia-china-challenge-u-s-nuclear-war-likely-future/. "Dr Paul Craig Roberts, the former U.S. Assistant Secretary of the Treasury for Economic Policy, said in a blog post that the United States was determined to block the rise of Russia and China. But neither of them will join the 'world's acceptance of Washington's hegemony.' Roberts notes that the U.S.'s attempt to contain Russia is the key reason for the crisis 'Washington has created in Ukraine.' Paul Craig Roberts, head of the Institute of Political Economy, said that Washington's aggression and propaganda have convinced Moscow and Beijing that Washington intends war. It has prompted Russia and China to form a strategic alliance to counterbalance the U.S. might. Dr. Roberts believes that Russia and China will not accept the 'vassalage status' that Germany, France, the UK, Canada, Japan, Australia and many other countries have accepted. Washington's arrogance of its self-image as an 'exceptional, indispensable' country with hegemonic rights over other nations has laid the groundwork for a war. Unless the U.S. dollar and power collapses, 'nuclear war is our likely future,' said Dr. Roberts. Besides military exercises, Russia and China have been stitching economic alliances to move closer to each other."

16 Cf. John Bolton, "Facing Reality on Iran," *National Review*, September 2015. http://www.aei.org/publication/facing-reality-on-iran/?utm_source=paramount&utm_medium=email&utm_content=AEITHISWEEK&utm_campaign=Weekly082915. "But neither wishful thinking nor outright deception can change the fundamental strategic reality. That facing reality is unpalatable politically does not mean we can imagine another reality into existence."

17 Henry Kissinger and George P. Shultz, "The Iran Deal and Its Consequences," *Wall Street Journal*, April 7, 2015. http://www.wsj.com/articles/the-iran-deal-and-its-consequences-1428447582. Subsequent events are confirming their misgivings. See Marc A. Thiessen, "Another secret Iran deal exposed", AEI, September 2, 2016.

http://www.aei.org/publication/another-secret-iran-deal-exposed/?utm_source=paramount&utm_medium=email&utm_content=AEITODAY&utm_campaign=090716. "First we learned last year that the Obama administration made a secret side deal with Iran which allowed the regime to effectively inspect itself – collecting its own soil samples, instead of IAEA inspectors, at the Parchin military complex."

"Then we learned last month that the Obama administration made a secret $400 million ransom payment to Iran, in which 'wooden pallets stacked with euros, Swiss francs and other currencies were flown into Iran on an unmarked cargo plane' on the very same day that US hostages were released. Now it appears the Obama administration has cut yet another secret deal with Iran – this one allowing Iran to evade some of the restrictions on its nuclear program."

18 Cf. Former Secretary of Defense, Paul Wolfowitz, "Obama's Gift to Iran," *AEI*, April 24, 2015. http://www.aei.org/publication/obamas-gift-to-iran/?utm_source=paramount&utm_medium=email&utm_content=AEITODAY&utm_campaign=042415. Citing Ali Younesi, formerly Iran's Minister of Intelligence and currently a senior adviser to President Hassan Rouhani, via Michael Morell, the former deputy director and acting director of the CIA, Wolfowitz asserts that "Iran's ambition is to become a regional hegemon – in short, to reestablish the Persian empire." "President Obama recently expressed a hope that 'the Iranian people begin to recognize that' if they stopped 'engaging in a whole bunch of proxy wars around the region, by virtue of its size, its resources and its people [Iran] would be an extremely successful regional power.' But hope is not a strategy. And a nuclear deal which concedes so much of what the Iranian regime has been demanding, and which provides it with enormous additional resources to pursue its threatening activities, is unlikely to produce such a change in attitude. It seems more likely to do the very opposite."

19 Cf. John Bolton, "The New Nuclear Arms Race: The Iranian Negotiations have Accelerated the Likelihood of Proliferation, Not Reduced It," AEI, April 14, 2015. http://www.aei.org/publication/the-new-nuclear-arms-race-the-iranian-negotiations-have-accelerated-the-likelihood-of-proliferation-not-reduced-it/?utm_source=paramount&utm_medium=email&utm_content=AEITODAY&utm_campaign=041415. "Most dramatically, some speculate that the White House dreams the nuclear deal will trigger sweeping changes in Tehran, which will evolve from the 1979 Islamic Revolution's ideology and become a 'normal' Middle Eastern state. In reality, no other regional power believes evidence of such developments is even vaguely on the horizon. Ironically, Obama has succeeded in creating a rare unity of analysis between Israel and almost the entire Arab world. And, without a radical shift in the ayatollahs' philosophy (and, even more importantly, that of Iran's Revolutionary Guards, who actually control the nuclear-weapons program), there is no chance of a 'new Middle East' emerging. The last two years of negotiations – and the universally accepted perception of American weakness thereby conveyed – have accelerated a regional nuclear-weapons race. Once only likely after Iran actually tested a nuclear device or otherwise demonstrated unequivocally it possessed such devices, the arms race already has started."

20 Anthony Cordesman, "America's Failed Approach to Chaos Theory," *CSIS*, April 16, 2015. http://csis.org/publication/americas-failed-approach-chaos-theory. "The United States now faces a rapidly evolving world filled with new challenges at a

time when real-world defense planning is focused on budget cuts, when U.S. 'strategy' lacks plans and program budgets, and when talk of strategic partnership lacks clear and specific direction. Far too much U.S. strategic rhetoric is a hollow shell, while the real U.S. national security posture is based on sub-optimizing the budget around the fiscal ceilings set by the Budget Control Act (BCA), persisting in issuing empty concepts and strategic rhetoric, and dealing with immediate problems out of any broader strategic context. The end result resembles an exercise in chaos theory. Once one looks beyond the conceptual rhetoric, the reality is a steadily less coordinated set of reactions to each ongoing or new crisis: the strategic equivalent of the 'butterfly effect.' To paraphrase Edward Lorenz, the chaos theorist who coined the term, 'the present state determines a series of changes and uncertain adjustments in U.S. force postures and military actions in spite of the fact the approximate present does not approximately determine the future.' Put more simply, the United States has no clear strategy for dealing with Russia and Asia and is reacting tactically to the immediate pressures of events in the Middle East and Afghanistan without any clear goals or direction. Worse, these military tactical reactions are steadily more decoupled from the need to create an integrated civil-military strategy: Grab any short-term form of 'win' and ignore the need to 'hold' and build."

21 Ibid. The simplest challenge so far is Russia and Ukraine, but "simple" is a very relative term in today's world. The invasion of Crimea that Russia began in February 2014 put an end to the U.S. assumption that it could somehow focus on other parts of the world. The strategic situation has grown steadily more complex as Russia has pushed deeper into Ukrainian territory, creating new hostile world views like its color revolution and challenging the United States and Europe in other areas. It is unclear where Russia intends to stop its invasion of Ukraine and unclear that U.S. and European actions put forth thus far can halt the series of slow, slicing Russian gains. Sanctions have not halted Russia in Ukraine or deterred it from posing potential new challenges in the Baltic, Central Asia, and Middle East. NATO has so far done little to create a new deterrent to Russia, focusing on a "two percent solution" for increasing member country defense spending whose strategic objective is unclear and has little chance of being reached.

22 Dave Majumdar, "Putin's Missile Could Make U.S. Attacks on Iran Nearly Impossible," *Daily Beast*, April 13, 2015. http://www.thedailybeast.com/articles/ 2015/04/13/putin-s-missile-could-make-u-s-attacks-on-iran-nearly-impossible. html?utm_source=feedburner&utm_medium=feed&utm_campaign=Feed%3A+t hedailybeast%2Farticles+%28The+Daily+Beast+-+Latest+Articles%29.

23 Jeremy Bender, "The Nordic Countries Are Banding Together against Russia's Arctic Push," *Business Insider*, April 22, 2015. http://finance.yahoo.com/news/ nordic-countries-banding-together-against-155811212.html. "The Nordic countries, not generally known for their extreme foreign policies or their habit of overreacting to current events, have started to voice increasingly louder concerns over Russia's role in the Baltics and the Arctic." Andrew Kramer, "Russia Stakes New Claim to Expanse in the Arctic," *New York Times*, August 4, 2015. http:// www.nytimes.com/2015/08/05/world/europe/kremlin-stakes-claim-to-arctic-expanse-and-its-resources.html. "Russia formally staked a claim on Tuesday to a vast area of the Arctic Ocean, including the North Pole. If the United Nations committee that arbitrates sea boundaries accepts Russia's claim, the seabed will

be subject to Moscow's oversight on economic matters, including fishing and oil and gas drilling, though Russia will not have full sovereignty. Under a 1982 United Nations convention, the Law of the Sea, a nation may claim an exclusive economic zone over the continental shelf abutting its shores. If the shelf extends far out to sea, so can the boundaries of the zone. The claim Russia lodged on Tuesday contends that the shelf extends far north of the Eurasian land mass, out under the planet's northern ice cap. Russia submitted a similar claim in 2002, but the United Nations rejected it for lack of scientific support. So this time, the Kremlin has offered new evidence collected by its research vessels. It even dispatched a well-known Arctic explorer, Artur N. Chilingarov, to take a miniature submarine to the sea floor directly below the North Pole, scoop up a soil sample and plant a Russian flag made of titanium there. In a statement posted on its website, the Russian Foreign Ministry said the claim would expand Russia's total territory on land and sea by about 1.2 million square kilometers, or about 463,000 square miles."

24 Sergei Karaganov, "New Configuration of the Global Landscape," *Valdai*, April 16, 2015. http://valdaiclub.com/russia_and_the_world/76760.html.

25 Graham Allison and Dimitri Simes, "Russia and America: Stumbling to War," *National Interest*, April 20, 2015. http://nationalinterest.org/feature/russia-america-stumbling-war-12662?page=8. Graham Allison is director of the Harvard Kennedy School's Belfer Center for Science and International Affairs and a former assistant secretary of defense for policy and plans. Dimitri K. Simes, the *National Interest*'s publisher, is president of the Center for the National Interest (formerly the Nixon Center). Dimitri Simes, *After the Collapse: Russia Seeks Its Place as a Great Power*, New York: Simon and Schuster, 1999.

26 Tyler Rogoway, "Russia Warns of Border Buildup as USAF Chief Says F-22 Are an Option," *Fox*, June 17, 2015. http://foxtrotalpha.jalopnik.com/russia-warns-of-border-buildup-as-usaf-chief-says-f-22-1711607134. Max Delany, "Russia Cites 'Threats' as Nuclear Arsenal Boosted," *AFP*, June 17, 2015. http://news.yahoo.com/russia-add-over-40-missiles-nuclear-arsenal-putin-134813487.html. " 'This year, the size of our nuclear forces will increase by over 40 new intercontinental ballistic missiles that will be able to overcome any, even the most technologically advanced, missile defence systems,' Putin said at the opening of an exhibition of military hardware outside Moscow."

27 Christopher Clark, *The Sleepwalkers: How Europe Went to War in 1914*, London: Allen Lane, 2013; Cf. Thomas Laqueur, "Some Damn Foolish Thing," *London Review of Books*, Vol. 35, No. 23, December 5 (2013): 11–16; Allison and Simes, "Russia and America: Stumbling to War." "At present, the most urgent challenge is the ongoing crisis in Ukraine. There, one can hear eerie echoes of the events a century ago that produced the catastrophe known as World War I."

28 Barbara Tuchman, *The Guns of August*, New York: The Macmillan Company, 1962.

29 Graham Allison, *Essence of Decision: Explaining the Cuban Missile Crisis*, New York: Little, Brown, 1971; Graham Allison, Albert Carneseale, and Joseph Nye Jr., eds., *Hawks, Doves and Owls: An Agenda for Avoiding Nuclear War*, New York: W.W. Norton, 1985; Graham Allison and Gregory Treverton, eds., *Rethinking America's Security: Beyond Cold War to New World Order*, New York: W.W. Norton, 1992; Graham Allison, *Avoiding Nuclear Anarchy: Containing the Threat of Loose Russian*

Nuclear Weapons and Fissile Material, Cambridge, MA: MIT Press 1996; Graham Allison, *Nuclear Terrorism: The Ultimate Preventable Catastrophe,* New York: Times Books/Holt, 2004.

30 "US, Ukraine start military training, defying Russian fury", *Yahoo,* April 20, 2015. http://news.yahoo.com/us-ukraine-start-military-training-defying-russian-fury-112519186.html. "The 300 U.S. Army paratroopers involved in the training traveled to Ukraine last week and will be working alongside 900 national guardsmen." "The exercises, dubbed 'Fearless Guardian-2015,' sparked an enraged reaction from Russia, which described them as a potential cause of destabilization."

31 Allison and Simes, "Russia and America: Stumbling to War." "In the United States and Europe, many believe that the best way to prevent Russia's resumption of its historic imperial mission is to assure the independence of Ukraine. They insist that the West must do whatever is required to stop the Kremlin from establishing direct or indirect control over that country. Otherwise, they foresee Russia reassembling the former Soviet empire and threatening all of Europe."

32 Simes, *After the Collapse.*

33 Allison and Simes, "Russia and America: Stumbling to War." "Russia's political environment, at both the elite and public levels, encourages Putin to escalate demands rather than make concessions. At the elite level, Russia's establishment falls into two camps: a pragmatic camp, which is currently dominant thanks principally to Putin's support, and a hard-line camp. The Russian public largely supports the hard-line camp, whom one Putin adviser called the 'hotheads.' Given Russian politics today, Putin is personally responsible for the fact that Russia's revanchist policies are not more aggressive. Put bluntly, Putin is not the hardest of the hard-liners in Russia.

"While none of the 'hotheads' criticize Putin, even in private conversations, a growing number of military and national-security officials favor a considerably tougher approach to the United States and Europe in the Ukraine crisis. This is apparent in their attacks on such relatively moderate cabinet officers as Vice Prime Minister Igor Shuvalov and Foreign Minister Sergey Lavrov. From their perspective, the moderates fail to comprehend the gravity of the U.S.-European challenge to Russia and hold futile hopes that things can change for the better without Russia surrendering to an unacceptable and degrading foreign diktat. They recommend shifting the game to areas of Russian strength – by using military force to advance Russian interests as Putin did in Crimea and to pressure the West into accepting Moscow on its own terms."

34 Ibid.

35 Cf. Graham Allison, "The Thucydides Trap: Are the U.S. and China Headed for War? *The Atlantic,* September 24, 2015. "The defining question about global order for this generation is whether China and the United States can escape Thucydides's Trap. The Greek historian's metaphor reminds us of the attendant dangers when a rising power rivals a ruling power – as Athens challenged Sparta in ancient Greece, or as Germany did Britain a century ago. Most such contests have ended badly, often for both nations, a team of mine at the Harvard Belfer Center for Science and International Affairs has concluded after analyzing the historical record. In 12 of 16 cases over the past 500 years, the result was war. When the parties avoided war, it required huge, painful adjustments in attitudes and actions on the part not just of the challenger but also the challenged. Based on the current trajectory, war

between the United States and China in the decades ahead is not just possible, but much more likely than recognized at the moment. Indeed, judging by the historical record, war is more likely than not. Moreover, current underestimations and misapprehensions of the hazards inherent in the U.S.-China relationship contribute greatly to those hazards. A risk associated with Thucydides's Trap is that business as usual – not just an unexpected, extraordinary event – can trigger large-scale conflict. When a rising power is threatening to displace a ruling power, standard crises that would otherwise be contained, like the assassination of an archduke in 1914, can initiate a cascade of reactions that, in turn, produce outcomes none of the parties would otherwise have chosen.

"War, however, is not inevitable. Four of the 16 cases in our review did not end in bloodshed. Those successes, as well as the failures, offer pertinent lessons for today's world leaders. Escaping the Trap requires tremendous effort. As Xi Jinping himself said during a visit to Seattle on Tuesday, 'There is no such thing as the so-called Thucydides Trap in the world. But should major countries time and again make the mistakes of strategic miscalculation, they might create such traps for themselves.'"

36 Allison and Dimitri Simes, "Russia and America: Stumbling to War." "To recognize the potentially catastrophic consequences of war with Russia does not require paralysis in addressing the challenge of a resurgent but wounded Russia. The United States has a vital interest in maintaining its credibility as a superpower and in assuring the survival and security of its NATO alliance – and thus of every one of its NATO allies. Moreover, in international politics, appetites can grow quickly if fed by easy victories.

"The Russian president's currently limited objectives in Ukraine could become more expansive if Russia does not face serious resistance. After all, the smooth annexation of Crimea led to an outburst of triumphalist rhetoric in Moscow about creating a new entity, Novorossiya, which would include eastern and southern Ukraine all the way to the Romanian border. The combination of resistance by local populations, the Ukrainian government's willingness to fight for its territory, and U.S. and EU sanctions quickly persuaded the Russian leadership to curtail this line of thinking. When a nation is prepared to fight for important interests, clarity about that determination is a virtue in discouraging potential aggression."

37 Ibid. "Americans would do well to recall the sequence of events that led to Japan's attack on the United States at Pearl Harbor and America's entry into the Second World War." "The Clinton administration misread an extended and bloody civil war in Yugoslavia before imposing its own shaky partition and angering Russia and China in the process. When George W. Bush decided to invade Iraq and replace Saddam Hussein's regime with a democratically elected one, he believed that this would, as he said, 'serve as a powerful example of liberty and freedom in a part of the world that is desperate for liberty and freedom.' He and his team held firmly to this conviction, despite numerous warnings that war would fragment the country along tribal and religious lines, that any elected government in Baghdad would be Shia-dominated and that Iran would be the principal beneficiary from a weakened Iraq. Next, the Obama administration joined Britain and France in a major air campaign in Libya to remove Muammar el-Qaddafi. The consequent chaos contributed to the killings of a U.S. ambassador and other American diplomats and to the creation of a haven for Islamic extremists more threatening than Qaddafi's Libya to its

neighbors and to America. In Syria, at the outset of the civil war, the Obama administration demanded the ouster of President Bashar al-Assad, even though he never posed a direct threat to America. Neither the Obama administration nor members of Congress took seriously predictions that Islamic extremists would dominate the Syrian opposition rather than more moderate forces – and that Assad would not be easy to displace."

38 Ibid. "This feeling is grounded both in Russian security concerns and in nearly uncontrollable sentiments about Ukraine and its Russian-speaking population. The growing popularity of the slogan Rossiya ne brosayet svoikh – Russia does not abandon its own – reflects these feelings and resembles Russia's pan-Slavic attitudes toward Serbia before World War I. One of us saw a powerful example of these emotions while watching a Russian talk-show discussion about Ukraine before a live audience. A Russian panelist declared that 'our cause is just and we will prevail' to thunderous applause. Importantly, the speaker, Vyacheslav Nikonov, is not only a member of the pro-Putin United Russia party and the chairman of the parliament's education committee. He is also the grandson of former Soviet foreign minister Vyacheslav Molotov, who made the same statement after Hitler attacked the USSR in 1941. Nikonov is known for reflecting establishment perspectives." "The director of the television network Rossiya Segodnya, Dmitry Kiselyov, has been more explicit, repeatedly warning, 'Russia is the only country in the world that is realistically capable of turning the United States into radioactive ash.' Russia's 2014 Military Doctrine emphasizes that Russia will use nuclear weapons not only in response to nuclear attacks but also 'in the case of aggression against the Russian Federation with the use of conventional weapons.' And, as a recent report of the European Leadership Network notes, there have been almost forty incidents in the past year in which Russian forces engaged in a pattern of provocations that, if continued, 'could prove catastrophic.'"

39 Ibid. "If the United States and the European Union would largely remove sanctions and restore business as usual, they would urge that Russia swallow its pride and reconcile. But if Russia is going to continue to be sanctioned, excluded from financial markets and denied Western technology, they say, then Russia should pursue its own independent path. Putin has yet to face a decisive moment that would require him to make a fateful choice between accommodating Western demands and more directly entering the conflict and perhaps even using force against Western interests outside Ukraine. And if that moment arrives, we may well not welcome his choice."

40 Ibid. "Putin drew a bright red line precluding the defeat of separatists in an interview with Germany's ARD television channel on November 17, 2014. Speaking rhetorically, he asked whether NATO wanted 'the Ukrainian central authorities to annihilate everyone among their political foes and opponents' in eastern Ukraine. If so, Putin declared categorically: 'We won't let it happen.' In every instance when the Ukrainian military seemed close to gaining the upper hand in the fighting, and despite U.S. and European warnings and sanctions, Putin has raised the ante to assure the separatists' success on the battlefield."

41 Ibid. "Though Russia's president has said less about Ukrainian accession to NATO, there can be no doubt that Ukraine's potential NATO membership is a preeminent Russian concern. One important reason for Moscow's willingness to let Donetsk and Luhansk go back under central Ukrainian control with a considerable degree

of autonomy is the Kremlin's desire for their pro-Russian populations to vote in Ukrainian elections and for their autonomous local governments to serve as a brake on Ukraine's road to NATO. Russia's political mainstream overwhelmingly supports preventing the emergence of a hostile Ukraine under NATO security umbrella less than four hundred miles from Moscow."

42 Ibid. "To recognize the potentially catastrophic consequences of war with Russia does not require paralysis in addressing the challenge of a resurgent but wounded Russia. The United States has a vital interest in maintaining its credibility as a super-power and in assuring the survival and security of its NATO alliance – and thus of every one of its NATO allies. Moreover, in international politics, appetites can grow quickly if fed by easy victories. The Russian president's currently limited objectives in Ukraine could become more expansive if Russia does not face serious resistance. After all, the smooth annexation of Crimea led to an outburst of triumphalist rheto-ric in Moscow about creating a new entity, Novorossiya, which would include east-ern and southern Ukraine all the way to the Romanian border. The combination of resistance by local populations, the Ukrainian government's willingness to fight for its territory, and U.S. and EU sanctions quickly persuaded the Russian leader-ship to curtail this line of thinking. When a nation is prepared to fight for impor-tant interests, clarity about that determination is a virtue in discouraging potential aggression."

43 Tim Marcin, "Despite Russian Aggression, US Apache Helicopters to Be Removed From Germany," *IBTimes*, April 20, 2015. http://www.ibtimes.com/despite-russian-aggression-us-apache-helicopters-be-removed-germany-1888549. "The move is a cost-saving transfer and comes as the United States has promised to back its allies amid increased aggression from Russia. The removal of 12 Apache helicopters is considered a significant reduction in the U.S. military presence in Europe."

15

Eternal Russia

The West resists hedging its presumption that this time will be the same. It continues pressing color revolutions, regime change, and a Western world order with two hands tied behind its back (straitjacketed economy and declining defense spending), ignoring enduring historical lessons for powerful political reasons. Politicians believe there is electoral advantage in prioritizing the financial community and social welfare entitlements over national security. They are prepared to accept the attendant security and economic risks, confident that they will find ways of muddling through, and hoping that the Kremlin will succumb to its internal contradictions. Their "motivated" belief that Russia is susceptible to color revolutions and regime change may be justified, but they are misjudging the Kremlin's tenacity, adaptability, economic robustness, military-industrial capabilities, and force projection potential, as well as the stultifying economic consequences of the West's misgovernment.

Russia's history is a testament to Muscovite tenacity. The notion that the West's duty to prevail assures that Cold War II will inevitably end the same way as Cold War I, with renewed partnership and Russia's transition to contemporary liberal democratic free enterprise, may seem plausible judged from the Gorbachev-Yeltsin interlude, but not from a half-millennial perspective. Russia has always been an autocracy and never had a true democratic government before or after Ivan the Great. Russia has had a great power imperial Muscovite culture for more than five centuries. It was exposed to Western ideals from the beginning of Muscovy. Italian architects influenced the design of Ivan the Terrible's Saint Basil cathedral, and the throne fancied itself the Third Rome.[1] Peter the Great promoted Western modernization and suppressed the "Old Believers" (*starovyery*).[2] Catherine the Great chirped about the Enlightenment and even toyed with the idea of establishing a constitutional autocracy.[3] Alexander II abolished serfdom in 1861, and

Lenin put the Soviet Union at the vanguard of Western-inspired communism. If he had prevailed, the "proletarian revolution" would have installed a "Western" world order that bore little resemblance to the global rule of law contemporary advocates have in mind. More recently, Gorbachev and Yeltsin spoke glowingly about democracy, competitive market economy, and new thinking without repudiating rent-granting and authoritarian rule, and of course Putin has reverted to the Kremlin's imperial future. In short, Russia has talked about Westernizing for more than 300 years (starting with Peter the Great), but always has chosen to modernize rather than Westernize, while retaining its Muscovite imperial mentality. The Kremlin suffers setbacks from time to time, but has never surrendered.

Western politicians who believe that this time will be the same in the sense that Russia eventually capitulates, partnering once again with America and the European Union and allowing itself to be submerged in the West's rule-of-law world order are probably whistling past the graveyard. Judged nearsightedly from the perspective of the past quarter century, one can understand why Western policy makers incline toward strategic patience, but not so in the long view, especially when Putin has grounds to believe that Washington and Berlin connived at destroying the Soviet Union and continue their double-gaming against Russia.[4]

Russia's history is a testament to Muscovite adaptability. Muscovite culture has survived, not because it is intransigent, but because it grudgingly accommodates to necessity. Kremlin rulers and their servitors adorn their palaces and minds with Western fashions and ideas, while protecting the Muscovite core. Enlightenment, socialist, and liberal democratic concepts empower Russians to glimpse the promised land; however, from the Muscovite point of view, Western ideas are only good starts. Western democracy is an inspired beginning, but proletarian and Surkovian democracy are better. Markets are good, but need strong state guidance and rent-granting support. Private ownership is desirable, but state ownership is more appropriate for the military-industrial complex and commanding heights. The rule of law is good, but the rule of Kremlin men is sublime. Russians have heard all the West's good news, but as public opinion polls confirm, this hasn't required the Kremlin to forego independent great power.

Russia's history is a testament to the Kremlin's ability to make its flawed economy suffice. Alexander Gerschenkron demonstrated that Russia's economy has always been economically backward vis-à-vis the developed West, recovering lost ground in spurts.[5] Ivan the Great imposed serf-slavery on Russia's peasantry when serfdom was crumbling in the West. Moscow relied on serf industrial labor when free labor fueled the industrial revolution. Tsars continued to shackle labor to the land after peasants were emancipated in 1861, at a time when labor mobility became a key driver of American and European economic growth. Nicholas II encouraged foreign direct investment in the heavy and natural resources extraction industries, and consumer goods markets turbocharged the economy in the 1890s. This was another late start. Lenin criminalized private ownership, markets, and entrepreneurship when the West embraced free enterprise, yet at the end of the day Abram Bergson, Simon Kuznets, and Angus Maddison showed that despite self-inflicted wounds, the Soviet Union found a way to narrow its per capita GDP gap with America in the period 1913–1991.[6] These estimates do not take adequate account of hidden inflation; nonetheless, the record shows that Russia's economic performance was often good enough to support Kremlin great power. Western intellectuals once knew this, but seem to have forgotten.

Russia's history is a testament to Russia's military-industrial prowess and force projection capabilities. The Kremlin steadily expanded its empire south, west, and east in the sixteenth, seventeenth, eighteenth, nineteenth, and twentieth centuries until 1991, when it shed nearly 30 percent of its accumulated territorial acquisitions. Peter the Great created a formidable military-industrial complex and defeated the Swedes at Narva. Napoleon sacked Moscow, only to have the favor returned in Paris.[7] Russia's defeat of Hitler and Stalin's occupation of Eastern and Central Europe hardly require retelling, and the Kremlin's tactical and strategic nuclear arsenals are at least as large as America's. From a long-run perspective, it is unreasonable to expect Russia to fade quietly into the night, especially when the *siloviki* feel that Gorbachev and his liberal court stabbed the USSR in the back, and Yeltsin stabbed Russia in the chest.

The West's history is a testament to 800 years of financial folly and periods of prolonged depression or secular stagnation, and periodic myopia about authoritarian threats.[8] The postwar macroeconomic mantra has been "never again" because Keynes has pointed the way toward perpetual state-managed prosperity. The state indeed possesses powerful fiscal, monetary, and financial instruments, fostering excess aggregate effective demand, however, this neither forestalled the 2008 global financial crisis nor prevented the secular stagnation that appears to have emerged thereafter.[9] Likewise, while the West won Cold War I with strategic patience, the same strategy backfired in the 1930s. Long-run economic and military perspectives apparently call for greater caution than Western leaders infer by too narrowly focusing on the Soviet Union's ignominious demise.

Gravitating toward Muscovy

Russia will never transition to democratic free enterprise or EU social democracy, if Putin has his druthers.[10] The Kremlin isn't rushing westward as Francis Fukuyama and Jack Matlock once supposed.[11] It is gravitating back to its autocratic roots in Ivan the Great's Muscovy, a trend partly obscured by the regime's carefully crafted Westernizing façade.[12] Putin's neo-Muscovite authoritarian ideal is a post-Communist market-assisted, patrimonial rent-granting, and planning regime designed to mobilize resources in the empire's service.[13] It is dominated by the power services (MD, FSB, MVD),[14] structurally militarized,[15] and grounded in Russian cultural traditions (including Orthodox Christianity). It resembles Peter the Great's, Catherine the Great's, Nicholas II's, and Nikita Khrushchev's modernizing autocracies, softened around the edges by incorporating liberal, democratic, and humane elements that promote competition, efficiency, and innovation, but not enough to classify Russia as a "normal" democratic middle-income country.[16]

Figure 15.1 clarifies the relationship between Putin's economic system and the Soviet model circa 1985 when Mikhail Gorbachev became general secretary of the Communist Party. Gregory Grossman dubbed the Soviet system a "command economy" because the State Economic Directorate governed by issuing orders to subordinate entities down a chain of command connecting ministries, and departments with firms, enterprises, and establishments.[17] These directives were approved by the Presidium of the Communist Party based on the State Planning Bureau's (Gosplan's) detailed suggestions (top-down planning), and enterprise *tekhpromfinplans* (bottom-up planning),[18] and had the force of law.[19] Red directors were supposed to obey these directives (targets), which is why the Soviets claimed Gorbachev's system was scientifically planned, administered, and controlled. This characterization, however, was misleading. Red directors were also co-governed by pragmatic administrative intervention, complex bonus incentive schemes linked to output, profits, product quality, and innovation,[20] and the de facto rationing of primary and intermediary inputs, subject to stringent State Bank (Gosbank)-enforced financial controls (Red directors operated in a cashless system).[21] The Soviets were compelled to employ these co-governing mechanisms because it was impossible to nano-plan 27 million products and corresponding primary and intermediate input supplies.

The command model in retrospect is best characterized as a plan-constrained (in the linear programming sense),[22] administratively coordinated, incentive- and rationing-driven system with stringent financial controls, given state wage

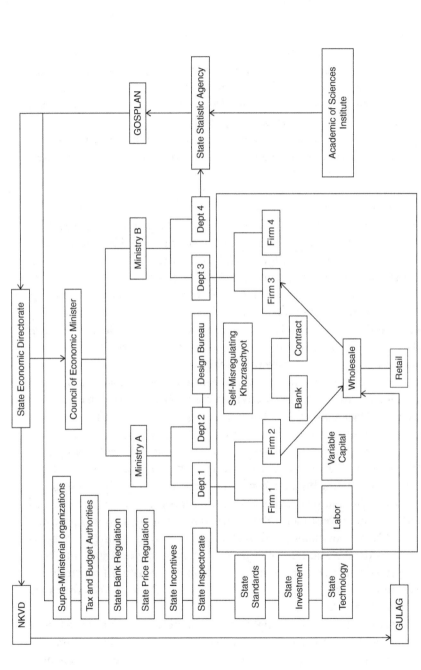

Figure 15.1 Putin's modified version of the Soviet plan-constrained, administratively coordinated, incentive- and rationing-driven system with stringent financial controls.

and price fixing, the criminalization of private property, markets, and entrepreneurship. It was a pragmatic device assuring overfull enterprise capacity
utilization,[23] overfull employment, price stability,[24] structural militarization, a
social safety net at the expense of profound microeconomic disequilibrium
that severely degraded economic freedom, efficiency, productivity, product
quality, economic growth,[25] and consumer welfare.[26] These deficiencies were
intrinsic to the plan-constrained, administratively coordinated, incentive- and
rationing-driven system, given state wage and price fixing, the criminalization
of private property, markets, and entrepreneurship, and were compounded
by unscrupulousness, power-seeking, anti-competitiveness, and willfulness
throughout the economic hierarchy.[27]

Putin's new economic model circa 2010 retains many of these features
in the military-industrial complex and many of Russia's nonmilitary state-
owned enterprises. This is illustrated by the central panel in Figure 15.1 for
firms 1 and 2. The core, however, has been supplemented by rent-granting
(oligarchy and kleptocracy) for firms 3 and 4 (energy and media sectors).
Oligarchs who emerged under Boris Yeltsin's reign and de facto operate
with insecure private property rights aren't required either to optimize or
satisfice in Herbert Simon's sense. Like their tsarist predecessors, they only
have to fulfill basic tasks and obsequiously display their loyalty to the *vozhd*.
If they displease the Kremlin, their rent-grants will be revoked and their
private property confiscated by means fair and foul.

Figure 15.1 also contains a third mechanism – the workably competitive
market for small and medium-sized enterprises, subject to Kremlin regulation.
It is depicted by links on the far left connecting the old Soviet regulatory bodies with private competitive firms (firms 5 and 6 not shown to avoid clutter).
This market was introduced by Yeltsin (*perekhod*), but Putin has improved it.[28]

The new architecture surpasses Gorbachev's scheme circa 1985 from
Moscow's viewpoint because it preserves the virtues of VPK command,
provides traditional servitor loyalty in the energy and media sectors, and
greatly enhances consumer utility, entrepreneurship, and growth potential
in the VPK and nonpublic goods sector. This improved mousetrap remains
inferior to democratic free enterprise,[29] but permits the Kremlin to continue prioritizing the military-industrial complex at reduced cost in terms
of consumer utility, growth, and civic repression. These characteristics are
baked into the system, not artifacts of fickle policy.

Tomorrow's Russia accordingly will be a more economically effective
autocracy with a Surkovian "sovereign democratic" façade (akin to communist "people's republics").[30] Vladimir Gel'man aptly describes the same phenomenon as "electoral authoritarianism."[31] The *vozhd* (leader/ruler), not the

people, will be sovereign. He (not she) will be above the law as expediency dictates.[32] He will be able to rule over Russia and its empire regardless of his formal title (president, prime minister, etc.),[33] and arbitrarily confiscate private property.[34] Putin's utopia will preserve state ownership and control over the nation's "commanding heights" – the military-industrial complex (VPK)[35] and the natural resources sector. They will be jointly governed by direct command-planning, managerial incentives, rent-granting, and workably competitive market outsourcing.[36] The Kremlin will employ fiscal, monetary, interest, and exchange rate policy, bank leveraging, mandates and edicts to macro-economically regulate the system, and it will harness private rent-granting, monopoly, oligopoly, and freehold property based on small-scale market competition in producer and consumer industries outside the direct control of the "commanding heights." This will prevent Russia from degenerating into an impoverished superpower.[37] The economy's core will be a flourishing military-industrial complex that will provide stable employment and modest GDP growth, just as it did during the Soviet era (1950–1978).[38] The regime will operate with a nonhereditary tsar under the rule of men, not a rule of law, even though Russia's executive, legislature, and judiciary will issue administrative edicts, promulgate laws, and render verdicts. Civil society will be increasingly repressed, but more open than it was under Gorbachev. Russians will enjoy greater personal liberty than communism allowed, including the rights to freely travel and engage in domestic and foreign for-profit business. Moscow's highways will be congested, contemporary skyscrapers and restaurants will abound, living standards will gradually improve, and the East-West per capita income gap will narrow as long as America and the European Union's economies are hobbled by secular stagnation.

Russia isn't going back to pauper communism, and won't reconstitute the USSR. Neither the Kremlin nor the American White House is interested in the proletariat. Moscow is creating an assertive but less strident empire on Russia's historical domain ruled by *siloviki* capable of advancing the Muscovite agenda (autocracy, rent-granting, and empire) in the long run.[39] Bolshevism was defeated, but the Kremlin remains ready, willing, and able to continue the civilizational battle with its western, southern, and eastern neighbors.[40]

Playing into the Power Services' Hands

Neither Washington nor Brussels desired the restoration of the power services, but they played directly into their hands. They pressed "shock therapy" (in today's parlance "hyper-austerity") that immiserated the Russian people and caused 3.4 million excess deaths.[41] They promised a "Grand

Bargain" (aid for transition),[42] but provided a pittance,[43] and tried to strip the Kremlin completely of its historical spheres of influence in the name of "globalization," while the West contradictorily applauded China's market communist strategy of public spending–driven economic growth. These results, regardless of motive, have discredited the West in the power services and the Russian public's eyes, despite Washington and the European Union's declared benign intentions.

The West denies that shock therapy was a failure. It sees no contradiction in having supported communist Chinese public spending–driven growth, while pressing austerity on Russia. It claims to have fulfilled its "Grand Bargain" obligations and insists that globalization takes priority over the Kremlin's notion of Russia's national interest.

Russia's power services and the majority of the Russian people understandably are unpersuaded. They take a less charitable view of the West's motivation and suspect foul play. They believe Gorbachev stabbed the Soviet Union in the back, and Yeltsin and the West stabbed Russia in the chest. Their view has traction, allowing the *siloviki* to discredit Russia's liberals and to set the Kremlin's political agenda for the foreseeable future.[44]

Compellence

This joust isn't novel. The Romanovs often skirmished with Europe for territory and influence. Nonetheless, it is worth noting that the Kremlin's shift away from "partnership" to confrontation is a striking departure from the Gorbachev-Yeltsin era. It can be dated symbolically to the 9/11 oil price shock that filled Russia's coffers, and coincided with Putin's initiatives restoring the power vertical and the nation's military might. Analysts detected the policy reversal immediately, but Western leaders brushed the transformation aside. George Bush looked into Putin's eyes, saw his soul, and knew that it was good.[45]

The Obama administration tried to nip the Kremlin's new assertiveness in the bud with its "reset" policy,[46] but failed, as the Kremlin's annexation of Crimea makes plain. Putin couldn't be gulled into accepting Western-orchestrated color revolutions as an acceptable foundation for Russian-American partnership.

Freeze, Rollback, Advance

The West didn't have to concern itself with the threat of Russian aggression during the 1990s. Yeltsin and his supporters wanted to move along the paths of transition and global integration. They voluntarily dissolved the Soviet Union and relinquished spheres of influence over Central and Eastern Europe and the Balkans. All the West needed to do was pretend that partnership was in the Kremlin's best interest.

Putin and the *siloviki* have rendered this strategy obsolete when judged from a five-century perspective, even though it appears validated by Cold War I. Once stung, twice shy. The Kremlin won't be snared again soon by the siren song of partnership. This is why the post–World War II outcome is apt to be a misleading guide to the immediate future, and the full historical record is more portentous.

The half-millennium experience suggests that America and the European Union won't be able to limit Russia's sphere of influence gains to Crimea; roll the clock back to March 17, 2014; or expect the Kremlin to passively accept the West's push for global transition on Moscow's turf in the new post-partnership age. Sweet talk won't sway Putin.

The West can prevail, but must rouse itself to steadfastly deal with the present danger. It cannot afford to build down its military forces, miss structure its warfighting capabilities, tolerate secular stagnation to indulge special insider interests, or presume that Russia is destined to be no more than a noisome regional power.[47]

Peace through Strength

A peace-through-strength approach, moreover, has an important hidden advantage. Instead of seeking to win by minimally accommodating the present danger, the West can nip Putin's challenge in the bud by making further aggression too risky and restoring America and Europe's liberal democratic ideals.

The West cannot achieve peace through strength today in Europe because it isn't strong enough. It has nuclear weapons, but cannot credibly use them. It could physically mobilize sufficient conventional forces to wage protracted war against Russia in Novorossiya and Crimea, but Germany, France, Italy, and the United Kingdom cannot forge the necessary political consensus.[48] It could wage all-out economic war against Moscow, but the Europeans can barely maintain the token sanctions already in place, and the discreetly veiled conflict between the European Union and "new Atlanticism" further degrades the possibilities of joint resolve.[49]

This means the West can achieve peace through strength in the age of Russian compellence only by mustering its will and by resolving to fundamentally change politics as usual instead of hewing the path of adaptive opportunism.[50] It must identify a set of domestic military, economic, and political measures sufficient to make Putin blink. The West's wealth and population advantages make peace through strength feasible, but this doesn't mean that it is likely to succeed because America and the European Union are reluctant to procure the right mix of military forces and maintain them at the requisite levels.[51] The European Union is still cutting its meager defense expenditures, not increasing them, and its expedient politics and economic policies are wishful thinking.[52] The West won't enhance budgetary, financial, and monetary discipline or improve competitive economic efficiency and long-term growth, even though it clearly knows better. It requires less-developed nations to follow the sound advice laid out in the "Washington Consensus," but as its author, John Williamson, wryly observes, it seldom practices what it preaches.[53]

The West won't engage in high-intensity economic warfare or radically modify its political culture, and therefore it cannot exert the requisite international leadership.[54] It can't even consistently ostracize Putin.[55]

These rigidities are serious handicaps in dealing effectively with a shrewd adversary like Putin because the Kremlin knows that the West is playing with only half a deck. America and the European Union should be able to negotiate and counter-compel on favorable terms, but only if they cease engaging the Kremlin with both hands tied behind their backs.[56]

Déjà vu All Over Again

The West's unwillingness to counter-compel Putin's quest to expand Russia's sphere of influence is "déjà vu all over again."[57] America, England, and France could have easily counter-compelled Hitler, Mussolini, and Hirohito had they embraced a peace-through-strength strategy in the mid-1930s. The potential is proved by America's "miraculous" war time economic recovery and rearmament after Japan attacked Pearl Harbor. Historians can endlessly debate whether America, England, and France should have discarded politics as usual to forestall the fascist threat, but they cannot deny that peace through strength could have been achieved if they had tried hard enough.

America, England, and France instead were content to rely on business as usual, treaties, negotiations, moral condemnations, platitudes, and miracles. They could have been saved from their own folly by Germany's, Italy's, and Japan's economic collapse, liberal palace coups, democratic revolutions,[58] or Westernization,[59] but weren't. The West today likewise is missing the forest for the trees. It refuses to acknowledge that Putin's tactics can be countervailed by taking unpalatable military, economic, and political decisions, and therefore cannot resolve the Kremlin's challenge with minimal losses and accommodation.[60]

Notes

1 Dmitri Shvidkovsky, *Russian Architecture and the West*, New Haven, CT: Yale University Press, 2007.
2 Old Believers had to pay double taxes and a separate tax for wearing a beard.
3 Geoffrey Hosking, *Russia: People and Empire*, Cambridge MA: Harvard University Press, 1997.
4 The notion that the West has acted in bad faith is vehemently denied by Anders Fogh Rasmussen, former prime minister of Denmark and secretary general of NATO. Anders Fogh Rasmussen, "The Kremlin's Tragic Miscalculation," *Project Syndicate*, November 3, 2015. "Russia's aggression against Ukraine is one of the great tragedies of our time, not only because of the tremendous human cost, but also because it is utterly pointless. Indeed, Russia's leaders fundamentally misjudged the West's intentions and created an entirely unnecessary confrontation that undermines both sides' interests. Russia and the West – with their closely interlinked economies and many overlapping political objectives in Europe and beyond – have much to gain from peaceful cooperation. But instead of working with Western powers to enhance shared prosperity, the Kremlin turned on its partners abroad. The reason was simple: Russia viewed the gradual enlargement of the European Union and NATO – achieved through their 'neighborhood' and 'open door' policies, respectively – as carefully orchestrated attempts to encircle and threaten it. According to Kremlin rhetoric, by welcoming former Soviet countries, the EU and NATO were explicitly attempting to weaken Russia. This interpretation ultimately drove Russia to respond to Ukraine's plans to sign an association agreement with the EU by annexing Crimea and attempting to create a 'frozen conflict' in eastern Ukraine. But Russia's interpretation was patently wrong – and I can say so with full authority. As Prime Minister of Denmark, I chaired the 2002 EU summit in Copenhagen, where European leaders agreed on the bloc's most expansive enlargement ever. And as Secretary General of NATO, I spent five years chairing the NATO-Russia Council to build cooperation with our largest neighbor." https://www.project-syndicate.org/commentary/russia-benefited-from-nato-enlargement-by-anders-fogh-rasmussen-2015-11#wqU9RtI3YmBmLHLw.99.
5 Alexander Gerschenkron, *Economic Backwardness in Historical Perspective*, Cambridge MA: Harvard University Press, 1963.
6 Abram Bergson and Simon Kuznets, co-editors, *Economic Trends in the Soviet Union*, Cambridge, MA: Harvard University Press, 1963.
7 Dominic Lieven, *Russia Against Napoleon: The True Story of the Campaigns of War and Peace*, London: Allen, 2010. The central point Lieven makes is that Russia owed its victory, not to the courage of its national spirit or to the coldness of the 1812 winter, as some French sources have argued, but to its military excellence, superior cavalry, the high standards of Russia's diplomatic and intelligence services, and the quality of its European elite. Thanks to the intelligence he obtained, Alexander was able to outwit Napoleon, anticipating his invasion.

8 Kenneth Rogoff and Carmen Reinhart, *This Time Is Different: Eight Centuries of Financial Folly*, Cambridge MA: Harvard University Press, 2012.

9 Adair Turner, *Between Debt and the Devil: Money, Credit, and Fixing Global Finance*, Princeton NJ: Princeton University Press, 2015. Steven Rosefielde, Masaaki Kuboniwa, and Satoshi Mizobata, eds., *Prevention and Crisis Management: Lessons for Asia from the 2008 Crisis*, Singapore: World Scientific 2012.

10 Andrei Tsygankov, "A Strong State: Theory and Practice in the 21st Century," Valdai Paper #15, May 15, 2015. http://valdaiclub.com/publication/77420.html. "The experience and goals of the Russian state The Russian state historically differs from all types mentioned above. The Orthodox Russian state sought to maintain a fair distribution of the social product and to protect subjects from the arbitrariness of landlords, governors and other officials. The Russian understanding of justice is focused on the economy and is based on the notion of communal fairness that took root after the baptism of Rus. When Russian rulers failed to ensure this fairness, people often fled to outlying regions or rose up against them. Russia also has a unique place in the world. Since Peter the Great, Russia has been known as a great power, even if it was not a central but a semi-peripheral state in the global economic system. Considering numerous external threats, Russian rulers never questioned the importance of maintaining its status as a great power and easily sacrificed their obligations to the people to maintain this status. Paradoxically, Russians consolidated around the state to defend their freedom from foreign incursions, even if this affected the internal components of freedom. Military might, imperial power and the ability to stand up against foreign incursions gradually turned from the elements necessary to protect national freedom into the end goals of state policy. The economically semi-peripheral Russian state increased taxes, invented new administrative methods of exploitation, and used poverty and serfdom to build up its army. The authorities disregarded the need for reforms, sometimes seeing them as a threat to the system of autocratic rule. As Georgy Vernadsky wrote, 'Autocracy and serfdom were the price the Russian people had to pay for national survival.' This heritage is preventing Russia from taking the European path. Other obstacles include the national political culture, the need to have a combat ready army and the need to mobilize public resources for accelerated economic growth. Therefore, the development of an effective state mechanism in Russia depends on improving the ability of the ruling class to deal with development and security tasks without becoming hostage to the interests of elite groups and without losing the connection to society. The modern Russian developmental state must be strong in order to reduce the distance from the leading global economies, fittingly respond to security threats and improve the people's standards of living, especially in the relatively remote and critically important regions of Siberia, the Far East, the Caucasus and Crimea. The attempts to create a decentralized and liberal Western-type system of government would only further consolidate Russia's economic lag and its oligarchic structure based on heavy reliance on raw materials. A weak Russian state would be unable to create internationally competitive industry. According to Immanuel Wallerstein (American sociologist), 'In those states in which the state machinery is weak, the state managers do not play the role of coordinating a complex industrial-commercial-agricultural mechanism. Rather they simply become one set of landlords amidst others, with little claim to legitimate authority over the whole.' On the

other hand, Russia certainly cannot revive the old types of strong power, such as autocracy or the system of Soviet government. Instead of trying to control business, the current Russian authorities should adopt clear rules for businesses and provide additional incentives for private initiative and foreign investment. The large-scale modernization reforms, which Prime Minister Pyotr Stolypin proposed over a century ago to integrate Russia into the global economy, are what Russia still needs. Russia's economic policy of the past 15 years has exhausted its potential. Vladimir Putin's Russia depends on energy exports, is operating predominantly based on the interests of influential political and economic groups and has not created mechanisms for sustainable social development. Its political class is not suited to the requirements of the state and its economic development. It did not use the relative prosperity of the 2000s to address fundamental economic and political issues. Russia's economic competitiveness is relatively low. Rampant corruption and the technological lag of Russian business compared to the West restrict the growth of budget revenue and hinder the strengthening of the state. The ineffectiveness of the current state machinery was laid bare by the ruble's devaluation in November and December 2014. The Western sanctions present not only risks, but also opportunities, in that they can encourage the development and diversification of foreign economic ties in Asia. The Ukrainian crisis increased the basis of internal support for the state and created conditions for a new consolidation of power. However, the authorities still cannot make a choice between continued maneuvering and building a developmental state. The opportunity will be wasted without a strong planning role on the part of the state, which must encourage private initiative, propose new large-scale projects and mobilize resources for their implementation. It must adopt a package of measures, including a resolute battle against corruption, create a legal framework for internal competition and support the most promising economic sectors to help their integration into the global economy. A strong state is necessary in order to improve the quality of Russia's elite and its political system. To improve the quality of the elite, it must not only offer material incentives, but also formulate political values that will help maintain a strong state. In addition to the opportunity to train abroad, Russia must also create a network of national universities for training patriotic national elites. Another key priority is a transition from hands-on management to a system of national 'primaries,' or the initial selection of members of the elite that would be acceptable to the main groups of the political class. This system has not yet been formalized, which is hindering the development of the institutional basis of Russia's political system. Considering the importance of maintaining the continuity of strong power in Russia, a leader whose nomination is coordinated with the main groups of the political elite and who is subsequently elected by a national vote will most likely remain in power for a relatively long time. And lastly, the Russian state is sufficiently mature for a transition from the system of managed democracy to competitive elections to regional and central bodies of legislative power. To prevent destabilization, a strong state must integrate more elements of both elite-aristocratic and democratic rule."

11 Jack Matlock, *Autopsy on an Empire: The American Ambassador's Account of the Collapse of the Soviet Union*, New York: Random House, 1995; Francis Fukuyama, *The End of History and the Last Man*, New York: Free Press, 1992; Francis Fukuyama, *Political Order and Political Decay: From the Industrial Revolution to the*

Globalization of Democracy, New York: Farrar, Straus and Giroux, 2014. Cf. Thomas Friedman, *The World Is Flat*, New York, Farrar, Straus and Giroux. 2007.

12 Steven Rosefielde, "'Back to the Future?' Prospects for Russia's Military Industrial Revival," *ORBIS*, Vol. 46, No. 3, Summer (2002): 499–510.

13 Mark Harrison, "Resource Mobilization for World War II: The U.S.A., U.K., U.S.S.R., and Germany, 1938–1945," *Economic History Review*, Vol. 41, No. 2 (1988): 171–192. Russia's imperial economy didn't always mobilize national resources. It fluctuated between periods of energetic modernization (Ivan the Great, Peter the Great, and Catherine the Great), and long interludes of indolence. See Alexander Gerschenkron, "Russia: Patterns and Problems of Economic Development, 1868-1958," in Gerschenkron, *Economic Backwardness in Historical Perspective* , 5–30.

14 Министерство обороны Российской Федерации (Ministry of Defence of the Russian Federation), Федеральная служба безопасности Российской Федерации (Federal Security Service of the Russian Federation), Министерство внутренних дел (Ministry of the Interior of the Russian Federation).

15 Vitaly Shlykov, *Kto Pogubilo Sovetskii Soiuz? Amerikanskaia Razvedka o Sovetskikh Voennykh Raskhodakh* (*Who Destroyed the Soviet Union? American Intelligence Estimates of Soviet Military Expenditures*), Voennyi Vestnik, No. 9, Moscow, September 2008. *Structural militarization* is a term Vitaly Shlykov coined to describe a productive system with a large embedded military-industrial sector capable of persuading government leaders to provide sufficient resources to deal with worst-case security threats.

16 Andrei Shliefer and Daniel Treisman, "Russia: A Normal Country," *Foreign Affairs*, March/April 2004. Cf. Steven Rosefielde, "Russia: An Abnormal Country," *European Journal of Comparative Economics*, Vol. 2, No. 1 (2005): 3–16.

17 Gregory Grossman, "Notes for a Theory of the Command Economy," *Soviet Studies*, Vol. 15, No. 2 (1963): 101–123; Richard E Ericson, "Command versus 'Shadow': The Conflicted Soul of the Soviet Economy," *Comparative Economic Studies*, Vol. 48 (2006): 50–76.

18 Technical, industrial, and financial plans.

19 Abram Bergson, *The Economics of Soviet Planning*, New Haven, CT: Yale University Press, 1964.

20 Joseph Berliner, *The Innovation Decision in Soviet Industry*, Cambridge, MA: MIT Press, 1976, 400–427.

21 George Garvy, *Money, Financial Flows, and Credit in the Soviet Union*, New York: NBER, 1977. http://www.nber.org/books/garv77-1.

22 Steven Rosefielde, *Russian Economy from Lenin to Putin*, New York: Wiley, 2007.

23 The state agreed to purchase everything enterprises produced (assured purchase), and prices were fixed to guarantee that firms made profits (and managers bonuses tied to them), even when output exceeded Pareto optimal levels.

24 Prices were fixed on average by the State Price Committee for ten years.

25 The system impaired optimal technology choice and criminalized entrepreneurship.

26 Bergson, *The Economics of Soviet Planning*. The Soviet system criminalized private property and markets. The diverse disequilibria generated by the plan-constrained, administratively coordinated, incentive- and rationing-driven system with stringent financial controls therefore weren't resolved by planning and couldn't be eliminated by the "invisible hand."

27 Steven Rosefielde and Ralph W. Pfouts, *Inclusive Economic Theory*, Singapore: World Scientific Publishers, 2014.

28 Andrei Yakovlev, "Russian Modernization: Between the Need for New Players and the Fear of Losing Control of Rent Sources," *Journal of Eurasia Studies*, Vol. 5, No. 1 (2014): 10–20.

29 Charles Sanders Peirce, *Pragmatism as a Principle and Method of Right Thinking*, ("Lectures on Pragmatism 1903), Stoneybrook: State University of New York Press, 1997; World Bank, *Doing Business 2015: Going Beyond Efficiency*, 2015. https://openknowledge.worldbank.org/bitstream/handle/10986/20483/DB15-Full-Report.pdf?sequence=1 Cf. Andrei Yakovlev, Anton Sobolev, and Anton Kazun, "Means of Production versus Means of Coercion: Can Russian Business Limit the Violence of a Predatory State?" *Post-Soviet Affairs*, 2013.

30 Masha Lipman, "Putin's "Sovereign Democracy," *Washington Post*, July 15, 2006. http://carnegieendowment.org/2006/07/15/putin-s-sovereign-democracy/ujs. "On the public relations side, one of the most influential Kremlin aides, Vladislav Surkov, met with Western journalists to explain that Russian 'sovereign democracy' is not much different from democratic practices of the Western countries. 'Sovereign democracy' is a Kremlin coinage that conveys two messages: first, Russia's regime is democratic and, second, this claim must be accepted, period. Any attempt at verification will be regarded as unfriendly and as meddling in Russia's domestic affairs." Lenin and Stalin claimed that Soviet democracy was a million times more democratic than Western parliamentary democracy because the Communist Party faithfully abided by the people's will.

31 Vladimir Gel'man, *Authoritarian Russia: Analyzing Post-Soviet Regime Changes*, Pittsburg: University of Pittsburg Press, 2015.

32 Appointment of Medvedev as president and as prime minister.

33 Russian presidents are constitutionally limited to two consecutive terms in office. Putin sidestepped the prohibition in 2007 by nimbly assigning Dmitry Medvedev as his presidential successor, appointing himself prime minister and ruling with the new title in his old capacity as *vozhd*.

34 Richard Sakwa, *Putin and the Oligarchs: The Khodorkovsky-Yukos Affair*, London: IB Tauris, 2014. "Russian Court Orders Seizure of Oligarch's Oil Stake," Yahoo!, October 30, 2014. https://www.yahoo.com/music/s/russian-court-orders-seizure-oligarchs-oil-stake-131057014.html. "A judge at Moscow's Arbitration Court ordered the return to the state of the stake held by billionaire Vladimir Yevtushenkov's holding firm Sistema in oil company Bashneft." Irina Reznik, "Putin's Next Takeover Target Is Oil Giant's $34 Billion Cash Pile," Bloomberg, May 11, 2015. http://finance.yahoo.com/news/putins-next-takeover-target-34-210000475.html. "A decade ago, Vladimir Putin's allies had Mikhail Khodorkovsky jailed and seized his Yukos Oil Co. Last year, they forced billionaire Vladimir Evtushenkov to hand over OAO Bashneft. Now they're coveting the biggest corporate treasure of all: OAO Surgutneftegas. The Siberian crude producer run for three decades by Soviet-trained Vladimir Bogdanov has amassed about $34 billion of cash, Bloomberg calculations based on company data released April 30 show. With sanctions over Ukraine having severed Russia from the global financial system, Putin is considering releasing some of Surgut's hoard, one he'd previously called untouchable, say three bankers close to the Kremlin who asked not to be identified because of the sensitivity of the

topic." "Russia Seizes Oligarch Assets in Crimea," *Euromaidan Press*, April 4, 2014. http://euromaidanpress.com/2014/04/12/russia-seizes-oligarch-assets-in-crimea/. "The Founder of 'Russia's Facebook' Explains how the Kremlin Took His Company Away," *Business Insider*, May 19, 2015. http://finance.yahoo.com/news/founder-russias-facebook-explains-kremlin-210500946.html. "The founder of Russia's most popular social network recently described to Mashable how he chose to flee his native Moscow after Kremlin loyalists wrested control of the company away from him. Pavel Durov, 30, seen by many as Russia's Mark Zuckerberg, created the website VKontakte – which had 69 million monthly users – before drawing the ire of Russian FSB agents when political protest pages began sprouting up. When Durov refused to shut down the page of activist Alexei Navalny, the FSB showed up at his door with automatic rifles, demanding to be let in."

35 Voenno-promyshlennyi kompleks (VPK). The name was changed to the Defense Industrial Complex, but in the Western literature it is often called MIC.

36 Steven Rosefielde, *The Russian Economy from Lenin to Putin*, New York: Wiley, 2007.

37 Henry S. Rowen, and Charles Wolf, Jr., *The Impoverished Superpower: Perestroika and the Soviet Military Burden*, Palo Alto, CA: ICS Press, 1990.

38 Rosefielde, *The Russian Economy from Lenin to Putin*.

39 It is unlikely that either Russia or China is intent on following in Hitler's footsteps. Michael Pillsbury paints a darker impression of Beijing's intentions. See Michael Pillsbury, *The Hundred-Year Marathon*, New York: Henry Holt and Co., 2015. Cf. Elizabeth Economy, (Review) "China's Secret Plan to Supplant the United States," *The Diplomat*, May 3, 2015. http://thediplomat.com/2015/05/chinas-secret-plan-to-supplant-the-united-states/.

40 Richard Sakwa, "A Bitter Anniversary," *Valdai*, May 8, 2015. http://valdaiclub.com/history/77300.html. "There are few more vivid manifestations of the deadlock in relations between Russia and the West than the effective boycott of attending the seventieth-anniversary victory celebrations in Moscow on 9 May." All this is witness to a breakdown in relations that is unprecedented in its depth, but also frightening in its lack of global vision." "All this attests to the dangers of the emerging new Atlanticism. Having blundered into confrontation over Ukraine, the Atlantic alliance is now trying to impose a bloc discipline on its members that is reminiscent of the worst periods of the Cold War. In some ways it is even worse, because even at the height of the Cold War Britain under Harold Wilson refused to participate in the Vietnam War, France under De Gaulle pursued its own vision of European continentalism, and West Germany established a fruitful energy relationship with Russia that endures to this day. Who can imagine these countries really standing up for an alternative vision of world order based on dialogue and recognition of difference against the US today?"

41 Steven Rosefielde, "Premature Deaths: Russia's Radical Transition," *Europe-Asia Studies*, Vol. 53, No. 8 (December 2001): 1159–1176.

42 Steven Rosefielde, "The Grand Bargain: Underwriting Catastroika," *Global Affairs*, Vol. 7, No. 1, Winter (1991): 15–35; Steven Rosefielde, "Beyond Catastroika: Prospects for Market Transition in the Commonwealth of Independent States," *Atlantic Economic Journal*, Vol. 20, No. 1 (March 1992): 1–8.

43 Steven Rosefielde, Vyacheslav Danilin, and Georgii Kleiner, "Deistvuiushaya Model' Reform i Ugroza Giperdepressii (The Russian Reform Model and the Threat of

Hyperdepression)," *Russian Economic Journal* (*Rossiiskii Ekonomicheskii Zhurnal*), No. 12 (1994): 48–55.

44 The West could have tempered its three-pronged strategy of smashing communism, pressing regime change, and pushing NATO expansion, but didn't. Had it done so, Russia's liberals might have stood a better chance of fending off the power services' onslaught, and denied Putin the ammunition he has seized to plausibly claim to Russian audiences that America and the European Union stabbed the motherland in the chest.

45 Jon Ward, "Bush Explains His Comment about Putin's Soul, Says Russian Leader 'Changed,'" *Daily Caller*, December 14, 2010. http://dailycaller.com/2010/12/14/bush-explains-his-comment-about-putins-soul-says-russian-leader-changed/.

46 The term *reset* applied to Russia refers to the Obama administration's policy of restoring the Bill Clinton-era strategy of transforming the Kremlin from an adversary to a trustworthy partner worth of munificent assistance (Grand Bargain), after the Bush administration shifted to a "containment" strategy (2002–2008) to counter increased Russian geopolitical aggressiveness. American policy makers bent over backward to accommodate the Kremlin, with nothing positive to show for it. See "Our Friends the Russians: The Kremlin Picks a Fight with America in Time for Elections." *Wall Street Journal*, Review and Outlook, December 2, 2011. "One of the foreign policy priorities of the Obama Administration was to 'reset' relations with Russia. How's that working out? Dmitry Medvedev, the placeholder for Vladimir Putin in the presidency, gave one indication last week. He declared that Russia may deploy 'strike forces' and aim mid-range Iskander missiles at Europe. He also threatened to pull out of the 2010 New Start arms accord, which is supposed to be the hallmark achievement of the 'reset.' The excuse for Mr. Medvedev's tantrum is the long-planned missile defense shield for Europe. Once deployed in 2020, it's designed to stop a limited number of missiles from Iran and doesn't diminish Russia's nuclear deterrent. The Obama administration scaled back the shield to please Russia in 2009, and with Russian agreement in return for the U.S. signing up to New Start, but now apparently that's not enough. On Tuesday Mr. Medvedev opened a new Russian early-warning radar in the Kaliningrad enclave between Poland and Lithuania and said: 'When they tell us – "It's not against you" – I would like to say the following: "Dear friends, the radar launched today isn't against you either. But it's for you and for fulfilling the tasks we have set."' Moscow's ambassador to NATO this week amplified this message by threatening to close the transport route through Russia that the U.S. and its allies use to supply troops in Afghanistan. This so-called northern corridor was another touted achievement of the 'reset.' Then there's Russia's veto of a Security Council resolution to sanction Syria and its continuing arms sales to the regime of Bashar Assad. Moscow also resists putting any new pressure on Iran's nuclear bomb makers. But the lesson for the U.S. concerns the limits of friendship with an authoritarian government that has no interest in being a strategic partner with the West." Cf. Leon Aron, "A Tormenting in Moscow," *AEI*, April 12, 2012. "Hence, we now see an anti-American propaganda the likes of which, in crudeness and shamelessness, we have not seen since 1985. Witness a 'documentary' on a state-controlled national television channel, shortly after McFaul came to Moscow, in which his writings on democracy promotion were used to bolster an accusation that, in essence, he was sent by the CIA to foment a color revolution. Thus the

calling out of Secretary of State Hillary Clinton as a 'signaler' to anti-Putin opposition. And finally, an utterly base 'Anatomy of the Protest' documentary (on the same NTV network) that showed allegedly U.S. officials distributing money and cookies (yes: evil, wanton democracy cookies) to the anti-Putin protesters. Welcome to Moscow, Mr. Ambassador..."

47 "Barack Obama: Russia Is a Regional Power Showing Weakness over Ukraine," The *Guardian*, March 25, 2014. http://www.theguardian.com/world/2014/mar/25/barack-obama-russia-regional-power-ukraine-weakness. "President Barack Obama has described Russia as no more than a 'regional power' whose actions in Ukraine are an expression of weakness rather than strength."

48 Philippe Migault, "NATO, the Wolf in Sheep's Clothing," *Valdai*, May 19, 2015. http://valdaiclub.com/europe/77540.html. "NATO is a defensive alliance established as it was in 1949. NATO will go to war, if a member of the alliance is attacked by an external power. I don't sit in the Kremlin, but to my knowledge, Russia does not intend to attack any of the NATO countries. And I'm sure that nobody in Paris, Berlin, or Rome has intention to make war with Russia." "We must at first point out that the NATO military build-up in Eastern Europe is rather limited, for a very simple reason. For example, at least 350 American soldiers take part in the maneuvers in Romania. Roughly two companies. This is far from the logic of the US forces build up. Certain statements made by several NATO member states about strengthening of their military budget should be considered as purely cosmetic. Political statements are often very firm from the diplomatic point of view, but are not followed by concrete actions from the military point of view. Their effects are sometimes anecdotal and do not constitute real threat to Russia." Philippe Migault, senior research fellow at the French Institute for International and Strategic Affairs (IRIS).

49 Richard Sakwa, "The New Atlanticism," *Valdai Papers*, No. 17, May 2015.

50 Desmond Lachman, "Eurozone Debt Crisis: A Spanish Wake-Up Call for Europe," *AEI*, May 27, 2015. http://www.aei.org/publication/eurozone-debt-crisis-a-spanish-wake-up-call-for-europe/?utm_source=paramount&utm_medium=email&utm_content=AEITODAY&utm_campaign=052715. "Last weekend's dismal local election results in Spain should be a wake-up call for Europe." "This will almost certainly raise questions in markets as to whether Spain will stay the course of economic adjustment. Making matters more serious yet is the fact that this uncertainty would be occurring at the very time that the Greek crisis is coming to a head and that Portugal is headed to general elections in October, where the anti-austerity Socialist Party is ahead in the polls. The Spanish local election result is also all too likely to have an important bearing on the already fraught Greek negotiations with the IMF and Greece's European creditors, since those creditors will not wish to give the radical Podemos Party a leg up in the forthcoming Spanish general election by being too generous to Greece and thereby allowing Podemos to campaign on the platform that it pays to stand-up to Spain's European taskmasters. With Greek Prime Minister Alexis Tsipras having little room for maneuver in making concessions to Greece's European creditors for fear of splitting his already divided Syriza Party, the last thing that Europe needed was to lose its room for maneuver for fear of the broader fallout of making any concessions to Greece ahead of the forthcoming

Spanish general elections." Dalibor Rohac "Do the Right Thing: Which Greek Politician Will Tell Greek Voters the Truth?" *AEI*, May 26, 2015. "Many Greeks agree that the real problem is political, not economic. 'No politician will ever dare to do what is needed,' a Greek friend told me. Another one, a former government official, thinks that 'the difference between the successful reformers of Eastern Europe and Greece is that in Eastern Europe, people were dissatisfied with the status quo. In Greece, everybody just wants to go back to how things were before 2010.'" http://www.aei.org/publication/do-the-right-thing-3/?utm_source=paramount&utm_medium=email&utm_content=AEITODAY&utm_campaign=052715.

51 Sakwa, "The New Atlanticism." "In the wake of the Ukraine crisis there is increased emphasis on 'burden-sharing' within the alliance. After 1991 most of the European partners cashed in the 'peace dividend' and cut defence spending, whereas the US maintained and indeed after 9/11 greatly increased the proportion of GDP devoted to defence. Currently, only three EU NATO countries spend the recommended two per cent of GDP on defence: the UK, Greece and Estonia. The Newport (Wales) summit of NATO on 4–5 September 2014 represented an attempt to kick-start NATO and was accompanied by commitments to increase defence spending. The final Declaration absolved NATO of all responsibility for the Ukraine crisis, and instead asserted that 'Russia's aggressive actions against Ukraine have fundamentally challenged our vision of a Europe whole, free and at peace' (Article 1). The summit adopted the NATO Readiness Action Plan that envisaged the rotation of forces in Central and Eastern Europe, but in keeping with the 1997 NATO-Russia partnership agreement, did not envisage the stationing of NATO forces permanently in the region. 14 Ukraine was not granted the special partnership with NATO that it sought, yet the trans-democratic language of the Declaration only intensified the processes that had provoked the crisis in the first place. The summit signalled the end of post-Cold War aspirations for a united Europe."

52 Judy Dempsey, "Judy Asks: Is the European Neighborhood Policy Doomed?" Carnegie Europe, May 20, 2015. http://carnegieeurope.eu/strategiceurope/?fa=60138&mkt_tok=3RkMMJWWfF9wsRojuKXPZKXonjHpfsX56OsvXqGg38431UFwdcjKPmjr1YYBRcJ0aPyQAgobGp5I5FEIQ7XYTLB2t60MWA%3D%3D. "Can anyone even say what the European Neighborhood Policy (ENP) is? The EU's current review of the ENP must be unsparing – the union's approach to both its Southern and its Eastern neighbors is a mess of inconsistency and wishful thinking. When the policy was last reviewed, in 2010–2011, the EU decided that the ENP needed 'a strong focus on the promotion of deep and sustainable democracy.' That included free and fair elections, freedom of expression, of assembly, and of association, judicial independence, the fight against corruption, and democratic control over the armed forces. Since then, of the sixteen countries covered by the ENP, two (Libya and Syria) have fallen into near anarchy; one (Egypt) has had a military coup; and repression of civil society and the media has worsened in several, including Azerbaijan. With a few honorable exceptions (Georgia, Israel, and Jordan), most states are profoundly corrupt, according to the corruption indices published by Transparency International, an NGO. A few ENP countries have made progress toward democracy (Tunisia and Ukraine) but remain vulnerable to internal and external challenges."

53 John Williamson, "What Washington Means by Policy Reform," in John Williamson (ed.), *Latin American Adjustment: How Much Has Happened?* Washington, DC: Peterson Institute for International Economics, Chapter 2, 1990. https://www.wcl.american.edu/hracademy/documents/Williamson1990What WashingtonMeansbyPolicyReform.pdf. "Washington's record is likewise imperfect in other areas discussed above. On the first criterion, that of controlling the fiscal deficit, the U.S. record of the 1980s is poor. It is true that the federal deficit has been falling since 1985, especially as a proportion of GNP, and that the operational deficit is now only some 1 percent of GNP, which is within the range consistent with continued solvency of the public sector. However, the fiscal deficit remains too large for macroeconomic balance, given the low private saving rate in the United States. The excessively high fiscal deficit results in the maintenance of high real interest rates and an unsustainably large current account deficit, with consequential burdens on debtors, discouragement of investment, nurturing of protectionist sentiment, and the continuing threat of a 'hard landing.'"

54 Moisés Naim, "America's Self-Inflicted Wounds," *Atlantic*, May 20, 2015. http://carnegieendowment.org/2015/05/20/america-s-self-inflicted-wounds/i8tr?mkt_tok=3RkMMJWWfF9wsRojuKXPZKXonjHpfsX56OsvXqGg38431UFwdcjKPmjr1 YYBRcJ0aPyQAgobGp5I5FEIQ7XYTLB2t60MWA%3D%3D. "Larry Summers, a former U.S. treasury secretary recently wrote, 'As long as one of our major parties is opposed to essentially all trade agreements, and the other is resistant to funding international organizations, the U.S. will not be in a position to shape the global economic system.'" Cf. Joseph Nye, *Is the American Century Over? (Global Futures)*, New York: Polity, 2015.

55 Julie Pace, "Putin Getting Left Out of G-7 Meeting, but not Much Else," *AP*, May 30, 2014. http://news.yahoo.com/putin-getting-left-g-7-meeting-not-much-070534002.html. "But despite vows from Obama and his European counterparts to isolate Putin as long as the crisis in Ukraine remains unresolved, the Russian leader is still a central player in major international affairs, including the U.S.-led nuclear talks with Iran."

56 Jim Talent, "Why Would the President Threaten to Veto Much-Needed Additional Defense Funds?" AEI, June 15, 2015. http://www.aei.org/publication/why-would-the-president-threaten-to-veto-much-needed-additional-defense-funds/?utm_source=paramount&utm_medium=email&utm_content=AEITODAY&utm_campaign=061615. "A showdown is looming in Washington over the National Defense Authorization bill and the Appropriations bill for the Department of Defense. At stake is whether the Congress is able to make any progress this year on repairing the damage which defense cuts have done to the armed forces and the nation's security. The Budget Control Act of 2011, also known as sequestration, had the effect of cutting a trillion dollars from the ten-year budget plan which secretary of defense Bob Gates recommended before he left office in 2011. Coming on the heels of a decade of hard fighting and chronic underfunding of the military's capital accounts, the sequester is a disaster in progress. It has resulted in severe shortfalls in day-to-day readiness across the services, and if continued, will make it nearly impossible in the future to restore readiness, maintain personnel end strength at an adequate level, or recapitalize the armed forces." "President Obama recognizes the need for more defense funding in principle, but is threatening to veto both the Defense

Authorization and Appropriations Bills on the grounds that Congress is not also increasing non-defense spending. In other words, the president is holding defense hostage to his domestic-spending priorities."

57 "It's déjà vu all over again." Berra explained that this quote originated when he witnessed Mickey Mantle and Roger Maris repeatedly hit back-to-back home runs in the Yankees' seasons in the early 1960s.

58 The Soviet constitution of 1936 and the Russian constitution of 1993 affirm all the principles Samuel Huntington includes in his "ideal of the West." "We, the multinational people of the Russian Federation, united by a common fate on our land, establishing human rights and freedoms, civic peace and accord, preserving the historically established state unity, proceeding from the universally recognized principles of equality and self-determination of peoples, revering the memory of ancestors who have conveyed to us the love for the Fatherland, belief in the good and justice, reviving the sovereign statehood of Russia and asserting the firmness of its democratic basic, striving to ensure the well-being and prosperity of Russia, proceeding from the responsibility for our Fatherland before the present and future generations, recognizing ourselves as part of the world community, adopt the CONSTITUTION OF THE RUSSIAN FEDERATION." http://www.constitution .ru/en/10003000-01.htm. Samuel Huntington, "The West: Unique, Not Universal," *Foreign Affairs*, Vol. 75, No. 6 (November/December 1996): 28–46.

59 Russian Westernization remains a possibility. Segments of Russian society have supported aspects of Westernization since the eighteenth century. Some like Peter the Great and Westernizers (*zapadniki*) like Pyotr Chaadayev and Aleksandr Herzen were drawn to industrial modernization. The *zapadniki*'s rivals were Slavophiles like Fyodor Dostoyevsky who advocated "return to the land" (*pochivennichestov*). On the technocratic aspect of the *zapadniki*, see W. H. G. Armytage, *The Rise of the Technocrats: A Social History*, London: Routledge, 2013. Catherine the Great championed Western culture, and others advocated democracy or democratic socialism. Most Russians identify themselves as Western, even though they value their cultural distinctiveness. Many Russians had high, if vague hopes for Westernization when the Soviet Union was dissolved, and tried to keep the faith during Russia's hyperdepression. They felt vindicated during the early phase of Putin's modernization drive (2000–2008), and may do so again, when the economy rebounds.

60 The West has a strong hand, but seldom plays its cards adroitly. It had victory in its grasp when Soviet leaders opted for auto-euthanasia, but chose instead to ravage Russia's economy with "shock therapy" (Washington Consensus) in order to assure that communism's coffin was sealed shut. Steven Rosefielde, "Rethinking Western Advice on Transition: Why Policymakers Don't Listen," *Problems of Post-Communism*, Vol. 48, No. 3, May-June (2001): 3–9.

Conclusion

Russia's vendetta-driven annexation of Crimea and its ensuing surrogacy war against Ukraine will mark the beginning of the end of the West's post-Soviet ascendency unless America and the European Union swiftly get their houses in order. The conflict has exposed the hollowness of commitments made in the 1975 Helsinki Final Act to the sovereignty of European states; the 1990 Charter of Paris to democracy, and the 1994 Budapest memorandum to security assurances to Ukraine in exchange for the surrender of its nuclear weapons.[1] It has punctured the balloon of Western globe-utopia and fixed the probable high watermark of its unipolar moment. The final configuration of the new multipolar terrain is hazy, but Russia is apt to become a potent rival of the West in a resuscitated great game.

The West is no longer master of double-gaming illusions because it misplayed its hand. Instead of exerting the self-discipline essential for realizing the potential of democratic free enterprise, American and EU politicians chose to construct and manage international affairs as political expediency dictated, glossed with platitudes and idealist rhetoric.[2] The results, driven by a pan-gloss "duty to prevail" have been toxic to the West's ideal rule of global law. Democracy (people's rule) has been transformed into the rule of political insiders. Secular stagnation has replaced economic vigor, inequality has widened, mass immigration from the Third World is destabilizing Europe, and financial markets have become crisis prone.[3] Prudent geostrategic engagement has yielded to adventurist "color revolutions" in Ukraine and elsewhere across the globe. NATO expansion has become provocative, while Western leaders refuse to parry Russia's rapid rearmament and assemble the forces required to defeat Kremlin-RMA combined arms assaults on targets of opportunity in Novorossiya and the Baltic States during what appears to be a 2018–2020 window of vulnerability.[4]

The upshot of these adverse developments is a negative turn in the correlation of forces that not only emboldens the Kremlin, but validates Putin's Crimean (and Syrian) gambits. Putin is now firmly convinced that the effete, double-gaming West, misguided by cognitive dissonance and motivated reason, cannot compel him to annul Crimea's annexation, relinquish gains in Novorossiya and South Ossetia, or prevent further predation.

The damage may be irreversible soon unless the West quickly gets its house in order, or regime change transforms Moscow. The West nonetheless remains unafraid of the big bad wolf. It is banking on punitive sanctions and regime change rather than developing more promising countermeasures because it cannot acknowledge its political paralysis. American and EU leaders remain steadfastly in denial, refusing to face reality. They don't believe that the Russians could be coming, continue to insist that the world play by their rules, and disregard those who call their wishful thinking into question. They place the entire blame for the renewed Cold War on Russia, pontificate about rule-based globalization, moralize, persuade, shame, cajole, posture, bluster, threaten reprisals, bully, impose sanctions, make symbolic gestures, and may even slightly increase defense spending, but lack the will to act prudently. This means that despite assertions of national interest, the West is seriously self-constrained. It cannot go to the brink of conventional or nuclear war in Novorossiya and the Baltic states as Russia is prepared to do, and won't re-empower democratic free enterprise. Western leaders are wedded to business as usual both in Russia's backyard and in insider economic governance, and it will take an immense effort by public intellectuals or a catastrophe to sober them up.[5]

When the West isn't in denial, it finds solace in "strategic patience." Perhaps, Russia will go the way of the dodo. It is clearly at risk. Autocrats often are colossuses with clay feet. Some Kremlin insiders are sympathetic to the West's values. Most Russians still aspire to achieve Western living standards. Corruption is endemic.[6] Russia's population is a small fraction of the West's. Its technologies are inferior, productivity subpar, and growth prospects uninspiring, and declining natural resources prices are constraining public spending.[7] These vulnerabilities could prove decisive.

Nonetheless, the odds are slender that the Kremlin will be swept into the dustpan of history by regime change any time soon. Putin, like all mortals, must eventually exit center stage, but the *siloviki* are entrenched. There are three compelling reasons for this judgment. First, the Russian people, as the old Soviet-era joke goes, now know that although Karl Marx was wrong about communism, he was right about capitalism! They may not fully comprehend the post-Soviet experience, but suffered enough during

Yeltsin's transition years to realize that the West isn't a panacea. Second, Putin has crafted a better market Muscovy. Russia isn't the Soviet Union, or even Tsar Nicholas II's market autocracy. Putin has blended Muscovite economic rent-granting tied to arms procurement in the Petrine tradition with a modern, diversified, workably competitive VPK and consumer goods market. The result does not measure up to the West's democratic competitive market ideal, but the gap is narrower when the benchmark is America's and European Union's secularly stagnant reality.[8] Third, the power services, Putin's most likely successors learned a lesson that they won't soon forget about Gorbachev's and Yeltsin's "liberalism." They will fight hard to forestall a reprise of *perestroika* (radical economic reform), *perekhod* (transition), and *novoe myshlenie* (new thinking). Their motto is never again.

Consequently, if the West continues to tie its own hands, Russia could be in a position to expand its sphere of influence without condemning itself anew to impoverished superpower.[9] The Kremlin has the capacity to gradually improve living standards without abandoning Putin's geostrategic agenda,[10] mollifying the population as Nazi Germany successfully did by appealing to national dignity and sacrifice, peppered with tangible material progress and a social safety net. Cold War II therefore is apt to be protracted, and if it ends peacefully like Cold War I, the resulting global division of influence should be better for the West than the Yalta settlement because Latvia, Lithuania, and Estonia will probably retain their independence. Finland won't be re-Finlandized, and the Visegrad Group (Czech Republic, Hungary, Poland, and Slovakia), Romania, and Bulgaria are likely to permanently escape the Kremlin's orbit.

Washington and Brussels, moreover, can further improve their positions. The West can strengthen the appeal of democratic free enterprise and weaken Putin's counter-influence by reducing its democratic deficit and radically downsizing big government. It can craft a credible military counterforce in Europe by focusing defense spending on the Russian threat, scaling back defense budgetary frills, waste, fraud, and abuses hidden in bloated military pensions, "welfare" and environmental programs, antidrug-trafficking activities, and affirmative action entitlements. It can eschew Third World misadventures and seek strategic independence (the power to wage large-scale conventional war with miniscule nuclear risk).

Worse outcomes, however, cannot be precluded. If the West overplays its hand by continuing to rashly press "color revolutionary" and NATO expansion,[11] without creating a credible military deterrent, it could lose additional territory and cede hegemonic influence to the Kremlin. The West today probably can settle the Ukrainian imbroglio without sacrificing most of its post-Soviet geopolitical gains including the Baltics and Balkans. America and the European Union merely have to accept that the West doesn't have a monopoly on spheres of influence, national and global interest, wisely negotiating the particulars of Russia's share. But if they don't, losses may compound in Novorossiya, Georgia, the Baltic states, and beyond.

Inertia and denial favor doing more of the same, leaving scant room for meaningful negotiation. Jean Tirole recently has shown that optimal mutually beneficial compacts can be reached between principals (the West) and agents (Russia) when relations are amicably facilitated by sovereign solidarity.[12] Positive, but more restrictive results also can be achieved when principals try to discipline agents with "tough love."[13] However, when solidarity ("partnership") flies out the window, the game shifts from maximizing mutual benefit to inflicting maximum losses on adversaries. This game theoretic framework illuminates the present impasse. Partnership is dead and both sides are motivated by a duty to prevail. There is a possibility for a frozen conflict, but little more. The terms of engagement can be nudged forward by kind words and confidence building, nonetheless until one or both sides relent, the most that can be accomplished is Cold Peace.

The right democratic strategy for public intellectuals, therefore, under these constraints is to promote a framework for Détente II that weans both sides from confrontation and nudges them toward Cold Peace.[14] It is a vehicle for de-escalation and confidence building that may lead to mutual accommodation beyond the status quo – not the ultimate goal of either party. Détente II isn't on the table despite Obama's tactical alliance with Putin against IS in Syria because Russia and the West intend to prevail. Neither is willing to make fundamental concessions. Russia wants its sphere of influence formally acknowledged and enlarged; the West wants partnership on its terms. It is precisely this impasse that makes Détente II an essential first step toward Cold Peace. Both sides can easily persuade themselves that strategic patience or aggressive probing is better than compromise, without appreciating that the cumulative expected costs of Cold War II far outweigh expected benefits. Détente II isn't a panacea, but is better than unreasoned tenacity. It alone offers the prospect of reduced tension and gradual attitude change essential for reconciliation.

Détente II isn't failsafe. It has no invisible hand to prevent Russia from continuing to press the correlation of forces in its favor, or the West from further diminishing counterforce capabilities in contested theaters of military operations, and intensifying secular stagnation. Détente's virtues are restricted to reducing the likelihood of catastrophic war, offering breathing room for constructing robust conventional force deterrence, reviving the West's economic vigor, and refurbishing its geopolitical appeal.

This means that America and the European Union under the umbrella of Détente II can continue espousing Rawls's neo-Kantian pipedream of a fair, impartial,[15] just, universal rule of law, while simultaneously preparing the groundwork for a new Westphalian East-West order where all parties pare their ambitions to facilitate geopolitical stability and peace, if the West fails to prevail.

A sound settlement requires the West to:

1. Tacitly acknowledge that it has no viable military option in Novorossiya and the Baltic states and won't fund one in the foreseeable future.
2. Acknowledge Russia's existing sphere of influence.
3. Accept Crimea's annexation as a fait accompli, pending some unforeseeable reversal of Kremlin fortunes.
4. Accept Moscow's unilateral dominium or condominium over parts of Novorossiya, including the possibility of forsaking Ukrainian EU and NATO membership.
5. Abandon its provocative promotion of color revolutions and regime change in Russia's sphere of influence.

Symmetrically, Détente II also means that Russia can continue espousing Surkovian democratic Muscovite imperial condominium, while simultaneously preparing the groundwork for a new Westphalian East-West order where all parties pare their ambitions to facilitate geopolitical stability and peace, if Russia fails to prevail.

A sound settlement from Putin's perspective requires the Kremlin to:

1. Tacitly acknowledge that it has no military option in Europe against NATO outside Novorossiya and the Baltic states and may not be able to create one in the future.
2. Acknowledge the West's prevailing sphere of influence.
3. Accept the independence of Kyiv and the Baltic states as a fait accompli, pending some unforeseeable reversal of their fortunes.
4. Accept the existing NATO and EU membership of former members of the Soviet sphere of influence.
5. Abandon the provocative promotion of pro-Kremlin revolutions and regime change in most of Novorossiya and throughout the West's sphere of influence.

The upshot of Détente II will be nonbelligerent Cold Peace. It is an interim consolation prize for both parties; not the best from the West's and

Russia's points of view. If Détente II fails, then the default position is a continuation of Cold War II.

The best outcome at the end of the day that neither side is yet prepared to contemplate is a solution to the Crimean imbroglio that facilitates the construction of a peaceful and harmonious global democratic multi-systemic world attuned to cultural sensibilities. Democratic free enterprise with appropriate social safety nets is best for the West, but may not be so for other cultures. The planet is lightyears away from this diversity-compatible globe-utopia, and any peaceful settlement of Cold War II will only be a small, but important step in the right direction.[16]

Notes

1 James Collins, "Daunting Challenges and Glimmers of Hope in Ukraine," *Carnegie Endowment for Peace*, November 20, 2015. http://carnegieendowment.org/2015/11/ 20/daunting-challenges-and-glimmers-of-hope-in-ukraine/im5z?mkt_tok=3RkM MJWWfF9wsRouuqvLZKXonjHpfsX56OsvXqGg38431UFwdcjKPmjr1YQITsJ0aPy QAgobGp5I5FEIQ7XYTLB2t60MWA%3D%3D.

2 Ibid. "This means most of all that Washington and its allies have to maintain Ukraine and the issues it presents to the broader region as central matters of concern. And support for a positive outcome in Ukraine has to receive the resources and attention adequate to the task at hand."

3 Steven Rosefielde and Quinn Mills, *Global Economic Turmoil and the Public Good*, Singapore: World Scientific Publishers, 2015.

4 Maria Kiselyova and Polina Devitt, "Russia to Deploy New Divisions on Western Flank, Form Nuclear Regiments," *Reuters*, January 12, 2016. http://news.yahoo .com/russia-says-create-three-divisions-western-flank-2016-092001552.html. Pavel Felgenhauer, "Putin Signs a National Security Strategy of Defiance and Pushback," January 7, 2016, *Eurasia Daily Monitor*, 13, 4. http://www.jamestown.org/programs/ edm/single/?tx_ttnews%5Btt_news%5D=44953&tx_ttnews%5BbackPid%5D=27&c Hash=27bc5fd6da889528c14e35fa5d8b0122&mkt_tok=3RkMMJWWfF9wsRous67 NZKXonjHpfsX56OsvXqGg38431UFwdcjKPmjr1YsHT8B0aPyQAgobGp5I5FEIQ 7XYTLB2t60MWA%3D%3D#.VpWi6o-cH4h.

5 Robert Skidelsky, "The Decline of the West Revisited," Project Syndicate, November 16, 2015. https://www.project-syndicate.org/commentary/terror-in-paris-symptom-of-western-decline-by-robert-skidelsky-2015-11#r8rSdw1XHiyHiysW.99. "In 1918, Oswald Spengler published *The Decline of the West*. Today the word 'decline' is taboo. Our politicians shun it in favor of 'challenges,' while our economists talk of 'secular stagnation.' The language changes, but the belief that Western civilization is living on borrowed time (and money) is the same.

"Why should this be? Conventional wisdom regards it simply as a reaction to stagnant living standards. But a more compelling reason, which has seeped into the public's understanding, is the West's failure, following the fall of the Soviet Union, to establish a secure international environment for the perpetuation of its values and way of life."

6 Mark Kramer, "High-Level Corruption in Russia," *Ponars*, Policy Memo 402, November 2015. "High-level corruption accounts for a much greater loss of public resources (estimates vary, but the evidence suggests around 90 percent or more). Diversion of state funds and appropriation of public assets have been especially salient under Putin. Even official spokesmen for the Putin administration have acknowledged that vast quantities of state funds are 'lost' (presumably diverted) every year, though this is presented mostly as a phenomenon of carelessness rather than of entrenched high-level corruption. Sergei Stepashin, the head of the Federal Accounting Chamber, told Interfax in November 2012 that a trillion rubles a year is diverted from federal procurements, but estimates by accounting specialists outside the government range much higher – up to 5 trillion rubles a year."

7 "Russia Announces New Budget Cuts Amid Oil Slide," *AFP*, January 13, 2016. http://news.yahoo.com/russia-announces-budget-cuts-amid-oil-slide-105539186.html. " 'We have agreed that ministries and (government) agencies ... will present their proposals to the finance ministry for optimising budget expenditure by around ten percent,' Finance Minister Anton Siluanov told an economic conference in Moscow, confirming media reports on Tuesday. 'We have to take well thought-out measures on how to bring the budget in accordance with the new realities,' he added. 'In the current difficult conditions, we must speak of a very thrifty, strict budget policy, in order not to end up with high deficit levels or a high volume of debt,' he said. Russia's 2016 budget is based on an oil price of $50 a barrel and a deficit of three percent, which President Vladimir Putin has ordered must not be exceeded. Crude prices on Tuesday dipped below $30 a barrel for the first time in over 12 years."

8 Jan Techau, "Four Predictions on the Future of Europe," *Carnegie Europe*, January 12, 2016. http://carnegieeurope.eu/strategiceurope/?fa=62445&mkt_tok=3RkMM JWWfF9wsRous6rLZKXonjHpfsX56OsvXqGg38431UFwdcjKPmjr1YsHRcZ0aPy QAgobGp5I5FEIQ7XYTLB2t60MWA%3D%3D.

9 Henry Rowen and Charles Wolf Jr., eds., *The Impoverished Superpower: Perestroika and the Soviet Military Burden*, Palo Alto, CA: ICS Publishers, 1990.

10 Martin Matischak, "Russia's Military Buildup Continues with Big New Fighter Jet Order," *Fiscal Times*, January 15, 2016. http://finance.yahoo.com/news/russia-military-buildup-continues-big-214600310.html. "Russia's military buildup shows no signs of slowing. Moscow recently ordered 50 twin-engine Sukhoi Su-35S multi-role fighters to bolster the country's air force."

11 "Russia Warns NATO over Montenegro Membership," *AP*, December 1, 2015. http://news.yahoo.com/russia-warns-nato-montenegro-invite-111359017.html.

12 Jean Tirole, "Country Solidarity in Sovereign Crises," *American Economic Review*, 2015, 105 (8): 2333–2363.

13 Steven Rosefielde and Yiyi Liu, "The Greek Debt Crisis: Rethinking Sovereign Solidarity," unpublished manuscript, September 2016.

14 The term is often used in reference to the general easing of the geopolitical tensions between the Soviet Union and the United States that began in 1969 as a foreign policy of U.S. presidents Richard Nixon and Gerald Ford called Détente; a "thawing out" or "unfreezing" at a period roughly in the middle of the Cold War. Détente was known in Russian as *разрядка* (*razryadka*, loosely meaning "relaxation of tension").

The period was characterized by the signing of treaties such as SALT I and the Helsinki Accords. Another treaty, SALT II, was discussed but never ratified by the

United States. John Lewis Gaddis, *The Cold War*, New York: Penguin Press, 2005; Jeremi Suri, *Power and Protest: Global Revolution and the Rise of Détente*, Cambridge, MA: Harvard University Press, 2003; Craig Daigle, *The Limits of Detente: The United States, the Soviet Union, and the Arab-Israeli Conflict, 1969–1973*, New Haven, CT: Yale University Press, 2012.

15 John Rawls, *A Theory of Justice*, Cambridge, MA: Belknap Press of Harvard University Press, 1971; Michael Sandel, *Justice: What's the Right Thing to Do?* New York: Farrar, Straus and Giroux, 2010.

16 Steven Rosefielde, *Asian Economic Systems*, Singapore: World Scientific Publishers, 2014.

BIBLIOGRAPHY

Acemoglu, Daron. *Introduction to Modern Economic Growth*. Princeton, NJ: Princeton University Press, 2009.

Acharya, Amitav. *The End of American World Order*. New York: Polity, 2014.

Adamsky, Dima. The Current State of Russian Strategic Thought in the Nuclear Realm, paper presented to the American Foreign Policy Council Conference on "The Russian Military in the Contemporary Perspective," held May 9–10 in Washington, DC, 2016.

Albats, Yevgenia and Fitzpatrick, Catherine A. *The State within a State: The KGB and Its Hold on Russia – Past, Present, and Future*. New York: Farrar Straus & Giroux, 1994.

Alexeev, Michael and Weber, Shlomo. *The Oxford Handbook of Russian Economy*. Oxford: Oxford University Press, 2012.

Allen, Robert. *Farm to Factory: A Reinterpretation of the Soviet Industrial Revolution*. New Brunswick, NJ: Princeton University Press, 2015.

Allen, Susan Hannah. The Domestic Political Costs of Economic Sanctions. *Journal of Conflict Resolution* 52, no. 6 (December 2008): pp. 916–944, esp. 916–917.

Allison, Graham. *Essence of Decision: Explaining the Cuban Missile Crisis*. New York: Little, Brown, 1971.

Window of Opportunity: The Grand Bargain for Democracy in the Soviet Union. New York: Pantheon, 1991.

Avoiding Nuclear Anarchy: Containing the Threat of Loose Russian Nuclear Weapons and Fissile Material. Cambridge, MA: MIT Press, 1996.

Allison, Graham and Blackwill, Robert. America's Stake in the Soviet Future. *Foreign Affairs* 70, no. 3 (1991): 77–97.

Allison, Graham and Treverton, Gregory, eds. *Rethinking America's Security: Beyond Cold War to New World Order*. New York: W.W. Norton, 1992.

Amsden, Alice; Kochanowicz, Jacek, and Taylor, Lance. *The Market Meets Its Match: Restructuring the Economies of Eastern Europe*. Cambridge, MA and London: Harvard University Press, 1994.

Aron, Leon. *Yeltsin: A Revolutionary Life*. New York: St. Martin's Press, 2000.

A Tormenting in Moscow. Washington, DC: American Enterprise Institute, 2012.

Aron, Raymond. *Opium of the Intellectuals*. Brunswick, NJ: Transaction Publishers, 2001.

Arrow, Kenneth. *Social Choice and Individual Values*, 2nd ed. New York: Wiley, 1963.

Aslund, Anders. *How Russia Became a Market Economy*. Washington, DC: Brookings Institute, 1995.

Russia's Capitalist Revolution: Why Market Reform Succeeded and Democracy Failed. Washington, DC: Peterson Institute of International Economics, 2007.

What Went Wrong and How to Fix It. Washington, DC: Peterson Institute of International Economics, April 2015.

Aslund, Anders and Layard, Richard. *Changing the Economic System in Russia*. London: Palgrave Macmillan, 1993.

Baker, Peter and Glasser, Susan. *Kremlin Rising: Vladimir Putin's Russia and the End of Revolution*. New York: Scribner, 2005.

Baldwin, Richard and Wyplosz, Charles. *The Economics of European Integration*, 4th ed. New York: McGraw Hill, 2012.

Baumol, William. *Business Behavior, Value and Growth, rev. ed.* New York: Macmillan, 1959.

Bell, Daniel. *The Cultural Contradictions of Capitalism*. New York: Basic Books, 1976.

The End of Ideology: On the Exhaustion of Political Ideas in the Fifties. Cambridge, MA: Harvard University Press, 2000.

Beltrami, Edward. *Mathematics for Dynamic Modeling*. Boston, MA: Academic Press, 1987.

Bergson, Abram. A Reformulation of Certain Aspects of Welfare Economics. *Quarterly Journal of Economics* 52, no. 1 (February 1938): 310–334.

Socialist Economics. In Herbert Ellis (ed.), *A Survey of Contemporary Economics*. Homewood, IL: Richard D. Irwin, 1948.

Soviet National Income and Product in 1937. *Parts I and II, Quarterly Journal of Economics* 64, nos. 2, 3 (May/August 1950), pp. 208–241, 408–441.

Reliability and Usability of Soviet Statistics: A Summary Appraisal. American Statistician 7, no. 3 (June–July 1953), pp. 13–16.

Soviet National Income and Product in 1937. New York: Columbia University Press, 1953.

Bergson, Abram (with Hans Heymann Jr.). *Soviet National Income and Product, 1940–1948.* New York: Columbia University Press, 1954.

Bergson, Abram. The Concept of Social Welfare. *Quarterly Journal of Economics* 68, no. 2 (May 1954): 233–252.

The Real National Income of Soviet Russia since 1928. Cambridge, MA: Harvard University Press, 1961.

The Great Economic Race. *Challenge Magazine* 11, no. 6 (March 1963): 4–6.

The Economics of Soviet Planning. New Haven, CT: Yale University Press, 1964.

Essays in Normative Economics. Cambridge, MA: Harvard University Press, 1966.

A Survey of Contemporary Economics. Cambridge, MA: Harvard University Press, 1966.

Market Socialism Revisited. *Journal of Political Economy* 75, no. 4 (October 1967): 655–673.

Planning and Productivity under Soviet Socialism. New York: Columbia University Press, 1968.

Comparative National Income in the USSR and the United States. In J. D. Daly (ed.), *International Comparisons of Prices and Output, Studies in Income and Wealth*, Vol. 37. New York: National Bureau of Economic Research, 1972, pp. 145–185.

Soviet National Income Statistics. In V. Treml and J. Hardt (eds.), *Soviet Economic Statistics*. Durham, NC: Duke University Press, 1972, pp. 148–152.

Soviet Economic Perspectives: Toward a New Growth Model. *Problems of Communism* 32, no. 2 (March–April), 1973, 1–10.

Social Choice and Welfare Economics under Representative Government. *Journal of Public Economics* 6, no. 3 (October), 1976, 171–190.

The Soviet Economic Slowdown. *Challenge Magazine* 20, no. 6 (January–February), 1978, 22–33.

Planning and Performance in Socialist Economies. London: Unwin and Hyman, 1989.

The USSR before the Fall: How Poor and Why? *Journal of Economic Perspectives* no. 5, Fall 1991, 29–44.

The Communist Efficiency Gap: Alternative Measures. *Comparative Economic Studies* 36, no. 1, Spring 1994, 1–12.

Bergson, Abram, Hazard, John, and Balinky, Alexander, et al. *Market and Plan in the U.S.S.R.: in the 1960s.* New Brunswick, NJ: Rutgers University Press, 1967.

Bergson, Abram and Kuznets, Simon. *Economic Trends in the Soviet Union.* Cambridge, MA: Harvard University Press, 1963.

Berle, Adolf and Means, Gardner. *The Modern Corporation and Private Property.* New York: Macmillan, 1932.

Berliner, Joseph. *The Innovation Decision in Soviet Industry.* Cambridge, MA: MIT Press, 1976.

Biddle, Stephen. *Military Power: Explaining Victory and Defeat in Modern Battle.* Princeton, NJ: Princeton University Press, 2006.

Bidwell, Percy W. Our Economic Warfare. *Foreign Affairs*, April 1942, 421–435

Birman, Igor. From the Achieved Level. *Soviet Studies*, 30, 2, 1978, 153–172.

Birman, Igor. *The Economy of Shortages.* New York: Chalidze Publications, 1983.

Blank, Stephen. *Does Russo-Chinese Partnership Threaten America's Interests and Policies in Asia?* Orbis, 60, 1, 2016.

Boldin, Valery. *Ten Years that Shook the World.* New York: Basic Books, 1994.

Browder, Bertrand Guay Bill. *Red Notice: A True Story of High Finance, Murder, and One Man's Fight for Justice.* New York: Simon and Schuster, 2015.

Campbell, Joseph. *Yellow Journalism: Puncturing the Myths, Defining the Legacies.* New York: Praeger, 2001.

Canuto, Octaviano. *The Commodity Super Cycle: Is This Time Different?* World Bank, Number 150.

Chickering, Rodger. *Imperial Germany and the Great War, 1914–1918.* Cambridge: Cambridge University Press, 2004.

Clark, John Maurice. *Competition as a Dynamic Process.* Washington, DC: Brookings Institution Press, 1961.

Clarke, John M. Toward a Concept of Workable Competition. *American Economic Review* (June 1940): 231–256.

Cohen, Stephen. *Failed Crusade: America and the Tragedy of Post-Communist Russia.* New York: W.W. Norton, 2015.

Should the West Engage Putin's Russia?: The Munk Debates. New York: House of Anansi Press, 2016.

Cooper, Julian. *Russia's State Armament Programme to 2020: A Quantitative Assessment of Implementation 2011–2015.* FOI, FOI-R--4239—SE, March 2016.

Corden, Warner Max. Boom Sector and Dutch Disease Economics: Survey and Consolidation. *Oxford Economic Papers* 36 (1984): 362.

Dahl, Robert. *Polyarchy: Participation and Opposition.* New Haven, CT: Yale University Press, 1971.

Dallago, Bruno and Rosefielde, Steven. *Transformation and Crisis in Russia, Ukraine and Central Europe: Challenges and Prospects.* London: Routledge, 2016.

Dawisha, Karen. *Putin's Kleptocracy.* New York: Simon and Schuster, 2014.

De Grauwe, Paul. *Economics of Monetary Union.* New York: Oxford University Press, 2000.

Dorfman, Robert, Samuelson, Paul, and Solow, Robert. *Linear Programming and Economic Analysis.* New York: McGraw Hill, 1958.

Ellman, Michael. Russia's Current Economic System: From Delusion to "Glasnost." *Comparative Economic Studies* (2015): 1–18.

Ericson, Richard E. Command versus "Shadow": The Conflicted Soul of the Soviet Economy. *Comparative Economic Studies* 48 (2006): 50–76.

Escribà-Folch, Abel and Wright, Joseph. Dealing with Tyranny: International Sanctions and the Survival of Authoritarian Rulers. *International Studies Quarterly* 54, no. 2 (June 2010): 334–359.

Fainsod, Merle. *How Russia Is Ruled.* Cambridge, MA: Harvard University Press, 1963.

Felshtinsky, Yuri. *The Corporation: Russia and the KGB in the Age of President Putin.* New York: Encounter Books, 2009.

Feshbach, Murray. *Russia's Demographic and Health Meltdown. In Russia's Uncertain Economic Future.* Washington, DC: Joint Economic Committee of Congress, 2002.

Festinger, Leon. *A Theory of Cognitive Dissonance.* Palo Alto, CA: Stanford University Press, 1957.

Field, Mark. *The Health and Demographic Crisis in Post-Soviet Russia: A Two Phase Development.* New York: St. Martin's Press, 2000.

Firth, Donald and Noren, James. *Soviet Defense Spending: A History of the CIA Estimates 1950–1990.* College Station: Texas A&M University Press, 1998.

Fisher, Irving. *The Theory of Interest.* Clifton, NJ: Augustus M. Kelley, 1930.

Fite, Brando. *U.S. and Iranian Strategic Competition: The Impact of China and Russia.* Washington, DC: Center for Strategic and International Studies, March 2012.

FitzGerald, Mary. Marshal Ogarkov and the New Revolution in Soviet Military Affairs. *Defense Analysis* 3, no. 1 (1987): 13–19.

Frankel, Jeffrey A. *The Natural Resource Curse: A Survey.* NBER Working Paper No. 15836, March 2010.

Friedman, Thomas. *The World Is Flat.* New York: Farrar, Straus and Giroux. 2007.

Fukuyama, Francis. *The End of History and the Last Man.* New York: Free Press, 1992.

    America in Decay: The Sources of Political Dysfunction. Foreign Affairs, September/October 2014, 5–26

    Political Order and Political Decay: From the Industrial Revolution to the Globalization of Democracy. New York: Farrar, Straus and Giroux, 2014.

Furr, Grover. *Khrushchev Lied. The Evidence That Every "Revelation" of Stalin's (and Beria's) Crimes in Nikita Khrushchev's Infamous "Secret Speech" to the 20th Party Congress of the Communist Party of the Soviet Union on February 25, 1956, Is Provably False.* Kettering, OH: Erythros Press & Media. 2011.

Furr, Grover. *The Murder of Sergei Kirov: History, Scholarship and the Anti-Stalin Paradigm.* Kettering, OH: Erythros Press & Media. 2013.

Gaddis, John Lewis. *The Cold War: A New History.* New York: Penguin, 2005.

Gaidar, Yegor. *The Economics of Russian Transition*. Cambridge, MA: MIT Press, 2002.
State and Evolution: Russia's Search for a Free Market. Seattle: University of Washington Press, 2003.
Collapse of an Empire: Lessons for Modern Russia. Washington, DC: Brookings Institution Press, 2007.

Gaidar, Yegor, McFaul, Michael, and Miller, Jane Ann. *Days of Defeat and Victory*. Seattle: University of Washington Press, 1999.

Gaidar, Yegor and Pöhl, Karl Otto. *Russian Reform/International Money (Lionel Robbins Lectures)*. Cambridge MA: MIT Press, 1995.

Gaidar, Yegor and Vasiliev, Sergei. *Ten Years of Russian Economic Reform*. London: Centre for Research into Post Communist Economies, 1999.

Gaidar, Yegor *The Economics of Russian Transition*. Cambridge, MA: MIT Press, 2002.

Garvy, George. *Money, Financial Flows, and Credit in the Soviet Union*. New York: National Bureau of Economic Research, 1977.

Gates, Robert. *Duty: Memoirs of a Secretary at War*. New York: Alfred A. Knopf, 2014.

Gel'man, Vladimir. *Authoritarian Russia: Analyzing Post-Soviet Regime Changes*. Pittsburg, PA: University of Pittsburg Press, 2015.

Gerschenkron, Alexander. The Rate of Industrial Growth in Russia since 1885. *Journal of Economic History* 7-S (1947): 144–174.
Economic Backwardness in Historical Perspective. Cambridge, MA: Harvard University Press, 1962.

Gessen, Masha. *The Man Without a Face: The Unlikely Rise of Vladimir Putin*. New York: Riverhead, 2012.

Giles, Keir. Russia's "New" Tools for Confronting the West: Continuity and Innovation in Moscow's Exercise of Power, Chatham House, The Royal Institute of International Affairs, March 2016.

Gigerenzer, Gerd and Selten, Reinhard. *Bounded Rationality*. Cambridge, MA: MIT Press, 2002.

Glazyev, Sergei and Douglas, Rachel B. Genocide: Russia and the New World Order. *Executive Intelligence Review*, 1999.

Goldman, Marshall. *The Piratization of Russia: Russian Reform Goes Awry*. London: Routledge, 2003.

Gorbachev, Mikhail. *Perestroika: New Thinking for Our Country and the World*. New York: Harpercollins, 1987.

Grossman, Gregory. Notes for a Theory of the Command Economy. *Soviet Studies* 15, no. 2 (1963): 101–123.

Halper, Stefan. *The Beijing Consensus: How China's Authoritarian Model Will Dominate the Twenty-First Century*. New York: Basic Books, 2010.

Haran, Olexiy. *Disintegration of the Soviet Union and the US Position on the Independence of Ukraine*. Belfer Center, Discussion Paper 95-09, 1995.

Harrison, Mark. Resource Mobilization for World War II: The U.S.A., U.K., U.S.S.R., and Germany, 1938–1945. *Economic History Review* 41, no. 2 (1988): 171–192.

Hoffer, Eric. *The True Believer: Thoughts on the Nature of Mass Movements*. New York: Harper Perennial Modern Classics, 2002.

Hoffman, Frank. *Conflict in the 21st Century: The Rise of Hybrid War*. Arlington, VA: Potomac Institute for Policy Studies, 2007.

Hybrid Warfare and Challenges. JFQ: *Joint Force Quarterly*, 2009, 34–48.

Hosking, Geoffrey. *Russia: People and Empire.* Cambridge, MA: Harvard University Press, 1997.

Hotelling, Harold. Demand Functions with Limited Budgets. *Econometrica*, no. 3 (1935).

Howe, James. Future Russian Strategic Nuclear and Non-nuclear Forces: 2022, paper presented to the American Foreign Policy Council Conference on "The Russian Military in the Contemporary Perspective," held 9–10 May in Washington, DC, 2016.

Huntington, Samuel. *The Clash of Civilizations and the Remaking of World Order.* New York: Simon & Schuster, 1996.

The West: Unique, Not Universal. *Foreign Affairs* 75, no. 6 (November/December 1996), 28–46

Ikenberry, G. John. *Liberal Leviathan: The Origins, Crisis, and Transformation of the American World Order.* Princeton, NJ: Princeton University Press, 2011.

Itzkowitz Shifrinson, Joshua R. Deal or No Deal? The End of the Cold War and the U.S. Offer to Limit NATO Expansion. *International Security*, 40, no. 4 (Spring 2016), 7–44.

Jacoby, Russell. *The End of Utopia: Politics and Culture in an Age of Apathy.* New York: Basic Books, 2000.

Jahn, Beate. *Liberal Internationalism: Theory, History, Practice.* London: Palgrave Macmillan, 2013.

Kaempfer, William and Lowenberg, Anton. The Theory of International Economic Sanctions: A Public Choice Approach. *American Economic Review* 78, no. 4 (December 1988): 786–793.

Kaempfer, William; Lowenberg, Anton, and Mertens, William. International Economic Sanctions against a Dictator. *Economics and Politics* 16, no. 1 (March 2004): 29–51.

Kahneman, Daniel. Maps of Bounded Rationality: Psychology for Behavioral Economics. *The American Economic Review* 93, no. 5 (2003): 1449–1475.

Kaiser, Wolfram and Starie, Peter. *Transnational European Union: Towards a Common Political Space.* London: Routledge, 2009.

Kaldor, Nicholas. Professor Chamberlin on Monopolistic and Imperfect Competition. *The Quarterly Journal of Economics* 52, no. 3 (May 1938): 513–529.

Kantorovich, L. V. *The Best Use of Economic Resources.* Cambridge, MA: Harvard University Press, 1965.

Kaplan, Robert. *The Revenge of Geography: What the Map Tells Us about Coming Conflicts and the Battle Against Fate.* New York: Random House, 2010.

Karasik, Theodore and Nichols, Thomas. *Novoe myshlenie and the Soviet Military: The Impact of Reasonable Sufficiency on the Ministry of Defense.* Santa Monica, CA: Rand, 1989.

Kasparov, Garry. *Winter Is Coming: Why Vladimir Putin and the Enemies of the Free World Must Be Stopped.* New York: Public Affairs, 2015.

Kenen, Peter B. *Toward a Supranational Monetary System.* 1967.

Kennedy, David M. What "W" Owes to "WW": President Bush May Not Even Know It, but He Can Trace His View of the World to Woodrow Wilson, Who Defined a Diplomatic Destiny for America That We Can't Escape. *The Atlantic Monthly* 295, no. 2 (March 2005).

Keynes, John Maynard. *The General Theory of Employment, Interest and Money.* London: Macmillan Cambridge University Press, for Royal Economic Society, 1936.

Khlevniuk, Oleg and Favorov, Nora. *Stalin: New Biography of a Dictator*. New Haven, CT: Yale University Press, 2015.

Kipp, Jacob. Russia, the European Union, and the Ukrainian Crisis: A European or a Eurasian affair? In John McGowan, Gert Guri, and Bruno Dallago; (eds.), *A Global Perspective on the European Economic Crisis*. London: Routledge, 2016, 259–274.

Koestler, Arthur. *Darkness at Noon*. New York: Scribner, 2006.

Kogan, Eugene. *Russian Military Capabilities*, Tiblisi Georgia: Georgian Foundation for Strategic and International Studies, 2016.

Kotkin, Stephen. *Stalin Volume 1: Paradoxes of Power, 1878–1928*. New York: Penguin, 2014.

Koyama, Yoji. *EU's Eastward Enlargement: Central and Eastern Europe's Strategies for Development*. Singapore: World Scientific Publishers, 2015.

Kratsev, Ivan and Leonard, Mark. Europe's Shattered Dream of Order. *Foreign Affairs* 94, no. 3 (May/June).

Krugman, Paul R. *It's Baack: Japan's Slump and the Return of the Liquidity Trap*. Washington, DC: Brookings Institution Press, 2008.

Krugman, Paul R. *The Return of Depression Economics and the Crisis of 2008*. New York: W. W. Norton Company, 2009.

Kurtzweg, Laurie Rogers. *Measures of Soviet Gross National Product in 1982 Prices*. Joint Economic Committee of Congress, Washington, DC, November 1990.

Laffont, Jean-Jacques and Martimort, David. *The Theory of Incentives: The Principal-Agent Model*. Princeton NJ: Princeton University Press, 2002.

Legvold, Robert. Review of Ten Years that Shook the World. *Foreign Affairs*, July/August 1994, 174–175.

Leijonhielm, Jan and Westerlund, Fredrik eds. *Russian Power Structures: Present and Future Roles in Russian Politics*. FOI-R-2437-SE, Stockholm, December 2007, pp. 71–96.

Lektzian, David and Souva, Mark. An Institutional Theory of Sanctions Onset and Success. *Journal of Conflict Resolution* 51, no. 6 (November 2007): 848–871.

Lermontov, Mikhail. *A Hero of Our Time: The Fatalist*. 1841.

Lider, Julian. The Correlation of World Forces: The Soviet Concept. *Journal of Peace Research* 17, no. 2 (June 1980): 151–171.

Lieven, Dominic. *Russia Against Napoleon: The True Story of the Campaigns of War and Peace*. London: Allen, 2010.

Lipset, Seymore. *Political Man: The Social Bases of Politics*. London: Heinemann, 1983.

Lipsey, Richard and Lancaster, Kelvin. The General Theory of Second Best. *Review of Economic Studies* 24, no. 1 (1956): 11–32.

Litvinenko, Alexander and Felshtninsky, Yuri. *Blowing Up Russia: The Secret Plot to Bring Back KGB Terror*. New York: Encounter Books, 2007.

Liu, Yiyi and Steven Rosefielde. Public Private Partnerships: Antidote for Secular Stagnation? In Steven Rosefielde, Masaaki Kuboniwa, Satoshi Mizobata, and Kumiko Haba, eds., *EU Economic Stagnation and Political Strife: Lessons for Asia*. Singapore: World Scientific Publishers, 2016.

Lodge, Milton and Taber, Charles. *Three Steps toward a Theory of Motivated Political Reasoning. In Arthur Lupia, ed., Elements of Reason: Cognition, Choice and Bounds of Rationality*. Cambridge University Press, 2000.

Lupia, Arthur, ed. *Elements of Reason: Cognition, Choice and Bounds of Rationality*. Cambridge University Press, 2000.

Lynch, Allen. *The Soviet Study of International Relations.* Cambridge: Cambridge University Press, 1989.

Makarov, Valerii and Kleiner, Georgii. Barter v ekonomike perekhodnovo perioda: Osobennosti i tendentsii. *Ekonomika i Matematicheskie Metody* 33, no. 2 (1997): 25–41.

Maki, Dennis and Spindler, Z. A. *The Effect of Unemployment Compensation on the Rate of Unemployment in Great Britain. Oxford Economic Papers,* New Series 27, no. 3 (1975): 440–454.

Malia, Martin. *The Soviet Tragedy: A History of Socialism in Russia, 1917–1991.* New York: Free Press, 1994.

Mankoff, Jeffrey. *Russian Foreign Policy: The Return of Great Power Politics.* New York: Rowman & Littlefield, 2009.

Marinov, Nikolay. Do Economic Sanctions Destabilize Country Leaders? *American Journal of Political Science* 49, no. 3 (July 2005): 564–576.

Marx, Karl. *Das Kapital.* 1867.

Matlock, Jack. *Autopsy on an Empire: The American Ambassador's Account of the Collapse of the Soviet Union.* New York: Random House, 1995.

McFaul, Michael and Stoner-Weiss, Kathryn. Mission to Moscow: Why Authoritarian Stability Is a Myth. *Foreign Affairs,* January/February 2008.

McKinnon, Ronald I. Optimum Currency Areas. *American Economic Review* 53, no. 4 (September 1963): 717–725.

McKinnon, Ronald I. *The Order of Economic Liberalization: Financial Control in the Transition to a Market Economy.* Baltimore, MD: John Hopkins University Press, 1991.

Meade, James. *Trade and Welfare,* London: Oxford University Press, 1955.

Mearsheimer, John. Why the Ukraine Crisis Is the West's Fault: The Liberal Delusions That Provoked Putin. *Foreign Affairs* 90 (September/October 2014), 77–89

Mend, Sarah. The View from Above: An Insider's Take on Clinton's Russia Policy. *Foreign Affairs,* July/August 2002.

Menon, Rajan and Rumer, Eugene B. *Conflict in Ukraine: The Unwinding of the Post-Cold War Order.* Cambridge, MA: MIT Press, 2015.

Milgrom, Paul and Roberts, John. The LeChatelier Principle. *American Economic Review* 86, no. 1 (1996).

Mundell, Robert A. A Theory of Optimum Currency Areas. *American Economic Review* 51 (September 1961).

Nove, Alec. *The Soviet Economic System.* London: Allen and Unwin, 1977.

Ofer, Gur. Abram Bergson: The Life of a Comparativist. *Comparative Economic Studies,* no. 47 (2005).

Ogarkov, N. V. *Vsegda v golovnosti k zashchite Otechestva,* Moskva 1982.

Ogarkov, N. V. *Istoriya Uchit vditel'nosti.* Moskva 1985.

Olson, Mancur. Dictatorship, Democracy, and Development. *The American Political Science Review* 87, no. 3 (September 1993): 567–576.

Orwell, George. *Nineteen Eighty-Four.* London: Martin Secker & Warburg Ltd. London, 1949.

Owen, Jones. *The Establishment – And How They Get Away With It.* London: Allen Lane, 2014.

Oxenstierna, Susanne, ed. *The Challenges for Russia's Politicized Economic System.* London: Routledge, 2015.

Pallin, Vendil and Nygren, Bertil, eds. *Russian Defense Prospects.* New York: Routledge, 2012.

Piketty, Thomas. *Capital in the Twenty-First Century.* Cambridge, MA: Harvard University Press, 2014.

Pillsbury, Michael. *The Hundred-Year Marathon.* New York: Henry Holt and Co., 2015.

Pipes, Richard. *The Formation of the Soviet Union: Communism and Nationalism, 1917–1923.* Cambridge, MA: Harvard University Press, 1964.

Politkovskaya, Anna. *Putin's Russia: Life in a Failing Democracy.* New York: Holt, 2007.

Pontecorvo, G., Shay, R. P., and Hart, A. G., eds. *Issues in Banking and Monetary Analysis.* New York: Holt, 1967.

Popov, Vladimir, Polterovich, Viktor, and Tonis, Alexander. *Resource Abundance: A Curse or Blessing?* – DESA Working Paper No. 93, June 2010.

Mechanisms of Resource Curse, Economic Policy and Growth. NES Working Paper # WP/2008/082.

Popper, Karl. *Unended Quest: An Intellectual Autobiography.* London: Routledge, 2005.

The Open Society and Its Enemies. Princeton, NJ: Princeton University Press, 2013.

Conjectures and Refutations: The Growth of Scientific Knowledge. London: Routledge, 2014.

The Myth of the Framework: In Defence of Science and Rationality. London: Routledge, 2014.

Putin, Vladimir, Gevorkyan, Nataliya, and Timakova, Natalya. *Vladimir Putin First Person: An Astonishingly Frank Self-Portrait by Russia's President.* New York: Public Affairs, 2000.

Rawls, John. *A Theory of Justice.* Cambridge, MA: Belknap Press of Harvard University Press, 1971.

Rayfield, Donald. *Stalin and His Hangmen: The Tyrant and Those Who Killed for Him.* New York: Random House, 2005.

Razin, Assaf and Rosefielde, Steven. Currency and Financial Crises of the 1990s and 2000s. *CESifo Economic Studies* vol. 57, no. 3 (2011): 499–530.

A Tale of a Politically-Failing Single-Currency Area. *Israel Economic Review* 10, no. 1 (2012): 125–138.

What Really Ails the Eurozone?: Faulty Supranational Architecture. *Contemporary Economics* 6, no. 4 (December 2012): 10–18.

The European Project after Greece's Near Default. *Israel Economic Journal,* 2016.

Reinhart, Carmen and Rogoff, Kenneth. *This Time Will Be Different: Eight Centuries of Financial Folly.* Princeton, NJ: Princeton University Press, 2009.

Renz, Bettina. Russian Military Capabilities after 20 Years of Reform. *Survival,* 56, no. 3, 2014, 61–84.

Robbins, Lionel Charles. *An Essay on the Nature and Significance of Economic Science.* London: Macmillan, 1932.

Rogoff, Kenneth and Reinhart, Carmen. *This Time Is Different: Eight Centuries of Financial Folly.* Cambridge, MA: Harvard University Press, 2012.

Romer, David. *The "Solow Growth Model" in Advanced Macroeconomics.* New York: McGraw-Hill, 2011.

Rosefielde, Steven. *False Science: Underestimating the Soviet Arms Buildup.* New Brunswick, NJ: Transaction Press, 1987.

The Grand Bargain: Underwriting Catastroika. *Global Affairs* 7, no. 1 (Winter 1991): 15–35.

Beyond Catastroika: Prospects for Market Transition in the Commonwealth of Independent States. *Atlantic Economic Journal* 20, no. 1 (March 1992): 1–8.

The Grand Bargain: Underwriting Katastroika. *Global Affairs* 7, no. 1 (1992): 15–35.

The Civilian Labor Force and Unemployment in the Russian Federation. *Europe-Asia Studies* 52, no. 8 (December 2000): 1433–1447.

Premature Deaths: Russia's Radical Transition. *Europe-Asia Studies* 53, no. 8 (December 2001): 1159–1176.

Rethinking Western Advice on Transition: Why Policymakers Don't Listen. *Problems of Post-Communism* 48, no. 3 (May–June 2001): 3–9.

Back to the Future? Prospects for Russia's Military Industrial Revival. *ORBIS* 46, no. 3 (Summer 2002): 499–510.

The Riddle of Postwar Russian Economic Growth: Statistics Lied and Were Misconstrued. *Europe-Asia Studies* 55, no. 3 (2003): 469–481.

Russia: An Abnormal Country. *European Journal of Comparative Economics* 2, no. 1 (2005).

Russia in the 21st Century: The Prodigal Superpower. Cambridge: Cambridge University Press, 2005.

Illusion of Transition: Russia's Muscovite Future. *Eastern Economic Journal* 31 no. 2 (Spring 2005): 283–296.

Tea Leaves and Productivity: Bergsonian Norms for Gauging the Soviet Future. *Comparative Economic Studies* 47, no. 2 (June 2005): 259–273.

Turmoil in the Kremlin: Sputtering Toward Fortress Russia. *Problems of Post-Communism* 53, no. 5 (September/October 2006).

Russian Economy from Lenin to Putin. New York: Wiley, 2007.

The Illusion of Westernization in Russia and China. *Comparative Economic Studies,* 49 (2007): 495–513.

Russian Rearmament: Motives Options and Prospects. In Jan Leijonhielm and Fredrik Westerlund, eds., *Russian Power Structures: Present and Future Roles in Russian Politics,* FOI-R-2437-SE, Stockholm, December 2007, 71–96.

Review of Andrey Vavilov, the Russian Public Debt and Financial Meltdowns. New York: Palgrave Macmillan, 2010.

Inclusive Economic Theory: Distinguishing "Second Best" from "Second Worst" Economic Behavior. *Higher School of Economics Journal (HSE), Moscow,* 2015, 30–44.

Russian Military, Political and Economic Reform: Can the Kremlin Placate Washington? U.S. Army War College, Carlisle Barracks, May 14–15, 2014.

Russia's Military Industrial Resurgence: Evidence and Potential. U.S. Army War College: Carlisle Barracks, 2016.

Rosefielde, Steven and Dallago, Bruno. *Transformation and Crisis in Central and Eastern Europe: Challenges and Prospects.* London: Routledge, 2015.

Rosefielde, Steven, Danilin, Vyachaslav, and Kleiner, Georgii. Deistvuiushaya Model Reform i Ugroza Giperdepressii. The Russian Reform Model and the Threat of Hyperdepression. *Russian Economic Journal (Rossiiskii Ekonomicheskii Zhurnal),* no. 12 (1994): 48–55.

Rosefielde, Steven and Hedlund, Stefan. *Russia since 1980: Wrestling with Westernization.* Cambridge: Cambridge University Press, 2008.

Rosefielde, Steven, Kuboniwa, Masaaki, and Mizobata, Satoshi, eds. *Prevention and Crisis Management: Lessons for Asia from the 2008 Crisis.* Singapore: World Scientific Publishers, 2012.

Rosefielde, Steven and Liu, Yiyi. Limits of Country Solidarity in Sovereign Crisis. *Singapore Economics Review,* 2017.

Rosefielde, Steven and Mills, Quinn. *Master of Illusion.* Cambridge: Cambridge University Press, 2007.

 Democracy and Its Elected Enemies: American Political Capture and Economic Decline. Cambridge: Cambridge University Press, 2013.

 Global Economic Turmoil and the Public Good. Singapore: World Scientific Publishers, 2015.

Rosefielde, Steven and Pfouts, Ralph W. *Inclusive Economic Theory.* Singapore: World Scientific Publishers, 2014.

Rosenberg, Alexander. *Mathematic Politics or Science of Diminishing Returns.* Chicago: University of Chicago Press, 1994.

Rowen, Henry and Wolf, Charles, Jr. *The Impoverished Superpower: Perestroika and the Soviet Military Burden.* San Francisco, CA: Institute for Contemporary Studies, 1990.

Rubinstein, Ariel. *Modeling Bounded Rationality.* Cambridge. MA: MIT Press, 1998.

Rumsfeld, Donald. Transforming the Military. *Foreign Affairs* 81, no. 3 (May/June 2002): 20–32.

Sachs, Jeffrey and Warner, Andrew. The Curse of Natural Resources. *European Economic Review* 45, nos. 4–6 (2001): 827–838.

Sakwa, Richard. *Putin: Russia's Choice.* Abingdon, Oxon: Routledge, 2007.

 Frontline Ukraine: Crisis in the Borderlands. London: I.B. Tauris, 2014.

 Putin and the Oligarchs: The Khodorkovsky-Yukos Affair. London: I.B. Tauris, 2014.

Samuelson, Paul. *Foundations of Economic Analysis.* Cambridge, MA: Harvard University Press, 1947.

 The Lechatelier Principle in Linear Programming. Santa Monica, CA: Rand Corporation, 1949.

 An Extension of the Lechatelier Principle. *Econometrica* 28 (1960).

Sandel, Michael. *Justice: What's the Right Thing to Do?* New York: Farrar, Straus and Giroux, 2010.

Sarotte, Mary Elise. A Broken Promise? What the West Really Told Moscow about NATO Expansion. *Foreign Affairs* 90 (September/October 2014), 96.

Schapiro, Leonard. *Communist Party of the Soviet Union.* New York: Vintage, 1960.

Schmitt, Carl. *Legality and Legitimacy.* Durham, NC: Duke University Press, 2004.

Schneider, Mark B. Russian Nuclear Weapons Policy and Programs, the European Security Crisis, and the Threat to NATO, paper presented to the American Foreign Policy Council Conference on "The Russian Military in the Contemporary Perspective" held May 9–10 in Washington, DC, 2016.

Schroeder, Gertrude. *The Soviet Economy on a Treadmill of Reforms. In Soviet Economy in a Time of Change.* Washington, DC: Joint Economic Committee of Congress, 1979.

Schroeder, Gertrude and Denton, Elizabeth. An Index of Consumption in the USSR. In *USSR: Measures of Economic Growth and Development, Washington, DC: Joint Economic Committee of Congress,* December 8, 1982, 217–401.

Schumpeter, Joseph. *Capitalism, Socialism and Democracy.* New York: Harper and Brothers, 1942.

Selten, Reinhard. What is Bounded Rationality? In Gerd Gigerenzer and Reinhard Selten, eds., *Bounded Rationality The Adaptive Toolbox,* Cambridge, MA: MIT Press, 2002.

Sen, Amartya. Personal Utilities and Public Judgements: Or What's Wrong with Welfare Economics. *Economic Journal* 89, no. 355 (1979): 537–588.

The Idea of Justice. London: Penguin, 2010.

Service, Robert. *Stalin.* Cambridge, MA: Belknap/Harvard University Press, 2005.

Shatalin, Stanislav. *Transition to the Market: 500 Days.* Moscow: Arkhangelskoe, 1990.

Shiller, Robert. *Irrational Exuberance.* Princeton, NJ: Princeton University Press, 2000.

Shleifer, Andrei. *A Normal Country: Russia after Communism.* Cambridge, MA: Harvard University Press, 2005.

Shleifer, Andrei and Treisman, Daniel. Russia: A Normal Country. *Foreign Affairs,* March/April 2004, 20–38.

Shleifer, Andrei and Vishny, Robert. *The Grabbing Hand: Government Pathologies and Their Cures.* Cambridge, MA: MIT Press, 2000.

Shlykov, Vitaly. Globalizatsiia voennoi promyshlennosti – imperativ XXI veka. *Otechestvennye zapiski.* No. 5 (2005): 98–115.

Nazad v budushchee, ili Ekonomicheskie uroki kholodnoi voiny. *Rossiia v Global'noi Politike.* Tom 4, No. 2, Mart–April' (2006).

Nevidimaia Mobilizatsii. *Forbes.* No. 3, March (2006): 1–5.

Shvidkovsky, Dmitri. *Russian Architecture and the West.* New Haven, CT: Yale University Press, 2007.

Simes, Dimitri. *After the Collapse: Russia Seeks Its Place as a Great Power.* New York: Simon and Schuster, 1999.

Simon, Herbert. A Behavioral Model of Rational Choice. *The Quarterly Journal of Economics* 69, no. 1 (February 1955).

A Behavioral Model of Rational Choice. In Herbert Simon, *Models of Man: Social and Rational – Mathematical Essays on Rational Human Behavior in a Social Setting,* New York: Wiley, 1957, 241–260.

Models of Man: Social and Rational-Mathematical Essays on Rational Human Behavior in a Social Setting. New York: Wiley, 1957.

Models of Bounded Rationality. Cambridge, MA: MIT Press, 1982.

A Mechanism for Social Selection and Successful Altruism. *Science* 250, no. 4988 (1990): 1665–1668.

Bounded Rationality and Organizational Learning. *Organization Science* 2, no. 1 (1991): 125–134.

Sinovets, Polina and Bettina Renz. Russia's 2014 Military Doctrine and Beyond: Threat Perceptions, Capabilities And ambitions. Research Paper (Rome, IT: NATO Defense College, Research Division), July 2015.

Solow, Robert. A Contribution to the Theory of Economic Growth. *Quarterly Journal of Economics Oxford* 70, no. 1 (February 1956): 65–94.

Technical Change and the Aggregate Production Function. *Review of Economics and Statistics* 39, no. 3 (1957): 312–320.

Solzhenitsyn, Aleksandr. *The Gulag Archipelago, 1918–1956: An Experiment in Literary Investigation (Volume One).* New York: Basic Books, 1997.

Steigerwald, David. *Wilsonian Idealism in America.* Ithaca, NY: Cornell University Press, 1994.

Stevens, Paul. Resource Impact: Curse or Blessing? A Literature Survey. *Journal of Energy Literature* 9, no. 1 (2003): 3–42.

Stoner-Weiss, Kathryn. *Resisting the State: Reform and Retrenchment in Post-Soviet Russia.* Cambridge: Cambridge University Press, 2006.

Stoner-Weiss, Kathryn and McFaul, Michael. *Domestic and International Influences on the Collapse of the Soviet Union (1991) and Russia's Initial Transition to Democracy (1993).* CDDRL WORKING PAPERS, Number 108, March 2009.

Sutela, Pekka. *The Road to the Russian Market Economy.* Helsinki: Kikkimora, 1998.

Sylvan, D. A. and Voss, J. F., eds. *Problem Representation in Political Decision Making.* London: Cambridge University Press, 1998.

Swan, Trevor. Economic Growth and Capital Accumulation. *Economic Record* 32, no. 2 (November 1956): 334–361.

Taber, Charles. *The Interpretation of Foreign Policy Events: A Cognitive Process Theory.* In D. A. Sylvan and J. F. Voss, eds., *Problem Representation in Political Decision Making.* London: Cambridge University Press, 1998.

Talbott, Strobe. *The Russia Hand: A Memoir of Presidential Diplomacy.* New York: Random House, 2003.

Thurow, Lester. *Zero Sum Society.* New York: Basic Books, 1980.

Tikhomirov, Vladimir. Capital Flight from Post-Soviet Russia. *Europe Asia Studies* 49, no. 4 (1997): 591–615.

   Capital Flight: Causes, Consequences and Counter-Measures. In Klaus Segbers, *Explaining Post-Soviet Patchworks 2.* Aldershot, UK: Ashgate, 2001.

Tirole, Jean. Country Solidarity in Sovereign Crises. *American Economic Review*, 2015.

Tisdell, Clem. *Bounded Rationality and Economic Evolution: A Contribution to Decision Making, Economics, and Management.* Cheltenham, UK: Brookfield, 1996.

Treisman, Daniel. *Putin's Silovarchs.* Orbis, 2007.

Tuchman, Barbara. *The Guns of August.* New York: The Macmillan Company, 1962.

Turner, Adair. *Between Debt and the Devil: Money, Credit, and Fixing Global Finance.* Princeton, NJ: Princeton University Press, 2015.

Twigg, Judith L. and Schechter, Kate. *Social Capital and Social Cohesion in Post-Soviet Russia.* New York: M. E. Sharpe, 2003.

Ullman, Harlan and Wade, James. *Shock and Awe: Achieving Rapid Dominance.* Washington, DC: National Defense University, 1996.

Von Clausewitz, Carl. *On War.* London: Oxford University Press, 2007.

Von Hayek, Fredrich A. *Collectivist Economic Planning: Critical Studies on the Possibilities of Socialism.* London: George Routledge & Sons, 1935.

Von Mises, Ludwig. *Socialism.* London: Jonathan Cape, 1936.

Voyennaya doktrina Rossiyskoy Federatsii. Военная доктрина Российской Федерации [Military Doctrine of the Russian Federation]. scrf.gov.ru (in Russian). Moscow: Security Council of the Russian Federation. 2010-06-25 [presidential decree 2010-06-25].

Weber, Max. *Economy and Society.* Berkeley: University of California Press, 1978.

Williamson, John. *What Washington Means by Policy Reform.* In John Williamson, ed., *Latin American Adjustment: How Much Has Happened?* Washington, DC: Peterson Institute for International Economics, 1990.

   Development and the "Washington Consensus." *World Development* 21 (1993): 1239–1336.

   What Washington Means by Policy Reform. Washington, DC: Peterson Institute for International Economics, Chapter 2, November 2002.

Wittgenstein, Ludwig. Logisch-philosophiche Abhandlung. *Annalen der Naturphilosophie (Leipzig)* 14 (1921): 185–262.

　　Tractatus logico-philosophicus. New York and London, 1922.

Wolf, Jr. Charles, and Rowen, Henry. *The Impoverished Superpower: Perestroika and the Soviet Military Burden.* San Francisco, CA: Institute for Contemporary Studies, 1990.

World Bank, *Doing Business* 2015: *Going Beyond Efficiency, 2015.*

Yakovlev, Andrei. Russian Modernization: Between the Need for New Players and the Fear of Losing Control of Rent Sources. *Journal of Eurasian Studies* 5, no. 1 (2014): 10–20.

Yakovlev, Andrei; Sobolev, Anton, and Kazun, Anton. Means of Production versus Means of Coercion: Can Russian Business Limit the Violence of a Predatory State? *Post-Soviet Affairs,* 2013.

Index